LEADERSHIP AND HUMAN BEHAVIOR

Class of 2003 Edition

UNITED STATES NAVAL ACADEMY
Department of Leadership, Ethics and Law

Edited by

LCDR Gene R. Andersen, USN

W. Brad Johnson, Ph.D.

LT Eric M. Thomas, USN

PEARSON CUSTOM PUBLISHING

Excerpts taken from:

Psychology, Second Edition,
by Saul Kassin
Copyright © 1998 by Prentice-Hall, Inc.
A Pearson Education Company
Upper Saddle River, New Jersey 07458

Psychology, Second Edition,
by Stephen F. Davis and Joseph H. Palladino
Copyright © 1997, 1995 by Prentice-Hall, Inc.

Leadership in Organizations, Fourth Edition,
by Gary Yukl
Copyright © 1998, 1994, 1989, 1981 by Prentice-Hall, Inc.

Human Relations: Interpersonal, Job-Oriented Skills, Sixth Edition,
by Andrew J. DuBrin
Copyright © 1997 by Prentice-Hall, Inc.

Interpersonal Skills for Leadership,
by Susan Fritz, F. William Brown, Joyce Povlacs Lunde and Elizabeth A. Banset
Copyright © 1999 by Prentice-Hall, Inc.

Psychology: An Introduction, Tenth Edition,
by Charles G. Morris and Albert A. Maisto
Copyright © 1999, 1996, 1993, 1990, 1988, 1985, 1982, 1979, 1976, 1973 by Prentice-Hall, Inc.

Printed in the United States of America

10 9 8 7 6 5 4 3 2 1

Please visit our website at www.pearsoncustom.com

ISBN 0–536–02546–0
BA 990258

PEARSON CUSTOM PUBLISHING
160 Gould Street/Needham Heights, MA 02494
A Pearson Education Company

Copyright Acknowledgments

Contents

1 *Introduction*

Objectives

1. Explain the course policy statement, course requirements and instructor policy statement.

2. Outline the introductory material presented during Plebe Summer.

3. Explain "The Great Man Theory" of leadership study and describe some of its deficiencies.

Ramage's Rampage

E

This text was created for NL112, the Naval Academy's flagship course in Leadership and Psychology. NL112 is a rigorous introductory course which focuses on developing a deeper understanding of one's own behavior and the behavior of others. NL112 emphasizes key concepts from the science of human behavior and demonstrates their relationship to leadership success by stressing their application to your life as a midshipman, as an officer and as a leader of character serving our nation.

Great leaders from military history have recognized the significance of studying and managing human behavior. Consider the words of General of the Army Omar Bradley: "A leader should possess human understanding and consideration for others. Soldiers are intelligent, complicated beings who will respond favorably to human understanding and consideration. By these means, their leader will get maximum effort and loyalty from them."

Psychology, or the science of human behavior, is a relatively young science. The American Psychological Association only recently celebrated its centennial. Widespread application of psychology in the military dates back to World War I, when psychologists were organized to assist in the selection and classification of recruits—primarily through the administration of mental tests. During World War II, 25% of all American psychologists served in the military—again screening and classifying new personnel or treating psychiatric reactions in military or Veterans Administration hospitals. From WWII to the present, the application of psychological science to the mission of the military has grown exponentially.

Scientifically established psychological principles are now routinely applied to the selection, classification and assignment of military personnel, to the evaluation and improvement of leadership effectiveness, to the management of individual and group behavior, to designing military equipment and environments and to consultation for mental health problems. Human behavioral science is also critical to such specialized military areas as propaganda, hostage negotiations, prisoner of war concerns and profiling of world leaders.

NL112 will prepare you to lead more effectively by giving you a basic understanding of human development, personality traits and styles, principles of followership, cognitive functioning and memory, learning principles, stress and stress management, motivation, social influences and basic interpersonal and self-management skills. Most of the course material can be readily applied both to yourself and to those you lead.

NL112 is designed to emphasize the leadership applications of critical concepts in human behavior to make a you a more effective leader in the United States Navy. Given a military case or situation, you should be able to use your understanding of human behavior to assess why people are behaving as they are, whether their behavior is likely to persist, how it could be changed and how to go about most effectively intervening in the situation.

[handwritten margin notes:]
USS Parche
Skipper Commander Ramage (Capt Red) 31 USNA Grad
cmd no action
Snipe hunt
hammer head & steel head
Lopsided fight

Ramage's Rampage

Wilbur Cross

Every officer and man aboard the U.S.S. *Parche* was frustrated and disgusted, but perhaps no one more so than the submarine's skipper, Commander L. P. Ramage. From conning tower to engine room the word went the rounds, "The Old Man's in a hell of a mood." He was up there on the tiny bridge now, glowering into the night, his thoughts fiery enough to match the red hair that gave him the nickname "Captain Red."

The reason behind the frustration was that *Parche,* on her second war patrol in July, 1944, should have been boring in for a kill on some juicy Jap shipping. Instead, she was looping back and forth off Cape Enigaño north of the Philippines chasing phantoms in what the crew caustically referred to as a "snipe hunt." A large Japanese convoy had been reported by sister ships of the *Parche,* but so far the sonarmen, radarmen and lookouts had not picked up even the suspicion of a trail.

"It looks like a dull evening," muttered the port lookout as night began to fall on the 30th and the sea stretched on all sides placidly and seemingly unmolested by any other ships of war. "With a nice moon coming up, how'd you like to be out here paddling your girl in a canoe?"

By way of answer the starboard lookout spat over the side. It sure was frustrating to get a contact report secondhand and then not be able to raise so much as a blip on the radar screen. But there was no use talking about it. The Old Man looked unhappy enough as it was as he eased his tight, wiry frame down through the hatch manhole to see if radar had picked up anything yet.

The weeks, days and hours of monotony were almost over. But no one aboard the *Parche* could have guessed how much so at the moment when the quartermaster wearily wrote "July 31, 0100, no contact" in the logbook and wondered if they ever would get rid of their twenty-four fish during the patrol.

The U.S.S. *Parche,* along with the *Hammerhead* and *Steelhead* made up a wolf pack known as "Parks' Pirates." The standard joke was that they should have been called the "Head-hunters," since they were composed of *Hammerhead, Steelhead* and (referring to Ramage) redhead. On this patrol they had been assigned to an area known as "Convoy College" lying between Luzon and Formosa and so called because it was the sector in which wolf packs like the Pirates and Mickey Finns received basic training in how to pick off Japanese ships. Formosa was the point of convergence of six main Jap convoy lanes—from the Nipponese mainland and Shanghai to the north, from Hong Kong and Hainan to the west, and from Singapore and the Palau Islands to the south. Any submarine assigned to these waters was bound to sight potential prizes belonging to the Japanese Co-Prosperity Sphere—all that is except the *Parche* on her second patrol, which seemed to be flunking badly. Although she had set out more than five weeks before, she had not yet expended a single torpedo.

At 10:30 in the morning, July 30, *Steelhead* had sighted distant smoke from a convoy but could get no closer to investigate because of the heavy umbrella of air protection. The Japanese were throwing everything they could in the path of the American forces advancing through the Marianas, and air cover always consisted of plenty of Jap pilots ready to use suicide tactics. After a frustrating day of his own, her skipper, Commander D. L. Whelchel got off a message to Ramage, reporting the contact, figuring the *Parche* would be in a more advantageous position north of the convoy, where she could wait for darkness and slip in for an attack.

All that day and into the night the *Parche*'s radar and sonar probed the waters of the Philippine sea with only one result: Captain Red grew more and more impatient. At midnight he stood on the bridge, squinting through his binoculars across water made milky white in some patches by the light of a waning moon. There was not a silhouette of any kind to be seen anywhere, Frustration was setting in fast.

"A position report from *Steelhead,* sir," came the radio operator's report at thirty minutes past midnight.

"Where?"

"The reported Japanese convoy has changed course and is now some thirty miles to the southeast of us."

"Come to course 140 degrees true," muttered Ramage. "If we don't make contact soon, half the crew will be putting in for transfer." The sky, which had been dotted with clouds was becoming overcast, hiding the moon half of the time. The sky along the horizon looked squally.

At 0230 there was still no sign of the Japs, but at 0240 Ramage, discouraged because the moon was just setting and reducing his visibility to a few hundred yards, suddenly received a report that sent him hustling from the bridge down into the conning tower.

"Radar contact!"

"I've got to see it to believe it," said Ramage. He had full confidence in his chief electronics technician, John C. Gray, Jr., whom he referred to as "a fabulous guy and a master of precision," but he had been chasing ghosts so long he was ready to blow his redheaded top any minute. If he alerted the crew on another false alarm it would be sheer murder.

By the time he took one glance at the radar screen in the conning tower he was convinced and at 0246 the general-quarters alarm sounded. The *Parche* began closing fast, guided by radar until a visual contact could be made. This came half an hour later when, through scattered rain squalls, the dim shadows of Jap ships were picked up ahead. It was 0307.

By now the Japanese were fully alerted through their own radar and sonar devices. One of the escort ships fired warning flares signaling the convoy to begin evasive maneuvers and to aid the other escorts in converging on the enemy.

At this point commenced one of the most audacious engagements in the history of United States naval warfare as the lone sixteen-hundred-ton boat challenged and took on the entire convoy, any one of whose escorts, loaded with heavy armament, depth charges and torpedoes, could have meant death to a submarine.

Even more remarkable than the nature of the lopsided fight was the unique manner in which Captain Red Ramage chose to attack.

Ramage had graduated from the Naval Academy in 1931 and been assigned directly to destroyers. He quickly became familiar with hit-and-run tactics and methods of taking advantage of superior speeds and maneuverability in pressing an attack. And he had the temperament to go along with it. Ramage was not a big man, but he had the kind of fighting instinct that did justice to his red hair. When he made decisions, he made them fast, and accurately. He learned that a small ship that could catch a larger one off balance and press the attack had a distinct advantage that outweighed size alone. When he joined the submarine force, he never forgot what he had learned aboard the old cans.

At the time of contact, the *Parche* was proceeding south, with the convoy almost directly east of her. As Jap escorts closed in on the position where they knew the unseen submarine to be, Ramage tried a reverse spinner, heading west, then north and finally east.

"By God, Captain, look where we are," said the executive officer, Lieutenant Commander Woodrow W. McCrory, when the maneuver had been completed. "The rascals have changed course and are headed right into our laps." There was a touch of gleefulness in his voice.

The submarine, charging at twenty knots, and still on the surface, was now well *inside* the ring of escort vessels with the bows of several freighters and tankers dead ahead, all coming due west while the *Parche* headed east.

"Clear the bridge!" shouted Ramage. The two lookouts and the duty officers vanished quickly below, leaving only the captain and his quartermaster, whose duty it was to assist with the visual navigation.

"Things are getting pretty hot up there," said one of the lookouts. "The Old Man must be ready to take her down."

The lean and fiery Ramage had no such intention. Nothing was going to make him submerge—not while Ensign Gray at the radar had picked up what he interpreted as an escort vessel at six thousand yards, a second one at twelve thousand and ten potential targets within a distance of eighteen thousand yards.

At 0354 *Parche* began closing on a medium AK cargo vessel, with the quartermaster, George G. Plume, Jr., taking rapid bearings through the TBT (target bearing transmitter, a sighting device which transmits the relative bearings of ships to the conning tower each time the operator presses his "mark" button). But she had appeared so quickly out of the darkness there was not time to complete the bearing and fire bow tubes.

"Hard right!" ordered Ramage from the open bridge. If the *Parche* kept on course she would have plowed right into the enemy. As it was, she slid past with less than two hundred yards to spare. Ramage's idea was to make a complete circle and head for her from behind, bringing his bow tubes to bear.

The Jap ship opened up with everything she had and the sky was lit by streams of tracers and the flash of five-inchers.

"Let me know when you've got a firing setup," shouted Ramage into the intercom to the TDC (torpedo data computer) operator, Lieutenant F. W. Allcorn, Jr., his torpedo officer. "It's all lit up like Times Square up here."

"We've got it," replied Allcorn. "Target is tracking on the nose."

"Give her two," ordered Ramage. "That ought to put her out of misery."

Two torpedoes sped from the bow tubes and the AK began a desperate turn, which succeeded in avoiding them. In doing so, however, she moved directly into the path of an escort vessel charging toward *Parche* and unintentionally blocked the escort attack so that Ramage was free to select another target.

Torpedo Officer Allcorn, who had continued to track the AK until ordered otherwise, now found that the *Parche*'s 360-degree swing gave him another setup, this time on the after tubes.

"Give her one more for good measure, then," said Ramage. The third torpedo sped out into the black waters, this time finding the mark the other two had missed. In due time there was a dull explosion astern.

"I think we got her," said Ramage to Quartermaster Plume, but there was no time to stop for sight-seeing. Off to starboard, in the TBT sights, was what looked to be two small carriers in procession but immediately turned out to be tankers—juicy targets for any submariner. A scant three minutes later the *Parche* was closing in, bow pointed north.

"We've got the setup," said the torpedo officer, who had now switched targets, using the bearings from the quartermaster, and was "playing the organ" furiously—feeding range and bearing information into the torpedo data computer, which came up with the correct settings instantly.

"Hold her." Captain Red kept his eye on the silhouette of the closer of the two tankers as the *Parche*'s bow knifed into the seas at full speed and her tail sent up a

tankers spotted

sheet of white spray. The submarine was spotted now. He could hear the sound of alarm bells and knew Jap gunners were trying to get a bead on their enemy.

"Two thousand yards . . . 1500 . . . 1100 . . ." the radar operator called off the range readings rapidly, as the distance closed fast.

"Fire one!" shouted Ramage as the computer delivered data on the enemy's port bow. Using slight starboard rudder, Ramage was letting his boat swing to the right, toward his second target. "Fire two!" That was aimed at the belly of tanker number one. "Fire three!" That should hit just about at the quarter. "Fire four!" And one for the stern. Tankers were tough targets at all times and this one was too juicy to take chances on a miss for any reason—miscalculations, misfires, changes in speed.

On tanker number one the *Parche* had a perfect score. The bow was blown off by the seventh torpedo of the evening. The midsection exploded with a blinding sheet of fire from torpedo number five. And numbers six and seven tore the stern sections in half. She plunged under the Pacific with hardly any slackening in speed, leaving nothing but a burning patch of oil to serve as a fine torch for silhouetting the following ship.

"Hard right," ordered Ramage, his bare red head wet from light spray and heavy sweat. The second tanker, which had not altered course, was now in range but so close there was no time to reload any of the six bow tubes. *Parche* swung neatly around until her stern was aimed at the target.

"We've got a setup in the after tubes," said the Torpedo Officer.

"Fire all of them," came the order. Ramage had already expended one of the four stern torpedoes, and the other three sped toward target. A minute later Ramage, hanging onto the grab rails on the weather bridge, cursed when he realized the first shot had missed. The next two struck the tanker forward, slowing her down but not stopping her completely. Not bad: of the ten torpedoes loaded in the ten tubes at the start of the battle, he had missed with only three.

By now every man on the boat, whether actively working or on emergency standby, was following the action audibly as orders flashed over the intercom in each section of the *Parche*.

"Well, I guess the Old Man will have to take her down now," said a rookie engineman, making his first patrol on the *Parche*.

"You want to bet?" asked a heavily bearded chief, without looking up from a bank of meters in the maneuvering room.

"Sure. That last salvo was numbers eight, nine, and ten. Six fish from the bow and four from the stern. What have you got left?"

The rookie engineman would have been right—except for one unique fact: Commander L. P. Ramage was about to make history. Months before, on his first patrol with the *Parche* he had started training his torpedo-room crews in reloading torpedo tubes under the most extreme conditions, while the boat was making full speed on the surface, rolling and pitching, with the imminent possibility of having to crash dive. Never before had this type of operation been tackled by submariners, the standard practice being to dive deep, level off and run slowly when torpedoes were moved from stowage racks to loading cradles and thence into the tubes fore and aft.

The surface reload was not only extremely difficult but hazardous as well, for if a torpedo should get loose from its rack it would be a ton of unmanageable steel and explosives, crushing men and equipment like so many eggshells. On the *Parche*'s first patrol, Ramage had successfully loaded four torpedoes in the forward tubes while maneuvering on the surface for an attack.

Now, under more intensified battle conditions, and with the boat changing course frequently and at full speed, he was attempting the same surface reload maneuver.

Once it got under way he would not be able to take the *Parche* down without considerable delay to make certain no torpedoes were loose enough to be rendered dangerous by the angle of dive.

Thus far in the engagement Ramage had brazenly ignored the vessels which were probably echoing with Japanese profanity. The *Parche*'s unexpected speed and maneuverability on the surface and the extreme daring of her skipper kept the Japs outguessed at every turn. Whenever an escort would get a bearing on the *Parche*—an unusually difficult feat since she was one of the first boats to be painted a camouflage gray instead of the normally accepted black—one of the ungainly old *marus* milling around would bumble into her path. But even so, Ramage's position was being scorched by heavy automatic weapons fire, enough so that he kept getting madder and madder at the Japs all around him and refused to leave the bridge under any circumstances.

Down in the control room, the man at the Christmas tree, the board on which red and green lights indicated which valves were open and which shut, sat with sweat pouring down his face. "Upstairs," through the hatch, he could hear the thunder of enemy guns and often the tattoo of smaller caliber bullets along the steel superstructure. The diving officer, Lieutenant David H. Green, was rigged for diving the instant the order came down to the conning tower, but somehow he knew it would not come. Captain Red was having too much of a field day to give up now, with fourteen torpedoes left aboard.

"What's the matter with the Old Man?" a seaman asked nervously. "Are you sure he's still alive up there?"

Lieutenant Commander McCrory laughed, as hot steel rained overhead. He knew damned well Ramage had no intention of taking her down. As executive officer, he had been given a loose assignment as a free agent, wandering from compartment to compartment to check any snags in operations. No five men in other parts of the boat seemed as busy as any one man in the two torpedo rooms. Theirs was a labor of pure love as they heaved and sweated the torpedoes, as slippery as greased pigs, into the tubes. The hull rang with the clank of chain falls and bars and the muffled slamming of tube doors, as the deadly fish were slid into position.

"Well, lads," said the exec, "this is what we've been looking for. We're going for broke this time."

On the bridge Ramage had a few rough moments after the original ten fish had gone. How were the boys making out down below? He did not have long to think about it, because Quartermaster Plume was calmly lining up a medium-sized *maru* in the TBT. Ramage steadied himself with both hands outstretched on the grab rails, freckled face low and close to the intercom so that he could bark orders into it.

"More speed!" he shouted to the engine-room gang. "Give me everything you've got." He had to get to the *maru* before an escort got to the *Parche*.

"We can't squeeze another quarter knot out of her, sir," came the reply. "We're on flank already." What did the Old Man think he was doing—still riding one of those crazy cans?

"O.K., O.K. Forward torpedo room, how's the reload?"

"We've got two in, Captain."

"Stand by, then." The *maru* loomed closer. The torpedo officer had the setup now on the TDC. "Fire two!"

"Two torps on their way," came the reply an instant later. "We're commencing full reload."

"Left full rudder!" shouted Ramage, as the *Parche* started getting uncomfortably blistered by deck gunfire from the *maru*. The *Parche*'s new gray camouflage job was serving its purpose well, but the Jap gunners could still sight on the white fin of spray rising from the submarine's tail as she continued at top speed. "And make ready all tubes."

The *Parche* slewed around to port and away from target. A few seconds later came the two dull explosions that gave the submarine a satisfying shudder and aroused battle cheers from everyone aboard. The Japanese merchantman had taken both fish squarely in her guts. Jerry-built for war service, she simply broke in two. The tracers from her batteries fore and aft skewed crazily, those in the bow rising skyward and those in the stern *ping*ing into the sea as the two halves of the ship tilted inward and began to sink.

"We're ready to take her down any time you are," came a report from the control room to the bridge when Ramage announced they could chalk up another kill. Escorts were boring in now from several approaches.

"Hang on a bit longer," said Commander Ramage, his lean jaw thrust out with determination. He still had twelve torpedoes aboard. Thus far at least that destroyer training back in the early thirties had really paid off. It was doubtful any of the brass supervising those training courses in night torpedo attacks against cruisers and battleships would have dreamed the tactics could be used by anything but destroyers.

While the officers and men below sweated and labored at assignments no submariners in history had ever been called upon to perform, Ramage calmly completed his reverse spinner so he could head back again for tanker number two, which was still afloat despite the two fish that had struck her forward. Down in the conning tower, where some fourteen officers and men concentrated on their jobs, Seaman First Class Courtland C. Stanton was getting a little dizzy. Stationed at the wheel he had spun it for so many "hard rights" and "hard lefts," so many spinners and so many changes of compass direction, he felt like a cross-eyed man on a merry-go-round.

Ramage had to make a quick decision now— which suited his flaming temperament just right. *Parche* was headed due north at full speed, the tanker due west and about two thousand yards off his port bow. He could not wait for the reload in the bow tubes, but the after torpedo room reported it had three fish reloaded. Captain Red decided bold tactics were the best—he would bore right in under the tanker's stern, which was high in the water because of the sinking bow, then loose his stern tubes from the other side.

In a confusing montage of flaring oil and flashing tracers, the *Parche* passed directly under her stern while the surprised Jap gunners feverishly tried to break loose their after mount, jammed from the angle of the deck. Some five hundred yards beyond target, as *Parche* "opened out" for a stern shot, the stricken tanker fired every gun she had. It looked for a few seconds as though Ramage had pushed his luck too far. But he had estimated his chances with the cool precision of an officer who has had a dozen

Naval Academy photo courtesy of United States Naval Academy Photographic Laboratory.

years of tactical experience. His surprise maneuver was just radical enough, and the tanker's inclination just critical enough, so that none of her hot metal struck home in time.

"You got the setup?" asked the skipper impatiently after he had maneuvered *Parche*'s tail to bear on the tanker, like a scorpion preparing for a sting.

"Yes, sir," replied Torpedo Officer Allcorn.

"After torp room, look lively!"

"We're ready with three, sir," came the reply.

"Half speed," ordered Ramage. The engine-room telegraph clanged and there was a noticeable slackening in the boat's forward sprint. Firing torpedoes at anything above ten knots was a tricky business because of the speed factor in computing. Yet Ramage had challenged all precedent by firing his forward torpedoes at full speed—forcing them into the wall of water formed by the bow's twenty-knot lunge ahead. When it came to firing stern torpedoes, he had to slow to about ten knots so they would not have too much backward momentum at the instant of leaving the tubes.

"Half speed," repeated the engine room.

"O.K., after torp room, don't wait for invitations." Three fish raced from the *Parche*'s stern tubes, boiling along unseen about twenty-five feet below the surface of the dark Pacific. The range was eight hundred yards.

"One cigar! Two cigars! Three cigars!" The men howled with delight as each dull impact was transmitted through the water. The tanker, already crippled by the two haymakers in her bow, slid without protest under the waves, leaving behind nothing but burning fuel.

Ramage was beginning to feel a sense of accomplishment now, as he mentally computed all pertinent facts: he had just expended torpedoes thirteen, fourteen and fifteen. How many would the forward torpedo room have in the process of reload now?

Suddenly, as he concentrated on these things, a black shadow loomed off the starboard bow, a small, fast *maru* bearing down on the *Parche* with intent to ram.

"Enginehouse!" shouted Ramage. "Pour on all the oil you've got. I feel like a mouse at a bridge party up here!"

The *Parche* had now regained full speed, but Ramage saw he needed flank speed and then some to pull off his next maneuver. As he plunged directly northward, the *maru* bore in from the east, spraying automatic weapons fire.

The gap closed fast . . . three hundred yards, two hundred yards. Now she was scarcely as far away as the *Parche*'s own length, headed for the submarine's conning tower and bridge from directly abeam. Ramage glowered calmly at this instrument of destruction, like a bullfighter standing in defiance of a charging animal.

"Hard right! Emergency!"

Seaman First Class Stanton at the wheel was by this time thoroughly familiar in the techniques of operating the *Parche* like a PT boat. The *maru* passed by on Ramage's starboard side as the forward half of the submarine cleared her bows and the latter half slewed around with the agility of a water skier making a right-angle turn.

The Japanese officers and deck men were screaming first with jubilation when it looked like a sure bet that they would cut the submarine in two, then with frustration as *Parche* slid by. So close was the maneuver that there was less than fifty feet to spare.

The *Parche* was now boxed in on all sides by Japanese small craft and escorts, all firing indiscriminately and so close they must undoubtedly have done a good bit of overshooting and damaged their own ships. But Ramage's maneuver had been coldly calculated, and quartermaster Plume, swallowing hard, could see why the skipper had taken the gamble of holding course until he got past the would-be rammer. Dead ahead lay a large AP troop transport vessel.

"By God, sir, she's a honey," said the quartermaster. Since the Japanese vessel was coming bow-on and the *Parche* was such a narrow target, the Jap gunners could not depress their guns enough to let loose any heavy stuff. It was a tricky position for attack. Torpedoes would have to be aimed with extreme accuracy to make a strike.

"Bow torpedo room," Ramage spoke calmly into the intercom, "how many fish do you have ready?"

"Three, sir," came the reply, the talker gasping a little for breath this time. It must be 125 degrees in the torpedo rooms, with the deck slippery from dripping sweat. "But . . . we'll have a fourth secured . . . in a minute." The men were stripped to their skivvies.

"No time," said Ramage. "Stand by for three."

Ramage waited a few seconds as range and hearing estimates were flashed from the radar operator and the quartermaster at the TBT. So much at close quarters was the action during the entire engagement that at one point John Gray, the chief electronics technician, one of the coolest, most methodical men Ramage had ever seen under high pressure, had actually shut off the set to retune it because he complained that it was "25 yards off."

"O.K., Captain, I've got the setup," said Torpedo Officer Allcorn on the torpedo data computer.

"Fire one!" shouted Ramage. Both vessels continued to hold course, the troop transport probably because she offered a smaller target than if she should turn broadside and because she, too, was intent on ramming.

"Check your setup again," said Ramage, slapping the coaming with the broad palm of his hand. "That baby missed."

"Fire two! Fire three!" rang out as the *Parche* continued to close the range. They sped straight down the transport's throat. "Left full rudder, before we get run over!" The submarine, swinging away from the starboard bow, shuddered as the two fish struck home.

Captain Red still was not satisfied. That miss—only the fourth out of eighteen shots—had made him mad, and the big transport, though well down at the bow, looked as though she might still float long enough for the Japanese troops aboard to reach safety. The bow tubes were now empty, but the after torpedo room had one in its tube and ready to go.

Ramage slowed speed slightly as the *Parche* arced some eight hundred yards away from the big transport, then gave the firing order.

The seconds went by. Ramage gripped the coaming edge and counted to himself. Quartermaster Plume lifted his eyes from his sights to look back past the white fin of spray marking the *Parche*'s tail. Then came a thundering *wharroom!* and a flash directly amidships. There followed a weird clanging of deck machinery and the hollow reverberations of loose chunks of metal and equipment crashing about inside the enemy transport. Then she plunged beneath the waves. The time was 0442.

The only ships within range now were heavily armed escort vessels, all concentrating their fury on the *Parche* since there seemed to be nothing left of their own convoy to endanger by indiscriminate fire. It was getting too hot even for Captain Red and besides, with nineteen torpedoes gone, he only had five left in case he spotted a more worthy target during the remainder of his patrol. Reluctantly he decided to haul clear.

"Set course 330 degrees true, and let's put a little distance between us and this hornet's nest," he called down to the conning tower. "Dawn's beginning to break."

"Take her down," said the diving officer, wiping the sweat from his brow with relief at the order everyone had expected long before this.

As the dark Pacific changed to a mass of foam across the forward decks, Quartermaster Plume squeezed lithely through the manhole, followed immediately by

Ramage. Behind them the hatch slammed shut, cutting out the din of gunfire beyond. Ramage spun the wheel tight and stepped from the ladder to the conning-tower deck and into heat that seemed to make his red hair curl. Down below the crewmen paused in their labors and heaved sighs of relief as the depth-gauge needle showed the boat plunging deeper and deeper. There would be a period of shuddering depth charges, but that was strictly routine compared with what they had gone through.

The *Parche* had had quite a run, and so had Commander Ramage. McCrory, Allcorn, Gray and Plume were all to receive Silver Stars for Gallantry, and the *Parche* and her entire crew a Presidential Unit Citation for extraordinary heroism. And Commander L. P. Ramage was to become the first living submariner to receive the Congressional Medal of Honor.

As the official citation put it:

> The personal daring and outstanding skill displayed by the commanding officer in his series of attacks against a large, heavily escorted enemy convoy . . . is one of the outstanding attacks in submarine warfare. . . . Only exceptional seamanship, outstanding personal heroism and extreme bravery of *Parche*'s commanding officer saved this submarine from serious damage if not total destruction.

As Captain Red put it, when interviewed later by a newspaper reporter, "I got mad!"

From *Lejeune:*
A Marine's Life
1867–1942

Merrill L. Bartlett

To all Marines interested in the history of our Corps, and all others dedicated to researching and writing that history, a study of the nine-year commandancy of our 13th Commandant of the Marine Corps, Major General John A. Lejeune, will provide many insights into the changing character of our country and the changing mission of the Marine Corps. When World War I began, the United States was not quite yet a world power, even though it had interests in China, the Philippines, and Latin America. With its participation in and influence on the course of the war in Europe, America truly became an international force. Major General Lejeune received the promotion to Lieutenant General after his retirement when the billet for the Commandant of the Marine Corps was elevated to Lieutenant General rank.

When he assumed the commandancy in 1920, General Lejeune headed a Corps numbering approximately 17,400 men, a considerable reduction from what it had been in World War I. He envisioned a Marine Corps whose success depended on two factors: "first, an efficient performance of all the duties to which its officers and men may be assigned; second, promptly bringing this efficiency to the attention of the proper officials of the government and the American people." General Lejeune saw that this Marine Corps faced at least three major internal problems. First, there was the issue of educating officers for broader and more complex and technical duties than those which they had been assigned to before. At the same time, the Corps had to attract to its ranks a smarter, younger, and more easily motivated type recruit who would be able to fit into a changing Marine Corps. Finally, General Lejeune had to seek for the Marine Corps an appropriate role in the defense of the country and a mission which it alone could fill.

He looked to the future of the Corps and instinctively knew that the Corps could not revert to its prewar role and outlook. As the noted Marine Corps historian, Colonel Robert D. Heinl Jr., observed: "Lejeune understood this fact well, even though many other Marines did not. General Lejeune was not only a field soldier of high ability, and a beloved leader, but also a Marine of prescient, active intelligence."

After reviewing the prewar missions of the Marine Corps and how they were accomplished, the Commandant and his advisors correctly concluded that readiness was the standard which inevitably ensured the success of any mission to which Marines were assigned. He then took several steps to guarantee that the Corps would be ready. One was to establish the Marine Corps Schools at Quantico, where his officers would be educated in their profession. As a corollary, General Lejeune encouraged his officers to attend the excellent schools run by the Army at that time. As a result, many of those who attained senior officer rank in World War II were those who had attended and graduated from the Fort Benning Infantry School, or the Command and General Staff Course at Fort Leavenworth, or the Fort Sill Artillery Course, among others, as well as from Navy and foreign military institutions. For enlisted Marines, there was the Marine Corps Institute, established during the commandancy of General Lejeune's predecessor, Major General George Barnett, but nurtured and supported by Lejeune.

A major achievement attained during General Lejeune's tenure was the realignment of the Marine Corps into the East and West Coast Expeditionary Forces, leading to the establishment of the Fleet Marine Force in 1933, which, in turn, compelled the Corps to develop amphibious warfare doctrine and techniques.

We Marines today are the heirs of General Lejeune's legacy which he enunciated so well in Article 38 of the 1921 edition of the *United States Marine Corps Manual*:

> In every battle and skirmish since the birth of our Corps, Marines have acquitted themselves with great distinction, winning new honors on each occasion until the term Marine has come to signify all that is highest in military efficiency and soldierly virtue.
>
> This high name of distinction and soldierly repute, we, who are Marines today, have received from those who preceded us in the Corps. With it, we also received from them the eternal spirit which has animated our Corps from generation to generation and has been the distinguishing mark of the Marines in every age. So long as that spirit continues to flourish, Marines will be found equal to every emergency in the future, as they have been in the past, and the men of our Nation will regard us as worthy successors to the long line of illustrious men who have served as "Soldiers of the Sea" since the founding of the Corps.

These words of General Lejeune are as valid today as they were when he first wrote them. And succeeding generations of Marines will find them as timely as well.

A. M. GRAY
General, U.S. Marine Corps (Retired)
Commandant of the Marine Corps (1987–1991)

Lejeune: Midshipman. In the two decades following the Civil war, the Marine Corps (numbering only 92 officers and 1,871 enlisted men in 1876) undertook the most intense reforms since its founding. Plagued with desertions and morale problems with the Corps' largely foreign-born enlisted force, and buffeted by demands from some Navy officers for the removal of leathernecks from the ships of the fleet, Colonel Commandant Charles G. McCawley sought to improve the professional starch of the crops. Commissioning better-educated officers became an important part of the reform effort; one critic of the Corps' junior officers suggested that USMC meant "useless sons made comfortable." Between 1883 and 1897, all of the 51 new second lieutenants for the Marine Corps came from the graduating classes of the U.S. Naval Academy. Most of the midshipmen accepted by the Marine Corps stood too low academically to be commissioned in the Navy and thus faced either discharge to civilian life or commissions as second lieutenants. Nonetheless, the Marine Corps profited from this influx of new officers with superior intelligence and more inclination to accept the smaller of the naval services for a full career.

When the class of 1888 returned to Annapolis in the late spring of 1890 from its post-graduation cruise, most midshipmen had already made up their minds as to service selection: Navy line or engineering, or the Marine Corps. Although he ranked thirteenth in his class, John Archer Lejeune raised his standing for the purposes of service selection to sixth following a spectacular performance on the post-cruise examinations. Thus, senior Navy officers were understandably bemused and nonplussed when the feisty Louisianan requested assignment to the Marine Corps. At first rebuffed by Navy superiors, one of whom admonished him by exclaiming, "Frankly, Mister Lejeune, you have altogether too many brains to be lost in the Marine Corps." He persisted and obtained a second lieutenant's commission only after the intervention of his senator.

Lejeune: Junior Officer to World War I. For the first two decades of his service in the Marine Corps, Lejeune's assignments reflected what had become routine for junior officers since 1798—sea or foreign duty alternating with stints at naval stations in the United States. Unlike most of his contemporaries, however, he chose marriage at a young age and began a family. Many of his peers adopted lifestyles of hard-drinking womanizers, claiming the lengthy periods at sea or abroad forced them to remain perpetual bachelors. As he matured, Lejeune became increasingly devout and moralistic.

When Colombian officials balked at President Roosevelt's heavy-handed political maneuvering to obtain a cross-isthmus canal, the United States opted to force the issue by coming to the aid of the Panamanian rebels. In November of 1903, Lejeune and his battalion marched ashore to reinforce other landing parties on the explosive scene. Lejeune's Marines patrolled the streets of Colon and otherwise kept the peace. Officially, the American forces received orders to protect the railway transiting the isthmus; no matter what transpired between the Colombian authorities and the Panamanian rebels, the United States demanded the right of neutral transit and intended to enforce that prerogative by armed force if necessary. Lejeune directed that each of his Marines carry a full canteen of water whenever leaving camp because of the variety of water-borne diseases endemic to the region. In addition, he required every man to sleep under a mosquito net because of the prevalence of malaria and yellow fever. He restricted liberty hours and placed the bordellos along the railway lines off-limits. Demanding that every Marine pay particular attention to personal hygiene, Lejeune and his officers inspected the battalion three times a week.

A chance assignment as a student at the Army War Collage in 1909–10 opened new vistas. He probably began his quest for the commandancy then at the urging of the president of the college, who relayed rumors that the helm of the Marine Corps might pass to a staff officer due to the lack of distinguished applicants. Although

Lejeune was too junior to be considered seriously for the Corps' highest post, either in 1910 or 1913–14, the idea that one day he might head the Marine Corps never disappeared.

On 7 November 1910, Lejeune assumed command of Marine Barracks, New York. Command of the large barracks tested Lejeune's mettle as a leader. When he arrived, he found that its desertion rate numbered the highest in Marine Corps. The strength of the barracks varied between four hundred and five hundred men, many of whom were recruits undergoing basic training; the remainder provided security for the naval station. Lejeune learned that most of the Marines had liberty following the noon meal, unless assigned to guard duties. Alarmed by the scandalous desertion rate, he cracked down immediately.

Determining that the proliferation of saloons and bordellos in the neighborhoods outside the barracks contributed to the problem, he required all hands to appear in a formation at reveille. Following breakfast, physical training and drill appeared on the schedule. An inspection of the mess hall revealed the food to be bland and unappetizing and little improvement over what he had tasted as a second lieutenant in Portsmouth. Finally, Lejeune enjoined his officers to make the training interesting rather than perfunctory; as an example, he added athletics to the training schedule and required non-swimmers to take lessons at a nearby YMCA pool. Idleness or "bunk fatigue" plagued the command and he was determined to stop it.

Reforms Marine Barracks [handwritten marginal note]

Almost immediately, his reforms bore fruit. When he assumed command in 1910, the desertion rate had reached 8.5 percent, but the following year, it dropped to 5.5 percent; and each year thereafter, the percentage dropped further. Although Lejeune's performance and that of his command pleased the commandant and his staff, his determined character ruffled Navy feathers in Brooklyn. Soon after assuming command, Lejeune asked the commandant of the Navy Yard, Rear Admiral Eugene Leutze, for permission to fly the flag in front of the Marine barracks. Leutze denied the request, opining that only one flag would be flown and that in front of his own headquarters. Lejeune notified the Commandant of the Marine Corps, who in turn passed the matter on to the Secretary of the Navy. A ruling arrived in Brooklyn that overturned Leutze's edict, reinforcing Lejeune's reputation as a stickler for the details of service custom and not an officer appeased simply by seniority.

Following a superlative performance as a regimental commander during the landing at Veracruz, Mexico, in 1914—although he failed to receive one of the several specious awards of the Medal of Honor—Lejeune became the assistant to the Commandant, Major General George Barnett. By then, Lejeune had captured the eye and respect of the Secretary of the Navy Josephus Daniels.

Lejeune: World War I. Almost from the beginning of America's declaration of war in 1917, Lejeune pressed for orders to join the American Expeditionary Forces (AEF) in France. As a brigadier general, he assumed that he would be given command of a brigade of infantry. Because of wartime expansion, Congress authorized the promotion of an additional major general for the Marine Corps. Lejeune received a second star in the summer of 1918. Surprising both Army and Navy observers, General John J. Pershing gave Lejeune command of the Second Division, AEF.

Lejeune became the first Marine Corps officer to command an entire division. Lejeune believed that he received the coveted assignment because of his superlative performance at the Army War College; many of his former classmates and instructors served in the highest councils of the AEF. Lejeune led the Second Division, AEF, during the offensive of St. Mihiel, Mont Blanc, and Meuse-Argonne, breaking the stalemate of years of trench warfare; he commanded the Second Division, AEF, during its deployment as an occupation force along the Rhine River after the German surrender. At the time, Lejeune reflected on the superb record of his command, feeling especially proud of his fellow Marines. The Second Division earned a record unequalled by a division in the AEF; the division had captured more enemy soldiers and had advanced farther against the enemy than any other division. The casualty figures—the Second Division suffered 5,150 leathernecks and doughboys killed in action and another 18,066 wounded; the final drive for the Meuse-Argonne to end the War had cost the Allies more than 120,000 casualties, but together they had captured forty-seven German divisions—troubled him. He expressed this concern in a letter to his successor: "The Marine Corps has just cause to feel proud of its brigade . . . there isn't much left of the original crowd. The hospitals are full of wounded."

Lejeune: Post-World War I.   Upon returning to the United States in October 1919, Lejeune assumed the position of commanding general at Quantico, Virginia. He found the installation in shambles because of frantic preparations for wartime service. Besides seeing to repair of the physical plant, Lejeune had plans for his Marines based on the personal criticisms over the way the war had been fought. Lejeune returned from the western front convinced that military personnel needed more education. At the enlisted level, he believed the men to be bored and over-trained to the point of disinterest in the military profession. The antimilitary attitude following World War I exacerbated the problem. Many Marines wondered how their military training would help them succeed in the difficult post-war employment situation. With Butler's assistance, Lejeune introduced a novel solution to the problem of educating and training Marines.

Lejeune suggested that his Marines would perform better if officers reduced the hours of purely military training. More than two hours of military training in the classroom or on the drill field each day made the average enlisted man muscle-bound and stale. In Lejeune's program, Quantico-based Marines trained, drilled, and performed routine maintenance from reveille until the noon meal. In the afternoon, they had the opportunity to study one of three vocational subjects: automotive mechanics, music, or clerical skills. Lejeune's plan attracted immediate support, both from within and outside the Corps.

Lejeune: Commandant of the U.S. Marine Corps.   A year after Lejeune's return from Europe in 1919, Secretary Daniels—the appointee of a Democratic administration—stunned the Washington naval and political circles by ousting Major General Barnett from the commandancy of the Marine Corps. The appointment of Lejeune, well-known for his support for the Democrats, produced considerable controversy. Barnett's Republican backers attempted to prevent Lejeune's confirmation as the thirteenth Commandant of the Marine Corps but failed.

Although Lejeune received his appointment as Commandant of the Marine Corps in an atmosphere rife with acrimony and recrimination, he provided the soothing balm to alleviate the pain and outrage felt by the ousted incumbent and his Republican supporters. Whereas Secretary Daniels continued to humiliate Barnett and exacerbate the controversy, Lejeune, a canny political infighter whose down-home Louisiana charm masked his shrewdness, suggested the solution that put the difficulty to rest.

The nine years that Lejeune held the reins of the Corps remain the least known and appreciated. During these lean years of America's military and naval entrenchment, he redirected the focus of Headquarters Marine Corps (HQMC) from its traditional concern over manpower and budgetary matters toward operational planning. Seizing on the prophesy of War Plan Orange—envisioning a conflict with Japan—he directed his subordinates to begin operational planning so as to prepare for the employment of amphibious forces in the event of a naval war in the Pacific.

While the genesis of modern amphibious doctrine is rightly attributed to the visionaries of the 1930s, Lejeune's stewardship during the lean years of the Harding-Coolidge retrenchment of the 1920s set the stage. Although plagued with congressional requests for personnel and budgetary reductions, and despite a continuation of traditional commitments overseas or in support of the fleet, Lejeune managed to steer a steady course for the Marine Corps through a period of intense and unrealistic cuts.

By the 1920s, the ranks of the officer corps had become badly split. One group, led by the frenetic Brigadier General Smedley Butler, wanted a Marine Corps led not by the intellectuals from Annapolis or the war colleges but by seasoned campaigners with tropical sweat stains and powder burns on their uniforms. Another faction, festooned with decorations earned on the battlefields of France, demanded recognition and preferential treatment for their heroic service. A third clique sought a Marine Corps led by officers with intellect and vision to prepare for its assault mission in support of the fleet.

This last coterie—composed largely of Annapolitans—sought the transformation of the Marine Corps from a rather colorful and quaint light infantry corps d'elite into a modern amphibious force. Intellectually and professionally, Lejeune sided with the visionaries. Yet he took pains to not appear to belong to any faction, because the ideological dispute had the potential to engulf the officer ranks in disruptive acrimony. The political debris resulting from the abrupt ouster of Barnett in 1920 still hung heavy over the Marine Corps. Lejeune and his senior officers could not likely weather another public inquiry into the machinations of its leaders—however popular, professional, or colorful. Lejeune's career encompassed what many naval historians consider to be an important and overlooked era in the history of the U.S. Marine Corps. As the new American Navy embraced the technology of the twentieth century, leatherneck participation in modernization became tenuous at best. Clinging to the traditional task of providing ships' guards and small landing parties no longer justified the existence of a separate naval service. Lejeune had the intellect and vision to realize that the Marine Corps' future remained with the fleet. The era of colonial infantry assignments for his beloved leathernecks slipped into the Marines' colorful history. When the Joint Army and Navy Board gave the amphibious assault mission to the Marine Corps during Lejeune's commandancy it marked the end of the colonial infantry era for the Corps and the beginning of the golden age of amphibious warfare.

Lejeune's impact on the Marine Corps is perhaps best embodied in the landing of the First Marine Division in the Solomon Islands during the year of his death. By planning and preparing for large-scale Marine involvement in the event of war with Japan, Lejeune set the stage for the genesis of amphibious doctrine in the years after his commandancy. Although the *Tentative Manual for Landing Operations* did not appear until after Lejeune relinquished the helm of the Corps, his vision and leadership established the basis for the most important era in leatherneck history. Without his foresight and persistence, Lejeune's Marines might have spent the golden age of amphibious warfare manning detachments in the warships of the fleet and providing forces for defense battalions on lonely island outposts—missions rapidly becoming antiquated and redundant.

Lejeune's tenure at the helm of the Marine Corps established the basis for the commandants of the 1930s to complete the codification of a modern naval mission.

Lejeune's professional life encompassed the far-reaching changes of this important era and linked his name with the evolution of a modern Marine Corps. Not since the lengthy tenure of Archibald Henderson has a Commandant had such an impact on the Marine Corps.

Lejeune: Recollections. Lejeune's Louisiana charm worked wonders on almost everyone whom he encountered, even Navy superiors who often came to loggerheads with him over peccadillos of service custom and seniority or Army officers who bridled over his unwillingness to adopt a style of leadership based on intimidation and threat. An aide-de-camp recalled Lejeune admonishing a young soldier for an unbuttoned blouse: "Son, General Pershing would give me hell if I went around with my blouse unbuttoned." Sitting on a promotion board, Lejeune and other board members heard a young officer describe his duties as a guard officer. One board member professed ignorance as to the meaning of "gahd," to which Lejeune replied: "Mister Vandergrift is from the South; he spells 'gahd' correctly as 'g-u-a-r-d' but pronounces it correctly as 'gahd'."

Before an accident in 1932 affected his ability to articulate, Lejeune claimed a fair amount of respect and admiration for his strong and stirring extemporaneous speeches. On 31 October 1921, Lejeune brought the annual convention of the Amer-

"Right There" A U.S. Marine 2nd Lt. confirms the enemy's position given him by his corporal.
Official U.S. Navy Photo.

ican Legion to its feet in thunderous applause. Comparing the heroic deeds of the Marine Corps to those of the French Foreign Legion that charged against the forces of Austria and Russia in the Battle of Wagram, Lejeune quoted Marshall Ney: "Hear them shoot; see them charge! It's in their blood! It's in their blood!" On 12 January, 1922, he addressed the officers at Quantico to explain his goals. Trumpeting his motto, "In time of peace, prepare for war," Lejeune admonished his audience to assist in his aims. In an emotional plea, he referred to the Corps' priceless heritage , and reminded his listeners that it had come to them from the heroic dead. In closing his address, the Commandant offered advice on leadership, a favorite theme: "Discipline must be maintained; military punctilio observed; but there is also the obligation to deal justly, fairly, kindly, and honorably with those who are under our command; and to serve loyally and faithfully those who command us." Then, Lejeune pointed directly to his officers for emphasis: "This obligation is mutual."

After more than four decades in uniform—military cadet at Louisiana State University, midshipman at the U.S. Naval Academy, graduated midshipman in the fleet, and as an officer in the Marine Corps—Lejeune had acquired fundamental ideas about citizenship, morality, duty to the Corps and country, and the high standards expected of a Marine Corps officer. His support for the idea of duty above and beyond the norm was exemplified by such actions as taking the pledge of temperance even before Prohibition was enacted.

2 *The Naval Professional*

Objectives

1. Describe the naval officer in terms of the characteristics of a professional.

2. Explain the relationship between standards and readiness and list some consequences of failing to maintain standards.

Professionalism

Is It Really a Profession?

Vice Admiral James Calvert

It is late at night and the half-dark corridors of the hospital are deserted. Their black-and-white checkered floors recede in both directions without interruption except for the occasional red glow of an exit light. Overhead, a framed glass panel soundlessly flashes the call numbers of doctors wanted somewhere within the hospital. The same numbers appear again and again, always in the same sequence, apparently always without success.

An open door on the corridor leads into a waiting room in which a young man, in shirtsleeves and with tousled hair, smokes a cigarette and paces restlessly back and forth. The room has a depressing, institutional look with its garish fluorescent light; one of the tubes is faulty, but the constant hum and occasional blink go unnoticed by the young man, who adds another cigarette to the already-full ashtray.

He moves to the door and once more studies the electric call sign with its incessantly repeating sequence of numbers. He wonders if the doctors are really needed and, if so, why someone doesn't go and get them. Do the doctors ever look at the sign? Are they even in the hospital? Are they being called for his wife?

Moving away from the door, the young man looks at his watch and realizes that hours have gone by since he should have heard from the delivery room. What is going on? Is his wife safe? And what of the baby, their first child?

What is it that permits a scene similar to this to be enacted many times each night across our land and almost always achieve a happy ending? Why does our young man entrust all that he holds dearest in the world to the skill and knowledge of a stranger whose competence he has no way to judge? What is the source of such faith in another man?

The answer lies in a single term: professional standards. Our society insists on certain standards of training and professional competence before it permits a man to present himself to the public as a doctor of medicine. These standards are nationwide; they enable an expectant father to spend his cheerless night of waiting with the knowledge that professional standards exist which go far toward ensuring that his wife and new child are in competent hands.

He cannot, of course, be certain. Tragedies do occur, doctors do make mistakes, and some cases are beyond human help—but the heavy probability is on the side of competence. The professional pride and standards of the medical profession are important and tangible assets in our society.

The doctor of medicine remains the primary and best example of the professional man in the United States today. His qualifications for that title and the rewards deriving from it go relatively unchallenged. But what of the other professions? How sure is their title? How firm their standard?

Naval Academy photo courtesy of United States Naval Academy Photographic Laboratory.

Perhaps we ought to examine this word "professional" to obtain a firmer grasp of its meaning and importance. First of all, there is little doubt that the word is of increasing interest and importance in our nation today. As our society becomes more complex, it becomes more professionalized; the proportion of professional men within our population has more than quadrupled within the last century. No title is more sought after, none holds more prestige than that of a profession. Other occupations, such as business, may receive greater income; others, such as entertainment, may receive more public notice; but none has greater prestige.

Those who have studied the sociology of the professions in our country are continually struck by the efforts of fringe occupations to claim professional status. Librarians, insurance salesmen, personnel administrators, city managers, YMCA secretaries, beauticians, accountants, publicity men, investment counselors, and a host of others all make arguments for their professional status, all strive to achieve this magical term of approval and prestige. Practically all of these people are serious and well-intentioned; they genuinely believe that their occupations deserve the term "profession" and also believe, perhaps not incorrectly, that the standards and ideals of those following their occupation will improve if only the term "profession" can be applied.

Any young person contemplating a career today has every reason to ask about its professional status. What, then, about the military occupation? Is the often-used phrase "the military profession" really meaningful? There is little doubt that the military officer's occupation is, at least traditionally, thought of as a profession. For example, the *Oxford Shorter Dictionary,* in defining the word "profession" states, among other things: "Applied specifically to the three learned professions of divinity, law and medicine; also the military profession." Although those military officers who aspire to professional status might look rather gloomily upon their separation from the word "learned" in this definition, the fact remains that a host of other aspirants to the magical term are not even mentioned.

What are the essential characteristics of the professional man? Bernard Barber, a sociologist who has done much work in this field, sees four:

1. A high degree of general and systematic knowledge.
2. Primary orientation to the community interest rather than self-interest.
3. A high degree of self-control of behavior through codes of ethics.
4. A system of rewards, both monetary and honorary, which are primarily symbolic and not a means to some end of individual self-interest.

Samuel Huntington, who has written extensively on the professional status of the military, sees three attributes of importance in estimating the professional status of any occupation:

1. Expertise in a significant field of human endeavor.
2. Responsibility to use that expertise in a manner beneficial to the functioning of society.
3. A sense of belonging to a corporate body which stands apart from the layman and at the same time enforces certain standards of competence and conduct.

The basic concepts revealed in these two lists of professional characteristics are similar. Knowledge, responsibility, and self-regulation stand out. The insistence upon knowledge, expertise, competence, learning, or skill in some field not understood by the general public is particularly striking.

However, many occupations can claim special knowledge. The characteristic of responsibility toward the welfare of the community in some significant area of its concern restricts the concept considerably. This is the factor that eliminates the public relations man, the beautician, and others from serious consideration. It also eliminates the professional athlete or the professional entertainer, traditional users of the word "professional" in an altogether different context.

Nevertheless, such occupations as investment counseling and estate planning can make serious claim to highly specialized knowledge and responsibility for vital concerns of the individual; it is the third attribute, that of a recognizable corporate organization which enforces certain standards of competence and conscience upon its practitioners, that narrows the field so severely.

We have then, it appears, three basic concepts: specialized knowledge in some significant field; responsibility to use that knowledge primarily in the interest of others; and membership in a recognized group dedicated to enforcing certain standards and capable of granting meaningful rewards. What of the naval officer's occupation in this light?

It is immediately apparent that to term every naval officer a true professional would be out of the question. A newly commissioned ensign, possessed of a college degree and a few weeks of training in an officer candidate school, possesses no specialized knowledge in a field of significance to the community. His status is not comparable to that of the new doctor, or even to that of the new intern.

On the other hand, to deny that there are officers who possess all of the characteristics we have outlined would also be wrong. One cannot deny that a successful general or admiral serving as, say, one of our unified commanders responsible for command of all United States armed forces over a large geographic area of the world is a professional in the deepest sense of the word. We are forced to conclude that some naval officers are professionals and some are not.

But we must not jump to the conclusion that it is only length of service that makes the difference. Is the officer who has decided to spend his active career in the Navy

July 3, 1996. . . . North Atlantic salt spray soaks Sailors on board USS Mitscher (DDG 57) during refuel operations with USS Enterprise (CVN 65).

Official U.S. Navy photo.

Comparing and Contrasting ensign to admiral

automatically a professional? I think the answer must be an emphatic no; indeed, the term "professional soldier" connotes the very opposite of some of those attributes we have considered vital.

But if the new ensign is denied the title and it is granted to the admiral holding high command, then where is the dividing line? Does it come suddenly, at some given rank? Before we can answer this question, we must define the essential ingredients of naval professionalism. To begin with, it is apparent that the subject of knowledge, of learning, of expertise, is of great importance. It is perhaps in this area that the military officer is most often challenged in his quest for professional status.

What is it that the admiral knows and the ensign does not? I believe his knowledge can be broken down into four broad categories: sea knowledge, technological competence, command ability, and staff competence.

Sea knowledge is the foundation of the naval profession, and although there are many naval officers who do not possess it, they cannot be considered professional in our sense of the word. Much of this knowledge is mundane, and rarely is it of an intellectual nature. It starts with the sea itself, its characteristics, and its behavior under various conditions of weather; it includes the behavior of ships in the sea, an awareness of what is dangerous and what is not, a knowledge of when to take precautions and how to calculate at sea. It also covers such matters as piloting and navigation, tides and currents, and a capacity to judge where ships can go safely and where not, which waters are minable and which not, where submarines can be expected and where they cannot operate, how ships are handled in formation or when approaching a mooring, in short, all the intrinsic capabilities and limitations of ships.

Some of this sea knowledge is almost folklore, and much of it is shared by rough and uneducated men in may parts of the world in ships of every type and description. Taken alone, it cannot be considered professional knowledge in any learned sense of the word; combined with other elements of military professionalism, it is of the essence.

Our second category, that of technological competence, is a more difficult matter. It has become a commonplace to observe the swiftly growing complexity of modern weapons. How much of the technology involved can we expect a professional naval officer to know? Can the Polaris submarine commanding officer leap, like Walter Mitty, to the side of his non-operating digital computer or nuclear power-plant component and unerringly put his finger on the source of the trouble, repairing it if necessary with a hastily converted part of an old fountain pen? No, not really.

But true professionalism, to say nothing of the successful and safe operation of our modern ships and planes, does require a significant amount of technological knowledge so complex that some very professional officers of the past might have been sorely pressed to meet this requirement. It is necessary, for one thing, to distinguish between operational knowledge and maintenance ability. To know how to start up or turn on equipment, operate it successfully, and turn it off is an altogether different matter from knowing how to repair it, as housewives have been proving with automobiles for decades.

Unlike the housewife, however, the modern naval officer depends upon his highly technical equipment to take him places where not only his own life but the lives of hundreds of his men depend upon its successful operation. It is obvious that his competence to judge whether certain equipment can or cannot operate safely or can or cannot be successfully repaired at sea, affects his ship's safety. Clearly this takes knowledge beyond the turn-it-on, turn-it-off category—and that knowledge alone can become bewilderingly complex with some of our new equipment.

The naval officer of today faces a real challenge in the area of technological competence. The temptation to specialize is strong, and yet the true specialist in technological matters cannot be considered a professional naval officer in our sense. On the other hand, to expect every naval officer to have a complete knowledge of all the Navy's equipment is expecting too much. The field has become too large.

Fortunately, there are common characteristics in many types of modern equipment. A sound knowledge of practical electronics is almost a professional necessity; the fundamental principles of capacitances, inductances, relays, amplifiers, rectifiers, solid-state devices, and cathode-ray applications pervade our Navy today the way rope, tar, and canvas did a century and a half ago. They are part of our professional equipment, and a basic understanding of their principles and applications will go a long way toward explaining the fundamental working of much of our new naval equipment.

More and more, the naval officer must understand the principles of metallurgy in order to make sound judgments about his ships, his planes, his missiles, and their capabilities and limitations. Indeed, the limitations of more and more weapons and vehicles are being determined by this field of knowledge. An understanding of what things can and cannot be safely welded at sea, what machinery may be hastily put into service in an emergency and what must, under any circumstances, be carefully warmed up—these and a host of other matters of importance to a commanding officer often depend upon a basic understanding of metallurgical principles.

In sum, while no one person can be competent in the operation and maintenance of all of the modern Navy's equipment, the professional naval officer needs to be sufficiently well grounded in engineering principles to make sound judgments without relying entirely on the advice and counsel of others.

Our third element of naval professionalism, command ability, like our first, is peculiarly of the sea. Command of a warship at sea is an experience without an exact counterpart in any other occupation. The elements of initiative, judgment, self-reliance, imagination, responsibility, and leadership brought into play here come very close to being unique.

But command of single ships is only a part of the naval officer's required professional command experience. When ships begin to work in company, problems of tactics, communication, and command become complex. Command over groups of ships at sea is a step in the development of the naval professional that requires both a thorough knowledge of the sea itself and of single-ship command.

As the naval officer becomes proficient in broad command at sea, he will inevitably become involved in our fourth level of professional knowledge: that of the staff. Commanders of large numbers of ships and aircraft need assistance in the discharge of their duties, and naval staffs are organized with this in mind. Even more complex, however, is the type of staff required to run our unified commands and joint task forces. The naval officer who would serve usefully in this area must have a knowledge of Army and Air Force organization and theory as well as that prescribed for joint use. A unified command staff or joint task force staff is a complex and intricate affair. Certain groups of these men are expert in supply, transportation, and personnel matters; others in the gathering of intelligence; and still others in the overall task of plan-

Seated in his uniquely covered chair, Captain Bill Synder, commanding officer USS COWPENS (CG 63), takes his ship out of San Diego harbor.
Official U.S. Navy photo.

ning large operations. These are all professional skills, and the naval officer who aspires to professionalism must understand them; they are not peculiar to the sea, but they are increasingly important in the joint command of our armed forces.

These four elements, then, in my view, are the ingredients of naval professionalism. Experience with each is necessary to the whole of professional knowledge. But, even if attained, this knowledge comprises only the first of our three attributes. What of the other two: orientation to community interest and membership in a corporate body capable of self-control and the dispensing of rewards?

In regard to its orientation to the community interest, there is not much that need be said about the naval officer's occupation. It has no other aim. It is entirely devoted to the protection and furtherance of the national community; those of its members who use it for other purposes have, by definition, divested themselves of any claim to professionalism.

Let us pass on to the third characteristic, membership in a corporate body of useful and significant powers. Our best hope in this area is to trace the evolution of those institutions which give the naval profession its distinguishing characteristics today: its ability to select its own leaders, its provision of adequate procurement and retirement procedures, the development of its schools and colleges, its achievement of an intellectual credo, and its evolution of those ideals and aspirations which separate a profession from other means of earning a livelihood. A profession must have a history; by its very nature, it is evolved, not created at one fell swoop.

A Guy I Want to Work For

Theodore Rockwell

One of the Admiral's former right-hand men tells how the tactics of Rickover and his staff influenced candidates for the Naval Nuclear Propulsion Program.

As each nuclear-powered ship approached the date of initial criticality, her skipper knew he would soon experience a Naval Reactors Crew Quiz. This was part of the process by which Rickover satisfied himself, and then reported to the U.S. Atomic Energy Commission, that the training and the performance of this crew were up to the standards necessary to start up a nuclear reactor and take it to sea. This would not be the only such inspection, but it would be the first on the ship, and the skipper would have done everything he could to get ready for it. A typical crew quiz ran about as follows: First, a call came from Bob Panoff, Rickover's submarine project officer, and the inspection was scheduled for a Friday night, to continue on into the weekend, as long as it took.

Panoff, Jack Grigg, and I made up a typical team for those early inspections. Grigg was Rickover's instrumentations and controls expert. I had the title of technical director. . . .

Panoff started right in. "I want to get right into this. We have a long evening ahead us. As I think you heard, we had one crew quiz on the prototype, and we interviewed the people alone so they wouldn't be intimidated by the presence of their officers. But then the officers had trouble believing that their people had done so badly. The officers didn't say so, but it was clear that they were convinced their men had all the answers and we must have tricked them or asked misleading questions. So tonight I'm asking your permission to have one or more of you present for all of the questioning. That way you'll be able to judge the results firsthand. Do you have any objection to that?"

The skipper replied. "No problem. I'm confident about our state of training, and if there is anything wrong, I want to see it myself."

Panoff continued. "Fine. Despite what you may have heard, it's not our purpose to terrorize your people. This is a technical quiz, not a psychological one. We'll keep the questions straightforward, and the men can ask for clarification without prejudice. But we expect them to know the technical material thoroughly. I'm sure you've heard Admiral Rickover say that any one detail, followed through to its source, will usually reveal the general state of readiness of the whole organization. Take the spare parts system, for example. The way parts are inventoried, stored, accessed, and reordered can be quite revealing of the whole organization." He pulled a little widget out of his pocket and asked, "Do you know what this is, Captain?" The skipper and his engineer looked at it carefully. "Do you use these on this ship?"

The engineer was ready with an answer, "Yes, sir. It's a . . ." Not waiting for a reply, Panoff asked, "How long would it take to get another one? Here, in the wardroom."

"They're stored in the yard, sir. Over in Siberia—one of the new buildings at the north end of the yard."

"How long?"

"Oh, I suppose we could have one within the hour."

"And if it were an emergency?"

"Half an hour, sure."

Panoff looked at his watch and said simply, "Go!"

"I beg your pardon?"

"You now have 29 minutes, 55 seconds left."

"Yes, sir!" The engineer jumped to his feet and ran out the door.

The skipper wanted to insert a caution. "It's late Friday evening, you realize. He may have trouble getting the right people at the yard. They keep all that stuff under heavy security."

"Can you guarantee that you won't have any emergencies on weekends, Captain?"

"No, sir. We may have to change our arrangements with the yard to handle things like this. Mr. Rockwell, I've been thinking about that radiation drill you pulled on the prototype last week. They phoned us about it. You had them take wipe samples on various surfaces, and they found high radioactive contamination. So they called a radiation alert. But you told them to go outside and check the hoods of some parked cars. And they were even higher. Those poor guys figured they'd blown a fuel element and were about to shut the whole place down and evacuate. Then you told them it was probably fallout from weapons tests. And they checked and found out it was. Is that just because they're out there in the desert, closer to the testing sites, or is that going to be a problem for me, too?"

I asked, "Did you try it here? You could make the same sort of test yourself, you know."

"No, sir. We just haven't had time."

"You would find that you got about the same results. In fact, the radiation levels from weapons testing fallout are higher, almost anywhere in the Northern Hemisphere, than we have set for a radiation alert on the ships. You should find lower contamination levels in your engine room than in the parking lot outside. You just have to be aware of that, and not call a false alarm. In case of doubt, you have procedures for differentiating between various radioisotopes. That should pin it down."

Panoff asked, "Have your men been briefed on the meaning of the colors of the various indicating and warning lights?"

The engineer had now come back from setting up the parts search, and he handled Panoff's question. "Lights? Yes, sir. I handled that myself. The complete spectrum, I called it, from on to caution to warning to danger. They ought to know that cold, sir."

"We'll see, won't we?" said Panoff. "Let's go."

Grigg had already left to go over electrical and control questions with appropriate crew members, accompanied by the executive officer. The skipper and the engineer ducked through the watertight door into the corridor, following Panoff. A noncommissioned officer was standing watch over some machinery with a large number of red and green lights. The engineer smiled reassuringly at the sailor, then did a double take as he looked at the lights.

Panoff asked, "Chief, do you understand the color system for machinery lights?"

"Yes, sir."

"Will you please explain what you have here?"

"Yes, sir. Glad to," replied the chief. "When I got here last week, these lights were all sorts of colors. You wouldn't believe it. Red, blue, yellow, green. Everything. Even white ones. But I got them all in order."

Naval Academy photo courtesy of United States Naval Academy Photographic Laboratory.

The engineer could control himself no longer. "My God, Chief! What in the world have you done?"

Panoff cut him off. "Please let him answer. Please explain your system, Chief."

"Yes, sir. Well, you see, red is for port and green is for starboard. So all the lights for the port valves and the port pumps are red, and the starboard ones are green. See how clear it makes it? You can't get the wrong one that way."

"Thank you, Chief. That will be all."

The engineer said grimly, "Chief, I want to see you in the wardroom when this is over. Don't go anywhere."

Panoff said gently, "There'll be more, Lieutenant. The night is young yet."

They went down the passageway to the next watchstander. I stopped to quiz him, and Panoff went through another door with the skipper, into the engine room. The engineer stayed with me.

"Sailor," I said, "I understand you're qualifying for reactor operator."

"Yes, sir. But I'm not finished yet."

"I understand. You've completed theoretical school?"

"Yes, sir. At Bainbridge."

"And prototype school?"

"Yes sir. And I'm qualifying for the various watch-stations here on the boat—or ship, we're supposed to call it. I can't get used to a submarine being a ship, sir."

"I'd like to check you out on some basic thermodynamic theory," I said. "Is that OK?"

"Yes, sir. I guess I'm about as ready as I'll ever be."

"Do you know what Charles's Law is?"

"I forget which is Charles's and which is Boyle's. One is temperature and the other is pressure."

"I don't care whether you remember their names. I just want to be sure you know what they mean. Suppose we have a sealed tank, full of a perfect gas. Is air a perfect gas?" I asked.

"Any gas follows the perfect-gas law pretty well unless it's under very high pressure," said the sailor.

"Well, air does, anyway. So let's say this tank has a pressure gauge on it that reads 10 PSIG. Do you know what that means?"

"Yes, sir, 10 pounds per square inch gauge pressure."

"Right. And let's say it has a temperature gauge that reads 70° Fahrenheit. Now let's say we heat it up until the temperature reads 140° Fahrenheit. What do you expect the pressure gauge to read? Will it change?"

"Yes, sir, it will go up. Boyle's or Charlie's Law says that if you double the temperature in a sealed system with perfect gas in it, the pressure will double too, so the gauge will read 20, right? . . . You look as if that's not right."

"Well, let's think about it a little more," I said. "Suppose there's a second temperature gauge on the tank, and this one reads Celsius. Let's see, 70° Fahrenheit would be about 20° Celsius. And 140° Fahrenheit would be about [mumble, mumble] 60° Celsius. So the Fahrenheit gauge says you've doubled the temperature, but the Celsius gauge says you've increased it threefold. Which is right?"

The sailor now looked baffled. "Gee, now I'm really confused. Wait a minute. I got it! From 70° to 140° Fahrenheit isn't doubling. You gotta start figuring from absolute zero, which is 273° below zero in Celsius. I don't remember what it is in Fahrenheit."

"Now we're getting somewhere," I said, getting into it. "Suppose we figured out how much heat it took to double the temperature, then the pressure would go to 20 pounds, right?" The sailor nodded. "But now let's start with the pressure gauge reading zero. We add the heat to double the pressure, but how do you double zero?"

But the sailor didn't bite on that one. "No, I'm with you now. The pressure gauge isn't showing an absolute number either. It reads zero at atmospheric pressure, which is about 15 pounds per square inch absolute. So if you doubled the pressure, the gauge would go to 30 PSI absolute pressure, or 15 PSI gauge pressure. That's right, isn't it?" He looked pleadingly at me. "Look, Mister, I'm not stupid. They just didn't teach us this sort of thing in school."

I was completely conciliatory. "You did OK. It's clear you're not stupid. And you're not ignorant, either. But you've got me worried about the schools."

While this was going on, the chief previously questioned was relieved of the watch, accompanied by the engineer, and I went back to quiz the replacement. The chief was looking at a sheaf of papers that he sheepishly tried to stuff into his pocket when he saw me approaching.

"Whatcha got, Chief?" I asked.

Embarrassed, the chief looked helplessly to the engineer, who said, "Tell him, Chief."

Crewmen on board USS Baltimore (SSN 704) stand by with a grappling hook to snag a mail shipment being lowered by an SH-60 Seahawk helicopter.
Official U.S. Navy photo.

"It's a crib sheet, sir. A list of questions we got from the guys at the prototype after their quiz. That isn't really cheating, is it?"

"No, because it won't do you any good. We just want to know if you understand what you're doing. What would you like to be asked about? What do you know best?"

"I just finished studying the charging procedure, sir. Ask me about that."

"OK, Chief, tell me about it. What do you do?"

"Well, when the water level in the pressurizer gets below this point here, I turn on the charging pump by throwing this switch. And I keep watching the waterlevel gauge, and I turn it off when it gets up to here."

"So what is the maximum amount of water you have to pump in, in inches of water level?" I asked.

"We try to keep it within four inches, sir. We normally don't like it to get any further off than that."

"How long should it take to raise the water level four inches, Chief?"

"Ten minutes, sir."

"Suppose I think it's 20 minutes. How would you check that?"

"I can find that right in the manual, sir. It will only take a few minutes to look that up. But I'm sure ten minutes is right."

He started pawing frantically through the manual, but I cut in. "Suppose you can't find it in the manual. Is there any other way you could check it?"

"I'd ask the other chief, sir. He's pretty smart, and he's been around longer than I have."

"Chief, I'm trying to get down to fundamentals. You taught math at the school, didn't you?"

The chief was puzzled by this turn in the conversation. "Yes, sir."

"Could you calculate from first principles how long it should take to pump four inches of water into that pressurizer?"

"What do you mean, sir? What first principles?"

"Chief, can you calculate the volume of a cylinder four inches high and the diameter of the pressurizer? And could you convert that volume into gallons? And, knowing the gallons per minute the charging pump can deliver, could you calculate how long it would take to deliver that volume of water? Could you?"

"Oh, yes, sir. That's the sort of problem I gave my students all the time."

"Then do it right now."

"Now, sir?"

"Now. Let me see you do it."

The chief pulled a piece of paper out of the drawer and quickly scratched out some figures. He then took out a slide rule and, after a few deft movements, wrote down an answer. With a smile of relief he turned to me and said, "See? Ten minutes."

"The point is, Chief, that you triggered around with every possible way of getting that answer except by a simple calculation. And you showed that you can calculate it in a few seconds. Why would you do everything else but? Why wouldn't you just calculate it?"

"I guess I just never think of math when I'm on the job. School is school, but this is the real world. That's what they kept telling us at the prototype school."

I jumped at that one. "*What* did they keep telling you at the prototype?"

"Geez, I guess I stuck my foot in it. I probably shouldn't be telling you this . . ."

"Tell him," said the engineer.

"On the very first day the instructors say, 'Forget about all that crap you learned at theoretical school. This is the real world.' Pardon me, but that's what they said, sir."

I responded with great sadness. "Oh, brother! Chief, I'm not mad at you. Thanks for telling me. But we're going to have to do something. If *you* don't ever think of using what you teach, we certainly can't expect your students to."

I turned to walk away, but the chief called after me, hesitatingly, "Sir, I have to tell you something."

"Yes?"

"I want you to know something. I was in the Navy for nearly 15 years before this program came along. I was a typical sailor, like in the movies. You know the type. If the average human being uses 10% of his brain, I was using 1%. Everybody figured sailors were supposed to be stupid, and who were we to argue? Now I'm working

Review for 1-31

Charasties of Rammage, Lajune, Rickover

Bravery
confidence
Perperation
Perserverance
Knowledge

Professionalism
commitment
Responsibility
Loyaly to office/oath/country

4 types of knowledge
Commandability
Technical
Knowledg of the sea
Capabilitys of crew

Naval Academy photo courtesy of United States Naval Academy Photographic Laboratory.

my tail off, but I'm alive. Y'know, I'm actually a thinking human being. And I think about how I just threw away 15 years of my life because nobody kicked my ass. You know what really woke me up? On my old ship we didn't have toasters, 'cause sailors are too dumb to work toasters, right? So we had cold, hard, dry toast from the galley. Then one day we had toasters on the tables. And I asked around, How come? And you know what I found out? They said Captain Rickover had told the top Navy brass that if sailors were smart enough to run a nuclear power plant, they could damn well run a toaster. And I said, there's a guy I want to work for. And I— well, I wanted you to know that you've done a lot for a lot of guys, 'cause I wasn't the only one. Thanks."

He turned away, and I was really touched. But all I could say was, "Thanks, Chief. I really appreciate your telling me that. Good luck to you."

Saturday continued along in the same vein. In the evening, Panoff came in from the engine room with word that Admiral Rickover had arrived and was waiting for us in the wardroom. So we hurried to the wardroom and seated ourselves at the table. The Admiral asked, "Have you finished with your quiz?"

. . . The results were reviewed with him and with the skipper, the exec, and the engineer. After making sure that all of the points had been made clear and that none of them was being contested by the ship's officers, Rickover signed off with a simple statement: "Well, Commander, from what you've just heard you can see you've got a lot of work to do. Your men are not as well trained as you thought. How is it that a couple of outsiders can come onto your ship and, in a few hours, find out more than you know about conditions here? Do you think I would let that happen on my ship? If you had spent last weekend like we spent this one, this never would have happened."

We departed into the night, to plan another crew quiz.

Mr. Rockwell worked directly for Admiral Rickover from 1949 to 1964 in the Naval Nuclear Propulsion Program and was his technical director for the last ten of those years. After leaving Naval Reactors, he and two colleagues established MPR Associates, an engineering firm. He is currently in private practice.

3 *What Makes Us Tick—*
Why Leaders Need to Understand Human Behavior

Objectives

1. Explain why a knowledge of human behavior is valuable to a military leader.

2. Define the terms cultural intelligence, hierarchy, and human network.

Exercise in Futurity: As War Looms, the Marines Test New Networks of Comrades

Joel Garreau, *Washington Post* staff writer

OAKLAND, Calif.—The drive-by massacre was a thing of beauty, the militiamen rejoiced as they roared back to the village. The arrogant infidel Marines had been caught lounging. It was as if those young Americans had dismissed the 15 wool-capped warriors of the Furzian Liberation Army on a truck full of garbage cans as no possible threat.

Well, the impertinent imperialists would not soon forget this lesson. They'd rue the day their leaders decided to send them to the country of Green to offer "earthquake assistance." If they had come in peace, why had the Marines massed below the Furzian village the previous day? And why, when the Furzian snipers tried to frighten them away, did they respond by defiling the Temple of Monad searching for weapons?

The FLA counterattack had been textbook. The militiamen had backed their garbage truck right into the heart of the Marines' humanitarian assistance feeding station. Then they'd whipped the lids off the trash cans, reached in and grabbed their hidden weapons, and within seconds a score of Marines were "dead." How jubilant were the militiamen as they sped back to the village!

Then they rounded the last curve. Suddenly, martyrdom flashed before their eyes. Three armored vehicles full of Marines blocked their way. The FLA men had no cover. What could they do? Thinking fast, they pumped their arms and started chanting, "We love America! We love America!"

It worked. Word of the massacre had not yet made it to these Marines, despite the elaborate electronic gear strapped to their chests. So the grunts smiled, waved, and let the Furzians pass. The militiamen raced up the hill to hand off their weapons to those practiced in hiding them. Then they melted into the crowd of civilians.

Chalk up another learning experience for the U.S. Marine Corps. For mercifully, this was not a real mission in, say, Kosovo, but an experiment called "Urban Warrior" staged in California last week.

33

Naval Academy photo courtesy of United States Naval Academy Photographic Laboratory.

As American forces mass off the Balkans, the lessons couldn't be more timely. The exercise was designed to see if one of the big ideas of the Information Age—human networking—could help the Marines fight successfully in cities. It was about how an old-fashioned hierarchy like the Marine Corps could transform itself into a spider web to confront unconventional forces like those found in Haiti, Somalia—and, of course, Kosovo.

The Marines were surprised again and again during this Urban Warrior exercise, and not just by the "militiamen." The Marines were equipped with, for example, tiny experimental computers on their chests that were supposed to provide them unprecedented views of the battlefield, and instantaneous connection to awesome firepower. Those are going to have to be sent back to the drawing board. On the other hand, cheap off-the-shelf radios performed so well they will become part of the American battle kit as soon as possible.

But the real lessons were rarely about gear. They were about psychology. What the Marines repeatedly came away with were new insights into how humans must behave to thrive in the chaos and speed of the 21st century. They also gained a new reverence for adaptability and innovation. For, they reminded themselves again and again, "the plan goes out the window with the first shot."

San Francisco Blues

The first thing the Marines learned was that if they were going to try to hit the beach at a place with complex tribal rituals—for example, the San Francisco Bay area—they would have to become much more sophisticated about cultural intelligence. Otherwise, they would repeatedly get their butts kicked for not understanding how legions of apparently docile residents might suddenly rise up with one mighty political roar if a baby seal were threatened with being sucked into landing craft rotors and exhaled as a cloud of pink mist.

In the city of San Francisco, a January grass-roots uproar prevented the Marines from conducting one of their exercises in the city's exquisitely beautiful Presidio area. They moved it to Oakland. But then, only hours before the landing craft were scheduled to arrive for the first operation in Monterey, the California Coastal Commission refused to allow use of the beach there because of a similar flap.

"For some it was the sea otters, for others it was the snowy plover eggs that might be tromped by the boots of the troops, for others it was images of American troops storming ashore in the homeland," observed John Arquilla of the Naval Postgraduate School in Monterey, author of "The Advent of Netwar."

"It was simply something unacceptable to a large part of the local community. The network came together extremely rapidly and very informally. It was a wonderful case for conducting an information operation well ahead of any exercise and engagement. They didn't do their homework. If they had taken a look at the Web page of the University of California at Santa Cruz, and realized Angela Davis was on the faculty, they'd get an idea of what the Marines would kick up. In some ways it was a replay of what happened in Somalia. The information campaign, the management of perceptions, was what was really going on."

"I don't actively seek pain—I really don't," said Col. Gary W. Anderson, chief of staff of the Marine Corps Warfighting Lab, which set up the Urban Warrior experiment. "But we certainly got it."

Anderson felt particularly wronged because for months the Marines had dutifully gotten permission to conduct their exercises from all the hierarchies they thought they had to deal with—the mayor, the police, the fire department. Basically, the Marine mind-set was that those must function something like a Marine hierarchy—in control of all they surveyed.

This profound lack of understanding had consequences.

The loss of the landing craft didn't stop the Marines. But switching to helicopters put a substantial dent in the show. Most of the attack force wasn't allowed to land because of low-hanging clouds and fog that triggered self-imposed safety and noise restrictions designed to protect civilians.

"Normally, cultural intelligence is simpler than this," Anderson acknowledged. "Normally, we go into a country that's in some fatal stage. We work with those who are with us, and shoot those who are not.

"The part that's missing here is that you can't shoot the Coastal Commission," he added ruefully.

Marine Capt. Anthony Henderson (right), Commander of Lima Company, Battalion Landing Team 3/2, briefs his Marines prior to a Tactical Recovery of Aircraft and Personnel (TRAP) mission aboard USS Wasp (LHD1).
Official U.S. Navy photo.

Hardware and Humans

The Marines did come up with some very pleasant surprises.

They discovered, for example, that if they gave a bunch of 19-year-old corporals some cheap, fast, convenient ways of talking with one another, these young people could organize a small war quite splendidly without necessarily consulting their elders.

The smallest Marine unit currently given a radio is a platoon—about 40 men. It's primarily used to keep in touch with the hierarchy—the commanders. For communications down to the small unit, the Marines use hand signals and shouts. This means several things: The 13-man squads have to stay fairly close together—within sight or hearing—to coordinate effectively. Stealth is a problem when your sergeant is yelling at you. And rarely does anyone go off on his own to solve a problem because then he'd lose touch with the larger force. "If you had an element forward, the only way you knew what they were doing is when you heard the gunshots," said Lt. Michael Hudson of Concord, Calif.

But for this exercise, the denizens of the Warfighting Lab found—in the back pages of a yachting magazine—some Motorola radios the size of a deck of playing cards, with headset earpieces and microphones. They were rugged, waterproof, short-range and cost $85. The lab bought several hundred.

The results were miraculous. Corporals made strategy on the fly just by talking to other corporals and not relying on the hierarchy.

"We had to take down a building at night with visibility zero, and we couldn't be detected," exulted Cpl. Daniel Rhoades, 21, of Alexandria. "We'd have no idea what's going on without these radios."

The grunts had absolutely no interest in giving those radios back.

The fact that they were an instant hit with the troops was instructive to the planners who had also provided the squads with those little chest-mounted computers with vast capabilities to network to all the assets of the Corps. That computer network is designed not only to help solve complex problems with one keystroke, like calling in fire on a target without hitting nearby friendly troops, but is also supposed to help anticipate complicated logistical problems like understanding where, how and when to deliver "beans, bullets and Band-Aids"—food, ammunition and medical supplies—slightly before units realize they need them.

This first generation of computers was useful, the grunts reported. "There's no guesswork, like is he really on top of that hill?," said Lance Cpl. Edgar Castaneda, 21, of Silver Spring. "This creates a whole new military occupational specialty—'data warrior,'" said Cpl. Clinton Eppert, 20, of Cincinnati. "The quicker you make decisions, the more power you have."

Nonetheless, it was the rare Marine who wanted to mess around with a keyboard in the middle of a firefight. "In the heat of battle, adrenaline starts to rush," explained Lance Cpl. Royce Fields. Therefore, the hope for a revolution in "common tactical picture," in which the generals and the corporals had the same view of the battlefield at the same time, didn't really come about.

On one occasion, for example, a platoon was wiped out in the Furzian village and this highly significant event never made it onto the computer network because there was nobody left to type. These bugs were not exactly unexpected.

"The end-user devices are not good enough," agreed Jens G. Pohl, of Cal Tech San Luis Obispo, who masterminded the Marines' network. "In the next stage, voice recognition has to be part of it. What was decided this time was that first we have to show that some [network computer] assistance is possible. That has been established. Now it has to be much easier. We have to have maybe a lapel screen with voice recognition. Give us another two or three years and it will be a lot more sophisticated."

The other big concern was the security of the networks. When the Cali Cartel or the Italian Mafia makes use of its human networks, they are notoriously difficult to penetrate. Not so for the little chest computers. Anyone could knock a corporal over the head, grab his computer, assume his identity and head toward the generals with a hand grenade, appearing electronically to be one of the troops.

Pohl says that's a difficult problem, but he plans on installing software that would work like the agents American Express and AT&T have watching over your credit cards to notice any usage that doesn't match your profile. For example, Pohl had just received a call from AT&T canceling his credit card after its computers noticed a sudden raft of calls from pay phones to Guatemala on his account—not his usual pattern.

Uncharted Waters

The Marines have a saying that came up again and again last week: "Speed is life." It was originally coined by aviators to describe the winning strategy in dogfights. But the Marines were startled to discover that Silicon Valley corporate leaders use exactly the same phrase to describe success at the punishing pace of business on the Net. Only a week before Urban Warrior was scheduled to open in Monterey, Col. Robert E. "Rooster" Schmidle, commanding officer of the attack force, was faced with an array of problems that normally would take months to solve. He couldn't wait for hierarchical results—underlings bringing the problems to him and waiting for orders. Instead, he was forced to try a new strategy: "I said to my executive officer, Frank Difalco, I want you to go into Monterey as the forward command element. And his question to me was, 'Well, what do you want me to do?'

"I said, 'I dunno.'

"I said, 'I want you to just go into the points of pressure. You'll know it when you see it.' He wanted a specific mission. And he's a very experienced officer—a lieutenant colonel. 'Tell me who you want me to talk to.' he said. I said, 'You'll know.'"

Schmidle was intentionally avoiding the classic Marine hierarchical command style. It worked. Difalco came back with a long list of problems solved.

"The point is I believe that individuals matter. That a certain individual at a certain point changes the course of everything that occurs. It's the great-man theory of history."

The importance of a crucial individual node in a network is only one of the surprises encountered in this new world. Another is the emergent behavior of the group—a behavior that is more than the sum of its parts.

On board the USS Coronado, which was anchored at Pier 35 in San Francisco for much of the Oakland exercise, "Rooster" Schmidle operated his main Experimental Combat Operations Center (ECOC). All computer screens and gray paint, it looked a little like the bridge of the Starship Enterprise. Its electronic network offered the commander an unprecedented ability to learn what was going on in the battlespace in real time. Sometimes it produced spooky results.

"When we're busy and things are really percolating, there's guys leaning over computers and they're yelling back and forth at each other. There's kind of a hum that starts in the COC when it's starting to operate as an entity unto itself. Yeah, they are alive."

Schmidle knows he's heading into strange territory, but he presses on.

"And when they are alive they have a . . . they have a . . . they think things. You know, it's groupthink, but it's not groupthink in a bad way. When we talk about being on the same wavelength, that's what we're talking about."

The Human Network

Far and away the most important lessons the Marines learned were that while all our futures will include revolutionary technology, meant to unite us into human networks, the real challenge is not the technology. It's figuring out the human strategies, tactics, training and organization that will quickly transform all those silicon wafers and batteries into effective human power.

Take Lt. Col. Robert J. Abblitt, for example. By the end of last week's exercises, he had bags under his eyes that hung down like the side pockets of his cargo pants. So much had been going on so fast for so long that the head of the Future Operations Branch of the Warfighting Lab had been catching sleep only in snatches.

"My most depressing time was the one where I was taken out of my world—taken out of the playbox." He meant that he had to leave his trailer full of computers displaying the battle for three hours to show a bunch of VIPs around.

"When I came back, I was so far behind the power curve because so much had happened."

How did he handle it? He could have pored over the information in the computers, drilling down through hour after hour of records. But that would have taken forever, without any guarantee that he'd find the important stuff. Instead, he picked up the phone and turned to his human networks.

"I've developed some relationships that have taken many years. The ethic is 'Don't let a buddy down.' Well, you know, when we're dealing with our own personal helmet fires here, I call my friends over in the battlefield. I ask them what's going on and they get me up to speed.

"My source of survival has been my close and tight friendships," Abblitt said as he sat surrounded by the Pentagon's most sophisticated electronic miracles.

"It's the most exciting thing I've seen."

4 *The Science of Human Behavior*

Objectives

1. List some advantages and disadvantages of the three types of psychological measurement (self-reports, behavioral observations, and archival records).

2. Describe the major approaches to research design in the behavioral sciences (descriptive studies, correlational studies and experiments).

3. Describe behavioral science experiments which answer questions of importance to leaders.

Scientific Methods

What are scientific methods, and why are they important? Is it better to study people in a laboratory or in natural settings? Why do psychologists devise subtle measures of behavior when they can just ask people about themselves? What ethical concerns have been raised about using human subjects in research? What about the use of animals?

It happens all the time. I'll see a report on the evening news, a magazine story, or an ad for a new product, and I'll react with a mixture of curiosity and skepticism. For example, I've heard that students can raise SAT scores 150 points by taking a test-preparation course, that a full moon triggers bizarre behavior, that workaholics drive themselves to an early grave, that pornography incites rape, and that girls start talking before boys do. Some of these claims are true; others are not. My reaction is always the same: "Hmm. Interesting," I'll say to myself. "But prove it!"

Many of us are drawn to psychology because people are fascinating and the subject matter is important. What unifies psychology as a discipline, however, is its commitment to scientific methods. A basic goal in science is one that should be modeled by everyone: critical thinking. Critical thinking is a skill, and it's also an attitude. The objective of scientific inquiry is to generate creative ideas and entertain these ideas with an open mind—but, at the same time, to be cautious, to demand that all claims be tested, and to scrutinize the results. The "art" in science is to achieve a balance between these competing objectives. It's good to be creative but not intellectually sloppy. Similarly, it's good to be critical, even skeptical, but not close minded. The key to thinking like a psychologist is learning how to walk these fine lines. And that means knowing something about psychology's methods of research.

The first important step in research is to formulate a hypothesis to be tested. As discussed earlier, you already have many intuitive theories on psychological issues. Everyone does. When I was choosing a graduate school, I had to decide whether or not to leave town to go to the best possible program—which meant leaving behind a girlfriend. What should I do? What effect would distance have on our relationship? One friend was certain he knew the answer: "Absence makes the heart grow fonder." Those words of encouragement made sense to me until a second friend said with equal certainty, "Out of sight, out of mind." Just what I needed. Two contradictory theories, both derived from common sense.

Psychological theories are more formal than the hunches we come up with in everyday conversation. A **theory** is an organized set of principles that describes, predicts, and explains a phenomenon. One can derive a theory from logic, a world

> *"At the heart of science is an essential tension between two seemingly contradictory attitudes—an openness to new ideas, no matter how bizarre or counterintuitive they may be, and the most ruthless skeptical scrutiny of all ideas, old and new."*
>
> —CARL SAGAN

theory An organized set of principles that describes, predicts, and explains some phenomenon.

41

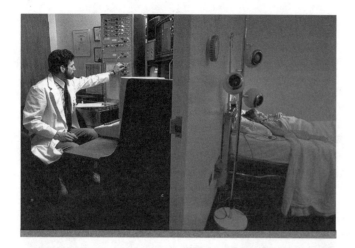

There are two types of research settings. In a laboratory study, behavior is observed in a controlled environment—such as a sleep laboratory (above). In field studies, people are observed in the street and in real-world settings (below).

hypothesis A specific testable prediction, often derived from a theory.

laboratory research Research conducted in an environment that can be regulated and in which subjects can be carefully observed.

field research Research that is conducted in real-world locations.

event, a personal experience or observation, another theory, a research finding, or an accidental discovery. Some theories are broad and encompassing; others account for only a thin slice of behavior. Some are simple; others contain a large number of interrelated propositions. In all cases, a theory should provide specific testable predictions, or **hypotheses**, about the relation between two or more variables. Researchers can then test these hypotheses to evaluate the theory as a whole.

There is no magic formula for determining how to test a hypothesis. In fact, as we'll see, studies vary along at least three dimensions: (1) the setting in which observations are made, (2) the ways in which psychological variables are measured, and (3) the types of conclusions that can be drawn. Let's separately examine each of these dimensions.

Research Settings

There are two types of settings in which people can be studied. Sometimes, data are collected in a laboratory, usually located at a university, so that the environment can be regulated and the subject carefully observed. **Laboratory research** offers control, precision, and an opportunity to keep conditions uniform for different subjects. For example, bringing volunteers into a sleep lab enables the psychologist to monitor their eye movements and brain-wave activity, record the exact time they fall asleep, and get dream reports the moment they awaken. Likewise, bringing a parent and child into a special playroom equipped with hand-picked toys, two-way mirrors, a hidden camera, and a microphone enables the psychologist to record every word uttered and analyze every nuance of their interaction. To study the way juries make decisions, I recruit people to serve on mock juries so that I can videotape and later analyze their deliberations.

Laboratory research is common in science. NASA physicists construct special chambers to simulate weightlessness in space; chemists generate chemical reactions in the test tube; botanists study plant growth in the greenhouse; and meteorologists use wind tunnels to mimic atmospheric conditions. Similarly, psychologists often find it necessary to simulate events in a laboratory. There is, however, a drawback. Can someone sleep normally in a strange bed with metal electrodes pasted to the scalp? Will a parent and child interact in the playroom the way they do at home? Do mock juries reach verdicts the same way real juries do? Possibly not. Being an artificially constructed world, the laboratory may elicit atypical behavior.

The alternative is **field research** conducted in real-world locations. The psychologist interested in sleep and dreams may have subjects report back periodically on their experiences. The parent and child could be visited in their own home. And jurors could be questioned about their decision-making process after a trial is over. The setting chosen depends on the behavior to be measured. Indeed, psychologists have observed people in city streets, classrooms, factories, offices, singles bars, subways, dormitories, elevators, and even public restrooms. To understand behavior in real-world settings, there is no substitute for field research. Unfortunately, the psychologist "out there" cannot control what happens to his or her subjects or measure with precision all aspects of their experiences. That's why the most fruitful approach is to use both laboratory and field settings.

Psychological Measurements

Regardless of where observations are made, many different types of measurements can be taken. These types fall into three categories: self-reports, behavioral observations, and archival records. These three types of observations, and the advantages and disadvantages of each, are summarized in Table 4.1.

Self-Reports   One way to assess a person's thoughts, feelings, or behavior is to go right to the source and ask. This is the method of **self-report**. Through interviews, questionnaires, or diaries, people are asked to report on their behavior, perceptions, beliefs, attitudes, and emotions. Self-reports are quick and easy to get. The information, however, can be inaccurate and misleading.

There are two problems with self-reports. First, people sometimes distort their responses in order to present themselves in a favorable light. It's hard to get anyone to admit to failures, mistakes, and shortcomings. Studies show, for example, that people tend to overestimate their own contributions to a joint effort (Ross & Sicoly, 1979), report after the occurrence of an event that they knew all along it would happen (Hawkins & Hastie, 1990), hide their feelings of prejudice (Crosby et al., 1980), and overestimate the accuracy of their own predictions (Dunning et al., 1990). Thus, when James Shepperd (1993) asked college students about their SAT scores and then checked their academic records, he discovered that they overestimated their actual scores by an average of seventeen points.

self-report A method of observation that involves asking people to describe their own thoughts, feelings, or behavior.

Table 4.1	Three Ways to "Observe" People		
METHOD	**DESCRIPTION**	**ADVANTAGES**	**DISADVANTAGES**
Self-reports	Ask people to report on themselves in interviews, surveys, or questionnaires.	People often reveal inner states that cannot be "seen" by others.	People distort self-reports to present themselves in a favorable light. People are not always aware of their own inner states.
Behavioral observations	Observe behavior firsthand, openly or covertly, sometimes using special tasks or instruments.	Behavior can be measured objectively.	Inner states can only be inferred from behavior, not actually seen. People may behave differently if they know they are being observed.
Archival records	Observe behavior secondhand, using available records of past activities.	The behavior occurs without the biasing presence of an observer	Records of past activities are not always complete or accurate.

Behavioral observation is critical to psychology. In this study, a four-month-old baby is tested to see if she knows that an object in motion will not stop in midair.

A second problem with self-report data is that even when respondents try to be accurate, they are often limited in their ability to do so. Long ago, Freud noted that people block certain thoughts and wishes from awareness. And studies show that people often lack insight into the causes of their own behavior (Nisbett & Wilson, 1977). In a surprising illustration of the limits of self-reports, Stanley Coren (1993), an expert on left-handedness, notes that when he asks people if they're right- or left-handed, 7 percent answer incorrectly. "One man who confidently reported that he was a right-hander, when tested to see which hand he used to throw a ball, aim a dart, cut with scissors, and the like, performed every single action with his left hand. His only detectable right-handed activity was writing."

Self-report measures are common in psychology, sometimes even essential. As you read through this book, however, you'll see that researchers often go out of their way to collect data in more subtle, indirect ways. Now you know the reason: The source is not always the best source.

Behavioral Observations   It is said that actions speak louder than words—and many researchers would agree. Many years ago, the Nielsen ratings of TV shows (which determine the cost of advertising and success of programs) were derived from the results of surveys and diary forms mailed to viewers. Realizing that these self-reports are flawed, however, Nielsen Media Research recently installed "People Meters" in 5,000 sample households across the country to electronically record what viewers are watching, when, and for how long.

behavioral observation A form of research that is based on the firsthand observation of a subject's behavior.

In psychology as well, the major alternative to self reports is firsthand **behavioral observation**. To animal researchers, the pressing of a bar, the running of a maze, and the consumption of food pellets are important behaviors. Sucking, smiling, crying, moving the eyes, and turning the head are significant sources of information for those who study infants. As for those who study adults, psychologically relevant behaviors range from the blink of an eye to the choice of a career. Even changes in internal states (such as respiration, heart rate, eye movements, brain waves, hormone levels, muscle contractions, and white blood-cell activity) can be monitored with the use of special instruments.

Behavioral observation plays a particularly important role in the study of subjective experience. One cannot crawl under a subject's skin and see what's on his or her mind. But researchers can try to infer various internal states from behavior. It is usually (though not always) safe to assume, for example, that recognition reveals the presence of a memory, that solving difficult problems reveals intelligence, and that the person who breaks into a cold sweat and runs at the sight of a snake has a fear of snakes.

archival research A form of research that relies on existing records of past behavior.

Archival Records   A third way to collect information about people is to conduct **archival research** that involves examining records of past activities instead of ongoing behavior. Archival measures used in psychology include medical records, birth rates, literacy rates, newspaper stories, sports statistics, photographs, absenteeism rates at work, personal ads, marriages, and divorce. A major advantage of these kinds of measures is that by observing behavior secondhand, researchers can be sure that they did not influence the subjects by their presence. An obvious limitation is that existing and available records of human activity are not always complete or detailed enough to be useful.

Archival measures are particularly valuable for examining cultural or historical trends. For example, Coren (1993) wanted to know if right-handedness was always dominant among humans (today, roughly 90 percent of the population is right-handed). So he went through a collection of art books and analyzed 1,180 drawings, paintings, and engravings that depicted an individual using a tool or a weapon. The drawings ranged from Stone Age sketches dated 15,000 BCE to paintings from the year 1950 CE. Yet Coren found that 90 percent of all characters were portrayed as right-handers—and that this percentage was the same thousands of years ago as in the twentieth century.

Research Designs

Regardless of how and where the information is obtained, researchers use **statistics** to summarize and then analyze the results. In some cases, statistical tests are used simply to describe what happened in terms of averages, percentages, frequencies, and other quantitative measures. In other cases, analyses are used to test inferences about people in general and their behavior. More about the use of statistics in psychological research is available in the Appendix of this book. For now, it is important to note that the types of conclusions that are drawn are limited by the way a study is designed. In particular, three types of research are used: descriptive studies, correlational studies, and experiments.

statistics A branch of mathematics that is used for analyzing research data.

Descriptive Research   The first purpose of research is simply to *describe* a person, group, or psychological phenomenon through systematic observation. This goal can be achieved through case studies, surveys, and naturalistic observations.

Case Studies   Sometimes it is useful to study one or more individuals in great detail. Information about a person can be obtained through tests, interviews, first-hand observation, and biographical material such as diaries and letters written. **Case studies** are conducted in the hope that an in-depth look at one individual will reveal something important about people in general. The problem with case studies is that they are time consuming and often are limited in their generality. To the extent that a subject is atypical, the results may say little about the rest of us.

case studies A type of research that involves making in-depth observations of individual persons.

Nevertheless, case studies have played an influential role in psychology. Sigmund Freud based his theory of personality on a handful of patients. Behaviorist John Watson used a case study to try to debunk psychoanalysis. Swiss psychologist Jean Piaget formulated a theory of intellectual development by questioning his own children. Neuroscientists gain insights into the workings of the brain by testing patients who have suffered brain damage. Cognitive psychologists learn about memory from rare individuals who can retain enormous amounts of information. Psycholinguists study language development by recording the speech utterances of their own children over time. Intelligence researchers learn about human intellectual powers by studying child prodigies, chess masters, and other gifted individuals. Social psychologists pick up clues about leadership by analyzing biographies of great leaders. And clinical psychologists refine the techniques of psychotherapy through their shared experiences with individual patients. When an individual comes along who is exceptional in some way or when a psychological hypothesis can be answered only through systematic, long-term observation, the case study provides a valuable starting point.

Surveys   In contrast to the in-depth study of one person, **surveys** describe an entire population by looking at many cases. In a survey—which can be conducted in person,

survey A research method that involves interviewing or giving questionnaires to a large number of people.

In 1948, newspapers projected that Dewey defeated Truman for president. As Truman basked in his victory, pollsters realized that their pre-election predictions were based on nonrandom samples of voters. Most polls were conducted by phone—and more Republicans than Democrats had phones.

epidemiology The study of the distribution of illnesses in a population.

random sample A method of selection in which everyone in a population has an equal chance of being chosen.

over the phone, or through the mail—people can be asked various questions about themselves. Surveys have become very popular in recent years and tell us, for example, that 95 percent of all American men and women have sexual fantasies (Leitenberg & Henning, 1995), that 96 percent believe in God (Golay & Rollyson, 1996), that 49 percent daydream about being rich (Roper Reports, 1989), and that 75 to 80 percent are generally happy (Diener & Diener, 1996). In case you've been wondering, 37 percent of women and 18 percent of men squeeze the toothpaste tube from the bottom (Weiss, 1991).

Surveys are sometimes necessary for the purpose of describing psychological states that are difficult to observe directly. For example, this method is an important tool in **epidemiology**—the study of the distribution of illnesses in a population. How many children are awakened by nightmares? What percentage of college students are plagued by test anxiety? How common are depression, alcoholism, and suicide? These kinds of questions are vital for determining the extent of a problem and knowing how to allocate health-care resources. Surveys are also useful for describing sexual practices. With AIDS spreading at an alarming rate, it's important to know how sexually active people are, whether they use condoms, and whether some segments of the population are more at risk than others. Today, surveys are so common, and the results have such significant implications, that the method (which, after all, relies on self-report) should be carefully scrutinized. Two factors are particularly important: who the respondents are and how the questions are asked.

To describe a group, any group—males, females, college students, redheads, homeowners, Americans, or all registered voters—researchers select a subset of individuals. The entire group is called the *population*; the subset of those questioned constitutes a *sample*. For a survey to be accurate, the sample must be similar to or representative of the population on key characteristics such as sex, race, age, region, income, and cultural background. Short of questioning everyone in the population, the best way to ensure representativeness is to use a **random sample**, a method of selection in which everyone has an equal chance of being chosen. Survey researchers usually pick names arbitrarily from a phone book or some other list. This seems like a reasonable strategy (and the larger the sample, the smaller the margin of error), but no sample is perfect. Not everyone has a telephone, some people have unlisted numbers, and some people who are called may not be home or may refuse to participate. In the 1948 U.S. presidential election, pollsters nationwide predicted that Thomas Dewey would defeat Harry Truman by a wide margin. Yet Truman won. The problem was that most polls were conducted by phone—and at the time, more Republicans than Democrats had phones. For a sample to accurately reflect its parent population, it must be selected in a manner that is random, not biased.

A second factor to consider is the wording of questions and the context in which they are asked (Tourangeau et al., 1991). The following examples illustrate the point.

- When survey respondents were asked about "assisting the poor," only 23 percent said that too much money was being spent. Yet among those asked about "welfare," 53 percent gave this negative response (*Time*, 1994).

- College students tried to estimate the distance from New York City to San Francisco (3,200 miles). Among those who were first asked if the distance is more or less than 1,500 miles, the average estimate was 2,600. Yet among those first asked if the distance was more or less than 6,000 miles, the average estimate was 4,000 (Jacowitz & Kahneman, 1995).

- Subjects who were asked whether "People should have the freedom to express their opinions publicly" were more likely to say *yes* when the previous question was about the Catholic Church than after a question about Nazis (Ottati et al., 1989).

- Eighty-eight percent of subjects thought condoms were effective in stopping AIDS when condoms were said to have a "95 percent success rate." However, when condoms were said to have a "5 percent failure rate," only 42 percent of the subjects were similarly optimistic (Linville et al., 1992).

Naturalistic Observations A third descriptive approach is to observe behavior as it occurs in the real world. **Naturalistic observations** are common in anthropology, where field workers seek to describe a culture by living in it for long periods of time. Psychologists use this method as well to study parents and their children, corporate executives, factory workers, nursing-home residents, and others.

Naturalistic observation is particularly common among ethologists, who study the behavior of animals in their natural habitats. For example, Jane Goodall has spent more than thirty-five years watching chimpanzees in African jungles (Goodall, 1986; Peterson & Goodall, 1993). She has observed their social structure, courting rituals, struggles for dominance, and child-rearing practices. She also saw the chimps strip leaves from twigs and use the twigs to fish termites out of nests—a finding that disproved the widely held assumption that only humans are capable of making tools. In another program of research, Dorothy Cheney and Robert Seyfarth (1990) observed vervet monkeys in Kenya and discovered that these monkeys behave as if they know the kinship bonds within their group, use deception to outsmart rivals, and use vocal calls in ways that are more sophisticated than was previously expected. To truly understand primates, and perhaps their similarities to humans, one has to observe their behavior in the wild—not captive in a zoo or laboratory.

naturalistic observation The observation of behavior as it occurs naturally in real-world settings.

correlation A statistical measure of the extent to which two variables are associated.

Correlational Studies Description is a nice first step, but science demands much more. A second goal is to find connections, or correlations, between variables so that one factor can be used to predict another. Correlational research is reported in psychology—and in the news—with remarkable frequency. Consider a few examples: The more violence children watch on TV, the more aggressive they are. Men with high testosterone levels are more prone to crime and violence. College graduates earn more money than nongraduates. The more optimistic people are, the less often they get sick. Adults who exercise regularly live longer than those who do not. People who are shy have fewer friends than those who are outgoing. So what do these statements of correlation *really* prove? And what do they not prove?

A **correlation** is a statistical measure of the extent to which two factors are associated. Expressed in numerical terms, *correlation coefficients* range from +1 to –1. A positive correlation exists when the two variables increase or decrease together, in the same direction. The link between TV violence and aggression is positive—more of one means more of the other; so are the correlations between testosterone and aggression, education and income, exercise and longevity. In contrast, a negative correlation exists when an increase in one variable is accompanied by a decrease in the

Naturalistic observation is a common form of descriptive research. For many years, Jane Goodall has observed champanzees in the wild.

other, and vice versa. The link between optimism and illness is in a negative direction, as is the one between shyness and friendships.

Correlation coefficients vary not only in direction but also in strength. The higher a correlation is, regardless of whether it is positive or negative, the stronger the link is between variables. Correlations that are very low—near zero—indicate that two variables are independent. Contrary to popular opinion, research shows, for example, that there is no correlation between phases of the moon and criminal activity, between an eyewitness's confidence and accuracy, or between intelligence-test scores in infancy and adulthood. In short, full moons, confident witnesses, and infant test scores cannot be used to predict crime, accuracy, or adult IQ. As shown in Figure 4.1, the direction and strength of a correlation can be represented in a **scatterplot**.

Correlational studies serve an important function: Based on existing associations, researchers can use one variable (or more) to make *predictions* about another variable. Before interpreting correlations, however, two important limitations should guide the cautious scientist. First, correlations between psychological variables are seldom perfect. Human beings are complex and their behavior is multidetermined. If you know a boy who spends twenty hours a week watching war movies, professional wrestling, or MTV's heavy-metal cartoon, *Beavis and Butt-Head*, you might predict that he gets into fights at school. But the positive correlation between TV violence exposure and aggressiveness is far from perfect, and you may well be wrong. Similarly, not every optimist is healthy and not every college graduate brings home a hefty paycheck. Unless a correlation is close to 1, it can be used only to make general statements of probability, not predictions about specific individuals.

There is also a limit to the types of conclusions that can be drawn from correlational evidence. It's tempting to assume that because one variable predicts another, the first must have caused the second. Not true. This interpretation is an error frequently committed by laypeople, college students, the news media, and sometimes even researchers themselves. Think about the correlations described earlier. Now, admit it: Didn't you assume that exposure to TV violence *causes* aggression, that testosterone fuels violence, that a college diploma brings financial reward, that optimism fosters health, that exercise prolongs life, and that shyness inhibits friendships? Regardless of how intuitive or accurate these conclusions may be, there's a cardinal rule of statistics: *Correlation does not prove causation.*

scatterplot A graph in which paired scores (X, Y) for many subjects are plotted as single points to reveal the direction and strength of their correlation.

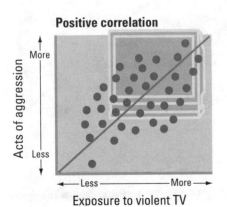

Positive correlation

Acts of aggression — More / Less

Exposure to violent TV — Less / More

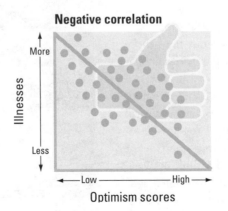

Negative correlation

Illnesses — More / Less

Optimism scores — Low / High

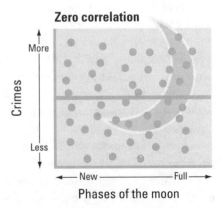

Zero correlation

Crimes — More / Less

Phases of the moon — New / Full

FIGURE 4.1 Visualizing correlations   Scatterplots provide a graphic representation of the observed relationship between two variables. The graphs above illustrate a positive correlation (left), a negative correlation (center), and a zero correlation (right). Each point locates the position of a single subject on the two variables. The solid straight lines show what the correlations would look like if they were perfect.

It's important to know and understand this rule. It does not mean that correlated variables are never causally related, only that the link may or may not be causal. Think again about our examples, and you'll see there are other ways to interpret these correlations. Sure, it's possible that TV violence (X) triggers aggression (Y). But based solely on the observation that these two variables go hand in hand, it's also possible that the causal arrow points in the opposite direction—that children who are aggressive (Y) are naturally drawn to violent TV shows (X). Or perhaps both variables are caused by a third factor (Z), such as the absence of involved parents at home.

Reconsider our other examples, and you'll further appreciate the point. Perhaps people become optimistic because they are healthy or are shy because they lack friends. As for the fact that college graduates earn more money than nongraduates, being smart or coming from an upper-middle-class family (Z) may both propel a student through college (X) and lead to financial success (Y). In a similar vein, maybe adults who exercise live longer because they also tend to smoke less, drink less, and eat healthier foods (see Figure 4.2).

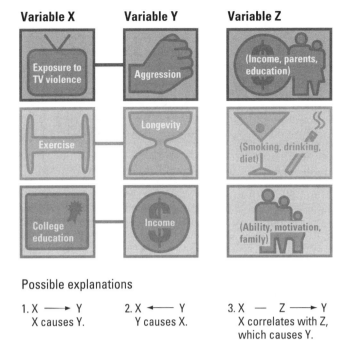

Possible explanations

1. X ——→ Y
   X causes Y.
2. X ◄—— Y
   Y causes X.
3. X — Z ——→ Y
   X correlates with Z, which causes Y.

FIGURE 4.2 **Explaining correlations** There are three possible ways to explain the association between two variables, X and Y. Look at the examples above and consider possible alternatives (Z refers to extraneous variables).

Experiments Correlation allows prediction, but to *explain* a relationship between variables, one needs a more exacting method of research: the scientific experiment. In an **experiment**, the psychologist seeks to establish causal connections by actively controlling the variables in a situation and measuring the subject's behavior. The factor an experimenter manipulates (the proposed cause) is called the **independent variable**, so named because it can be varied on its own—"independent" of any other factors. The behavior that is being measured (the proposed effect) is called the **dependent variable** because it is said to "depend" on the experimental situation. If you were to test the hypothesis that exposure to TV violence causes aggression, TV violence would be the independent variable, and aggression would be the dependent variable.

The purpose of an experiment is to focus on a causal hypothesis—by manipulating the independent variable, keeping other aspects of the situation constant, and observing behavior. A true experiment contains two essential sets of ingredients. The first is control over the independent variable and use of a comparison group. Second is the random assignment of subjects to conditions. By means of these ingredients, any differences in behavior can logically be traced back to the independent variable.

experiment A type of research in which the investigator varies some factors, keeps others constant, and measures the effects on randomly assigned subjects.

independent variable Any variable that the researcher manipulates in an experiment (the proposed cause).

dependent variable A variable that is being measured in an experiment (the proposed effect).

experimental group Any condition of an experiment in which subjects are exposed to an independent variable.

control group The condition of an experiment in which subjects are not exposed to the independent variable.

Control and Comparison I heard a report on the radio recently that half of all couples who live together before marriage later get divorced. "Wow, that's high," I said to a friend. "I wonder why." Then it hit me. "Wait a second. Isn't there a 50 percent divorce rate in the United States?"

In order to evaluate the significance of a number, you have to ask the question "Compared to what?" In its most basic form, a typical experiment compares subjects who are exposed to the independent variable with others, similarly treated, who are not. Subjects who receive the treatment make up the **experimental group**; the others constitute the **control group**. To the extent that the two groups differ in

"I'm down to two hundred and sixty-three packs a day."

behavior, the difference can then be attributed, with varying degrees of certainty, to the independent variable. The key is to *vary one factor, keep other aspects of the situation constant, and measure the effect.* To test the hypothesis that TV violence triggers aggression, for example, researchers bring children into the laboratory, show rock'em–sock'em films to half of them (the others would watch nonviolent films or else nothing at all), and measure subsequent aggression in a laboratory or field setting (Wood et al., 1991).

The comparison between an experimental and a control group provides the building blocks for more complex experiments. There are three ways to expand upon this basic two-group design. The first is to create more than two levels of the independent variable. Instead of comparing the presence and absence of TV violence, for example, one might form three groups by varying the amount, or "dosage," of exposure (high, medium, low). Second, researchers can manipulate more than one independent variable in the same experiment. For example, they might vary not only the amount of exposure but also the context in which the violence is portrayed (cartoons, films, or sports). The separate and joint effects of these variables can then be evaluated. The third way to increase the complexity of an experiment is to use more than one dependent variable, or to measure the dependent variable on more than one occasion. In our example, aggression could be measured both before and after subjects watch TV.

Random Assignment   The second essential ingredient of an experiment is that subjects be assigned to conditions in an arbitrary manner. **Random assignment** ensures that all participants in a study have an equal chance of being put into an experimental or control group. If I were to show *Beavis and Butt-Head* to children in one school and *Free Willy* to those in another school, it would later be impossible to know whether observed differences in aggression were produced by this exposure or whether they reflect instead differences that exist between the schools. Similarly, if I were to let the children pick their own condition ("Which show would you rather see?"), observed differences might mean that those who chose the violent show were more aggressive to begin with.

By flipping a coin to determine which children in a sample are in the experimental and control groups, a researcher can neutralize individual differences. Assuming that enough subjects are recruited, the two conditions would contain roughly equal numbers of male and female children as well as rich and poor, active and passive, and bright and dull. To similarly evaluate the health benefits of exercise, one might recruit volunteers and assign half of them randomly to take part in an experimental aerobics program. Chances are that both the exercise and the no-exercise groups would then have an equal mixture of men, women, smokers, health-food eaters, couch potatoes, and so on. Then if exercisers turn out to be healthier, the reason would be clear.

> *"No amount of experimentation can ever prove me right; a single experiment can prove me wrong."*
>
> —ALBERT EINSTEIN

Overview of Major Research Approaches

Leadership as a subject of research and the many different conceptions of leadership have created a vast and bewildering literature. Attempts to organize the literature according to major approaches or perspectives have been only partially successful. One of the more useful classification system is according to the types of variables emphasized in a theory or study. Major lines of research include: (1) trait approach, (2) behavior approach, (3) power-influence approach, and (4) situational approach. Occasionally a theorist or researcher will include more than one of these leadership variables, and this integrative approach can be viewed as a fifth line of research. Each approach and how it is reflected in the organization of the book are described.

Trait Approach

One of the earliest approaches for studying leadership was the trait approach. The trait approach emphasizes the personal attributes of leaders. Underlying this approach was the assumption that some people are natural leaders who are endowed with certain traits not possessed by other people. Early leadership theories attributed managerial success to extraordinary abilities such as tireless energy, penetrating intuition, uncanny foresight, and irresistible persuasive powers. Hundreds of trait studies were conducted during the 1930s and 1940s to discover these elusive qualities, but this massive research effort failed to find any traits that would guarantee leadership success. One reason for the failure was a lack of attention to intervening variables in the causal chain that could explain how traits could affect a delayed outcome such as group performance or leader advancement. The predominant research method was to look for a significant correlation between individual leader attributes and a criterion of leader success, without examining any explanatory processes. However, as evidence from better designed research slowly accumulated over the years, researchers have made progress in discovering how leader attributes are related to leadership behavior and effectiveness.

Behavior Approach

In the 1950s researchers became discouraged with the trait approach and began to pay closer attention to what managers actually do on the job. The behavior research falls into two general subcategories. One subcategory is research on the nature of managerial work. This research examined how managers spend their time, and described the content of managerial activities in terms of content categories such as managerial roles, functions, and responsibilities. The research on managerial work relies mostly on descriptive methods such as direct observation, diaries, job description questionnaires, and anecdotes obtained from interviews.

Another subcategory of research on managerial behavior compares the behavior of effective and ineffective leaders. The preferred research method has been survey research with behavior description questionnaires. In the past 40 years, hundreds of studies have examined the correlation between questionnaire measures of leadership behavior and measures of leadership effectiveness. A much smaller number of studies have used laboratory experiments, field experiments, or critical incidents to determine how effective leaders differ in behavior from ineffective leaders.

Much of the behavior research is concerned with finding ways to classify behavior that will facilitate our understanding of leadership.

Power-Influence Approach

Power-influence research examines influence processes between leaders and other people. Like most of the research on traits and behavior, some of the power-influence research also has a leader-centered perspective with an implicit assumption that causality is unidirectional (leaders act and followers react). This research seeks to explain leadership effectiveness in terms of the amount and type of power possessed by a leader and how power is exercised. Power is viewed as important not only for influencing subordinates, but also for influencing peers, superiors, and people outside the organization, such as clients and suppliers. The favorite methodology has been the use of survey questionnaires to relate leader power to various measures of leadership effectiveness.

Other power-influence research has used questionnaires and descriptive incidents to determine how leaders influence the attitudes and behavior of followers. The study of influence tactics can be viewed as a bridge linking the power-influence approach and the behavior approach. Different influence tactics are compared in terms of their relative effectiveness for getting people to do what the leader wants.

Participative leadership is concerned with power sharing and empowerment of followers, but it is firmly rooted in the tradition of behavior research as well. Many studies have used questionnaires to correlate subordinate perceptions of participative leadership with criteria of leadership effectiveness such as subordinate satisfaction, effort, and performance. Laboratory and field experiments have been used to compare autocratic and participative leadership. Finally, descriptive studies of effective managers have examined how they use consultation and delegation to give people a sense of ownership for decisions.

One major issue addressed by power-influence research is the way power is acquired and lost by various individuals in a group. In addition to research on power acquisition by individuals, there has been research on power acquisition by organizational subunits and coalitions. The latter research seeks to understand why some subunits or coalitions are able to exert more influence over strategy decisions and the allocation of scarce resources.

Naval Academy photo courtesy of United States Naval Academy Photographic Laboratory.

Situational Approach

The situational approach emphasizes the importance of contextual factors such as the nature of the work performed by the leader's unit, the nature of the external environment, and the characteristics of followers. This approach has two major subcategories. One line of research treats managerial behavior as a dependent variable, and researchers seek to discover how this behavior is influenced by aspects of the situation such as the type of organization or managerial position. The research investigates how managers cope with demands and constraints from subordinates, peers, superiors, and outsiders (e.g., customers, government officials). The primary research method is a comparative study of two or more situations in which managerial activities or behaviors are measured with leader behavior description questionnaires, job description questionnaires, or direct observation. Researchers seek to discover the extent to which managerial work is the same or unique across different types of organizations, levels of management, and cultures. Even though this comparative research was not designed to identify what behavior is effective in what situation, it is relevant for understanding managerial effectiveness because effectiveness depends on how well a manager resolves role conflicts, copes with demands, recognizes opportunities, and overcomes constraints.

The other subcategory of situational research attempts to identify aspects of the situation that "moderate" the relationship of leader behaviors (or traits) to leadership effectiveness. The assumption is that different behavior patterns (or trait patterns) will be effective in different situations, and that the same behavior pattern (or trait pattern) is not optimal in all situations. Theories describing this relationship are sometimes called "contingency theories" of leadership. The contingency theories can be contrasted with "universal theories" of leadership effectiveness, which specify an optimal pattern of behavior for all situations.

Integrative Approaches

Another line of influence research attempts to explain why the followers of some leaders are willing to exert exceptional effort and make personal sacrifices to accomplish the group objective or mission. The effectiveness of a leader is explained in terms of influence on the way followers view themselves and interpret events. Effective leaders influence followers to have more optimism, self-confidence, and commitment to the objectives or mission of the organization. Most theories of charismatic and transformational leadership identify behaviors and traits that facilitate the leader's effectiveness. In contrast to other approaches in leadership research, follower perceptions and attributions are also considered to be important for understanding leadership effectiveness. The same behavior by a leader may have a different effect on followers depending on the situation, the history of interaction between the leader and followers, and the way the behavior is interpreted by followers.

5 A Basis for Trust— Early Human Development

Objectives

1. Describe the basic formation of temperament, trust and attachment.

2. Apply your understanding of early psychosocial developmental tasks to the concerns and problems of junior personnel.

3. Describe the importance of trust in effective military leadership.

4. Define "special trust and confidence" and explain how it will apply to you as a future junior officer.

Psychosocial Development

If you break the word *psychosocial* down into its two components, *psycho* and *social*, you have a good idea of what this section covers. We consider the development of the individual's own, unique personality (*psycho*) as well as factors that influence the ability to interact with the other people (*social*). Such abilities begin at an early age. For example, social behaviors begin to emerge by the time the child is a year old (Moore & Corkum, 1994).

Temperament

Physicians Alexander Thomas and Stella Chess (1980) were struck by the differences they observed in their own children; those differences were apparent even in the first few weeks of life. They were also impressed by the lack of any correlations between environmental influences, such as parental attitudes and practices, and the child's psychological development. They decided to study the causes and consequences of differences in *temperament*. Temperament is the "how" of behavior: its quickness, ease of approach to new situations, intensity, and mood. A child's temperament is revealed in measures of activity level, regularity of biological functions, approach to or withdrawal from new situations, adaptability to new or altered situations, intensity of reaction, quality of mood, distractibility, and attention span and persistence. Thomas and Chess identified three different types of temperament:

1. *Easy children* (40 percent) were regular, had a positive approach to new situations, and were highly adaptable to change. Their mood was mild to moderate and predominantly positive.
2. *Slow-to-warm-up children* (15 percent) displayed a combination of intense, negative responses to new stimuli with slow adaptability even after repeated contact.
3. *Difficult children* (10 percent) were irregular, nonadaptable, and usually characterized by intense negative mood.

As you can see from the percentages, not all children fit easily into one of these three groups.

Heredity seems to play an appreciable role in determining temperament (Goldsmith & Gottesman, 1981; Thomas & Chess, 1980). Level of activity is especially enduring; in one study, the children who were most active 4 days after birth were also most active 8 years later (Korner et al., 1985). Difficult children are most vulnerable to behavior problems in early and middle childhood. Most of them improve with parental counseling and other therapeutic measures. A study of the enduring temperament of babies born in Finland also emphasized the importance of parental views (Lehtonen, Korhonen, & Korvenranta, 1994).

Although the work of Thomas and Chess has made important contributions to our understanding of temperament, it is not the only approach. For example, David Buss and Robert Plomin (1984) view temperament in behavior-genetic terms: temperament is inherited and forms the core of the individual's personality. Moreover, Buss and Plomin feel that there are only three dimensions of temperament: activity level, sociability, and emotionality.

Another view was suggested by Mary Rothbart and Douglas Derryberry (1981). These investigators view temperament in terms of reactivity (excitability or arousability) and regulation (processes such as approach-avoidance, inhibition, or attention that modulate reactivity). Rothbart and Derryberry have proposed six temperamental dimensions: activity level, soothability, fear, reactions to frustration, smiling and laughter, and duration of orientation.

Despite these different views of temperament, research has shown that an infant's temperament remains remarkably stable as the child gets older (Goldsmith, et al., 1987). The most stable aspects of temperament appear to be sociability, emotionality, and level of activity (Goldsmith & Campos, 1982; Kagan, Reznick, & Snidman, 1987). Such stability suggests that temperament may influence the development of personality and the attachments that infants form with their caregivers.

Personality Development

Both Sigmund Freud and Erik Erikson developed theories of personality development based on the idea that childhood experiences leave lasting marks on an individual's personality. Whereas both theorists felt that the personality develops in a series of orderly stages and that childhood experiences are important, they differed in their emphasis. Freud stressed the individual's biological makeup, whereas Erikson stressed social interactions.

Sigmund Freud.   During the late 1800s and early 1900s, Sigmund Freud radically influenced the way psychologists viewed the development of personality. Freud was the first person to propose that the first few years of life are crucial to personality development. Freud's theory was concerned with the manner in which children resolve conflicts between their biological urges (primarily sexual) and the demands of society, particularly those of the parents. Freud viewed these conflicts as a series of developmental stages determined largely by the child's age. For example, he felt that during the first year of life, the mouth is the source of pleasure and sensual gratification. During this *oral stage,* the attitudes of the mother who breast-feeds her child and the timing of weaning are thought to have a significant effect on the psychological development of the infant. Freud was the first individual to propose a stage theory of personality development. Moreover, he believed that each stage had the potential to affect the personality of the developing child.

Erik Erikson.   Erik Erikson (1902–1994) also proposed a stage theory of personality development. Unlike Freud, however, Erikson did not stress the need to resolve conflicts created by biological needs. According to Erikson, our personality is molded by the way we deal with a series of psychosocial crises that occur as we grow older. A **psychosocial crisis** occurs when a psychological need conflicts with societal pressures and demands. Different cultures present different obstacles to the resolution of these psychosocial crises. Hence certain developmental paths will be more appropriate in one culture than in others.

Babies experience two psychosocial crises. The first occurs from birth until about 1½ years of age, when the infant is establishing a pattern of **basic trust versus basic mistrust.** Put another way, can infants trust their environment? Will food be there when they are hungry? Will their diapers be changed? Will other sources of pain and discomfort be alleviated? The person who usually attends to the child's needs, the primary caregiver, plays a major role in the development of basic trust and mistrust. Consistent, loving caregivers facilitate the development of a sense of trust. Having trust in one's caregivers and one's environment is very important for developing trust in oneself. That is, infants who trust their caregivers and their environment begin to develop a sense that they are all right and that they fit into their environment in an appropriate manner.

Between the ages of about 1½ and 3, children deal with a second psychosocial crisis, **autonomy versus shame and doubt. Autonomy** is the feeling that we can act independently and that we are in control of our own actions. Children start on the road to either autonomy or shame and doubt by developing a sense of how their behavior is controlled or determined. If children feel that their behavior is not under their control but is determined by other people or external forces, they develop an external sense of control. Doubt and shame concerning one's ability to function frequently accompany an external sense of control. For example, if the parents always insist on feeding a child, the child may begin to doubt his or her ability to perform this important activity.

If children develop a sense of being in charge of what happens to them, they have developed an *internal* sense of control, or *autonomy*. The relationship between sense of control and autonomy is straightforward: The greater a child's internal sense of control, the greater the independence he or she will feel and exhibit.

The developing sense of independence allows children to begin doing things on their own. They decide what, when, and with whom they will play. This developing independence is the hallmark of the "terrible twos" and often brings children into conflict with their parents over such issues as what to eat and when to go to bed (Kopp, 1982). One cannot deny that the development of independence is necessary, yet it is also clear that the sense of independence must be achieved within certain rules and constraints. For example, children who are allowed to feed themselves in any manner they desire without being taught that throwing food is wrong may find it difficult to adapt to other social rules.

The child's growing sense of morality forms the basis for Erikson's third psychosocial crisis, **initiative versus guilt.** A developing sense of right and wrong leads children to evaluate the consequences of the behaviors in which they might engage. Some behaviors, such as playing by the rules and obeying one's parents, can produce desirable consequences; others, such as cheating or not obeying one's parents, produce undesired consequences. To resolve this conflict successfully, children must take the initiative to adopt behaviors and goals that they enjoy *and* that society values. To do otherwise leaves the child (and later the adult) feeling guilty and fearful because his or her behaviors may not be appropriate or valued.

To make such decisions about the consequences of our behavior, we must successfully resolve the first two psychosocial crises: basic trust versus basic mistrust and autonomy versus shame and doubt. Unless children have some degree of trust in

psychosocial crisis Developmental problem or obstacle that is created when a psychological need conflicts with the demands of society

basic trust versus basic mistrust Erikson's first psychosocial crisis (birth to 1½ years), in which children learn through contact with their primary caregiver whether their environment can be trusted

autonomy versus shame and doubt Erikson's second psychosocial crisis (1½ to 3 years), in which children develop a sense of whether their behavior is under their own control or under the control of external forces

autonomy The feeling of being able to act independently and having personal control over one's actions

initiative versus guilt Erikson's third psychosocial crisis, in which children begin to evaluate the consequences of their behavior

their own ability to take action, they will always be afraid of undertaking a new project or behavior.

industry versus inferiority Erikson's fourth psychosocial crisis, in which children begin to acquire the knowledge and skills that will enable them to become productive members of society

The importance of developing a sense of competence also underlies Erikson's fourth psychosocial crisis, **industry versus inferiority**. Once children have developed basic trust, autonomy, and initiative, it is time to learn the skills and acquire the knowledge that will allow them to become productive members of society. The acquisition of such skills and knowledge reflects the development of industry. If an individual is to become a productive member of society, the lessons taught in school must be learned, and learned well.

Erikson suggests that there are four additional psychosocial crises that continue beyond childhood; they are discussed in the next chapter. Although critics point out that Erikson's theory lacks precision, supporters note that it captures the reality of the changes that occur as we grow and develop throughout the life span. In addition, it is generally conceded that Erikson's theory is far more optimistic than Freud's.

If you read the sections about Freud and Erikson carefully, you noticed that personality develops in the context of significant other people, usually the parents. The attachments children form to their parents play a major role in shaping their developing personality.

Attachment

attachment Intense, reciprocal relationship formed by two people, usually a child and an adult

Attachment refers to an intense, reciprocal relationship occurring between two people, usually a child and an adult. The first experimental studies on the effects

	Study Chart	
	Crises of Psychosocial Development during Childhood, as Proposed by Erik Erikson	
CRISIS	**APPROXIMATE AGE**	**CHARACTERISTICS**
Basic trust versus basic mistrust	Birth to 1½ years	Child learns whether to trust the environment. Ability to trust the environment is important for the development of trust in oneself.
Autonomy versus shame and doubt	1½ to 3 years	Child develops a sense of control. The sense that control is internal (autonomy) helps the child develop independence. The sense that control is external fosters shame and doubt and hinders the growth of independence
Initiative versus guilt	3 to 7 years	Child experiences conflict between the behaviors he or she wants to engage in and a growing sense of morality and begins to question whether certain behavior is right or good.
Industry versus inferiority	7 to 10 years	To become a productive member of society, the child must master certain skills and acquire a basic amount of knowledge. Successful learning and skill acquisition lead to the development of a sense of competence.

Source: Erikson, 1954.

of attachment were reported by psychologists Harry and Marguerite Harlow (Harlow & Harlow, 1962). Approximately 8 hours after birth, baby monkeys were separated from their mothers. The baby monkeys were raised in experimental chambers, where they were exposed to an inanimate object that served as a surrogate (substitute) mother. Some of the surrogate mothers were plain wire cylinders; others were covered with soft terrycloth. Some of the infant monkeys were allowed to come into contact with both types of objects. When a bottle was attached, the baby monkey could be "fed" by the wire or cloth-covered "mother."

The Harlows found that the infant monkeys showed a definite preference for the soft, cloth-covered mother. For example, when confronted by a strange and frightening situation, they ran to the cloth-covered mother for safety and security. The monkeys showed this preference even when they were fed by the plain wire mother; apparently, the contact comfort and warmth provided by the terrycloth were more important determinants of attachment than the provision of nourishment.

Although the Harlows' research demonstrated the role of contact comfort, it is clear that attachments are most often formed between children and their parents or primary caregivers. Parents and primary caregivers can return or reciprocate the love and affection that the child brings to the relationship. Inanimate objects do not return affection; the cloth mother provided only contact comfort and warmth.

In addition to demonstrating the importance of contact comfort, the Harlows also found that raising baby monkeys in isolation in the laboratory had a detrimental effect on their social behavior (Suomi & Harlow, 1972; Suomi & Ripp, 1983). When the laboratory testing was complete, the juvenile animals were returned to a colony with other monkeys. However, the experimental monkeys did not adapt well in the colony. They avoided contact, fled from touch, curled up and rocked, or tried to attack the biggest, most dominant monkey in the group (often getting seriously injured in the process). Thus a major conclusion of the Harlows' research was that even though attachment was important, it did not ensure normal social development. Environmental contact (nurture) with members of one's own species is needed for this kind of development.

Mary Salter Ainsworth observed the reactions of human infants confronted by strange situations (Ainsworth et al., 1978). At birth, infants are equipped with behaviors such as crying that promote closeness to a caregiver and operate to activate caregiving behaviors. "At first," Ainsworth (1989) notes, "these attachment behaviors are simply emitted, rather than directed toward any specific person, but gradually the baby begins to discriminate one person from another and to direct attachment behavior differentially" (p. 710).

Once attachment occurs, it can take several forms. One way to determine the kind of attachment a baby has developed is to observe the baby's reaction to being put in a strange situation. When Ainsworth and her colleagues did just that, they found that most babies (66 percent) were *securely attached*. When their mother was present to provide security and support, securely attached babies explored and investigated their environment. A smaller group (20 percent) of babies did not want to be held; they also did not want to be put down. They ignored their mother or greeted her casually on her return. In fact, they seemed to interact with a stranger the same way they did with their mother. Such babies are termed *avoidant*. A third group (about 12 percent) consisted of *anxious-ambivalent* babies (see also Cassidy & Berline, 1994) who became almost panic-stricken when their mother left. This panic reaction began before the mother left. When the mother returned, the baby actively sought, but at the same time actively resisted, contact and comfort.

It is important to remember that attachment is not a one-way process: The infant is only one-half of the interaction. The personality and temperament of the caregiver must also be considered. For example, the emotion and affect of the caregiver are related to the infant's pattern of attachment (Goldberg, MacKay-Soroka, & Rochester, 1994). Mothers of secure infants responded more frequently and were attentive to the full range of their baby's affective display, whereas mothers of avoidant infants were less responsive, especially to their baby's negative affect. Mothers of anxious-ambivalent babies were especially responsive to their baby's negative displays but unresponsive to positive displays.

The percentages of different types of attachment may vary from culture to culture (Van Ijzendoorn & Kroonenberg, 1988). For example, more German infants than infants in the United States, Israel, or Japan are anxiously attached. Cultural practices such as German parents' stressing autonomy at an earlier age may produce such differences: they are not interpreted as deficiencies. However, sleeping out of the home in communal arrangements, such as those found in Israeli kibbutzim, may lead to insecure attachments (Sagi et al., 1994).

Infants' attachment styles are well documented, but not much is known about how these styles may influence individuals' behaviors as adults. Psychologists Judith Feeney and Patricia Noller (1990) found a relationship between the attachment style reported by the parents of college students and the students' preferred type of interpersonal relationship as adults (see also Vormbrock, 1993). For both men and women, there was a link between reported infant attachment style and preferred type of adult relationship. Securely attached babies grew into adults who had trusting attitudes toward others. Anxious-ambivalent babies were more dependent and in need of commitment in their relationships as adults. Babies with the avoidant style of attachment were more likely to mistrust others and feel uncomfortable in close relationships as adults. Likewise, it has been found that early attachment patterns can affect the behaviors of adults as old as 85 (Crose, 1994). Moreover, Diane Benoit and Kevin Parker (1994) have shown that an attachment style can persist through at least three generations: We treat our children much as we were treated as children. Finally, a longitudinal study of German children (Wartner et al., 1994) indicates that the lasting effects of attachment style occur across cultures.

The Father's Role

We have repeatedly described the attachment established between an infant and its mother. What about the father? Do fathers form attachments with their children? There is some basis for the emphasis placed on the mother-infant attachment. As David Lynn (1974) has pointed out:

> One of the factors eroding the father's position in the family is the nature of work today in urban-industrial societies. Fathers now work away from the home, so that a degree of father absence is taken for granted. . . . In our society the absence of the father through death or divorce can be considered simply an extreme on the prevailing continuum of father absence. (p. 6)

Despite this father-absent pattern, infants do establish attachments with their fathers at about the same age that they form attachments with their mothers (Fox, Kimmerly, & Schafer, 1991). The types of interactions displayed by fathers to their infants may differ from those shown by the mother. Fathers are more likely to invest their time playing with their children than in cleaning or feeding them (Hossain & Roopnarine, 1994). However, it appears that delaying having children until the father is older (i.e., age 35 or older) results in the father's spending more time with the child, having higher expectations for the child, and being more nurturant (Heath, 1994).

Culture and Fatherhood. The father-absent pattern is not found in all cultures. For example, in the Chinese patriarchal (father-dominated) family, the most important relationship is between a father and his sons. Other cross-cultural research has found that infants in all cultures become attached to their parents despite widely varying child-rearing practices (Sagi, 1990). For example, in Israel, many people live in communal kibbutzim. Children visit with their parents for several hours around dinnertime, and their parents can drop in to see them throughout the day, but most of their time is spent in a day-care arrangement in which adult workers serve as their caregivers. When tested for attachment, these kibbutz-reared children are found to be quite attached to their parents, although the percentage of anxious-ambivalent children among them is higher than the norm in the United States.

In general, fathers tend to spend more time with their sons than with their daughters. Some psychologists (e.g., Pedersen, Rubenstein, & Yarrow, 1979) have found that a boy's cognitive development may be positively influenced by interaction with his father. As the number of dual-career and single-parent families increases, fathers are taking a more active role in caring for their babies.

Studies of Swedish (Lamb et al., 1982) and American (Belsky, Gilstrap, & Rovine, 1984) families have shown that the parent's sex is a more important determinant of parent-child interaction than employment status and parental role. Mothers are more likely to have direct physical contact with infants (such as kissing, hugging, and holding them) than fathers are. Moreover, fathers spend only 20 to 35 percent as much time as mothers in one-on-one interaction with their children (Lamb et al., 1987). Because of increased employment among mothers and shrinking family size, this trend seems to be reversing itself; fathers are assuming more responsibility and spending more time caring for their children (Poussaint, 1990), even in cultures where such nurturance runs counter to the prevailing style (Nugent, 1991).

Trust as a Basis for Leadership

Admiral J. Paul Reason

Let's talk about a critically important dimension of leadership. And that is: *trust*. Trust in yourself, your peers, your superiors, and—one day—your subordinates. Right now each of you in this hall is surrounded by about one thousand people you trust. You occupy a truly unique environment, almost unheard of in any other professional arena. As midshipmen, you share a code of honor, suffer similar hardships, exult over similar victories, and undergo an intense and fatiguing regimen of study and physical exertion. You trust each other, your academy classmates, implicitly, without reserve. To lose that special relationship, a classmate of '02 must earn your distrust.

Breaches of trust are taken very seriously, because without trust, your professional and social community cannot function at its best—if at all. It's the same way in the fleet. You will have to extend the same sort of trust to your fellow officers, and they will have to trust you in the same way. You will rely on their sense of honor and their professional competence; they will rely on yours.

An effective wardroom of officers is composed of people who trust each other with their careers and even their lives. They share the same mission and the same experiences. In the most literal sense possible, they are "all in the same boat."

When newly minted ensigns report to the fleet, trust is the basis of the relationship between them and their superiors. New ensigns trust the experience, wisdom, and integrity of their senior officers. Senior officers put their faith in the new ensigns. Of course, there is a gap in experience and age, so there is always an element of "show me" on the part of the superior, with the burden of proof on the junior.

As far as professional competence goes, a new ensign's superiors are really putting faith in the Navy's—and Naval Academy's—ability to select and train new officers. They are putting faith in the new ensign's potential to learn quickly, to handle stress, to make decisions, to accomplish the mission—whatever that mission is. But—and this is most important—they always trust that the new ensign, or "butter bar" lieutenant, is an officer of honor, with unquestioned integrity.

Perhaps the most challenging thing for a new officer to handle is the special dimension of trust between the young leader and those who are *led*. There are two aspects to this.

First, the young ensign must *earn* the trust of those he or she leads. Take a ship, for example. Sailors look at the captain, the XO, the department heads, the chiefs, and the leading petty officers, and they assume that these people—by virtue of their rank and experience—deserve to be trusted and obeyed.

But the brand-new, inexperienced division officer is another matter. True, by virtue of billet and rank, the Div-O is owed obedience. But the new officer, with less active duty time than all but the most junior Sailors, must build moral authority and trust over time, as a result of constant, daily interaction with Sailors.

How fair are you? Are you competent in your job? Do you really listen well? How dedicated are you? Are you an enthusiastic leader? Do you express yourself clearly? How steady are you under pressure? Sailors think about all of these things as they evaluate their division officers.

On the other hand—and this is the second aspect of trust—the new leader must trust subordinates *immediately* right off the bat. That is a risk, but it is a *necessary*, unavoidable risk. You must have the self-confidence, intelligence, and education to deal with it.

Do not let yourself be seduced into thinking that those who are "like you"—whether in terms of ethnicity, religion, sex, politics, social status, level of education, etc.—are more worthy of trust than others. If there's anything I've learned in my lifetime as a naval officer, it's that you really can't judge a book by its cover. I've been reminded of the truth of that proverb over and over again.

To trust your Sailors better, *learn* about them individually. Don't just read their service jackets. Talk to them. Find out about them as people—what they care about, what their goals are, what their needs and fears are. You can do this without becoming unduly familiar, but do this you must.

My point is that you must be willing to take the risk to trust those you lead. And *that* requires self-confidence, otherwise known as trust in yourself. To trust yourself, you must know yourself—your strengths and limitations—and to be worthy of trust you must be honorable, competent, and readily responsible for your every judgment and your every action.

The Navy operates on trust. We can't do without it.

Can trust be risky? You bet. It's so risky that society at large has done practically everything it can to *erase the need for trust*. Every business requires a contract and a signature . . . "Put it in writing," they say. "Let's see it on paper." In fact, "trust no one" becomes the lesson many people learn in our society.

Yet trust is the bedrock of our profession as naval leaders. Your word is your bond. You say "Aye, aye, sir," to an order, and your captain trusts it will be done. Everyone knows about the Navy's superior technology and training, but the real secret of our success is that we trust our Sailors, our superiors, and each other.

Does trust risk failure? Yes, because it risks *success*. This proverb is also true: "nothing ventured, nothing gained." That is how you have to look at it.

Now, when you arrive at your first duty station, you will be pumped up and ready to go. You'll have a plan for your success. You're going to get qualified in record time. Your division will be the best on the ship, or in the squadron.

Just remember these words by Mike Tyson. Yeah, Mike Tyson isn't the world's smartest man; he's not Naval Academy material. But he did say something right . . . years ago when he was being interviewed before his fight with Leon Spinks, a reporter told Tyson, "You know, Spinks has a plan for how to fight you." Tyson replied, "They all got a plan—until they get hit."

Naval Academy photo courtesy of United States Naval Academy Photographic Laboratory.

Naval Academy photo courtesy of United States Naval Academy Photographic Laboratory.

You'll get hit. There will be challenges you haven't dreamed of. You'll have to meet them head on, and you'll have to trust others as they trust you. You'll have to improvise, adapt, and overcome.

And yes, you may fail. I'm not talking only about flunking an inspection, grounding a ship, or not accomplishing a mission. Those things happen, and you take your licks for mistakes that you—or even your people—make, and you move on. Sometimes the penalties are large, even career-ending (hopefully not life-ending), but that's the nature of the profession. So be it.

No, worse yet—by far—is failure in character. Did you take a short cut, and lie or cheat your way out of a tough spot? Did you betray a trust to make yourself look good? Did you do something that only you know about, but that you know was wrong, a violation of the Navy's core values? Were you weak when you should have been strong? Cowardly when you should have been brave?

Now *that's* real failure. It might be noticed, or it might not be. It might be punished, or it might not be. Doesn't matter. You have to rebuild yourself if it ever happens to you. As a person of honor, you owe it to yourself and to those you lead and serve.

How do you rebuild? One step at a time, one day at a time, with determination and courage. It may be painful and it may be humiliating, but just do it. You'll be the better for it.

Don't dwell on your failure—that's childish and selfish.

Don't ignore your failure—that's arrogant and dishonest.

But be *mindful* of your failure and learn from it, and never do it again.

Everything I've discussed is pretty deep stuff. It can even be overwhelming—believe me, I know. I, too, have made mistakes. It's okay.

But remember that you are *never* alone. You are a member of a team, and that team wants to see you succeed and grow. Your classmates, and all midshipmen—and later on Sailors, chiefs, and your fellow officers (peers and seniors)—*want* you to be a good officer, and they will help you. Trust them. Learn from them.

There will be tough times, but you will succeed more than you fail.

Always keep in mind, even in the worst possible moments, these simple words by Sir Winston Churchill: "Never give in, never give in, never, never, never, never—in nothing, great or small, large or petty—never give in except to convictions of honor and good sense."

I cannot say it better. If you keep those words in mind, you will do just fine, and I will have complete confidence—I will *trust*—that our great Navy is in the best possible hands: your hands!

6 The Metamorphosis of Plebes into Officers— Adult Human Development

Objectives

1. Describe the process of identity formation and the major developmental tasks of adulthood and explain how this knowledge would shape your approach to leading subordinates in the fleet.

2. Evaluate your own stage of psychosocial development as it relates to Erickson's psychosocial crises.

3. Explain how the Naval Academy environment will likely cause your psychosocial development to differ from what you would experience at a civilian college.

4. Describe some of the leadership challenges related to psychosocial development in a military with 50% of its personnel in the 17–25 year old range.

Personality and Social Changes

Adolescence

In Chapter 5 we described Erik Erikson's theory of psychosocial development and saw that four psychosocial crises are experienced before the end of childhood. Erikson's fifth psychosocial crisis deals with **identity versus identity confusion**. For the adolescent, who is experiencing a major growth spurt and developing signs of adulthood, the search for an identity and a place in society is most important (Erikson, 1975). It can also be extremely frustrating. For some individuals, the search for an identity may not end for years; for others, it never ends.

The new roles open to the adolescent are influenced by ethnic and racial background, geographic locale, family values, and societal values. It is quite unlikely that a 15-year-old girl from rural Nebraska will see her place in society in the same way as a 15-year-old girl from Los Angeles. Being raised on a farm in a small town in the Midwest gives one a different view of possible societal roles than does being raised in a major metropolitan area (Holland & Andre, 1994). Although both adolescents search for a place in society, their perceived options are quite different. The same could be said for the comparison of adolescents in the United States with adolescents in other countries. For example, in the United States, young people tend to choose an occupation, whereas many adolescents in other cultures do not have a say in what their occupation will be. In some countries, such as Italy, the parents' occupation will likely become that of their children.

Possible Outcomes of Identity Formation. In some instances, the frustrations of this stage of development may cause adolescents to accept uncritically the values and desires of their parents. In this situation, called **foreclosure**, the adolescent's own unique identity is not allowed to develop. Consider Willard, a successful but frustrated surgeon. Willard grew up in a small town in southwestern Oklahoma. As a boy, he enjoyed electronics and building radios. He could easily have become an electronics engineer. However, he became a doctor because that was the occupation his family chose for him; nobody asked him what he wanted to do with his life.

Some adolescents find the identity expected of them unacceptable but are unable to replace it with an acceptable alternative. In such situations, the adolescent may develop a **negative identity** by adopting behaviors opposite to those that are expected. For example, Ken's family always expected that he would become a lawyer. After a rebellious college career and a frustrating semester of law school, Ken dropped out of school; he now drives a cab.

Identity diffusion occurs when the adolescent has few goals and is generally apathetic about schoolwork, friends, and the future (Archer & Waterman, 1990). The individual lacks an identity and is not motivated to find one.

identity versus identity confusion Erikson's fifth psychosocial crisis, in which the adolescent faces the task of determining his or her identity and role in society

foreclosure Uncritical acceptance of parental values and desires; hampers the development of a unique identity

negative identity Adoption of behaviors that are the opposite of what is expected

identity diffusion Failure to develop an identity because of lack of goals and general apathy

moratorium Period during which an adolescent may try several identities without intending to settle on a specific one

Finally, some adolescents may go through a period in which they try out several identities without intending to settle on a specific one. It is as if a **moratorium** had been called on actually selecting an identity. The years spent in college may be viewed as a moratorium. A student may sample several different subject areas before settling on a major and choosing a career.

Adolescent Peer Groups. During adolescence, the peer group promotes a sense of identity and defends against identity confusion. The peer group can have a pronounced influence on an adolescent's attitudes, values, and behaviors. Belonging to groups such as the French club, the hiking club, or an athletic team may have a positive influence. However, not all adolescent groups help develop a strong and productive sense of identity and an appropriate adjustment to society. For example, the prevalence of teenage gangs has added to the crime and violence found in the nation's cities (Williams, Singh, & Singh, 1994).

Colorado psychologists Cynthia Tennant-Clark, Janet Fritz, and Fred Beauvais (1989) investigated the effects of adolescent participation in groups focusing on the occult. They defined occult participation as "belief in supernatural powers such as magic, . . . , witchcraft or Satanism, and the practice of rituals associated with their beliefs" (p. 758). Adolescents who scored high in knowledge of occult rituals, literature, games, and paraphernalia were more likely to be involved with substance abuse, have a poor self concept, and harbor negative feelings about the future. Adolescents who participate in occult activities may have difficulty adjusting to the demands of a society that does not condone such behaviors (Clark, 1994). Although we cannot say whether such participation causes problems like drug abuse and low self-esteem or whether those problems drive adolescents to participate in occult practices, it is clear that such groups are likely to have a negative influence.

The importance of appropriate models for the adolescent was also clear in a study conducted by Judith Brook and her colleagues (1989). Their participants were 278 college students and their older brothers. All of the participants completed a questionnaire that dealt with the use of drugs by themselves, their parents, and their peers. The results indicated that drug use may be influenced by peers, parents, and older siblings but that these three sources do not exert the same degree of influence. "Drug modeling by peers and siblings was found to have a greater association with younger brother drug use than did drug modeling by parents" (p. 70). Likewise, John W. Graham, Gary Marks, and William B. Hansen (1991) reported that modeling by peers was related to cigarette smoking and alcohol use by seventh-grade boys and girls. Frequency of drug use among adolescents is related to frequency of parental drug use (Anderson & Henry, 1994; Denton & Kampfe, 1994).

John Coleman (1980) highlighted three functions that make peer groups so important to the adolescent.

1. Through the process of experimentation, adolescents find out which behaviors and personality characteristics will be accepted and praised and which ones will be rejected. Peer groups provide the all-important feedback.

2. The peer group serves as a support group of contemporaries who are also experiencing the same social and physical changes.

3. Because adolescence is a period of questioning the behavior, standards, and authority of adults, it is hard for adolescents to seek help and advice from their parents. The peer group serves this important function.

Any peer group can serve these three functions. Hence it is important for adolescents to be associated with a positive peer group if they are to become contributing members of society.

Family Influences. The importance of the adolescent's peer groups should not lead you to believe that the family has ceased to have an influence; that is not at all the case. For example, Kenneth Felkers and Cathie Stivers (1994) found that family attitudes play a major role in determining whether adolescents, especially girls, develop eating problems such as anorexia nervosa and bulimia. Family relations are also an important variable in predicting juvenile delinquency (Hoge, Andrews, & Leschied, 1994). A study of Norweigan adolescents indicated that good family relations were important in producing good mental health and reducing depression in adolescents (Pedersen, 1994); a study of Canadian adolescents has also shown the importance of family perceptions of adolescents in protecting them against depression (McFarlane et al., 1994).

Making a Commitment. Adolescence is the stage of life in which individuals begin to make sustained personal commitments. Such commitments may be to another person, a religious cause, career preparation, or a social program. Commitments help the adolescent develop a sense of identity and accomplishment.

The decision to become sexually active represents a major personal commitment that has important consequences. Nowhere is the importance of this decision more clearly seen than in the case of teenage pregnancy (Bingham, Miller, & Adams, 1990; Raeff, 1994; Rauch-Elnekave, 1994). To understand the factors involved in teenage pregnancy, researchers conducted in-depth interviews with five 14-year-old African-American adolescents who were pregnant or had recently given birth (Pete & De Santis, 1990). The interviews revealed three key factors in the decision to become sexually active: (1) The partner was someone the young woman trusted; (2) the risk of pregnancy was not taken seriously (contraceptive devices were rarely, if ever, used); and (3) family relationships were less than ideal (there was no parent or other adult with whom to talk). These three characteristics are consistent with the self-centered and self-conscious adolescent thought patterns described by David Elkind (1984).

Pete and De Santis (1990) highlight a major implication of their research when they indicate that "young teenagers need assistance . . . in communicating with their parents and partners about sexual matters. Parents also need assistance in developing these communication skills" (p. 153). The importance of teenage mothers maintaining good communication with their parents is seen clearly in the area of child abuse. Teenage mothers who have poor support and poor communication are more likely to abuse their children than mothers who have good support and good communication (Haskett, Johnson, & Miller, 1994).

Marion Howard and Judith McCabe (1990) also provide some helpful suggestions for encouraging teenagers not to be sexually active. Their procedure includes teaching teenagers to understand the problems of sexual activity through role playing and learning how to say no. For example, the adolescent role-plays in various situations involving pressure to be sexually active and learns to say no. Role-playing the difficulties they are likely to face may help adolescents find it easier to say no when the real situation actually presents itself.

Early Adulthood

Along with the physical and intellectual changes that characterize adulthood come important personality and social changes. In the United States, the world is the

Popular bootcamp lore

intimacy versus isolation Erikson's sixth psychosocial crisis, in which the young adult faces the task of establishing a strong commitment to others (intimacy) or having to deal with isolation

Psychological Detective

What are some of the advantages of having children when you are in your mid to late twenties? Are there any advantages to becoming a parent at an earlier age? Write down some answers to these questions before reading further.

adults' oyster: they can make of it what they want. Career and lifestyle choices are almost unlimited. *Diversity* is a key word for the adult.

Intimacy versus Isolation. It may be difficult to believe that one can experience a psychosocial crisis when one is in the best of health and at the height of one's physical and intellectual powers. Yet this is exactly what Erikson suggests. He believes that young adults experience the crisis of **intimacy versus isolation**. *Intimacy* refers to the ability to make a strong commitment to other people. An individual who cannot establish intimate relationships becomes isolated. Adolescents who have developed a strong sense of personal identity and worth are better prepared to make the compromises and sacrifices required in a successful relationship. Those who lack a strong personal identity are likely to feel insecure and to avoid close relationships.

However, the development of a strong sense of personal identity and intimacy may take different courses for boys and girls. Susan Basow (1992) observes that according to Erikson's life span perspective, "the sexes diverge during adolescence: boys generally establish a strong autonomous identity before establishing an intimate relationship, whereas girls frequently establish an intimate relationship first and may never establish a strong autonomous identity" (p. 120).

Marriage and Children. A young adult who is able to establish intimate relationships faces a number of important decisions. Among those decisions are whether to marry or cohabit and whether to have children. Research on such topics as cohabitation has yielded some interesting results. Data from a sample of 180 college students indicated that the willingness to cohabit was shown by older students who had lower levels of religiosity, more liberal attitudes toward sexual behavior, and less traditional views of marriage and sex roles (Huffman et al., 1994).

Both marriage and cohabitation have benefits and costs. For example, married people are healthier and tend to be happier than unmarried people (Verbrugge, 1979). However, with nearly a million divorces granted each year in the United States, it is clear that marriage is difficult (Wallerstein, 1994) and may not always be beneficial or desirable. Although people who have divorced are likely to remarry, the rate of redivorce has increased to the point that there are now nearly as many redivorces as there are divorces (Norton & Moorman, 1987).

Whether and when to have children is another major issue of young adulthood that has both costs and benefits. Statistics show that the average age at which women have their first child has been rising since the 1960s.

If you wait until you are in your mid- to late twenties to have children, you will have greater earning power, and you will be able to provide a better lifestyle and education for your children. Your career goals will be more fully developed. Your role and responsibilities as a parent will be clearer, and you are likely to have more time to enjoy your children.

Most of the advantages of having children when one is younger are related to the effects of aging. Younger parents are likely to be more active and energetic than older parents; hence they may be able to deal with the demands of caring for a baby more effectively than older parents. Health is another age-related factor. As the age of childbearing increases, the health risks to both mother and child increase (Fryns, 1987). For example, the risk of having a child with Down syndrome increases from 1 in 2,000 for mothers age 25 to 1 in 40 for mothers age 45 and older. However, age is not the only factor that affects the decision to have children; career aspirations may also play a major role.

Consider the case of Nancy and Charles. Nancy aspires to become an electrical engineer, and Charles is planning a career in advertising. As a dual-career family, they have been forced to make compromises; sometimes their schedules conflict and create tension between them.

But there are also several potential benefits. The sharing of child-care responsibilities can result in a closer relationship between a father and his children. Compared to wives who do not work outside the home, the wife in a dual-career couple has additional opportunities to develop her skills and build identity and self-esteem. Because neither partner dominates the family in terms of responsibility and earning power, dual careers can lead to a more egalitarian relationship. However, dual careers can also result in a variety of problems, such as rivalry between husband and wife, conflicts between family and work roles, insufficient time to meet children's needs, and changes in family decision-making processes (Flanagan, 1990).

Career Development.   As this discussion suggests, career development is one of the major tasks young adults face. Until fairly recently, a discussion of career development would have dealt exclusively with men. This situation has changed: By 1986, more than half of the women in the United States were employed outside the home (Bianchi & Spain, 1986). Despite the dramatic increase in the number of women in the workforce, women continue to encounter barriers. Many more women than men are employed in clerical and sales positions (U.S. Department of Labor, 1985), and equity in salaries has not been achieved. However, like Nancy, the aspiring electrical engineer, more women are entering traditionally male-dominated fields.

Middle Adulthood

During middle adulthood, one's occupation takes on added significance. Because prestige, productivity, and earning power may never be greater, these are the "golden years" for many people. The importance of one's job during this stage has been revealed in two different types of research. One set of studies investigates what individuals feel they would do if they suddenly became millionaires. In one study, 80 percent of the participants said they would keep working (Harpaz, 1985). The other type of research deals with the effects of unemployment. Workers who have been laid off report feelings of depression, emptiness, and being lost (Kelvin & Jarrett, 1985).

Burnout.   Even during these golden years, however, a person can experience job problems and dissatisfaction.

For some individuals, employment during middle adulthood may be characterized by high levels of stress and frustration, eventually creating a condition known as *burnout*. **Burnout** is a feeling of emotional and physical exhaustion that interferes with job performance and can lead to reduced self-esteem and eventually to depression. (Christina Maslach, 1982, has provided an in-depth analysis of this phenomenon.) This condition is one of the hazards of high-stress occupations with long hours, such as medicine, police work, air traffic control, psychological counseling, teaching, and legal practice. For example, clinical psychologists who feet that they are no longer able to help their clients often experience burnout (Maslach, 1978).

Many students enter the field of psychology with the goal of becoming clinical psychologists. Although this occupation can be very rewarding, the typical day of a clinical psychologist at a mental health center may be very stressful. The psychologist will see at least four or five clients for psychotherapy. Conducting psychotherapy sessions is a draining experience. There will be at least one meeting pertaining to the operation of the mental health center. Each of the numerous phone calls from patients will require 10 to 15 minutes of the psychologist's time. If student interns are studying at the center, the psychologist may be asked to supervise them. Sometime during the day, the psychologist will have to find time to write up therapy notes and prepare complete written reports on each patient for use by the mental health center, the consulting psychiatrist, or the local judge. In short, there is too much to accomplish and not enough time in which to accomplish it. Is it any wonder that there is a high rate of burnout among clinical psychologists?

What can be done to prevent or alleviate burnout? Many experts suggest that taking vacations and breaks from the job can help. Sophia Kahill (1986) suggests that adopting realistic expectations about one's job, developing outside interests, and establishing a social support system can also help counteract burnout. Hobbies can help, too. Consider Mark, a clinical psychologist who is also an avid collector of baseball cards. This hobby helps counteract burnout in several ways. Reading magazines about cards and going to card shows takes his mind away from the pressures of work. It also puts him in touch with new friends and acquaintances who do not talk about work-related problems.

Midlife Crisis.

For some men in Western countries like the United States, middle adulthood brings with it the well-known midlife crisis (Levinson, 1986). The **midlife crisis** is a potentially stressful period that typically occurs during the mid-forties and is brought on when the individual comes to grips with his own mortality and begins to review his life and accomplishments. Dissatisfaction with one's life may be accompanied by the feeling that rapid action is needed to correct the situation or regain one's youth. Therefore, it is not uncommon for men who experience such a crisis to make radical changes in their jobs or lifestyles.

Consider the case of Paul. For a number of years, Paul was a successful business executive. His daily routine never varied, and most people saw him as rather dull. Then, at age 46, he made a dramatic change in his lifestyle. His gray and blue business suits and white dress shirts were replaced with bright-colored, trendy clothes. The family sedan was traded in for a small sports car. Many people are saying that Paul is not acting his age. What happened to cause these changes in Paul?

Paul's new car and flashy clothes suggest that he is undergoing a midlife crisis. Is it possible that he is trying to deny his advancing age by adopting symbols of youth? How satisfying and productive has his life really been?

Although some experts feel that few men can avoid the midlife crisis (e.g., Levinson, 1986), other research does not paint as bleak a picture. The percentage who

burnout Emotional and physical exhaustion that interferes with job performance

midlife crisis Potentially stressful period that occurs during the mid-forties and is triggered by reevaluation of one's accomplishments

experience the classic midlife crisis may be quite low (less than 15 percent), and a sizable proportion (over 30 percent) report a satisfying adjustment to midlife (Farrell & Rosenberg, 1981).

Research on midlife changes in women has revealed a different pattern (Reinke et al., 1985). For women, age-related stress tends to occur earlier, at age 30 rather than age 40 or 50. However, the likelihood of a midlife crisis appears to be decreasing as more women return to college and enter the labor force. College training and job satisfaction, in conjunction with family roles, provide important buffers against midlife difficulties (Baruch, 1984).

Erikson was not directly addressing the midlife crisis when he described the psychosocial crisis of middle adulthood, yet many of the same issues involved. Erikson believes that during our early forties we face the crisis of **generativity versus stagnation**. To be generative is to have concern for the next generation and for the perpetuation of life. Because teaching, coaching, and parenting reflect an obvious desire to share one's talents and knowledge, this concern is frequently expressed through such activities.

generativity versus stagnation Erikson's seventh psychosocial crisis, which occurs during middle adulthood and reflects concern, or lack of concern, for the next generation

Other Stresses during Middle Adulthood. As their children grow older and leave home to begin their own careers, middle-aged American parents must confront another challenge. During the hustle and bustle of the child-rearing years, communication between the parents may have diminished and in some cases faded entirely. Now that there are no children at home, the parents must become reacquainted. This adjustment is called the **empty nest syndrome**.

empty nest syndrome Period of adjustment for parents after all children have left home.

Several factors appear to be responsible for the increase in marital satisfaction following the departure of children. First, the family's financial situation improves, and there are fewer worries about financial matters (Berry & Williams, 1987). Second, the goal of raising a family has been achieved. Once the children have left home, many of the anxieties associated with this goal are reduced. Finally, there is more time for the husband and wife to do things together.

Another major stress that may occur during middle adulthood is having to provide care for one's aging parents. The stress of attending to the needs of elderly parents is heightened when the parents live with their children. Such strains can, and do, lead to violence. As many as 1 million cases of elder abuse may occur in the United States each year (Eastman, 1984). The magnitude of this problem and the intense stress it creates have led to the development of counseling and support groups for people who care for the elderly (Cantor, 1983).

In times of economic hardship, many young couples are forced to return home to live with their parents. Similarly, a daughter and her young children may return to live with her parents following a divorce. For parents who have adjusted to the empty nest, this newly refilled nest may be very stressful. Routines must be changed, and the needs and desires of additional family members must be addressed.

Psychological Detective

Many individuals report an improvement in marital satisfaction after their children have left home. What are some possible reasons for this increased satisfaction? Write down your answers before reading further.

Late Adulthood

Erikson's final personality crisis, **integrity versus despair**, occurs during late adulthood. To accept one's impending death, one must be able to put one's life in perspective and attach meaning to it. Achieving this goal results in a sense of wholeness or

integrity versus despair Erikson's eighth psychosocial crisis, which occurs during late adulthood; integrity reflects the feeling that one's life has been worthwhile; despair reflects a desire to relive one's life

integrity. People who are unable to find meaning in their lives may develop a sense of despair and anguish and wish they could have lived their lives differently.

Retirement. The crisis of integrity versus despair is reflected in the way an individual adapts to retirement. According to the American Association of Retired People (1992), more older Americans are choosing to retire than ever before. In addition, the age at which individuals retire is decreasing. Retirement may call forth visions of elderly people enjoying a vacationlike life in places with ideal climates such as Florida or Arizona. Although these images sell condominiums and retirement houses, they are not accurate. Retirement represents a major adjustment (Glick, 1980). Some individuals look forward to retirement and enjoy it greatly. For others, retirement is a time of frustration, anger, and possibly depression.

Why do people react so differently to retirement? A number of factors are involved. The keys to successful retirement include good planning and preparation, satisfaction with one's accomplishments, good health, and freedom from financial worries. Individuals who begin to attend to these issues during middle adulthood make the transition to retirement much more easily than those who do not.

The Kansas City Study. Erikson's final crisis might lead you to believe that there are only two personality types among the elderly—those who have achieved integrity in their lives and are reasonably satisfied and those who have not achieved integrity and are angry or despondent. The results of an extensive study of aging conducted in Kansas City by Bernice Neugarten and her colleagues (Neugarten, Havichurst, & Tobin, 1968) indicate that such a description may not be accurate. Through extensive interviews with 159 men and women ranging in age from 50 to 90, these investigators identified four main personality types: integrated, armor-defended, passive-dependent, and unintegrated. *Integrated* individuals (44 percent) have good cognitive abilities and generally lead active, complex, and satisfying lives. Individuals in the *armor-defended* category (25 percent) are achievement-oriented. They defend themselves against growing old and cling to the lifestyle of middle adulthood as long as possible. As long as they can maintain that lifestyle, they are satisfied with their lives.

The *passive-dependent* group (19 percent) comprises two types of individuals. People who are dependent on one or two others for their needs are categorized as *succorance-seeking*. As long as the support of those others is available, these people report a reasonably high level of satisfaction with life. Individuals who are inactive and have been passive throughout their lives are categorized as *apathetic*. These individuals typically report lower levels of satisfaction with their lives.

Unintegrated individuals (12 percent) fail to display a consistent or organized pattern of aging. Despite poor emotional and psychological control, such individuals are able to continue living in society, although with low levels of life satisfaction.

Over 90 percent of the elderly live in a community, not in an institution such as a nursing home. Most elderly people prefer to live in their own homes or apartments and maintain their independence as long as possible. With some careful planning, it is often possible to achieve this objective. Consider the case of Peggy, now 91, whose husband died 10 years ago. She continues to live in her own house, as she has for over 40 years. During the day a nurse assist her with meals and provides companionship, but Peggy is as independent as possible. Not all elderly people are able to live in their own homes in this style. Retirement villages and cooperative housing arrangements, in which elderly people share a house, enable them to live in a residential neighborhood. As the average life span increases, we can expect to see additional arrangements of this nature.

CRISIS	DEVELOPMENTAL PERIOD	CHARACTERISTICS
Identity versus identity confusion	Adolescence	The individual asks, "Who am I?" Adolescents seek to establish their sexual, career, and ethnic identities during this period. If these identities are not established, the individual will be confused about the roles he or she plays in the future.
Intimacy versus isolation	Early adulthood	Patterns of intimacy, companionship, and love are established during this period. Failure to develop such patterns results in an individual who lives in isolation from others.
Generativity versus stagnation	Middle adulthood	The individual's career and productivity reach a peak during this period. Families are formed, and children are raised. Failure to accomplish these objectives results in inactivity and stagnation.
Integrity versus despair	Late adulthood	One's life and its meaning are put in perspective. Individuals who feel that their lives lack meaning experience despair over unattained goals and unresolved problems.

The Making of Midshipman Me

Caroline Elizabeth Magee
Midn 1/C, USNA '95

Dedicated to all those who aided in the process

As I watch the tide of Naval Academy faces drifting past me officers, professors, and friends, friends who are themselves my teachers, my leaders, my support and my happiness—I realize that the face I know best is mine, and the best description of their faces I can offer is what of them is reflected in my own. I owe so many of the people I have encountered at USNA. A debt of gratitude, a debt of joy. A debt of myself—for without their collective influence, I would not be the person I am proud to be today. The marks of their presence in my life over these past four years are sketched indelibly into my features, my expressions. They reside forever in the nuances of my smile, in the inadvertent quirks of my features, in the gleams of remembered moments in my eyes.

Plebe summer Induction Day July 9 1991 I show up in my short muskrat-looking haircut and my old blue skirt and my nervous grin and nauseated stomach and they take me away and take my blood and take my picture and take my clothes and here I am running around without knowing where I'm going and my whole world is shaped by the plebe summer detailers, most of them between the ages of nineteen and twenty-one but they seem so much older, so much stronger and wiser and I want to be like them someday, so knowledgeable and sure and so prepared for the roles they will play at USNA and in the fleet itself. I answer to my squad leader first, Chad

Naval Academy photo courtesy of United States Naval Academy Photographic Laboratory.

Reed ("Mr. Reed, sir" to me). He watched us with his warm wise brown eyes and praised us when we did well, laughed when we amused him, but how I dreaded the clouding of disappointment in his face when we did not live up to his standards which were becoming our own. I watched with awed eyes Tom Baldwin, Sierra Company commander, who named us the "Scurvy Dogs" and led us through the weeks with confidence and compassion. I took from these two men (officers, now) their intensity, their honest attentiveness to their plebes, and their well-timed humor.

Third-class summer comes: a pack of midshipmen crawling over Quantico, Virginia in utilities. I was caught up in the mass of mids, humping heavy packs over rocky roads, sleeping with my head pillowed on an M-16, slithering through the mud of the Quigley. My classmates, yelling motivationally, barking encouragement, laughing when there was nothing else or nothing better to do. Before me and behind me, pushing me. I clambered up the Stairway to Heaven, a ladder of logs reaching into the hot June sky, and I know the only reason I outclimbed my fear of heights was the watchful, strength-willing, eyes of my compatriots. So when I returned to solid ground I was grinning, because I had somehow been more than I thought I was; and a new courage set in my jaw and an awe for the power of a team lit my eyes. That moment of triumph was directly connected to those around me; the fact of their presence challenged me to challenge myself. The support in their faces helped me to add fresh confidence to my own.

During my youngster year, the individual who influenced me most was Professor Thompson, who taught the required sophomore Western Civilization course. He was dynamic, enthusiastic, energetic. I wrote so furiously in his class that my pen felt like it was burning up the page. I felt my mind awaken, stretch itself to absorb as much information as possible. My eyes wide, my mouth forgotten and slack, I listened and scribbled notes. My face the mirror of his brilliance in the classroom. He intensified my desire to learn, to understand. He left me with a permanent expression of hunger for knowledge; with a sense of how much is available for me to learn, and how exhilarating the learning can be.

U.S. Marines conduct M-16 training at a target range in Agrigento, Sicily.
Official U.S. Navy Photo.

Second-class summer I sampled both the life of a sailor and that of a hybrid drill instructor/mom—more commonly referred to as a plebe summer detailer. Six female midshipmen were assigned to LST 1186 (USS *Cayuga*); the first females ever to board her (and the last, as she was decommissioned a year ago). I learned to create a professional face; I discovered how to work effectively and comfortably with a group of men who had never worked with women in such tight quarters. The experience was overwhelmingly positive; virtually every man, officer or enlisted, with whom I worked was exceptionally mature and perfectly able to work with six young women. I realized I did not have to hide my sense of humor and my smile or otherwise bury my personality in order to make shipboard integration work. My face showed its usual expressions; but I learned to be myself as a junior officer, not just a midshipman or student. I became aware of the subtle differences in my body language, speech, and mannerisms that emerged when I was working on the bridge. That summer I began to understand how to be at once a woman and an officer; to deny neither role, but to make their combination effective.

Training the Class of 1997 during plebe summer gave me another injection of confidence. I found a stern face, an expression that allowed no excuses for erroneous actions. I tried to soften it with compassion as necessary, following the example of

Naval Academy photo courtesy of United States Naval Academy Photographic Laboratory.

those who had trained me. I learned to forgive myself quickly and learn from my mistakes (of which there were indeed a few!) without burdening those I was leading with my sulking over my own embarrassment. I called cadences, created training exercises, counseled my plebes; all new duties to me, and all performed in public. I had to prevent my features from revealing my doubts; competence and confidence were all that could be projected.

My next remarkable phase of development came the following summer, my last summer as a midshipman. I acted as midshipman commanding officer on a 44-foot sloop cruising round trip from Annapolis, Maryland to Charleston, South Carolina. My crew consisted of six new youngsters and another first-class midshipman. We were supervised by two safety officers. One of them, Lieutenant Commander Luis Lopez-Mazzeo, a foreign exchange officer from Argentina's navy, soon became a powerful influence on my growth as a sailor and as a leader. He knew every detail about maintaining and repairing our boat, and I admire and hope to emulate his technical knowledge when I arrive at my first ship. He always had an ear or an eye open; watching us, ready to help if we required it. He slept little but exhaustion never became evident; his high energy level and enthusiasm pushed us all to keep putting forth maximum effort. I want to be as motivating to my own sailors some day; I want to infuse my face with his spirit and vitality, my mind with his knowledge. He helped me further define the type of officer I hope to become.

During that month of sailing, I developed a deeper sense of responsibility than I had ever known. In the middle of the night when all you can see is black, black sky and blacker waters, when you are moving with and at the mercy of God's wind and waves, you realize that your actions are directly related to whether you live or die; and to lose a person into that darkness would mean losing him forever. Safety became my utmost concern, which became evident in the new crease in my forehead. My next priority was ensuring that the crew was interested and involved in its work; not only for morale purposes, but because without their full attention to their duties someone could get hurt. These fresh concerns added shadows to my expression and circles under my eyes; but they also sent adrenaline pulsing through me as I considered how to teach them, how to make it work. My face shone with a combination of anxiety and exhilaration.

My first-class fleet cruise was spent on a destroyer tender, AD-37 (USS *Samuel Gompers*). This experience was critical, although I did not fully understand why at the time. I had planned on going into aviation, had little to no interest in living the sleepless life of a surface warfare officer. But I worshipped our Commanding Officer, and nothing he said to me left my mind easily. He let me conn during an UNREP, and I looked out at that oiler 140 feet away and I was amazed that I was driving. He did not coach me or prompt me. Just told me what to do and watched me do it myself. Following this session, he asked me what I was planning to do in the Navy. I replied that I hoped to fly. He looked at me with the faintest smile and said, "Well, you know, the Navy *is* ships," as if it were the most solid fact he knew.

And I agreed with him.

In that moment, mine became the face of a surface warfare officer, reflecting his passion for and belief in ships. In January 1995 when I selected CG-72, the USS *Vella Gulf,* as my first ship, I heard his voice echoing somewhere in my memory and I wished I could tell him of the choice I had finally made.

My final year at the United States Naval Academy has flown past; I struggle to absorb all I can from the people, these incredible people, whom I will no longer see regularly after May 1995. I want them to know they have helped me become who I am. My face as an ensign will not be the face I had as a plebe, and I owe that fact to the community in which I lived at Canoe U. I want to thank them, and thank this institution for holding them all in its walls and affording me the opportunity to grow along with my shipmates.

I look in the mirror at the bright pride in my eyes and the tiny confident smile on my lips. In my eyes which open into the caverns of my memory I see all who have helped me and educated me by both example and instruction over the past four years. As I behold the future with this face, they will be there with me. And although they may not promise fair winds and following seas, they have given me the fortitude to face whatever the oceans may offer.

7 Learning to Do the Right Thing— Moral Development

Objectives

1. Outline Kohlberg's theory of moral development and describe some major criticisms of it.

2. Apply Kohlberg's model to classic moral dilemmas and to moral dilemmas which you may face as a Naval officer.

Cognitive Development

Moral Reasoning   According to Piaget (1932), the adolescent's capacity for abstraction gives rise to a more mature form of **moral reasoning.** Piaget noticed that young children take rules literally, without regard for a person's intentions or motives or the circumstances. As far as the young child is concerned, the Little Leaguer who accidentally smacks a baseball into the windshield of a car is bad, and the parent who promises cookies only then to find the cupboard bare is a liar. Not until the age of ten or eleven do children think more flexibly about rules and evaluate others not just by what they do but *why* they do it. In this more advanced stage of reasoning, the Little Leaguer is not considered a bad person or the parent a liar for actions that produced negative outcomes they did not intend (Lickona, 1976; Strichartz & Burton, 1990).

Building on the idea that moral reasoning requires cognitive sophistication, Lawrence Kohlberg argued that adolescence is a particularly rich time of life for moral development (Kohlberg, 1981, 1984; Colby & Kohlberg, 1987). Kohlberg presented stories containing moral dilemmas to children, adolescents, and adults and asked them how these dilemmas should be resolved. To illustrate, consider the following classic story:

> In Europe, a woman was near death from cancer. One drug might save her, a form of radium that a druggist in the same town had recently discovered. The druggist was charging $2,000—10 times what the drug cost him to make. The sick woman's husband, Heinz, went to everyone he knew to borrow the money, but he could only get together about half of what it cost. He told the druggist that his wife was dying and asked him to sell it cheaper or let him pay later. But the druggist said, "No." The husband got desperate and broke into the man's store to steal the drug for his wife (Kohlberg, 1969, p. 379).

What do you think: Should Heinz have stolen the drug? Were his actions morally right or wrong, and why? Based on responses to stories like this one, Kohlberg proposed that people advance through three levels of moral thought, further divided into six stages. First, there is a *preconventional* level, in which moral dilemmas are resolved in ways that satisfy self-serving motives—so an act is moral if it enables a person to avoid punishment or obtain reward. Second is a *conventional* level, in which moral dilemmas are resolved in ways that reflect the laws of the land or norms set by parents and other sources of authority. Thus, an act is moral if it meets with social approval or maintains the social order. Third, adolescents and adults who attain Piaget's formal operational stage of cognitive development may also reach a *postconventional* level of moral thought, one based on abstract principles such as equality, justice, and the value of life. At this level, an act is moral if it affirms one's conscience—even if it violates the law. At each stage, there are possible reasons for and against stealing the drug (see Table 7.1).

moral reasoning The way people think about and try to solve moral dilemmas.

81

LEVELS	STAGES	IN FAVOR OF HEINZ'S STEALING THE DRUG	AGAINST HEINZ'S STEALING THE DRUG
I. Preconventional	Stage 1 *Punishment and obedience orienta- tion:* Motivation to avoid punishment	"If you let your wife die, you will get in trouble."	"You shouldn't steal the drug because you'll be caught and sent to jail if you do."
	Stage 2 *Instrumental rela- tivist orientation:* Motivation to obtain rewards	"It wouldn't bother you much to serve a little jail term, if you have your wife when you get out."	"He may not get much of a jail term if he steals the drug, but his wife will probably die before he gets out, so it won't do him much good."
II. Conventional	Stage 3 *Good boy–nice girl orientation:* Motivation to gain approval and to avoid disapproval	"No one will think you're bad if you steal the drug, but your family will think you're an inhuman husband if you don't."	"It isn't just the drug- gist who will think you're a criminal; everyone else will too."
	Stage 4 *Society-maintaining orientation:* Motivation to fulfill one's duty and to avoid feelings of guilt	"If you have any sense of honor, you won't let your wife die because you're afraid to do the only thing that will save her."	"You'll always feel guilty for your dis- honesty and law- breaking."
III. Postconventional	Stage 5 *Social-contract orientation:* Motiva- tion to follow ratio- nal, mutually agreed-upon princi- ples and maintain the respect of others	"If you let your wife die, it would be out of fear, not out of reason- ing it out."	"You would lose your standing and respect in the community and break the law."
	Stage 6 *Universal ethical principle orientation:* Motivation to uphold one's own ethical principles and avoid self-condemnation	"If you don't steal the drug, . . . you would have lived up to the outside rule of the law but you wouldn't have lived up to your own standards of con- science."	"If you stole the drug, . . . you'd con- demn yourself because you wouldn't have lived up to your own conscience and standards of honesty."

Source: Adapted from L. Kohlberg (1969). Stage and sequence: the cognitive-developmental approach to socialization. In D. A. Goslin (Ed.), *Handbook of socialization theory and research.* Chicago: Rand McNally.

Is this theory of moral development valid? Over the years, Kohlberg has drawn an enormous amount of attention, support, and criticism. To his credit, Kohlberg and others have found that as children and adolescents mature, they climb his moral ladder in the predicted order, without skipping steps (Colby et al., 1983; Walker, 1989). Figure 7.1 shows that although most seven- to ten-year-olds are preconventional in their moral thinking, many thirteen- to sixteen-year-olds reason in conventional terms. Interestingly, researchers find that very few adolescents—or even mature adults, for that matter—resolve moral issues on a postconventional level.

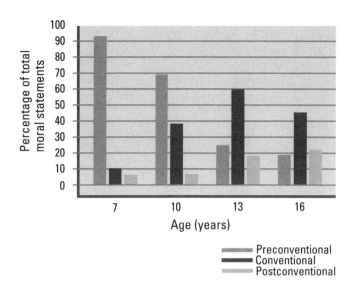

FIGURE 7.1 **Levels of moral reasoning** In response to standard moral dilemmas, most seven- to ten-year-olds are preconventional in their reasoning, while most thirteen- to sixteen-year-olds are conventional. Very few subjects resolved these dilemmas on a postconventional level (Colby et al., 1983).

Alternative Conceptions There are three major criticisms of Kohlberg's theory. The first is that his model is culturally biased. This is partly true. John Snarey (1985) reviewed forty-five studies conducted in twenty-eight countries and found that most children and adolescents—from Canada, Taiwan, Israel, Mexico, Turkey, and elsewhere—advanced at the same rate and in the same sequence through the first two levels. He also found, however, that only well-educated middle-class adults from complex urban societies consistently exhibited postconventional forms of morality based on abstract principles. When presented with Kohlberg's written dilemmas, many non-Westerners—including Tibetan Buddhist monks and respected village leaders from Kenya and Papua New Guinea—fail to reason at this third level. Why? In cultures that value friendship, belonging, and social responsibility more than rugged individualism, conventional moral reasoning is not only common but desirable. Thus, in a study that compared American and Indian children and adults, Joan Miller and David Bersoff (1992) found that in India, people operate by an alternative postconventional moral code in which obligation to a friend is more principled than obligation to justice.

A second criticism is that the model is gender biased. When Kohlberg first constructed his dilemmas, he tested only males and then used their responses as a moral yardstick. Yet according to Carol Gilligan (1982), women address moral issues "in a different voice." More concerned about compassion for others than about abstract rules, the female voice may be different, but it is not morally inferior. Gilligan's point has obvious intuitive appeal, but it lacks clear empirical support. On the one hand, public-opinion pollsters do find that women care more deeply than men about social issues and interpersonal relations. On the other hand, moral-development researchers find that women and men, on average, obtain very similar scores on Kohlberg's dilemmas (Rest, 1986; Walker, 1984). Also, in contrast to the assumption that people resolve moral dilemmas in set ways, as defined either by Kohlberg or by Gilligan, men and women are flexible in their reasoning. Studies by Dennis Krebs and his colleagues have shown that the kinds of moral judgments people make in real life depend on the situations they're in and the kinds of dilemmas they face (Krebs et al., 1991; Wark & Krebs, 1996).

Finally, many developmental psychologists have argued that Kohlberg's model is limited because morality consists of more than just an ability to think about hypothetical dilemmas in a manner that is cognitively sophisticated. Actions speak louder than words, say Kohlberg's critics. The real question is, does moral *reasoning* breed

empathy A feeling of joy for others who are happy and distress for those who are in pain.

moral *conduct*? Are the postconventional thinkers kinder, more caring, or more virtuous in their daily affairs than those who are lower on the cognitive ladder? Do society's model citizens and philanthropists use higher levels of moral reasoning than drug pushers, racists, mobsters, and corrupt business executives? Available research offers two answers to these questions.

First, moral reasoning and behavior are very often related. Juvenile delinquents tend to score lower on Kohlberg's dilemmas than normal adolescents, and those with higher scores tend to behave in ways that are considered even more moral (Blasi, 1980; Kurtines & Gewirtz, 1984). The second answer, however, is that it's entirely possible to live a moral life without "elitist" levels of cognitive reasoning. Think about Kohlberg's theory, then ask yourself: Are young children *amoral*, or less moral, than their cognitively superior parents? Children lack the cognitive equipment, but do they lack the emotional equipment underlying morality? According to Martin Hoffman (1984), morality in children is rooted in **empathy**—a capacity to experience joy for others who are happy and distress for those who are in pain. By this account, morality is present early in life. In the crib, infants often cry when they hear the sound of another baby crying. They feel no pain of their own, yet they are distressed, a possible sign of empathy. At less than two years old, babies have been observed giving food, toys, hugs, and kisses to others who show signs of distress—again, a possible sign of empathy (Zahn-Waxler et al., 1992). At the sight of a homeless person curled up on the floor of a bus station, even the preconventional young child reacts with sorrow and a desire to offer help (Damon, 1988; Eisenberg & Mussen, 1989).

As an alternative to Kohlberg's model of moral reasoning, Nancy Eisenberg (1992) argues that to predict changes in moral *behavior* it is better to examine how children and adolescents reason specifically about prosocial, helpful actions. So rather than present subjects of different ages with dilemmas that pit a rule against their own sense of right and wrong, Eisenberg presents situations in which the conflict is between one's own desires and the needs of another person. She then asks the subjects to choose a course of action and select among a set of reasons for engaging in that action. For example, subjects are asked to choose between getting an injured child's parents or going to a party, hoarding food after a flood or sharing with others, going to the beach or helping a friend study for a test, and so on.

Using a standard set of seven stories, and in longitudinal and cross-sectional studies, Eisenberg and others have found that prosocial reasoning follows a predictable developmental course. Preschool children are primarily hedonistic and self-centered in their responses; grade-school children are more other-oriented (but focused on what the person in need and others would think of them); and by late adolescence, there is an increase in feelings of guilt and sympathy, perspective-taking, and, ultimately, an inner sense of social responsibility. This pattern has been found in several countries—and there's a link between prosocial reasoning and helpfulness in actual behavior (Eisenberg et al., 1995; Carlo et al., 1996).

Moral Dilemmas in Law Each of us makes moral choices in our own lives and when called on to judge the actions of others, as when we sit on a jury. Juries have long been confronted with moral dilemmas like those constructed by Kohlberg. Before the Civil War, Northern juries regularly failed to convict people charged with aiding escaped slaves. During the turbulent Vietnam era, many juries refused to convict antiwar activists on political conspiracy charges. Today, cases involving battered women who retaliate against abusive husbands and crime victims who kill in self-defense present similar dilemmas. In cases like these, the jury has the power to vote its conscience—even if it means overruling or "nullifying" the law (Horowitz & Willging, 1991).

Particularly heart-wrenching are cases involving *euthanasia,* or assisted suicide—one of the most explosive moral and ethical issues of our time (Brigham & Pfeifer, 1996). Sometimes the issue involves physician-assisted suicide, as often practiced by Jack Kevorkian, a retired Michigan pathologist. As of the start of 1997, Kevorkian had presided over forty-six deaths. For three of these incidents, he was tried for murder—and in all three he was acquitted by a jury. Sometimes on trial are family members who are tried for what they say were acts of compassion on behalf of loved ones who were suffering, terminally ill, and pleading for death. In some instances, juries have used a postconventional morality, voting for acquittal on the ground that compassion takes precedence over the letter of the law. Yet in other instances, juries have voted to convict. Illustrating the conventional form of moral reasoning, a juror in one such case said, "We had no choice. The law does not allow for sympathy" (Associated Press, 1985).

The conflict in these events is profound: The law strictly prohibits assisted suicide, yet many people who are terminally ill and in agony desperately want to die. Is it morally superior to condone assisted suicide? No, not necessarily. Kohlberg was always quick to note that moral development is measured not by *what* decision is made but by *how* that decision is reasoned. Indeed, any juror, judge, physician, or family member can decide against assisted suicide for reasons that are either conventional ("The law prohibits this act, so it's wrong") or postconventional ("A human life should never be sacrificed"). It's a sad and ironic postscript in this regard that Kohlberg himself—who had a chronic parasitic infection that caused him excruciating stomach pain—committed suicide in 1987, before his sixtieth birthday. He had discussed his predicament with a close friend and had concluded that someone with social responsibilities to others ought to go on. But overcome with pain and deeply depressed, he drowned himself in Boston Harbor (Hunt, 1993).

The Story of Regulus

Retold by James Baldwin

This ancient story about the Roman general and statesman Marcus Atilius Regulus takes place in the third century B.C. during the First Punic War between Rome and Carthage. The legend of how Regulus kept his word immortalized him in Roman history.

On the other side of the sea from Rome there was once a great city named Carthage. The Roman people were never very friendly to the people of Carthage, and at last a war began between them. For a long time it was hard to tell which would prove the stronger. First the Romans would gain a battle, and then the men of Carthage would gain a battle; and so the war went on for many years.

Naval Academy photo courtesy of United States Naval Academy Photographic Laboratory.

Among the Romans there was a brave general named Regulus—a man of whom it was said that he never broke his word. It so happened after a while that Regulus was taken prisoner and carried to Carthage. Ill and very lonely, he dreamed of his wife and little children so far away beyond the sea; and he had but little hope of ever seeing them again. He loved his home dearly, but he believed that his first duty was to his country; and so he had left all, to fight in this cruel war.

He had lost a battle, it is true, and had been taken prisoner. Yet he knew that the Romans were gaining ground, and the people of Carthage were afraid of being beaten in the end. They had sent into other countries to hire soldiers to help them. But even with these they would not be able to fight much longer against Rome.

One day some of the rulers of Carthage came to the prison to talk with Regulus.

"We should like to make peace with the Roman people," they said, "and we are sure that, if your rulers at home knew how the war is going, they would be glad to make peace with us. We will set you free and let you go home, if you will agree to do as we say."

"What is that?" asked Regulus.

"In the first place," they said, "you must tell the Romans about the battles which you have lost, and you must make it plain to them that they have not gained anything by the war. In the second place, you must promise us that, if they will not make peace, you will come back to your prison."

"Very well," said Regulus. "I promise you that if they will not make peace, I will come back to prison."

And so they let him go, for they knew that a great Roman would keep his word.

When he came to Rome, all the people greeted him gladly. His wife and children were very happy, for they thought that now they would not be parted again. The white-haired Fathers who made the laws for the city came to see him. They asked him about the war.

"I was sent from Carthage to ask you to make peace," he said. "But it will not be wise to make peace. True, we have been beaten in a few battles, but our army is gaining ground every day. The people of Carthage are afraid, and well they may be. Keep on with the war a little while longer, and Carthage shall be yours. As for me, I have come to bid my wife and children and Rome farewell. Tomorrow I will start back to Carthage and to prison, for I have promised."

Then the Fathers tried to persuade him to stay.

"Let us send another man in your place," they said.

"Shall a Roman not keep his word?" answered Regulus. "I am ill, and at the best have not long to live. I will go back as I promised."

His wife and little children wept, and his sons begged him not to leave them again.

"I have given my word," said Regulus. "The rest will be taken care of."

Then he bade them goodbye, and went bravely back to the prison and the cruel death which he expected.

This was the kind of courage that made Rome the greatest city in the world.

Hobson's Choice: Responsibility and Accountability

The Wall Street Journal

In Charleston, SC down at the Battery there is a monument in a corner of the park that notes:

> *In 1952, USS HOBSON was in a collision with USS WASP (CVS-18) during mid-Atlantic exercises. HOBSON sank in less than four minutes taking with her 176 crew members. Crew members are listed on the plaque.*

Along with responsibility, as this famous editorial of 14 May 1952 points out, must go accountability. Without accountability, having to answer for what one has or has not done, either good or bad, one has no responsibilities. If an officer has no responsibilities for which he or she will be held accountable, followers will find it difficult, if not impossible, to place their confidence and trust in that leader.

One night past some thirty thousand tons of ships went hurtling at each other through the darkness. When they had met, two thousand tons of ship and a hundred and seventy-six men lay at the bottom of the sea in a far off place.

Now comes the cruel business of accountability. Those who were there, those who are left from those who were there, must answer how it happened and whose was the error that made it happen.

It is a cruel business because it was no wish of destruction that killed this ship and its hundred and seventy-six men: the accountability lies with good men who erred in judgment under stress so great that it is almost its own excuse. Cruel because no matter how deep the probe, it cannot change the dead, because it cannot probe deeper than remorse.

And it seems more cruel still, because all around us in other places we see the plea accepted that what is done is done beyond discussion, and that for good men in their human errors there should be afterwards no accountability.

We are told it is all to no avail to review so late the courses that led to the crash of Pearl Harbor: to debate the courses set at Yalta and Potsdam; to inquire how it is that one war won leaves us only with wreckage and with two worlds still hurtling at each other through the darkness. To inquire into these things, now, we are reminded, will not change the dead in Schofield Barracks or on Heartbreak Ridge, nor will it change the dying that will come after the wrong courses.

We are told, too, how slanderous it is to probe into the doings of a captain now dead who cannot answer for himself, to hold him responsible for what he did when he was old and tired and when he did what he did under terrible stresses and from the best of intentions. How futile to talk of what is past when the pressing question is how to keep from sinking.

Everywhere else we are told how inhuman it is to submit men to the ordeal of answering for themselves; to haul before committees and badger them with ques-

Official U.S. Navy photo.

tions as to where they were and what they were doing while the ship of state careened from one course to another.

The probing into the sea seems more merciless because almost everywhere else we have abandoned accountability. What is done is done and why torture men with asking them afterwards, why?

Who do we hold answerable for the sufferance of dishonesty in government, for the reckless waste of public monies, for the incompetence that wrecks the currency? We can bring to bar the dishonest men, yes. But we are told men should no longer be held accountable for what they do as well as for what they intend. To err is not only human; it absolves responsibility.

Everywhere, that is, except on the sea. On the sea there is a tradition older even than the traditions of the country itself and wiser in its age than this new custom. It is the tradition that with responsibility goes authority and with them goes accountability.

This accountability is not for the intention but for the dead. The captain of a ship, like the captain of a state, is given honor and privileges and trust beyond other men. But let him set the wrong course, let him touch ground, let him bring disaster to his ship or to his men, and he must answer for what he has done. No matter what, he cannot escape.

No one knows yet what happened on the sea after that crash in the night. But nine men left the bridge of the sinking ship and went into the darkness. Eight men came back to tell what happened there. The ninth, whatever happened, will not answer now because he has already answered for his accountability.

It is cruel, this accountability of good and well-intentioned men.

But the choice is that or an end to responsibility and, finally, as the cruel sea has taught, an end to the confidence and trust in the men who lead, for men will not long trust leaders who feel themselves beyond accountability for what they do.

And when men lose confidence and trust in those who lead, order disintegrates into chaos and purposeful ships into uncontrollable derelicts.

The enormous burden of this responsibility and accountability for the lives and careers of other men and often, the outcome of great issues, is the genesis of the liberality which distinguishes the orders to officers commanding ships of the United States Navy.

8 Becoming a Student of People— Personality Types

Objectives

1. Describe and distinguish personality traits and psychological types.

2. Discuss the meaning and significance of emotional intelligence in leadership.

3. Determine your psychological type and describe the implications for your relationships and leadership performance.

Personality

"We're not going to promote you to department head," said the vice president to the analyst. "Although you are a great troubleshooter, you've alienated too many people in the company. You're too blunt and insensitive." As just implied, most successes and failures in people-contact jobs are attributed largely to interpersonal skills. And personality traits are an important contributor to interpersonal, or human relations, skills. The subject of individual differences in personality must therefore be given consideration in any serious study of interpersonal relations in the workplace.

Personality refers to those persistent and enduring behavior patterns that tend to be expressed in a wide variety of situations. A person who is brash and insensitive in one situation is likely to behave similarly in many other situations. Your personality is what makes you unique. Your walk, your talk, your appearance, your speech, and your inner values and conflicts all contribute to your personality.

We will illustrate the importance of personality to interpersonal relationships in organizations by describing six key personality traits and psychological types related to cognitive styles. In addition, you will be given guidelines for dealing effectively with different personality types.

Six Major Personality Factors and Traits

Many psychologists believe that the basic structure of human personality is represented by five broad factors:

I. Extroversion
II. Agreeableness
III. Conscientiousness
IV. Emotional stability
V. Openness to experience

A sixth key personality factor, self-monitoring of behavior, has received much recent attention and is also included here. People develop all six factors partially from inborn tendencies and partially from being raised in a particular environment. For example, a person might have a natural tendency to be agreeable. Growing up in an environment in which agreeableness was encouraged would help the person become even more agreeable.

All six factors have a substantial impact on interpersonal relations and job performance. The interpretations and meanings of these factors provide useful information because they can help you pinpoint important areas for personal development. Although these factors are partially inherited, most people can improve their standing on them.

I. **Extroversion.** Traits associated with the extroversion factor include being social, gregarious, assertive, talkative, and active. An outgoing person is often described as extroverted, while a shy person is described as being introverted.

II. **Emotional stability.** Traits associated with the emotional stability factor include being anxious, depressed, angry, embarrassed, emotional, and worried. A person with low emotional stability is often referred to as neurotic or emotionally unstable.

III. *Agreeableness.* An agreeable person is friendly and cooperative. Traits associated with the agreeableness factor include being courteous, flexible, trusting, good-natured, cooperative, forgiving, softhearted, and tolerant.

IV. *Conscientiousness.* A variety of meanings have been attached to the conscientiousness factor, but it generally implies being dependable. Traits associated with conscientiousness include being careful, thorough, responsible, organized, and purposeful. Other related traits include being hardworking, achievement-oriented, and persevering.

V. *Openness to experience.* People who score high on the openness-to-experience factor have well-developed intellects. Traits commonly associated with this factor include being imaginative, cultured, curious, original, broad-minded, intelligent, and artistically sensitive.

VI. *Self-monitoring of behavior.* The self-monitoring trait refers to the process of observing and controlling how we are perceived by others. High self-monitors are pragmatic, and even chameleon-like actors in social groups. They often say what others want to hear. Low self-monitors avoid situations that require them to adopt different outer images. In this way their outer behavior adheres to their inner values. A low self-monitor can often lead to inflexibility. Do the quiz in Self-Assessment Exercise 8-1 to measure your tendencies toward self-monitoring.

Depending on the job, any one of the preceding personality factors can be important for success. Conscientiousness relates to job performance for many different occupations. Another important research finding is that extroversion is associated with success for managers and sales representatives. The explanation, of course, is that managers and salespeople are required to interact extensively with other people.

Psychological Types and Cognitive Styles

Personality also influences a person's **cognitive style**, or the mental processes used to perceive and make judgments from information. A knowledge of these cognitive styles can help you relate better to people because you can better appreciate how they make decisions. According to the famous psychiatrist Carl Jung, how people gather and evaluate information determines their cognitive style. Jung's analysis became the basis for a widely used test of personality and cognitive style called the Meyers-Briggs Type Indicator.

Gathering Information: To solve problems it is necessary to gather information. Two different styles of gathering information are sensation and intuition. **Sensation-type individuals** prefer routine and order. They search for precise details when gathering information to solve a problem. Sensation-type individuals prefer to work with established facts rather than to search for new possibilities. **Intuitive-type individuals** prefer an overall perspective—the big picture. Such people enjoy solving new problems. In addition, they dislike routine and prefer to look for possibilities rather than to work with facts.

Directions: Decide whether each of the following statements is more true or false for you. Circle T or F to indicate your answer.

1.	I find it hard to imitate the behavior of other people.	T	F
2.	My behavior is usually an expression of my true inner feelings, attitudes, and beliefs.	T	F
3.	At parties and social gatherings, I do not attempt to say and do things that others will like.	T	F
4.	I can only argue about ideas that I already have.	T	F
5.	I can make impromptu speeches, even on topics about which I have almost no information.	T	F
6.	I guess I put on a show to impress or to entertain people.	T	F
7.	When I am uncertain how to act in a social situation, I look to the behavior of others for cues.	T	F
8.	I'd make a good actor.	T	F
9.	I rarely ask my friends' advice on movies, books, or music.	T	F
10.	I sometimes appear to others to be experiencing deeper emotions than I actually am.	T	F
11.	I laugh more when I watch a comedy with others than when alone.	T	F
12.	In a group I am rarely the center of attention.	T	F
13.	In different situations and with different people, I often act like very different persons.	T	F
14.	I am not particularly good at making other people like me.	T	F

Scoring and Interpretation: To obtain your score, count one point for each False answer to statements 1, 2, 3, 4, 9, 12, and 14. Count one point for each True response to statements 5, 6, 7, 8, 10, 11, and 13. The higher your score, the stronger your tendencies toward self-monitoring. You are a high self-monitor if your score is 10 or higher; low if it is 5 or less. Refer to the text for the meaning of high and low self-monitoring.

Source: Adapted from Bernard Asbell, *What They Know About You* (New York: Random House, 1993).

When shopping for an automobile, a sensation-type individual would want to gather a large number of facts about such matters as miles or kilometers per gallon, provisions of the warranty, finance charges, and resale value. In contrast, the intuitive-type individual would be more concerned about the overall style of the car and how proud he or she would be as the owner.

Evaluating Information: The evaluation aspect of problem solving involves judging how to deal with information after it has been collected. Styles of information evaluation range from an emphasis on feeling to an emphasis on thinking. **Feeling-type individuals** have a need to conform and adapt to the wishes of others. Because of these tendencies, they try to avoid problems that might result in disagreements. **Thinking-type individuals** rely on reason and intellect to deal with problems. They downplay emotion in problem solving and decision making.

Assume that a team leader asks group managers their opinion of an idea for a new product. Feeling-type people in the group are likely to look for the good in the proposal and then express approval for the project. Thinking type team members are likely to be more independent in their evaluation of the new-product idea. As a result they will express their opinion whether or not it is what the manager wants to hear. (Notice that feeling-type people are high self-monitors, and thinking types are the opposite.)

The Four Cognitive Styles: The two dimensions of information gathering and evaluation are combined to produce a four-way classification of cognitive (or problem-solving) styles. Exhibit 8-1 lists the four styles and occupations well suited to them.[2] The four styles are as follows:

- Sensation/thinking
- Intuitive/thinking
- Sensation/feeling
- Intuitive/feeling

If you take the Meyers-Briggs Type Indicator, often available in career centers, you will be presented a diagnosis of your type. You can also study the four types and make a judgment as to your cognitive style. Recognizing your cognitive style can help you identify work that you are likely to perform well. For example, a person with an intuitive/feeling type is likely to be skillful in resolving customer complaints. The same person might not be well suited by temperament to bookkeeping.

Guidelines for Dealing with Different Personality Types

A key purpose in presenting information about a sampling of various personality types is to provide guidelines for individualizing your approach to people. As a basic example, if you wanted to score points with an introvert, you would approach that person in a restrained, laid-back fashion. In contrast, a more gregarious, lighthearted approach might be more effective with an extrovert. The purpose of individualizing your approach is to build a better working relationship or to establish rapport with the other person.

To match your approach to dealing with a given personality type, you must first arrive at an approximate diagnosis of the individual's personality. The following suggestions are therefore restricted to readily observable aspects of personality.

1. When relating to an *extroverted* individual, as suggested above, emphasize friendliness, warmth, and a stream of chatter. Talk about people more than ideas, things, or data. Express an interest in a continuing working relationship.
2. When relating to an *introverted* individual, move slowly in forming a working relationship. Do not confuse quietness with a lack of interest. Tolerate

---

Exhibit 8-1
Four Problem-Solving Styles and Work Matchup

Sensation/Thinking: Decisive, dependable alert to details	**Sensation/Feeling:** Pragmatic, analytical methodical, and conscientious
Accounting and bookkeeping Computer programming Manufacturing technology	Supervision Selling Negotiating
Intuitive/Thinking: Creative, progressive perceptive	**Intuitive/Feeling:** Colorful, people person, helpful
Design of systems Law, paralegal work Middle manager	Customer service Business communications Human resources

---

moments of silence. Emphasize ideas, things, and data more heavily than people.

3. When relating to a person who appears to be *emotionally unstable* based on symptoms of worry and tension, be laid back and reassuring. Attempt not to project your own anxiety and fears. Be a good listener. If possible, minimize emphasis on deadlines and the dire consequences of a project failing. Show concern and interest in the person's welfare.

4. When relating to an *agreeable* person, just relax and be yourself. Reciprocate with kindness to sustain a potentially excellent working relationship.

5. When relating to a *disagreeable* person, be patient and tolerant. At the same time, set limits on how much mistreatment you will take. Disagreeable people sometimes secretly want others to put brakes on their antisocial behavior.

6. When relating to a *conscientious* person, give him or her freedom, and do not nag. The person will probably honor commitments without prompting. Conscientious people are often taken for granted, so remember to acknowledge the person's dependability.

7. When relating to a person of low *conscientiousness*, keep close tabs on him or her, especially if you need the person's output to do your job. Do not assume because the person has an honest face and a pleasing smile that he or she will deliver as promised. Frequently follow up on your requests, and impose deadlines if you have the authority. Express deep appreciation when the person does follow through.

8. When relating to a person who is *open to experience,* emphasize information sharing, idea generation, and creative approaches to problems. Appeal to his or her intellect.

9. When relating to a person who is *closed to experience,* stick closely to the facts of the situation at hand. Recognize that the person prefers to think small and deal with the here and now.

10. When dealing with a person whom you suspect is a high *self-monitor,* be cautious in thinking that the person is really in support of your position. The person could just be following his or her natural tendency to appear to please others, but not really feel that way.

11. When dealing with a *sensation-type* person, emphasize facts, figures, and conventional thinking—without sacrificing your own values. To convince the sensation type, emphasize logic more than emotional appeal. Focus on details more than the big picture.

12. When dealing with an ***intuitive-type*** individual, emphasize feelings, judgments, playing with ideas, imagination, and creativity. Focus more on the big picture than details.

Emotional Intelligence

New research has updated and expanded the idea of practical intelligence, suggesting that how effectively people use their emotions has a major impact on their success. **Emotional intelligence** refers to qualities such as understanding one's own feelings, empathy for others, and the regulation of emotion to enhance living.[5] A person with high emotional intelligence would be able to engage in such behaviors as sizing up people, pleasing others, and influencing them. Four key factors included in emotional intelligence are as follows:

Self-awareness. Understanding one's feelings and using intuition to make decisions he or she can live with happily.

Management of feelings. Controlling impulsiveness, calming anxiety, and reacting with appropriate anger to situations.

Motivation. Drive, persistence, and optimism when faced with setbacks. (Motivation in the context of emotional intelligence is resiliency.)

Empathy. Understanding and responding to the unspoken feelings of others.

Social skill. Dealing effectively with emotional reactions in others, having smooth interactions with others, and having positive relationships with people.

Emotional intelligence thus incorporates many of the skills and attitudes necessary to achieve effective interpersonal relations in organizations. Most of the topics in this book, such as resolving conflict, helping others develop, and positive political skills, would be included in emotional intelligence.

From *Incredible Victory*

Walter Lord

Following the Japanese attack on Pearl Harbor and a succession of other Japanese victories over Allied forces in the Pacific and Indian Oceans in late 1941 and early 1942, the U.S. Navy's confidence had reached a low point. The Japanese, under Admirals Yamamoto and Nagumo, planned to strike a decisive blow by capturing the American air base on Midway Island at the far western end of the Hawaiian Island chain. In the early months of the war Americans had grossly underestimated the strength and willingness to take risks of their Japanese adversaries. With the battleship force that was the heart of the U.S. Pacific Fleet largely wiped out at Pearl Harbor, much of the Navy's hopes for victory in the short term rested with the two aircraft carrier task forces. Among these was Task Force 16, under the charismatic leadership of VADM William F. "Bull" Halsey. In the wake of Pearl Harbor and subsequent setbacks at the hands of the Japanese fleet, Halsey had emerged as a morale-building leader who symbolized the U.S. determination to strike back hard at the advancing Japanese.

U.S. commanders received excellent intelligence on the Japanese battle plans and were able to anticipate the attack on Midway. Despite being severely outnumbered, U.S. forces seemed finally to have all the pieces for victory in place until Admiral Halsey fell ill as TF-16 sprinted back from the Battle of the Coral Sea. He was hospitalized at Pearl Harbor less than a week before the Midway operation by order of Fleet ADM Chester Nimitz, and RADM Raymond Spruance was named as his relief to lead TF-16 into the most crucial battle in U.S. Navy history.

The differences in leadership styles and personality traits between Halsey and Spruance were readily noticeable. Halsey was a gung-ho aviator with an extremely gregarious personality and a personable leadership style. He held large, informal staff meetings and often made decisions intuitively. Spruance, on the other hand, was much more reserved, preferring small meetings and a more analytical approach to problem solving than Halsey. Spruance was faced with replacing the most revered officer in the Pacific Fleet on the eve of the pivotal battle of the war. Add to this the fact that he was a surface warfare officer taking over for an aviator in command of an aircraft carrier task force (while retaining the aviator's staff), and the leadership challenge he was confronted with is readily apparent.

The following excerpt summarizes some key events in the days leading up to Midway. A comparison of the leadership styles of these two very different men demonstrates the effect that different personality types can have on military organizations.

That same morning on the southwest horizon a single speck appeared . . . then 2 . . . 5 . . . 21 altogether, as Admiral Halsey's Task Force 16 pounded up from the Solomons. It had been an exciting trip back, full of speculation. Some, like Commander Ed Creehan, the *Hornet*'s engineering officer, had a good pipe line—his old shipmate Captain Marc Mitscher tipped him off. Others could only guess. On the *Enterprise* Ensign Lewis Hopkins of Bombing Squadron 6 noted that even the plane radio transmitters were wired off—it must be really big. Seamen on the destroyer *Balch* wondered why Commander Tiemroth had them working so hard rigging life lines and rescue nets—whatever it was, it looked dangerous.

The man who knew best was in no mood to see anyone. Admiral Halsey had come down with a skin disease, and the itch was driving him crazy. He tried everything—even oatmeal water baths—but nothing helped. He couldn't eat, he couldn't sleep. Completely exhausted, he now lay in his cabin, a bundle of nerves and temper.

At 11:33 A.M. the *Enterprise* entered Pearl Harbor channel, and was soon tied up at Ford Island. Dr. Hightower put Halsey on the sick list, but the Admiral—never a good patient—went over to CINCPAC anyhow. Nimitz took one look, ordered him to the hospital immediately. But first he wanted Halsey's recommendation on who should take over Task Force 16 for the coming battle. Without a second's hesitation, the normally ebullient Halsey named the man perhaps least like him in the entire Pacific fleet—the quiet, methodical commander of his cruisers and destroyers, Rear Admiral Raymond Ames Spruance.

Spruance himself had no inkling what was up. After his flagship *Northampton* made fast, he went around to the *Enterprise* to report to Halsey as usual. Only then did he find that the Admiral had been taken to the hospital. He joined the rest of the task force commanders as they sat in the flag cabin, restlessly waiting to learn who would take over.

Halsey's aide Lieutenant William H. Ashford arrived, sent by the Admiral to tip Spruance off. The place seemed a little public, so Ashford took the new commander into Halsey's bedroom and told him there. Spruance was thoroughly surprised. He was junior to several other possibilities, was a non-aviator, had never even served a day on a carrier. Yet he was used to following Halsey around the Pacific, and he'd have Halsey's fine staff to back him up.

He hurried to CINCPAC, where Nimitz formally told him of his appointment. A quick briefing followed on the Japanese advance; then the two men sat around planning the U.S. countermove. To Spruance there was only one thing to do: take the carriers and lie in wait northeast of Midway. Normally he might head northwest—straight for the Japanese—and engage them somewhere west of the atoll, but the stakes seemed too high. Even accepting that miraculous intelligence, the Japanese just might change their plans and go for Hawaii or the West Coast. Then he'd find himself caught on the wrong side of them, out of the fight and useless.

Naval Academy photo courtesy of United States Naval Academy Photographic Laboratory.

He could have it both ways by waiting in the northeast: he'd be safe against an end run, and he had a marvelous chance for an ambush.

It was fine with Nimitz.

Back on the *Enterprise*, Lieutenant Clarence E. Dickinson noticed his old Academy classmate Lieutenant R. J. Oliver coming up the gangway. Oliver was Spruance's flag lieutenant on the *Northampton*—what was he doing here? It turned out he was arranging to bring over the Admiral's personal gear. One way or another the news raced through the task force: Spruance was taking over; Halsey was on the beach.

It was hard to believe. In the past six months Bill Halsey had become a part of them. From the wreckage of Pearl Harbor, he had lifted them—both the frightened recruits and the disillusioned old-timers—and given them new faith in themselves. Gradually he gave them other things too—skills, strength, endurance, spirit. They knew all this, and they loved him for it. Even now they could picture him sitting up by the bow watching take-offs—they said he knew every plane. It was almost impossible to think of being without him.

Not that they disliked Spruance—they hardly knew the man—but that was just the trouble. There were stories that he was from the "gun club"—part of the conservative battleship crowd that looked down on the jaunty aviators and their sporty brown shoes. That sounded like bad news. As one long-time machinist's mate on the *Enterprise* later explained, "We had nothing against him, but we knew we had a black-shoe admiral in our midst."

The favorites were Glenn Miller, Tommy Dorsey and Mary Martin's "My Heart Belongs to Daddy," as the U.S. carrier *Enterprise* steamed northeast of Midway this same 2nd of June. Task Force 16 had been at sea six days now, and life off duty was, on the surface at least, fairly routine: all the usual phonograph records, cribbage games, bull sessions and occasional pranks. On the *Hornet* Chaplain Eddie Harp playfully swiped a much-prized case of grapefruit from Dr. Sam Osterloh; on the *New Orleans* Seaman A. M. Bagley resumed his hobby of beating Seaman F. Z. Muzejka at rummy.

On duty, the pattern seemed pretty normal too. The *Enterprise* "Plan of the Day" mechanically ticked off the chores for the 2nd: 0315 (ship's time), call the Air Department . . . 0325, early breakfast . . . 0350, flight quarters . . . 0500, launch first patrols . . . and so on, through a steady sequence of patrols out and in, watches on and off, until finally that inevitable salute to a dying day, "2049, blow tubes."

It was all very normal—yet not normal at all, for beneath the surface routine Task Force 16 seethed with a tumbling variety of emotions. "Lord! This *is* the real thing,"

Lieutenant Burdick Brittin breathlessly noted in his diary when the destroyer *Aylwin*'s sealed orders were opened May 29. And on the 30th his mind overflowed with awesome thoughts:

> We have history in the palm of our hands during the next week or so. If we are able to keep our presence unknown to the enemy and surprise them with a vicious attack on their carriers, the U.S. Navy should once more be supreme in the Pacific. But if the Japs see us first and attack us with their overwhelming number of planes, knock us out of the picture, and then walk in to take Midway, Pearl will be almost neutralized and in dire danger—I can say no more—there is too much tension within me—the fate of our nation is in our hands.

To Brittin even the men on the tankers seemed to sense that destiny rode with these ships. They all refueled on the 31st, and as the tankers slipped astern and out of the picture, their men lined the rails, showing thumbs up for Task Force 16.

There were other emotions too as the force plowed on. For some of the pilots there was that hollow, empty feeling as they thought of absolute radio silence and all that it meant—even if an engine conked out on patrol, they could no longer ask the ship for help. Others felt a strange tingle that harked back to college and the days of the big game. On the *Enterprise* dive bomber pilot Bill Roberts was normally scared before battle—but not this time. It was too exciting: the feeling of being in on the secret, of setting a trap, of watching and waiting. Others were just plain mad. Captain Marc Mitscher had a way of getting the *Hornet*'s men "up," and this time he pulled all the stops—"They are even bringing the guns they captured from us at Wake."

For Lieutenant Richard H. Best, commanding the *Enterprise*'s Bombing Squadron 6, there was a personal worry all his own. He had a wife and child in Honolulu, and he thought of them more than once as he sat in Admiral Spruance's cabin, listening to a special briefing on the Japanese plan. The Navy, he felt, was certainly banking a lot on all this neat, precise information—what if it was wrong? He finally asked Spruance what would happen if the Japanese bypassed Midway and came straight for Hawaii.

The Admiral looked at him for a full half-minute in silence, then finally said, "We just hope that they will not."

Best said nothing more—admirals were close to God in those days—but privately he felt this was a pious hope and a rather poor basis for committing all the available strength of the United States Navy.

Actually, of course, Spruance had very good reasons for the move he was making—he just didn't care to tell them. Far from banking on "pious hopes," he was a man with a passion for facts, who insisted on every scrap of evidence before making a decision. And far from failing to think things through, he never moved without weighing every possible consequence.

Nor did his long silence before answering Best mean uncertainty; he was just considering all the factors before speaking—another Spruance characteristic. On the one hand, here was a young officer who had asked a legitimate question; on the other, he was a pilot who might fall into enemy hands. It was clear which way the scales finally went.

USS Merrimack (AO 179) (center) provides fuel to US San Jacinto (CG 56) (left) and USS George Washington (CVN 72) (right) during replenishment at sea operations in the Arabian Gulf.

Official U.S. Navy photo.

Dick Best wasn't the only one who had trouble grasping this new Admiral. The whole staff found it hard to adjust. Halsey had been so outgoing; Spruance preferred channels. Halsey paid little attention to detail; Spruance spent hours poring over charts and plotting the course. Halsey left so much to their discretion; Spruance left so little. Halsey was so free-wheeling; Spruance so precise and methodical.

Morning coffee somehow symbolized the change. In the old days everyone just slopped it down together. But Spruance—a genuine connoisseur—brought his own green coffee beans aboard. Every morning he carefully ground it himself, made precisely two cups, and then courteously asked if some member of the staff cared to join him. In the end they drew lots, with the loser getting the honor, not because they disliked Spruance but because they couldn't stand his coffee.

Yet there was much more method to this little ritual than appeared on the surface. Spruance was trying to educate himself. A man with no carrier experience, he had only a week to learn the trade before facing the greatest master of them all, Isoroku Yamamoto. In his quest for knowledge he picked the brains of his staff at coffee or anyplace else.

A great walker, he also collared them one by one and paced the flight deck with them. Searching questions probed what they did, how they did it, how each job fitted into the whole. He walked their legs off, but with his great ability to absorb detail, he was learning all the time.

The walks went on, fair weather or foul . . . as the staff soon discovered. June 1 was a wretched day, damp and foggy. Flying was out, gunnery practice called off; just the wiry Admiral and his latest victim tirelessly trudging the wet, empty flight deck. Task Force 16 was now 345 miles NNE of Midway—marking time, waiting for Admiral Fletcher and the *Yorktown*.

9 Assessing and Understanding Personality

Objectives

1. Describe and give examples of the major components (five factors) of human personality.

2. Discuss methods of informal and formal assessment of personality traits and patterns.

3. Describe your salient personality traits and discuss how these will impact your leadership style and effectiveness.

4. Describe examples of the effects of personality traits and types on performance at the Naval Academy and in the Fleet.

The Trait Approach

What are the main goals in a trait approach to personality? What are the "Big Five"? How are personality tests like the MMPI constructed, and what are their strengths and weaknesses? What evidence is there for the role of genetic factors in personality? What's an introvert, what's an extravert, and in what fundamental ways do they differ?

In 1919, a twenty-two-year-old psychology student from Indiana wrote a letter to Sigmund Freud to say he'd be traveling in Europe and would like to meet. Freud was the master, known worldwide, and the student wanted to feel his presence and maybe talk for a while. A meeting was arranged, so the student took a train to Vienna, arrived on schedule, and entered the master's inner office. But Freud just sat there in silence, staring, waiting for his young, wide-eyed admirer to state his mission. Desperate to break the awkward stalemate, the student told about an incident he witnessed on the train that day involving a young boy who appeared to have a "dirt phobia." The boy complained that the seats were soiled and pleaded with his mother to keep dirty passengers from sitting nearby. The mother, it turned out, was a dominant, "well-starched" woman. Isn't that an interesting case? When the student finished telling his story, Freud paused, then leaned over and said in a soft voice, "And was that little boy you?"

Freud's young admirer was terribly embarrassed. Wishing he could disappear, he nervously changed the subject, babbled a bit, excused himself, and left. How could Freud have been so wrong? Was he so accustomed to analyzing the hidden motives of his anxious patients that he couldn't appreciate a man's simple curiosity? It turns out that the student was Gordon Allport, who went on to become one of the most important personality psychologists of all time. In an autobiography published the year he died, Allport (1967) said that this experience convinced him that before personality theorists search for deep, analytical explanations, they should start by trying to *describe* and *measure* the basic units of personality. In other words, first things first. This rule now guides what is known as the trait approach.

The Building Blocks of Personality

Working from the ground up, Allport and his colleague Henry Odbert (1936) combed through an unabridged English dictionary and came up with a list of 18,000 words that could be used to describe people. By eliminating synonyms, obscure words, and words referring to temporary states, they brought the list down to 4,500, then grouped words that were similar into about 200 clusters of related traits. For Allport, these **traits** were the building blocks of personality (though he was quick to point out that not all traits are relevant to all people, nor do they all have an influence on behavior).

trait A relatively stable predisposition to behave in a certain way.

To reduce Allport's list to a more manageable size and to construct a science of personality, Raymond Cattell (1965) used factor analysis, a statistical technique designed to identify clusters of items that correlate with one another. You may recall that this technique was used to distinguish among different aspects of intelligence. Cattell—who was a chemistry major in college—wanted to uncover the basic units of personality, much like chemistry's periodic table of elements. Are individuals who are passive also thoughtful, calm, and even-tempered? Do those who describe themselves as sociable also say they're easygoing, lively, and talkative? How many trait clusters are needed to fully describe personality? To answer these questions, Cattell collected people's ratings of themselves and others on various attributes, crunched the numbers through factor analysis, and found that personality consists of sixteen distinct units, which he called *source traits*. What distinguishes one individual from another, said Cattell, is that each of us has a unique combination of traits—high levels of some, and low levels of others—a pattern that is summarized by a personality "profile." To derive this profile, Cattell devised the Sixteen Personality Factors Questionnaire (16 PF), a 187-item scale that yields sixteen separate scores, one for each factor.

As factor analysis became more sophisticated, researchers began to notice that Cattell's model (and other existing models as well) could be simplified even further—and that five major factors often seemed to emerge from self-ratings, ratings of others, and an assortment of personality questionnaires. This **five-factor model** has emerged consistently in studies of children, college students, and older adults; in men and women; in different languages; and in testing conducted in the United States, Canada, Finland, Germany, Japan, Poland, the Philippines, China, and other countries. As a result, these factors have been called the Big Five (Goldberg, 1993; Digman, 1990; McCrae & Costa, 1997; Paunonen et al., 1992; Wiggins, 1996).

Not everyone agrees with the five-factor model. Cattell still believes that five factors are too few. Hans Eysenck, whom we will meet shortly, thinks five is too many. Others see five as the right number but disagree about how the factors should be described. For the most part, however, evidence in support of the five-factor model is mounting. As represented in Table 9.1, most researchers are now convinced that the best way to describe personality and individual differences is to find where people stand on the following traits: (1) neuroticism (a proneness to anxiety and negative affect); (2) extraversion (a desire for social interaction, stimulation, and activity); (3) openness (a receptiveness to new experiences and ideas); (4) agreeableness (a selfless concern for others); and (5) conscientiousness (a tendency to be reliable, disciplined, and ambitious).

New tests have been developed to measure these five broad traits (Costa & McCrae, 1992)—and to use the scores to make predictions about behavior. In one study, for example, Winfred Arthur, Jr., and William Graziano (1996) tested large numbers of college students and recruits from a temporary-employment agency and found that subjects who scored low rather than high on the conscientiousness trait were more likely to have received a moving violation and more likely to have been involved in an automobile accident. As we'll see on pages 116–117, the Big Five have also been used to predict performance in the workplace.

▣ Construction of Multitrait Inventories

As Allport had noted, the study of personality must begin not only with description but also with measurement. And so it did. One of the most important contributions of trait psychology is the construction of personality inventories, questionnaires

five-factor model A model of personality that consists of five basic traits: neuroticism, extraversion, openness, agreeableness, and conscientiousness.

Table 9.1 The "Big Five" Personality Factors

FACTOR	DESCRIPTION OF TRAITS
Neuroticism	Anxious vs. related
	Insecure vs. secure
	Emotional vs. calm
	Self-pitying vs. content
Extraversion	Social vs. withdrawn
	Fun-loving vs. sober
	Friendly vs. aloof
	Adventurous vs. cautious
Openness	Original vs. conventional
	Imaginative vs. down-to-earth
	Broad interests vs. narrow interests
	Receptive vs. closed to new ideas
Agreeableness	Good-natured vs. irritable
	Soft-hearted vs. ruthless
	Courteous vs. rude
	Sympathetic vs. tough-minded
Conscientiousness	Well-organized vs. disorganized
	Dependable vs. undependable
	Hardworking vs. lazy
	Ambitious vs. easygoing

designed to assess a whole multitude of traits (Wiggins & Pincus, 1992). Cattell's Sixteen Personality Factors Questionnaire is one such instrument. There are many others. The most widely used is the **Minnesota Multiphasic Personality Inventory,** or MMPI, a 550-item questionnaire originally developed in the 1940s to help in the diagnosis of psychological disorders (Hathaway & McKinley, 1983).

The MMPI is to personality measurement what the Stanford-Binet was to intelligence testing. Taking an empirical approach, Alfred Binet developed his test by generating a large number of problems, testing schoolchildren, and retaining those problems that were solved differently by fast and slow learners. The MMPI developers used a very similar strategy. They wrote hundreds of true-false statements, gave them to both normal adults and clinical patients with varying psychiatric diagnoses (depressed, paranoid, and so on), and then included in the final test only those items that were answered differently by the two groups—even if the content made little sense. The MMPI is filled with discriminating but odd items (for example, hysterical patients are more likely than others to answer *True* to "My fingers sometimes feel numb"). Indeed, satirist Art Buchwald once wrote a spoof of MMPI-like personality tests by creating his own items. Among them: "I think beavers work too hard," "Frantic screams make me nervous," and "My mother's uncle was a good man."

These MMPI scales have been used for more than fifty years. Many of the original items became dated, however, and the norms had been based on a predominantly white, rural, middle-class group of subjects. To bring the test up to date, new items were written and a more ethnically diverse cross-section of the United States was sampled. The result is a newer 567-item version known as MMPI-2 (Butcher et al., 1989; Butcher & Williams, 1992; Graham, 1990). As in the original test, MMPI-2

Minnesota Multiphasic Personality Inventory (MMPI) A large-scale test designed to measure a multitude of psychological disorders and personality traits.

contains the ten *clinical scales* shown in Table 9.2. Eight of these are designed to distinguish between "normals" and diagnostic groups. Two others are used to measure the traits of masculinity-femininity and social introversion. It also contains fifteen *content scales* that measure work attitudes, family problems, and other characteristics. In addition, the MMPI and MMPI-2 contain a set of *validity scales* designed to expose test takers who are evasive, confused, lying to make a good impression, or

Table 9.2 Clinical and Validity Scales of the MMPI

CLINICAL SCALES	DESCRIPTIONS	SAMPLE ITEMS
1. Hypochondriasis	Excessive concern about self and physical health, fatigue, a pattern of complaining	"I have a great deal of stomach trouble."
2. Depression	Low morale, pessimistic about the future, passive, hopeless, unhappy, and sluggish	"I wish I could be as happy as others seem to be."
3. Hysteria	Use of physical symptoms to gain attention from others or avoid social responsibility	"I have had fainting spells."
4. Psychopathic deviation	Disregard for social rules and authority, impulsive, unreliable, self-centered, has shallow relationships	"In school I was sometimes sent to the principal for cutting up."
5. Masculinity/Femininity	Identification with masculine and/or feminine sex roles	"I enjoy reading love stories."
6. Paranoia	Feelings of persecution and/or grandeur, suspiciousness, hypersensitivity, use of blame and projection	"I am sure I get a raw deal from life."
7. Psychasthenia	Anxiousness as exhibited in fears, self-doubt, worries, guilt, obsessions and compulsions	"I feel anxiety about something or someone almost all the time."
8. Schizophrenia	Feelings of social alienation, aloofness, confusion and disorientation, bizarre thoughts and sensations	"I often feel as if things were not real."
9. Mania	Hyperactivity, excitement, flakiness, elation, euphoria, and excessive optimism	"At times my thoughts race ahead faster than I could speak them."
10. Social introversion	Withdrawal from social contact, isolation, shyness, a reserved, inhibited, self-effacing style	"Whenever possible I avoid being in a crowd."
VALIDITY SCALES	**DESCRIPTIONS**	**SAMPLE ITEMS**
Cannot Say	Evasiveness, as indicated by a high number of noncommital, "Cannot say" responses	(None; this score consists of the number of "Cannot say" responses)
Lie scale	Tendency to present oneself favorably, not honestly, to fake a good impression	"I always tell the truth."
Infrequency scale	Tendency to "fake bad" by reporting unusual weaknesses and problems	"Everything tastes the same."
Correction	Subtle test-taking defensiveness, or lack of self-insight	"I have never felt better in my life than I do now."

defensive. Someone who answers *True* to many socially desirable but implausible statements such as "I never get angry" is assumed to be trying too hard to project a healthy image.

The MMPI-2 is easy to administer, and in contrast to the Rorschach and TAT, in which two examiners may reach different conclusions, the MMPI scoring is perfectly objective. Thus, a test taker's responses can be converted into a personality profile by computer. That's one reason why the test has been translated into more than 100 languages and is popular in both clinical and research settings. Test administrators must be cautious, however, about how to use the test and how to interpret the results. The test has good reliability and validity, but it is far from perfect (Helmes & Reddon, 1993). One needs to be particularly careful in interpreting the responses of test takers from subcultural groups that share different beliefs, values, ideals, and experiences. A pattern of responses may be normal in one culture and deviant in another.

Biological Roots of Personality

Many trait theories, even those that predate psychology's birth as a discipline, assume that there is a linkage between biological and personal dispositions. In the fifth century BCE, the Greek physician Hippocrates said that people could be classified into four temperament types, depending on which of their "humors," or body fluids, predominated: An excess of blood was associated with cheerfulness, black bile with sadness, yellow bile with anger, and phlegm with sluggishness. In the nineteenth century, German physician Franz Gall introduced phrenology, the pseudoscience that tried to link personality to brain structures that could be seen in the bumps on our head. Others used physiognomy, the idea that a person's character is revealed in the features of the face (for example, people with thin lips were said to be conscientious; those with thick lips, emotional).

Although these early theories were rejected, there is renewed interest in the connections between biology and personality. In 1954, William Sheldon studied thousands of adult men and concluded that there are three kinds of physique, each linked to a distinct type of personality. The *ectomorph*, said Sheldon, has a thin, frail body and a restrained, anxious, shy disposition. The *endomorph* has a soft, plump body and is relaxed, sociable, and easygoing. And the *mesomorph* has a strong, muscular build and is bold, assertive, and energetic. Sheldon reported high correlations between body types and personality, but his methods were flawed, and later research produced less impressive results.

Are there any biological underpinnings to personality? Yes, absolutely. Recall the nature–nurture debate and the twins study presented previously. For a wide range of traits, studies have shown that (1) raised together, identical twins are more similar than fraternal twins, and (2) twins raised apart are as similar as those raised in the same home. Taken together, a growing body of research suggests that personality differences in the population are 40 to 50 percent genetically determined (Bouchard, 1994; Loehlin, 1992; Tellegen et al., 1988; DiLalla et al., 1996). As shown in Figure 9.1, this result is consistent with the results of a recent study in which the Big Five personality factors were measured in 123 pairs of identical twins and 127 pairs of fraternal twins (Lang et al., 1996).

To the surprise of many psychologists, recent twin studies have revealed that there are also genetic links to characteristics that would seem to be determined entirely by personal experience. Specifically, identical twins are more similar than fraternal twins of the same sex in their attitudes toward sexuality, religion, and the death

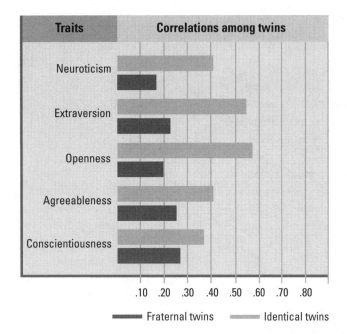

Traits	Correlations among twins
Neuroticism	
Extraversion	
Openness	
Agreeableness	
Conscientiousness	

.10 .20 .30 .40 .50 .60 .70 .80

━━ Fraternal twins   ━━ Identical twins

FIGURE 9.1 Genetic influences on personality Based on twin studies, these correlations provide estimates of the degrees to which various personality characteristics are inherited. Note that some traits have stronger genetic roots than others.

extravert A kind of person who seeks stimulation and is sociable and impulsive.

introvert A kind of person who avoids stimulation and is low-key and cautious.

"But, in the end, you will become bored with that, too."

Extraverts have a constant appetite for stimulation and arousal—and may become easily bored.

penalty (Tesser, 1993); in their vocational and personal interests (Lykken et al., 1993); and even in their risk of getting divorced (McGue & Lykken, 1992). Apparently, certain personality traits for which there is a genetic component predispose us to have certain types of experiences. It turns out, for example, that people who score high on measures of neuroticism, or anxiousness—for which there's a genetic basis—are more likely to get divorced than those who are low on this trait (Jockin et al., 1996).

Introversion and Extraversion

Psychologists may disagree over whether personality consists of 2, 5, 16, or 200 traits, but they all agree that the single most powerful dimension—one that can be seen in infants as well as adults, in cultures all over the world, and in questionnaires as well as behavior—is introversion–extraversion, one of the Big Five traits. The ancient Greeks and Romans noticed it, as have philosophers, physicians, and creative writers through the ages. Carl Jung wrote about individual differences on this dimension. So did Allport and Cattell. Even Pavlov said that some of the dogs in his classical-conditioning laboratory were more outgoing than others. But it was British psychologist Hans Eysenck who most clearly defined the trait, constructed a test to measure it, and proposed a provocative theory to explain its origin.

As described by Eysenck (1967), the typical **extravert** is someone who has many friends, likes parties, craves excitement, seeks adventure, takes chances, acts on the spur of the moment, and is uninhibited. In contrast, the typical **introvert** is low-keyed, has just a few close friends, shies away from stimulation, acts cautiously, and distrusts the impulse of the moment. Based on past writings, personal observations, and factor analyses of trait questionnaires, Eysenck developed a test that includes a measure of introversion and extraversion (see Table 9.3). Using this instrument, and others, researchers have found that extraverts are generally more talkative, prefer occupations that involve social contact, and take greater risks (Eysenck & Eysenck, 1985). The question is, What accounts for this broad and pervasive aspect of personality? To see whether you are an introvert or an extravert, go to Table 9.3 and answer the questions for yourself. If you said *yes* on most odd-numbered questions and *no* on the even-numbered ones in Table 9.3, you are relatively extraverted. If your answers are the other way around, then you're more of an introvert. Many people fall somewhere in the middle of the continuum.

Eysenck argues that individual differences are biologically rooted and that introverts have central nervous systems that are more sensitive to stimulation. According to Eysenck, people seek a moderate, comfortable level of CNS arousal. Introverts are easily overaroused, so they avoid intense sources of excitement. In contrast, extraverts are not so easily aroused, which leads them to approach high levels of excitement. Thus, it takes a more potent stimulus for the extravert to feel the "buzz." Research generally supports this hypothesis (Bullock & Gilliland, 1993; Eysenck, 1990). For example, one study showed that when drops of natural lemon juice are placed on the tongue, most introverts salivate more than most extraverts (Deary et al., 1988). Others have shown that introverts are more easily aroused by

Table 9.3 Are You an Introvert or an Extrovert?

1. Are you usually carefree?
2. Do you generally prefer reading to meeting people?
3. Do you often long for excitement?
4. Are you mostly quiet when you're with others?
5. Do you often do things on the spur of the moment?
6. Are you slow and unhurried in the way you move?
7. Would you do almost anything for a dare?
8. Do you hate being in a crowd who plays jokes on one another?
9. Do you enjoy wild parties?
10. Do you like the kind of work you need to pay attention to?

Source: H. J. Eysenck & S. G. B. Eysenck (1964). *Manual of the Eysenck Personality Inventory.* London: University of London Press.

Fulfilling a promise he had made to himself after he had to bail out of a plane during World War II, former president George Bush landed his second parachute jump in 1997, at age seventy-two. This high-risk activity epitomizes the sensation-seeking component of extraversion.

caffeine and other stimulants—and are less easily relaxed by alcohol and other depressants (Stelmack, 1990). In short, says Eysenck, each of us is born with a nervous system that predisposes us to either love or hate large crowds, bright lights, blaring music, fast cars, roller coasters, suspenseful movies, spicy foods, and other, more social stimulants.

As you can see, extraverts are not just more sociable and people-oriented than introverts. According to Marvin Zuckerman (1994), they are also more *sensation seeking*—a trait that leads people to drink, smoke, and use other drugs; seek out novel experiences; enjoy dangerous sports and other intense forms of stimulation; and gamble and take other risks for the thrill of it. As for the introvert, Elaine and Arthur Aron (1997) note that avoiding stimulating social situations is a smart and adaptive strategy for people sensitive to stimulation. In a series of studies, they found that subjects who described themselves as "highly sensitive" were more likely to report feeling overwhelmed by strong sensory input. Compared to others, they cry more easily, are more sensitive to daylight, are less tolerant of pain, are affected more by emotional films, and prefer country living to the city. Table 9.4

Table 9.4 What's Your Orientation to Stimulation?

SENSATION-SEEKING SCALE (Zuckerman, 1994)

1. I would like to try parachute jumping.
2. I like "wild" uninhibited parties.
3. I often like to get high.
4. I get bored seeing the same old faces.
5. I enjoy the company of people who are free and easy about sex.

HIGHLY SENSITIVE PERSON SCALE (Aron & Aron, 1997)

1. Do you startle easily?
2. Are you easily overwhelmed by strong sensory input?
3. Are you made uncomfortable by loud noises?
4. Do changes in your life shake you up?
5. Do you get rattled when you have a lot to do in a short amount of time?

presents sample items from the tests that are used to measure both sensation-seeking and sensitivity.

Interestingly, the rudiments of introversion and extraversion can be seen in the predispositions of infants shortly after birth. Over the years, Jerome Kagan (1994) and his colleagues have studied children who are *inhibited* and *uninhibited* in temperament (most fall between these two extremes). At sixteen weeks old, inhibited infants—compared to those who are uninhibited—are more easily distressed and cry more in response to hanging mobiles, human speech, intense odors, and other types of stimulation. At two years of age, inhibited children are fearful, wary of strangers, and avoidant of novel situations, while their uninhibited peers are outgoing, adventurous, and quick to approach strangers and new situations. At five years old, socially inhibited children are shy and more easily aroused by mildly stressful tasks—as measured by increases in heart rate, dilation of the pupils, and a rise in norepinephrine. They often have more tension in the face muscles and are more likely to have higher-than-average levels of cortisol, a hormone associated with physiological arousal during stress.

Not all inhibited infants grow up to become inhibited adults. But two additional lines of research suggest that temperament is a biological predisposition. First, Stephen Suomi (1991) observed that infant rhesus monkeys also differ in their behavior at birth. Suomi calls the inhibited monkeys "uptight" and the uninhibited ones "laid back." He finds that the uptight monkeys, who are shy and anxious, also have the same physical attributes as Kagan's inhibited human infants. Second, Janet DiPietro and her colleagues (1996) monitored heart rate and motor activity in thirty-one human fetuses for twenty weeks prior to their birth. They found, through follow-up reports provided by the mothers, that the most active fetuses were later fussier, more difficult, and less adaptable as six-month-old babies. Apparently, certain aspects of an infant's temperament can be detected even before birth.

Intersection

Personality and Business
Using Personality Tests in Personnel Selection

On Christmas Eve 1996, Dan Reeves resigned as head coach of the New York Giants football team. At his press conference, Reeves criticized the organization's draft practices for relying too heavily on the psychological tests that prospective rookies must take. "So how valid is a two-hour test?" he asked. "When a psychologist has more to do with the draft than you do as a head coach, I have a problem with that" (Rhoden, 1996).

Anyone who has applied for a desirable job knows that you sometimes have to climb hurdles and jump through hoops to get hired. It's a familiar routine. You submit a resume and a list of references, fill out an application, and perhaps take the "hot seat" in a face-to-face interview. You may even be asked to bring in samples of your work or take a standardized test of intelligence, vocational interests, or personality. When it comes to personnel selection in business and industry, there are numerous methods—all designed to predict performance in the workplace (Landy et al., 1994; Borman et al., 1997).

The use of personality tests for employment purposes has been a source of controversy. Can scores on trait inventories be used to predict worker productivity, motivation, satisfaction, loyalty, or other aspects of job performance? For many years, the MMPI was used to assess a candidate's personality—even though it had been developed for the purpose of diagnosing mental disorders, and even though there was no clear link between MMPI test scores and work performance (Guion, 1965). Questions were also raised about whether it was ethical, or a violation of privacy, to require the testing of all prospective employees. People are free to refuse to take a test as part of an application process, but 52 percent of personnel managers surveyed said they automatically reject applicants who refuse to take a test (Blocklyn, 1988).

For predictive purposes, many organizations have sought more "scientific" methods of evaluation. It has been estimated, for example, that 3,000 firms in the United States and many more in Europe use "graphology," or handwriting analysis, to predict job-relevant traits such as honesty, sales ability, and leadership potential (Rafaeli & Klimoski, 1983). But controlled research does not support the claim that handwriting can be used in this way. In one study, professional graphologists were asked to predict various aspects of job performance by analyzing the handwriting contained in the autobiographical sketches of bank employees. From these same materials, the researchers themselves also made predictions. A comparison of predicted and actual employee performance revealed that the graphologists were no more effective than were the researchers. They were no more accurate than they would have been by flipping a coin (Ben-Shakhar et al., 1986).

Dan Reeves the day he announced his resignation as head coach of the New York Giants. Reeves was critical of the organization for relying too heavily on "psychological tests" to make player selections.

Despite the initial problems and occasional misdirections, it now appears that certain personality tests can be used to predict a whole range of worker outcomes, including leadership potential, helpfulness, absenteeism, and theft (Goffin et al., 1996; Hogan et al., 1996). In particular, researchers have found that performance across different occupations can be significantly predicted by questionnaires that measure the Big Five personality factors. For example, extraverts are more likely than introverts to succeed as managers and salespersons, while workers in general benefit more from job training if they are high rather than low in their openness to new experiences. Recent reviews of this research have also revealed that, across the board, among skilled and unskilled workers alike, and in studies conducted in North America and Europe, conscientiousness—the trait of being dependable, responsible, organized, and persistent—is highly predictive of performance at work (Barrick & Mount, 1991; Tett et al., 1991; Salgado, 1997). Clearly, personality traits—not just measures of intelligence—are useful for predicting success and failure in the workplace (Goldberg, 1993; Hogan et al., 1996).

One criticism of personality testing for employment purposes is that, as motivated test takers, job candidates can fake their responses in order to present themselves in a positive light. This is a serious possible drawback. Imagine having applied for a job you really wanted, and all that stands in your way are the results of a personality questionnaire. Isn't it possible that you would cover up your flaws, consciously or not, according to what you see as desirable? And wouldn't this render your test results invalid? The answer is *yes* to the first question, but *no* to the second. Industrial/organizational psychologists have found that people do bias their responses in a socially desirable direction—but that this does not diminish the value of the personality tests. Apparently, the ability to present oneself favorably is a sign of emotional stability and conscientiousness—traits that are predictive of success at work (Barrick & Mount, 1996; Ones et al., 1996).

From *Introverts Abandon Ship*

Neal Thompson

Far from his South Carolina home, Gary Moody sat glassy-eyed and tremble-lipped amid the din of the Naval Academy dining hall as upperclassmen pummeled him for answers eluding him: You got a 1500 on your SAT but can't remember our names or what's for dinner?

"It's all about how hard you try, and I don't think you're giving it your all right now. Do you have a little bit more left in there?" asked Kerry George, a senior-ranking upperclassman.

"Ma'am, yes, ma'am," Moody said, making it sound more like a question. He left a half-eaten sandwich on his plate, knocked a fork to the floor and walked off, forgetting his towel.

"I thought he was going to cry," George said. "It amazes me how many guys will cry here."

It's not easy being a plebe. And that, sir or ma'am, is the whole point.

The first step in molding officers is weeding out the weaklings. But that is a delicate and imperfect process, and academy officials are increasingly concerned that their traditional initial testing of midshipmen's physical and emotional limits, plebe summer, may be burning off the most-promising freshmen.

Officials are considering using personality tests to identify potential dropouts they want to keep and then offering them some relief from the stressful regimentation of life in the academy and military.

When Moody and 1,250 classmates signed on as the Class of 2002, people spoke to them of honor, courage and commitment. Nobody mentioned such plebe summer realities as "plebe hack" and the ominous "Tango company." When those realities hit, 87 of them walked out the door.

Moody was among them. He and his near-perfect SAT score are back in South Carolina. Academy officials worry that they might have scared off a future admiral. Again.

Personality Plays a Role

Whether you weep or thrive at the academy depends largely on how you handle the stress of abusive upperclassmen, who returned to Annapolis last week, and the pressures of a heavy academic load, which begins next week. But academy officials are finding that personality type also plays a role. Extroverts, for example, thrive, they have found. Introverts, such as Moody, walk away.

Most Naval Academy students are extroverts, people who follow orders and need to be part of a group. But the Navy also needs independent introverts, people who can weather a month in a submarine on the ocean floor. Yet most dropouts are independent people who are not weak but disgusted with the military lifestyle.

Since 1986, incoming freshmen have taken the Myers-Briggs Type Indicator personality test, which measures how they interact with others and make decisions. In recent months, the academy has been exploring why certain types—sensitive, introverted thinkers—are three times more likely to drop out.

"Their personality tells them, 'I don't like being told when to get up in the morning, I don't like being told what to wear and where to stand,'" said Glenn Gottschalk, the academy's institutional research guru, who studies the students' test results.

The academy is considering what some alumni might consider sacrilege: attempting to reduce the dropout rate by accommodating the introverts.

"Extroverts are recharged and have their stress relieved by group activities, which we have a lot of here. The introvert has his stress relieved by reading a book, listening to music or taking a long run by themselves, which there's no time for," Gottschalk said.

For plebes of all personality types, surviving the first months of academy life is an intense exercise in managing stress, which comes in many forms.

Naval Academy photo courtesy of United States Naval Academy Photographic Laboratory.

There's "plebe hack," the chronic cough plebes sustain because of exhausted immune systems. There's "plebe funk," the result of too much sweat and too little shower time. And there are the injuries, mostly shin splints, that result from the rigorous exercise.

The pressure and temptation to leave are constant.

Heard at a 6 A.M. exercise session: "Come on, Smith! Don't wuss out. There's a girl over here kicking your butt and you're on your knees. There isn't room here for a weakling like you."

Heard at a training session on the academy's strict honor code: "If you don't want to buy into that [honor] and pay attention to these lectures, please do us all a favor and get out."

Heard from a plebe during an interpersonal relationship training class: "When are they going to stop breaking us down and start building us up?"

Another plebe: "He drove his shoulder into my back and it hurt. It's guys like that who make me say, 'Do I really want to be part of this institution?'"

As a result, the word "Tango" rings in plebes' ears during the summer.

Tango company is a remote section of the academy's dormitory, Bancroft Hall, that is used to "process out" the dropouts. Plebes can't just walk out the door. It takes a week or two to complete paperwork and interviews, to turn in their uniforms and to tell a dozen academy officials why they're leaving.

"Tango is looming over people's heads," said Michael Rea, a plebe from Stevensville. "It goes through everybody's mind. The fear that you don't have what it takes to become an officer, that you won't make it academically, that you won't make it physically."

For Rea, who chose the academy over Princeton and Brown universities, the key to surviving has been learning to quietly do his push-ups and to avoid drawing attention to himself, confronting his aggressors or questioning their tactics.

At the end of the first six weeks, plebes are allowed off campus for the first time during parents' weekend. Rea used his liberty to attend a party with family and friends, where he tried to describe the most unusual six weeks of his life.

"I haven't said to myself once, 'This makes no sense. This is pointless.' I've been angry and I've been frustrated. But stress management has been the key," he said.

"Because, if I dwell on my failures I'll be headed to Tango myself."

	The Facts	
YEAR	PLEBE SUMMER DROPOUTS	PLEBE YEAR DROPOUTS
1994	8.4%	11.0%
1995	7.4%	11.4%
1996	6.8%	11.3%
1997	7.4%	11.0%
1998	7.1%	n/a

Plebe Dropouts, 1986–1997, Based on Personality Type

Personality types are determined by Myers-Briggs Type Indicator: extrovert/introvert, E or I; intuitive/sensory, N or S; thinking/feeling, T or F; judgmental/perceiving, J or P.

- ISFP = 1.5% of all admissions, but 11.7% of ISFPs drop out during plebe summer; 22% drop out by the end of plebe year (ISFPs are the lowest percentage of the student body, but have the highest dropout rate)

- ESTJ = 18.3% of all admissions, but only 1.8% of ESTJs drop out during plebe summer; 8.3% drop out by the end of plebe year (ESTJs are the highest percentage of the student body but have the lowest dropout rate)

Source: Naval Academy

Nathaniel Hathaway also finds small, creative ways to cope. He has asked his mother to send granola bars and Gatorade. At night, after the lights go out at 10 P.M., he stays up an extra hour or two, catching up on his food intake and writing letters and journal entries.

"I did it, and I knew it was wrong. But I had so much to do during the day. There's just no time," said Hathaway, of Bowie.

Classes on Coping

The academy tries to help plebes deal with the lack of time and the extra pressures of a military education. They attend classes on anger and conflict resolution ("Conflict at USNA is inevitable and normal"), eating disorders ("Are you preoccupied with concerns about food, weight and body image"), and coping with stress ("Academy life is inherently stressful").

But Hathaway has seen classmates who simply haven't found a way to cope. Some have been on crutches all summer with shin splints, sprains or blisters. At one point this summer, 120 of them—10 percent—held "medical chits" that earned them light duty.

Those are often the ones who incessantly fume about coming to the academy just to please their mothers and fathers.

"Some people just shouldn't be here," Hathaway said.

But some freshmen don't realize that until they're crying into their pillows at night.

Those were the ones lined up outside Capt. Len Hering's door July 16, the first day plebes were allowed to drop out. Inside, Hering listened to their reasons:

"This is not the career for me."

"This is not what I expected of college life."

"This is not what the brochure said."

"A kid this morning said to me, 'I really like the Marine Corps' dress blue uniform.' That is not a reason to come to the Naval Academy," said Hering, plebe summer's officer in charge.

"One guy said, 'I must have been out to lunch.' Well, yeah. I guess so. Some people, a military life is just not for them."

They are the ones who went to see Keith Laganga, a senior chief petty officer who supervised Tango company this summer. Laganga said many dropouts were academic or athletic standouts unaccustomed to the failures common in plebe life, such as a poorly made bed.

'What'd You Expect?'

"I can't understand how you can go to the Naval Academy and not recognize that it's going to be regimented," Laganga said. "I mean, what'd you expect?"

By the end of the freshman year, more than one in 10 will have dropped out. By graduation, in 2002, three-fourths of the freshman class is likely to remain.

The academy is trying to determine whether it is accepting too many people destined to drop out, or whether it should be working harder to help them survive.

That's where the personality testing will play a larger role.

The Myers-Briggs tests categorize each person in one of 16 personality types. More than half of the incoming freshmen fall into three categories. Most are extroverts who are intuitive rather than sensitive and rely on facts, not feelings, to make decisions. Sensitive, feeling people made up 1 percent of the freshmen between 1990 and 1997, but 22 percent of them dropped out.

"There's not much room for feelings here," Gottschalk said. "We don't give them a chance to say, 'Gee, what do you think about that?' That's the epitome of what the military is not."

It is seen in the drill practice where plebes spend two hours in the sun, three times a week, wearing camouflage fatigues while learning how to face right and present arms.

Those who don't step in time and drop their rifles are called "individuals," which is not good at the academy, said Gunnery Sgt. Terrance Slaughter. "We call them an individual because they stick out from the rest of the platoon. We'll pull them off to the side," he said.

Four years ago, the academy tried to include more personal time during plebe summer to help the "individuals" unwind. But there were a record 102 dropouts "because the other extrovert types had more time to think 'Why am I here?'." Gottschalk said.

This summer, the academy used a "ramp up" approach, starting exercise and military training gradually, But the attrition rate remained about the same as in prior years.

The academy is thinking of telling dormitory supervisors, called company officers, which students are the independent-thinking introverts so that the officers can dole out duties tailored more to the possible dropouts.

The extra attention is important for the Navy because introverts become admirals at a higher rate than extroverts do, Gottschalk said.

"They're very productive members of the military once they assimilate. It just takes them longer," he said. "If we can just get them past the summer."

10 *Followership— The First Step in Leadership*

Objectives

1. Explain the rules of good followership exemplified in the readings: "The No-Name Company," "Damn Exec," and "A Message to Garcia."

2. Describe the difference between leadership and followership.

3. Explain the dual role of leader and follower with which Naval Officers are confronted and how to cope with it.

'The No Name Company': Self-Discipline and Followership

Self-discipline and followership, when combined in the same individual, form the basis for military leadership, as exemplified in this abridged version of the Vietnam story about "The No Name Company" which appeared in the January 1985 issue of Marines.

My R & R in Honolulu with my wife and child was like stepping through a time warp when compared to the horrors of war I had left only days before in Vietnam. A radio broadcast cancelling leave for all military personnel and ordering everyone to return to duty in Vietnam took me back through that time warp sooner than I had expected. I knew my wife wouldn't question why I believed I should return when no one knew I had heard the broadcast. No one knew but the two of us . . . and she realized that I had to go. We both knew that it was the Corps, the Corps, the Corps.

DaNang was always confusing, but on my arrival, I found chaos. Over one thousand military personnel, mostly Marines, were milling about, not knowing why their emergency leaves, R & R, or end-of-tour rotations home had been cancelled. The airport was a collection of people who were supposed to leave and people who were coming back, and no one was going anywhere.

Activity several hundred yards down the airfield caught my eye. A steady sortie of helicopters were landing, and Marines hurried out to discharge the cargo, which was stacked like cord along the edge of the taxiway in the hot Vietnamese sun. I watched for a while before I realized that the cargo being unloaded consisted of large black bags. Black plastic bags. Body bags. From that distance I counted several dozen. Whatever was happening was heavy with death.

That day at DaNang there was a loud chorus arising from the uncertainty and frustration of those who had left and then had been brought back early. In the midst of all the commotion, a tall Marine colonel tapped me on the shoulder and said, "Captain, I need to see you in my hootch."

I entered a strongback hut a few yards down the flight line and found five other young Marine officers. None of us knew what was about to happen. The colonel explained that the communists had launched a major offensive, which we now call the Tet Offensive. Regular North Vietnamese Army (NVA) regiments were headed straight for DaNang, which until then had been similar to a rear area. DaNang was short of defenders, and we were going to provide extra defense. We were to be company commanders.

"Let me get this straight. They put us inside these solid steel vehicles that weigh, oh . . . say 50 tons. Then we drive them off a perfectly good ship into a hundred fathoms of water. We miraculously bob to the top and drive safely to shore. You go first."

"I think you ought to know, sir," I advised the colonel, "I am a Comm O." The other officers responded similarly, and not one was an infantry officer.

"That makes no difference," the colonel said, "you're all Marines."

I knew then that I had a job to do, so I didn't stand around to chat with the other five officers who were in there as to what was going to be done or how it was going to be accomplished.

I walked out of the hut, grabbed the first sergeant and said, "Top, I've got a problem and I think you can help me solve it. We're going to have to form some companies here and what I'd like you to do is to have this mob fall into three ranks." Top said, "Aye, Aye, Sir," turned around, and at the top of his lungs yelled, "Fall in!"

Just as they were trained to do, these Marines who had been milling around became a military formation by falling in facing this first sergeant in three ranks. That's the way they were taught to do it. That's what I expected to happen. This mass of humanity began its transformation into a fighting unit.

He turned back to me and said, "Now what do you want me to do, Sir?"

I said, "I'd like you to have them count to 13 three times."

They counted down. We then had a random selection of three platoons of Marines. I began to think I would need a couple of admin types, maybe some corpsmen, some people who know logistics—I was flashing back to all I'd been taught about organization for combat in Basic School 12 to 15 months earlier. I asked him to get me some Marines for a headquarters group. He did, and then he dismissed the rest.

At that point I didn't have any officers, so I asked my first sergeant to pick the ranking staff NCO in each platoon and make him a platoon commander. I then called these platoon commanders front and center. They made quite a group! I had a master sergeant who was a cook, a baker by MOS; another master sergeant who was an intelligence chief; and one who was an admin chief. I had no one with an infantry MOS. The only one I knew was the baker. He was one of the most dedicated Marines I had ever known from the standpoint of believing in a support role, believing that his mission was just as important as the guy out on the point. Master Sgt. Cook was his name and, even though he was a baker, he would soon be on the point.

He and the other platoon commanders came over. I explained the circumstances to them and told them that we had been tasked to form a provisional rifle company. That's what the colonel had called it, "A provisional rifle company of III MAF." Since we were the first company formed, I gave us the name of 1st Provisional Rifle Company of III MAF. I told them that was what we would call ourselves. I asked the platoon commanders to get organized, to assign squad leaders and fire team leaders, and to get the names, ranks, and serial numbers of all our personnel. They did so and I had admin types put together a company roster. This process, from the time I started talking to the first sergeant until I had a platoon roster, took 20 minutes.

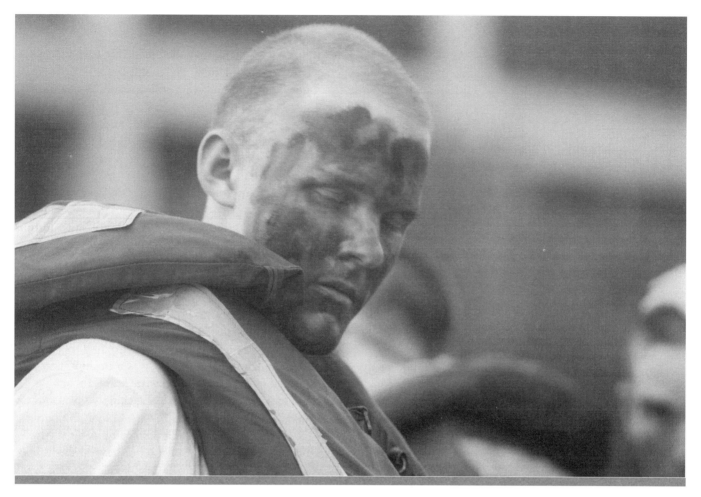

Naval Academy photo courtesy of United States Naval Academy Photographic Laboratory.

I went back to the colonel and reported to him that I had formed my company and asked what we were to do next. I heard him offer defense of the medical battalion, and I figured that if I had to get shot, I would rather be where someone could take care of me. It would be a mutual relationship: if we took care of them, they would take care of us.

The colonel said, "All right, that's where you'll go, to the medical battalion. You will be in defense of their perimeter."

I said, "Fine. But we don't have any weapons." It was 1600, and he directed me to take my new company across the road to the mess hall for hot chow and advised me that by the time I returned, the weapons would have been delivered. The Top marched them to the chow hall and had them back in one hour for muster. The company returned a little happier; they had food, a little bit of organization, and they were all accounted for at muster. No UAs. They still wondered what was going on.

As I learned information, I shared it with them. I think it is important to keep the troops informed. I told them that we had a mission and I thought it was important that we do it and do it to the best of our abilities because we were Marines. They responded without any grouching or grumbling. I explained that the weapons would be arriving shortly, and that we would mount out on "six bys." The colonel had since told me that we would be trucked out to the medical battalion which was on the other side of Hill 327, "Freedom Hill."

About the time I finished talking with them, up rolled some six bys, and in the back were big wooden crates full of brand new M-16 rifles. The troops were impressed with rifles that had not been fired and were still in crates. I was uneasy. They started passing rifles out just like you'd pass out beers at a party: come down the line and get one. Every Marine got one, including me. We were also issued five magazines, rounds for the magazines, and a cleaning rod. We placed the magazines inside our jackets, since we didn't have any web gear: we were not issued helmets or flack jackets, either. All we had were our jungle utilities.

I still didn't know the extent of the enemy situation, but after the gear was issued, I knew we were in a whole lot of trouble. After they issued me all this gear, no one came up to ask me to sign for it. That's trouble. When a military organization doesn't ask you to sign for gear, especially weapons, you know that people are more worried about getting the job done than having the paper work taken care of.

When we arrived in the medical battalion area, I reported to a Navy Captain who, when he saw me, was the happiest person I have ever seen. He didn't have many personnel to help him defend that area. I told him what I was there for and asked him to show me his positions and what he had for defense of the area. The dug-in positions had sandbags that could have interlocking fire. If we had been going to be there longer, I would probably have done much more with it. It was a position that had been there for a long time; it was adequate but nothing to write home about.

The first sergeant and I decided to handle the defense by placing two platoons on the line and keeping one back as a reaction force. I did not send out any patrols, because I had no maps. We were on 50 percent alert on the positions. One person was to be up all the time in all the positions. Being a "Comm O," I established something similar to a gun loop on artillery. We hooked in a telephone loop that went around the perimeter that we were defending and back to me, so I could talk to anyone at any of the phone positions. We had never worked together, we didn't know each other from Adam's house cat. If they got nervous about anything, I wanted them to talk to me before they did something. I told them not to just go shooting up the place. "I want good fire discipline, and I want you to talk to me about it first. If you see something or hear something talk to me."

We got the phones, wire, and other gear from the medical battalion. With the medical battalion's entrenching tools we improved our positions so more people could be up on the line. With a North Vietnamese Army regiment coming, I wanted to have plenty of firepower. We got it all done before it was completely dark. I was amazed that we were able to accomplish so much so quickly. Then again, I was working with Marines. If you ask Marines to accomplish something, they do it.

We set in for the night, and I periodically checked the lines. Soon the NVA began to probe. We were mainly probed by fire. Several fights erupted to our front with the units on our flanks. We maintained very good fire discipline and never gave away our entire position, since we did not return fire until I ordered it, and I only ordered it when we were being attacked. I only wanted to return fire when there was sufficient volume of fire coming in to justify it. I figured the enemy would not know our strength as long as we maintained fire discipline. In thinking about it later, it is amazing that we could maintain fire discipline with a group of men who had never fought together, and had only been an organized unit since shortly before supper. We did not even know one another's names.

It was to our advantage to keep our positions concealed until it was necessary to fire final protective fires. I was impressed with the troops. During the course of the

A Marine guards a hillside perimeter at Camp Pendleton as an LCAC heads to sea.
Official U.S. Navy photo.

night we never cranked off the first round. We took many rounds in the positions, but never in sufficient volume to justify firing all along our line.

Came the dawn and we were still there; life went on. The Navy captain was all smiles and couldn't tell us enough how he appreciated us. He provided rations and water and repeated thanks. While we caught up on our sleep, the medical battalion was hard at work, as incoming casualties were crowded all over the area. The rest of the day was spent improving our positions and checking on the troops. No one seemed to be nervous. Belonging to the 1st Provisional Rifle Company helped relieve the tension caused by the confusion, disappointment, and frustration of missing R & R, leave, and rotation.

The second night was a repeat of the first. Random incoming fire, probing minor fire fights, and excellent fire discipline by the 1st Provisional Rifle Company.

On the third day a messenger came out and told us the alert was over: "They are not coming; I don't know what happened to them." The answers to all my questions were the same, "I don't know." All I could find out was that we didn't have to be there anymore. We were ordered to return to our units.

I called the company together, and everyone who had answered the company's first muster was still there. I told them we were being relieved, and that I appreciated everything they had done. We got back on trucks and returned to the air strip. Supply personnel were there to pick up all our gear.

After we turned in our gear, we had a formation and I thanked these Marines one more time. All the individual baggage was stacked in a small warehouse, just where we had left it before departing for the medical battalion area. We retrieved our baggage and off we went. Those leaving the country checked out flights. I went to flight operations and caught a ride back to Quang Tri and reported back to my unit.

It is fantastic to see that it does work. I never felt we had done anything heroic or had turned back the thundering hordes. Our presence may have diverted the enemy to some other area or made them reconsider their action. The roster was written in longhand and never typed. No entries were made in any service recordbooks of the duty, and to my knowledge no record has ever been made of the existence of the 1st Provisional Rifle Company.

The 1st Provisional Rifle Company was formed out of chaos, existed on a tradition of training and discipline, took hostile enemy fire in trenches without helmets, maps, or artillery support, and was disbanded without any record. It functioned as a fighting unit because every man there knew he was part of the Corps, the Corps, the Corps.

Damn Exec

Lt. Commander Stuart D. Landersman

The Norfolk wind was streaking the water of Hampton Roads as Commander Martin K. Speaks, U.S. Navy, Commanding Officer of the USS Bowens (DD-891), stepped from his car, slammed the door, and straightened his cap. As he approached the pier head, a Sailor stepped from the sentry hut and saluted.

"Good morning, Captain."

"Good morning, Kowalski," answered Commander Speaks. He took pleasure in the fact that he knew the Sailor's name. Kowalski was a good Sailor. He had served his entire first cruise in the *Bowens* and did his work well.

The Captain noticed that, over his blues, Kowalski wore a deck force foul weather jacket, faded, frayed, dirty, and spotted with red lead. "Little chilly this morning," said the Captain as he walked by. "Yes sir, sure is," replied the Sailor with his usual grin.

As the Captain approached his quarterdeck, there was the usual scurrying of people, and four gongs sounded. "Bowens arriving," spoke the loudspeaker system, and Lieutenant (j.g.) Henry Graven, U.S. Naval Reserve, gunnery officer and the day's command duty officer, came running to the quarterdeck. Salutes and cheerful "Good mornings" were exchanged, and the Captain continued to his cabin.

Lieutenant Graven looked over the quarterdeck and frowned. "Let's get this brightwork polished, chief."

"It's already been done once this morning, sir," replied the OD.

"Well, better do it again. The Exec will have a fit if he sees it this way," said Graven.

"Yes sir," answered the OD.

As soon as Graven had left, the OD turned to his messenger, "Go tell the duty boatswain's mate that Mr. Graven wants the brightwork done over again on the quarterdeck."

Later that morning, Captain Speaks was going over some charts with the ship's executive officer, Lieutenant Commander Steven A. Lassiter, U.S. Navy. The Captain had just finished his coffee and lighted a cigarette. "Steve, I noticed our pier sentry in an odd outfit this morning. He had a foul weather jacket on over his blues; it looked pretty bad."

"Yes sir. Well, it gets cold out there, and these deck force boys have mighty bad-looking jackets," the Exec said.

The Captain felt the Exec had missed his point and said, "Oh, I realize they have to wear a jacket, but for a military watch like that, I'd like to see them wear pea coats when it's cold."

Lieutenant Graven was talking with a third-class boatswain's mate on the fantail when the quarterdeck messenger found him. When told that the executive officer wanted to see him, Graven ended his discussion with, "There, hear that? He probably wants to see me about the brightwork. I don't care how many men it takes to do it, the Exec told me to be sure to get that brightwork polished every morning."

The executive officer indicated a chair to Graven and asked: "How's it going these days?"

Lassiter had always liked Graven, but in the past few months, since he had taken over as senior watch officer, Graven seemed to have more problems than usual.

"Okay, I guess," Graven replied with a forced grin. He knew that things were not as they used to be. It seemed strange, too, because everyone on the ship had been so glad to be rid of the previous senior watch officer, that "damn" Lieutenant Dumphy. The junior officers even had a special little beer bust at the club to celebrate Dumphy's leaving and Graven's "fleeting up" to senior watch officer. Now the Exec was always after him. The junior officers didn't help much either, always complaining about the Exec. Maybe the Exec was taking over as "the heel" now that Dumphy was gone.

"That's good," said the Exec. "Here's a little thing that you might look into. These men who stand pier watches have to wear a jacket, but the foul weather jacket doesn't look good for a military watch. I'd like to see them wear their pea coats when it's cold." Graven had expected something like this, more of the Exec's picking on him. He responded properly, got up, and left.

Graven told his first lieutenant. "The Exec says the pier head sentries can't wear foul weather jackets anymore. If it's cold they can wear pea coats," he added.

"But the pea coats will get dirty, and then what about personnel inspections?" asked the first lieutenant.

"I don't know," Graven shook his head, "but if the Exec wants pea coats, we give him pea coats!"

"Pea coats!" said the chief boatswain's mate, "Who says so?"

"That's what the Exec wants," said the first lieutenant, "so let's give him pea coats."

"The Exec says pea coats for the pier sentries when it's cold," announced the chief to his boatswain's mates.

A third-class boatswain's mate walked away from the group with a buddy, turned and said, "That Damn Exec. First I got to have all my men polish brightwork on the quarterdeck, now they got to wear pea coats on sentry duty 'stead of foul weather jackets!"

Seaman Kowalski's relief showed up at the sentry booth at 1150. "Roast beef today," constituted the relieving ceremony.

"Good, I like roast beef," was the reply. "Hey, how come the pea coat?"

"Damn Exec's idea," said the relief. "We can't wear foul weather gear no more out here, only pea coats."

"Damn Exec," agreed Kowalski. "Captain didn't say nothin' when he came by."

"The Captain's okay, it's just that Damn Exec. He's the guy who fouls up everything," complained the new sentry.

Seaman Kowalski had just gone aboard the ship when Captain Speaks stepped out on deck to look over his ship. The quarterdeck awning shielded the Captain from the view of those on the quarterdeck, but he could clearly hear the conversation.

"Roast beef today, Ski."

"Yeah, I know, and we wear pea coats from now on."

"Whaddaya mean, pea coats?"

"Yeah, pea coats on the pier, Damn Exec says no more foul weather jackets."

"Well that ain't all, we got to polish this here brightwork 'til it shines every morning before quarters. Damn Exec says that too."

"Damn Exec."

Captain Speaks was shocked. "Why 'Damn Exec' from these seamen?" he thought. It was easy to see that the executive officer had passed the order along in proper military manner. It was easy to see that the junior officers, leading petty officers, and lower petty officers were passing it along saying "The Exec wants. . . ." That's the way orders are passed along. Why? Because "it is easy."

"All ship's officers assemble in the wardroom," the boatswain's mate announced on the loudspeaker system. Lieutenant Commander Lassiter escorted in the Captain. The junior officers took their seats when the Captain was seated. The executive officer remained standing. "Gentlemen, the Captain has a few words to say to us today."

The Captain rose and looked around slowly. "Gentlemen, we are continually exposed to words like administration, leadership, management, capabilities, organization, responsibilities, authority, discipline, and cooperation. You use these words every day. You give lectures to your men and use them, but if I were to ask each of you for a definition of any of these words I would get such a wide variety of answers that an expert couldn't tell what word we were defining. Some we probably couldn't define at all. We still use them, and will continue to use them as they are used in the continually mounting number of articles, instructions, and books we must read.

"If I were to ask any of you how can we improve leadership I would get answers filled with these words—undefined and meaningless.

"If we listed all of the nicely worded theories of leadership, studied them, memorized them, and took a test on them, we would all pass. But this would not improve our ability as leaders one bit. I can tell a story, containing none of these meaningless words, that *will* improve your leadership.

"In 1943, I was secondary battery officer in a cruiser in the South Pacific. In my second battle, gun control was hit and I lost communications with everyone except my 5-inch mounts. I could see that the after main battery turret was badly damaged

USS San Jacinto (CG 56) (left) takes on fuel from USNS Big Horn (T-AO 198) during replenishment at sea operations in the Central Mediterranean.
Official U.S. Navy photo.

and two enemy destroyers were closing us from astern. At the time my 5-inch mounts were shooting at airplanes. I ordered my two after 5-inch mounts to use high capacity ammunition and shift targets to the two destroyers closing from astern. 'But Mr. Speaks, we're supposed to handle the air targets; who said to shift targets?' my mount captain asked.

"There were noise and smoke and explosions that day, but the explosion that I heard and felt was not from a shell, but from those words of the mount captain.

"Those attacking destroyers got a few shots in at us before we beat them off. Maybe those shots found a target and some of my shipmates died. I never found out. There was too much other damage.

"I thought over the battle afterward and realized that this entire situation was my fault, not the mount captain's. I may have been responsible for the death of some of my shipmates because up to that day I always gave orders to my subordinates by attaching the originator's name to it.

"What does that mean? It means that it was the easy thing to do, to say, 'the gunnery officer wants us to shift targets.'

"In this peacetime world you may say that we no longer have this struggle on a life or death basis. Quick response does not mean life or death now, but it might tomorrow, or sometime after we've all been transferred elsewhere and this ship is being fought by people we don't know.

"Whether you're cleaning boilers, standing bridge watch, or administering your training program, it's easy to say 'The Exec wants' or 'Mr. Jones says.' It's the easy, lazy way: not the right way. You can sometimes discuss or even argue with an order, but when you give it to a subordinate, make him think it is coming from you.

"Giving orders the lazy way is like a drug. Once you start saying 'The ops officer wants' you will find yourself doing it more and more until you can't get a thing done any other way. Your men will pass along orders that way, too, and it will become a part of your organization right down to the lowest level. When some problem arises and you want action, you'll get 'Who wants this?' or 'Why should we?'

"Each of you ask yourself if you have given an order today or yesterday in the lazy manner. I think almost all of us have. Now ask yourself if that order really originated with the person who gave it to you, or did he receive it from a higher level? We never really know, do we, but why should we even care?

"In almost every unit the 'lazy' ordering starts on a particular level. From personal experience I can tell you that this can be an exact measure of the unit's effectiveness. If it starts at the department head level or higher it's a relatively bad outfit, and if it starts at the chief's level it's a relatively good outfit. You can find the level below which it starts by hearing a new title preceding a primary billet. 'Damn Exec' means that the executive officer is the lowest level giving orders properly. 'Damn division officer' means that the division officers are taking responsibility for the order.

"Here I am using some of those words, responsibility and authority, those undefined terms we want to avoid, but perhaps we have helped define them.

"To be more specific, every officer does some 'lazy' ordering, but we need to do it less and less. We must try to push the 'damn' title down as far as it will go.

"Let's push the 'damn officer' down all the way to the chiefs and below, then we will have a Damn Good Ship."

From
A Message to Garcia

Elbert Hubbard

This literary trifle, A Message to Garcia, *was written one evening after supper, in a single hour. It was on the twenty-second of February, Eighteen Hundred Ninety-nine, Washington's Birthday, and we were just going to press with the March* Philistine. *The thing leaped hot from my heart, written after a trying day, when I had been endeavoring to train some rather delinquent villagers to abjure the comatose state and get radioactive.*

The immediate suggestion, though, came from a little argument over the teacups, when my boy Bert suggested that Rowan was the real hero of the Cuban War. Rowan had gone alone and done the thing—carried the message to Garcia.

It came to me like a flash! Yes, the boy is right, the hero is the man who does his work—who carries the message to Garcia.

I got up from the table, and wrote A Message to Garcia. *I thought so little of it that we ran it in the Magazine without a heading. The edition went out, and soon orders began to come for extra copies of the March* Philistine, *a dozen, fifty, a hundred; and when the American News Company ordered a thousand, I asked one of my helpers which article it was that had stirred up the cosmic dust. "It's the stuff about Garcia," he said.*

The next day a telegram came from George H. Daniels, of the New York Central Railroad, thus "Give price on one hundred thousand Rowan article in pamphlet form—Empire State Express advertisement on back—also how soon can ship."

I replied giving price, and stated we could supply the pamphlet in two years. Our facilities were small and a hundred thousand booklets looked like an awful undertaking.

The result was that I gave Mr. Daniels permission to reprint the article in his own way. He issued it in booklet form in editions of half a million. Two or three of these half-million lots were sent out by Mr. Daniels, and in addition the article was reprinted in over two hundred magazines and newspapers. It has been translated into all written languages.

At the same time Mr. Daniels was distributing the Message to Garcia, Prince Hilakoff, Director of Russian Railways, was in this country. He was the guest of the New York Central, and made a tour of the country under the personal direction of Mr. Daniels. The Prince saw the little book and was interested in it, more because Mr. Daniels was putting it out in such big numbers, probably, than otherwise.

In any event, when he got home he had the matter translated into Russian, and a copy of the booklet given to every railroad employee in Russia.

Other countries then took it up, and from Russia it passed into Germany, France, Spain, Turkey, Hindustan and China. During the war between Russia and Japan, every Russian soldier who went to the front was given a copy of the Message to Garcia.

The Japanese, finding the booklets in possession of the Russian prisoners, concluded that it must be a good thing and accordingly translated it into Japanese.

And on an order of the Mikado, a copy was given to every man in the employ of the Japanese Government, soldier or civilian.

Over forty million copies of A Message to Garcia *have been printed. This is said to be a larger circulation than any other literary venture has ever attained during the lifetime of the author, in all history—thanks to a series of lucky accidents.*

—E.H.

1 December 1913

In all this Cuban business there is one man stands out on the horizon of my memory like Mars at perihelion.

When war broke out between Spain and the United States, it was very necessary to communicate quickly with the leader of the Insurgents. Garcia was somewhere in the mountain fastnesses of Cuba—no one knew where. No mail or telegraph message could reach him. The President must secure his co-operation, and quickly.

What to do!

Someone said to the President, "There is a fellow by the name of Rowan will find Garcia for you, if anybody can."

Rowan was sent for and given a letter to be delivered to Garcia. How the "fellow by the name of Rowan" took the letter, sealed it up in an oilskin punch, strapped it over his heart, in four days landed by night off the coast of Cuba from an open boat, disappeared into the jungle, and in three weeks came out on the other side of the island, having traversed a hostile country on foot, and delivered his letter to Garcia—are things I have no special desire now to tell in detail. The point that I wish to make is this: McKinley gave Rowan a letter to be delivered to Garcia; Rowan took the letter and did not ask, "Where is he at?"

> COL. ANDREW ROWAN, who performed one of the celebrated feats in the history of the American Army . . . carrying the message to Garcia . . . died Jan. 10, 1943 at San Francisco. He was 85.
>
> A Virginian who graduated from West Point in 1881, he executed minor military assignments in Central America, with the Army Information Bureau and as an attache, and was still a lieutenant at the age of 41 when he became famous.
>
> After his exploit . . . recognized some 20 years later by the award of the Distinguished Service Cross . . . he served in the Philippine campaigns, taught military science and tactics at Kansas State Agriculture College, and also served at Fort Riley, Kan., West Point, in Kentucky, and at American Lake, Washington. He was cited for gallantry in the Philippine action.
>
> After his retirement from the army, he spent the remainder of his life in San Francisco.

By the Eternal! there is a man whose form should be cast in deathless bronze and the statue placed in every college of the land. It is not booklearning young men need, nor instruction about this and that, but a stiffening of the vertebrae which will cause them to be loyal to a trust, to act promptly, concentrate their energies: do the thing— "Carry a Message to Garcia."

General Garcia is dead now, but there are other Garcias. No man who has endeavored to carry out an enterprise where many hands were needed, but has been well appalled at times by the imbecility of the average man—the inability or unwillingness to concentrate on a thing and do it.

Slipshod assistance, foolish inattention, dowdy indifference, and half-hearted work seem the rule; and no man succeeds, unless by hook or crook or threat he forces or bribes other men to assist him; or mayhap, God in His goodness performs a miracle, and sends him an Angel of Light for an assistant.

You, reader, put this matter to a test: You are sitting now in your office—six clerks are within call. Summon any one and make this request: "Please look in the encyclopedia and make a brief memorandum for me concerning the life of Correggio." Will the clerk quietly say, "Yes, sir," and go do the task?

On your life he will not. He will look at you out of a fishy eye and ask one or more of the following questions:

Who was he?
Which encyclopedia?
Where is the encyclopedia?
Was I hired for that?
Don't you mean Bismarch?

What's the matter with Charlie doing it?

Is he dead?

Is there any hurry?

Shan't I bring you the book and let you look it up yourself?

What do you want to know for?

And I will lay you ten to one that after you have answered the questions, and explained how to find the information, and why you want it, the clerk will go off and get one of the other clerks to help him try to find Garcia—and then come back and tell you there is no such man. Of course I may lose my bet, but according to the Law of Average I will not. Now, if you are wise, you will not bother to explain to your "assistant" that Correggio is indexed under the C's, not in the K's, but you will smile very sweetly and say, "Never mind," and go look it up yourself. And this incapacity for independent action, this moral stupidity, this infirmity of the will, this unwillingness to cheerfully catch hold and lift—these are the things that put pure Socialism so far into the future. If men will not act for themselves, what will they do when the benefit of their effort is for all?

A first mate with knotted club seems necessary; and the dread of getting "the bounce." Saturday night holds many a worker to his place. Advertise for a stenographer, and nine out of ten who apply can neither spell nor punctuate—do not think it is necessary to.

Can such a one write a letter to Garcia?

"You see that bookkeeper," said the foreman to me in a large factory.

"Yes; what about him?"

"Well, he's a fine accountant, but if I'd send him up town on an errand, he might accomplish the errand all right, and on the other hand, might stop at four saloons on the way, and when he got to Main Street would forget what he had been sent out for."

Can such a man be entrusted to carry a message to Garcia?

We have already recently been hearing much maudlin sympathy expressed for the "downtrodden denizens of the sweatshop" and the "homeless wanderer searching for honest employment," and with it all often go many hard words for the men in power.

Nothing is said about the employer who grows old before his time in a vain attempt to get frowsy ne'er-do-wells to do intelligent work; and his long, patient striving after "help" that does nothing but loaf when his back is turned. In every store and factory there is a constant weeding-out process going on. The employer is constantly sending away "help" that have shown their incapacity to further the interests of the business, and others are being taken on. No matter how good times are, this sorting continues: only if times are hard and work is scarce, the sorting is done finer—but out and forever out the incompetent and unworthy go. It is the survival of the fittest. Self-interest prompts every employer to keep the best—those who can carry a message to Garcia.

I know one man of really brilliant parts who has not the ability to manage a business of his own, and yet who is absolutely worthless to any one else, because he carries with him constantly the insane suspicion that his employer is oppressing, or intending to oppress him. He can not give orders, and he will not receive them. Should a message be given him to take to Garcia, his answer would probably be, "Take it yourself!"

Tonight this man walks the streets looking for work, the wind whistling through his threadbare coat. No one who knows him dare employ him, for he is a regular

Official U.S. Navy photo.

firebrand of discontent. He is impervious to reason, and the only thing that can impress him is the toe of a thick-soled Number Nine boot.

Of course I know that one so morally deformed is no less to be pitied than a physical cripple; but in our pitying let us drop a tear, too, for the men who are striving to carry on a great enterprise, whose working hours are not limited by the whistle, and whose hair is fast turning white through the struggle to hold in line dowdy indifference, slipshod imbecility, and the heartless ingratitude which, but for their enterprise, would be both hungry and homeless.

Have I put the matter too strongly? Possibly I have; but when all the world has gone a-slumming I wish to speak a word of sympathy for the man who succeeds, the man who, against great odds, has directed the efforts of others, and having succeeded, finds there's nothing in it: nothing but bare board and clothes. I have carried a dinner-pail and worked for day's wages, and I have also been an employer of labor, and I know there is something to be said on both sides. There is no excellence, per se, in poverty; rags are no recommendation; and all employers are not rapacious and high-handed, any more than all poor men are virtuous. My heart goes out to the man who does his work when the "boss" is away, as well as when he is at home. And the man who, when given a letter to Garcia, quietly takes the missive, without asking any idiotic questions, and with no lurking intention of chucking it into the nearest sewer, or of doing aught else but deliver it, never gets "laid off," nor has to go on a strike for higher wages. Civilization is one long, anxious search for just such individuals. Anything such a man asks shall be granted. He is wanted in every city, town and village in every office, shop, store and factory. The world cries out for such; he is needed and needed badly—the man who can "Carry a Message to Garcia."

11 *Followership in the Fleet—Senior Enlisted Seminar*

Objectives

1. Apply the principles of good followership to establishing a strong working relationship with enlisted personnel.

2. Explain the role of senior enlisted personnel in training junior officers.

The Sailors' Creed

I am a United States Sailor.

I will support and defend the Constitution of the United States of America and I will obey the orders of those appointed over me.

I represent the fighting spirit of the Navy and those who have gone before me to defend freedom and democracy around the world.

I proudly serve my country's Navy combat team with honor, courage and commitment.

I am committed to excellence and the fair treatment of all.

Naval Academy photo courtesy of United States Naval Academy Photographic Laboratory.

Rudder Orders

These guiding principles are the foundation upon which the entire Navy operates:

- People are the Navy's most valuable asset.
- The Navy must attract quality individuals.
- We encourage our people to make the Navy a career.
- We provide frequent recognition to deserving individuals and units.
- Our goal is to promote people to the highest grade or rank according to their abilities.
- We make duty assignments based on both the needs of the Navy and the needs of the individual.
- Some personal hardships may require reassignment or discharge from naval service.
- We provide leave for every member, liberty time away from work, all benefits allowed by law and seek to keep pace with changing economic conditions.
- Training and education are vitally important.
- We value and depend on professional input and ideas from all of our people.
- We do not tolerate discrimination, any form of sexual harassment, fraternization, or the illegal or improper use of drugs or alcohol.
- We provide timely, constructive written evaluations of performance.
- We strive to provide high quality, attractive, modern facilities for our people.
- We are committed to the safety of our people.
- We are accountable to standards of conduct, federal statutes and regulations.
- We look after the individual needs of our people.

Acad Grads, They Say You're Arrogant

Victor Rodriguez

Perhaps I've lead a sheltered life. It could be that I just never noticed before. I've heard all the jokes about Naval Academy graduates but the reality was that they weren't really any different from other officers.

Then I ran into a few of the latest group to hit the fleet. Not wanting to believe these young men were representative of what the Academy produced, I compared notes with a few old shipmates. Sadly it was true.

It seems that after four years of being "immersed in a naval environment" these young men had failed to absorb the very things that tens of thousands of enlisted people absorb in just two short months of recruit training. Conforming to standards

An aviator conducts a planeside brief with squadron technicians on the flight deck of USS George Washington (CVN 73).
Official U.S. Navy photo.

and being willing to learn. It is almost as if, after four years of paid-for-education, they think they have learned everything and don't have to take advice from anyone.

This became apparent to me when I made a recommendation to a young ensign about an item on his uniform prior to a personnel inspection. He was wearing a belt buckle with his officer's crest on it instead of the plain brushed one prescribed.

He promptly informed me that it was the division being inspected and not him. I tried to point out that he had to set the example for these young men and women, but he didn't want to hear anymore and let me know it. I kept my silence.

The inspecting officer was, and still is, *old Navy,* hard as nails and a firm believer in standards. In other words, he's the kind of captain that I love to work for. When the division officer presented the division, the captain looked him over and I could see the beginning of a scowl. This wasn't going to be pretty.

In a voice so low I could barely hear, I heard the captain ask my division officer how he could inspect the division when, as the division officer, he was out of uniform. The captain then asked me if I had advised my division officer on the proper wearing of his uniform. I said I had and noted that I'd even offered to loan him a spare. He turned back to the division officer.

Flight deck crew on board USS Theodore Roosevelt (CVN 71) rig a barricade.
Official U.S. Navy photo.

"Could you please explain to me why, when this master chief petty officer, who is charged with training division officers, advised you on the correct uniform, that you failed to take his advice? Why do I ask chiefs their opinion even after 25 years of service? I'll tell you why. It's because they understand reality. They know sailors and understand them more than anybody else."

The captain then had me present my division, and after a thorough look he finished with no discrepancies. The captain thanked me for my efforts and told everybody that they looked great and that it had been a pleasure to inspect them.

Later I caught up with my division officer as he was going over a few request chits that I had commented on. On two he had disagreed with me and insisted that I tell the sailors concerned that their request was not possible.

I reminded the ensign that only the CO could disapprove them. I also told him that he needed to give a reason why he was saying no. He took them up to the department head and later both chits were approved.

At lunch I ran into him at the exchange wearing a command ball cap. Now I reminded him that it wasn't authorized either. He complained a bit about having to buy a garrison cap before he left to go back to work.

So what was it I was doing with this brand-new ensign? Doing my best to train him despite his not wanting that. It was almost as if he thought he knew it all and couldn't possibly be aided in his job by someone of lower rank. Over the next several weeks, another thing became obvious. This individual and several others seemed to project that because they had been to Boat U, they were owed something special.

I knew I was doing my job and that my fellow chiefs were doing their jobs with their ensigns, but it just wasn't working.

A motto at the academy is "Excellence without arrogance." I'll settle for the excellence if I can get it. I can deal with arrogance if it's justified. With the ensign it wasn't.

In the meantime, I'm thinking about calling the fraud, waste and abuse hot line. I'm not getting my money's worth.

Victor Rodriguez is the pseudonym for a master chief petty officer in the Navy.

12 How We Make Choices—The Way The Mind Thinks

Objectives

1. List and explain the four basic problem-solving processes that we use to generate solutions.

2. Explain the benefits and liabilities of different problem-solving approaches.

3. Apply each of the problem-solving strategies to a given case.

Solving Problems

What are algorithms and heuristics, and how are they more efficient as problem-solving methods than trial and error? What's an analogy, and what makes it a powerful tool? Why do some psychologists believe in problem solving by insight—and why do others think insight is just an illusion? What are some of the "blind spots" that impair our ability to solve problems?

When you lock your keys in the car, play Scrabble, mediate a dispute between friends, or struggle to figure out a function on your computer, the solution you're looking for requires that you combine and manipulate concepts, often in new ways, to solve the problem or to make the necessary judgment. When a solution cannot simply be pulled from memory, it takes effort to obtain. As we'll see, it helps to view problem solving as a process that involves defining and representing the problem, then generating and evaluating possible solutions (Glass & Holyoak, 1986; Ellis & Hunt, 1989). These steps are not a fixed series of stages but rather are mental activities that are used in cycles. So if you're stuck on a problem and realize that you have not represented it correctly in the first place, you might start the process over again.

Representing the Problem

Many problems we encounter come to us in the form of words and concepts activated from semantic networks. Playing the TV game *Jeopardy!*, trying to recite the lyrics of an old song, and working on a crossword puzzle are some examples. But there are other ways as well to depict problems.

image A mental representation of visual information.

Mental Images Often people represent information through **images**, or mental pictures. To turn on the ignition of your car, do you turn the key to the right or to the left? What about the cold-water faucet in your kitchen sink? Which way do the hands of a clock move? (Yes, it's clockwise, but describe what that means.) What's the color of your psychology professor's eyes? And if you can picture a map of the world, which city is farther north, London or New York? To answer these questions, people generate visual images.

In the past, psychologists had to take people at their word when they said they had formed mental pictures. Today, there are more objective ways to study the "mind's eye"—and these new methods have confirmed that imagery is a pervasive aspect of human thought. Consider some specific examples. In one study, Margaret Intons-Peterson (1993) gave people verbal descriptions of simple line drawings, like the one in Figure 12.1, and found that the more rotations that were involved, the longer it took subjects to generate the image. This result suggests that people solve this problem by manipulating mental pictures of the described forms. In fact, the

139

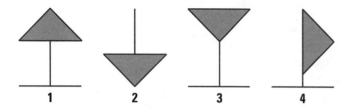

FIGURE 12.1 Mental-rotation tasks Imagine a capital letter *T*. Rotate it 90 degrees to the right. Put a triangle directly to the left of the figure so that it is pointing to the right. Now rotate the figure 90 degrees to the right. Got it? Now look at the images above and pick the correct one. You can check your answer by drawing the figure on paper or looking on page 148.

mental models Intuitive theories about the way things work.

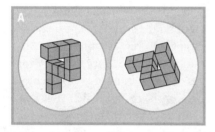

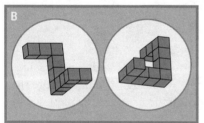

FIGURE 12.2 3-D mental-rotation tasks Look at the pairs of objects and try to determine whether the two objects in each pair are the same shape or different. Suggesting that people make these judgments by forming images, research shows that the more mental rotation is required to align two objects, the more time it takes people to make the judgment (Shepard & Cooper, 1982).

images we form are often like three-dimensional sculptures. Look at the pairs of objects shown in Figure 12.2. When people are asked to judge whether the paired objects are the same shape or different, they try to solve the problem by imagining one of the forms rotating into alignment with the other. The more mental rotation required to align the objects, the more time it takes people to make the judgment (Shepard & Cooper, 1982). Additional evidence concerning the nature of imagery comes from recent brain-scanning studies, where researchers have found that when subjects engage in tasks that require mental imagery, their brains become active in the same areas of the occipital cortex that are involved in vision (Farah, 1989; Isha & Sagi, 1995).

To the cognitive psychologist, it's now clear that mental images play a key role in human problem solving (Kosslyn, 1994). But is imagery a uniquely human thought process? Research in a newly developing area of animal cognition suggests not. In an intriguing experiment, depicted in Figure 12.3, Jacques Vauclair and others (1993) trained six wild baboons to move a cursor on a computer with the use of a joystick. In a series of trials, each subject then saw a sample stimulus flashed briefly on the screen (the letter *P* or *F*). This presentation was followed by two "comparison stimuli" that were rotated at varying degrees—one always matched the sample; the other was its mirror image. Using the joystick, the subject's task was to select the comparison stimulus that matched the original sample. Each correct response was rewarded with food. Could the baboons perform the necessary mental rotation to achieve this task? Yes. In contrast to what many psychologists would have predicted, the accuracy rate was 70 percent. And, as in humans, their performance varied according to the degree of rotation that was needed to make the comparison.

Mental Models   Do you understand how a virus spreads from one computer to another? Can you describe how an engine works? What about the economy: Do you know how the inflation and unemployment rates interact? At times, the problems that confront us can be best represented in the form of **mental models,** which are intuitive theories of the way things work. When accurate, these theories can be powerful tools for reasoning. By having specific mental models of how human beings, organizations, machines, and other things work, we can diagnose problems and then adapt accordingly (Gentner & Stevens, 1983).

Unfortunately, our mental models are often in error. Before reading on, try the problems in Figure 12.4. These problems are used to study *intuitive physics*—the mental models people have about the laws of motion. Research shows that people are poor intuitive physicists. Consider three common errors. First, many people wrongly believe in the "impetus principle" that an object set in motion acquires its own internal force, which keeps it in motion. So when asked to predict the path of a metal ball rolling through a spiral tube, a majority of subjects predicted that the ball would follow a curved path even after it exits the tube (McCloskey & Kuhl, 1983). A second error is the "straight-down belief" that something dropped from a moving object will fall in a straight vertical line. So when asked to predict the path of a ball dropped at shoulder height by a walking adult, most subjects wrongly assumed that the ball would fall straight down rather than in a forward trajectory (McCloskey et al., 1983). A third error is made in the "water-level task" shown in Figure 12.4. When shown a tilted glass or container filled with liquid, some subjects—including

FIGURE 12.3 **Can baboons mentally rotate objects?** In this apparatus, six baboons were trained to use a joystick to move a cursor. The sample form on the left would be shown and then subjects would have to choose the rotated form on the right that matched the sample. As evident from a 70 percent accuracy rate, these baboons were able to mentally align objects to make these judgments (Vauclair et al., 1993).

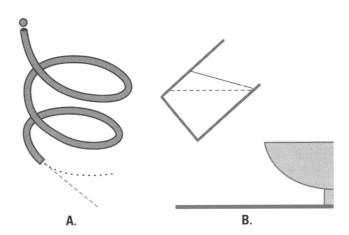

A.   **B.**

FIGURE 12.4 **Intuitive Physics** A. Subjects were asked to draw the path that a marble would take as it exited this curved tube. Most subjects incorrectly drew a curved path (*dotted line*) rather than the correct straight path (*dashed line*). Our mental models of motion are often wrong. B. In this task, subjects were asked to draw a line to illustrate the surface of water in the tilted container. Although the line should be depicted as perfectly horizontal to the ground, many people placed it at the tilted angle shown below.

many bartenders and waitresses—harbor the belief that the water surface tilts as well rather than remains horizontal to the ground (Hecht & Proffitt, 1995). Interestingly, physics students don't always perform better on these types of problems, suggesting that mental models can be difficult to change (Donley & Ashcraft, 1992).

Generating Solutions

Once a problem is represented through words, static images, or mental models, we try out possible solutions and test to see if they work. If the problem is solved, life goes on. If not, we return to the proverbial drawing board to come up with new ideas. There are many different ways to find solutions, but there are four basic problem-solving processes: trial and error, algorithms, heuristics, and insight.

Trial and Error **Trial and error** is the simplest problem-solving strategy there is, and it's often effective. Edward Thorndike, in 1898, studied animal intelligence by putting cats in a "puzzle box," placing food outside a door, and timing how long it took for them to figure out how to escape. At first, the cats tried various ineffective behaviors. They tried reaching with their paws, but the food was too far away. They scratched at the bars, but that did not work. They pushed at the ceiling, but that did not work either. Then they would literally stumble upon the solution (which was to step on a lever, which opened the door) and repeat that solution whenever they were in the box. The cats solved the problem by trial and error.

trial and error A problem-solving strategy in which several solutions are attempted until one is found that works.

Solution to Figure 12.1: The answer is (3).

As you can imagine, this aimless, hit-or-miss approach is not the most efficient way to proceed. Yet I must confess that when I tinker with my computer and run into problems, I often start pecking furiously at the keyboard or probing and clicking with the mouse, hoping that something I do will effect a change. Sometimes this strategy proves enlightening. For example, Thomas Edison—the most prolific inventor in American history—tested thousands of lightbulb filaments before stumbling upon the one that worked. The problem is that this strategy often takes too long or fails completely. If possible, it's better to take a more systematic, planned approach.

algorithm A systematic problem-solving strategy that is guaranteed to produce a solution.

heuristic A rule of thumb that allows one to make judgments that are quick but often in error.

means-end analysis A problem-solving heuristic that involves breaking down a larger problem into a series of subgoals.

Algorithms and Heuristics An **algorithm** is a step-by-step procedure that is guaranteed, eventually, to produce a solution. When you were taught in school how to solve two-digit addition problems or long division, you learned an algorithm. An alternative is to use **heuristics**, mental shortcuts, or rules of thumb, that may or may not lead to the correct solution. The "*I* before *E*" heuristic for spelling *I-E* words is a good example. To appreciate the difference between algorithms and heuristics, consider the following anagram problem: Unscramble the letters *L K C C O* to make a word. One strategy is to use an algorithm—to try all possible combinations by systematically varying the letters in each position. Sooner or later, you will form the correct word. An alternative is to use a heuristic. For example, you could try the most familiar letter combinations. A common ending for English words is *CK* so you might start with this combination and arrive quickly at the solution: *CLOCK*.

If algorithms are guaranteed to produce solutions, why not use them all the time? The reason is that algorithms are not always available, and sometimes they take too much time to be practical. Thus, chess experts do not consider all the possible moves on the board, because there are simply too many of them. This strategy is fine for high-speed computers such as "Deep Blue"—an IBM computerized chess master equipped with 512 processors acting in parallel to analyze millions of positions and moves per second. But great players must rely instead on heuristics, such as "Get control of the center of the board."

Some heuristics are general, in that they can be used to solve a wide range of problems. One important general heuristic is the **means-end analysis** (Newell & Simon, 1972). This involves breaking a larger problem into a series of subgoals. For example, let's say you are starting a new job Monday and have to get to work on time. You could solve this problem by driving your car to work, but your car needs repair. So you set a subgoal of getting your car repaired. But this might require other subgoals, such as finding a mechanic. For some problems, the nested subgoals can get quite complex and involved. In fact,

In February 1996, Garry Kasparov, the world chess champion from Azerbaijan, defeated IBM's chess master, Deep Blue. In a rematch played in May 1997, however, Kasparov lost to an even more powerful version of Deep Blue. Equipped with 512 microprocessors working in parallel, IBM's chess master was able to analyze two hundred million positions per second.

unless people carefully evaluate whether each step brings them closer to the end-point, it is possible to lose track of what part of the problem is actually being solved (Simon, 1975). The benefits of formulating subgoals can be seen in the *Tower of Hanoi problem*, shown in Figure 12.5.

Another powerful problem-solving heuristic is the use of **analogies.** If you have previously solved some problem that seems similar to a new one, you can use the old solution as a model. The trick is to recognize that the second problem resembles the first. By way of illustration, take a few minutes to try to solve the following "tumor-and-radiation problem" (Gick & Holyoak, 1980):

> Suppose you are a doctor faced with a patient who has a malignant tumor in his stomach. To operate on the patient is impossible, but unless the tumor is destroyed the patient will die. A certain kind of ray, at a sufficiently high intensity, can be used to destroy the tumor. Unfortunately, at this intensity the healthy tissue that the rays pass through on the way to the tumor will also be destroyed. At lower intensities, the rays are harmless to healthy tissue, but they will not affect the tumor. What type of procedure might be used to destroy the tumor using the rays without injuring healthy tissue?

Do you have the answer? If not, read the following "general-and-fortress" story:

> A small country was ruled from a strong fortress by a dictator. The fortress was in the middle of the country, surrounded by farms and villages. Many roads led outward from the fortress like spokes in a wheel. A rebel general vowed to capture the fortress. The general knew that an attack by his entire army would capture the fortress. He gathered his troops at the head of one of the roads, ready to attack the fortress. However, the general learned that the dictator had planted mines on each of the roads. The mines were set so that small bodies of men could pass over them safely, but any large force would detonate the mines. Not only would this blow up the road, but it would also destroy nearby villages. It seemed impossible to capture the fortress. But the general devised a plan. He divided his army up into small groups and dispatched each group to the head of a different road. When all were ready he gave the signal, and each group marched down a different road. Each group continued down its road to the fortress, so that the entire army finally arrived together at the same time. In this way, the general captured the fortress and overthrew the dictator.

Okay, now return to the radiation problem and try again. If you're still drawing a blank, here's a hint: Think of the general-and-fortress story as an analogy for the radiation-and-tumor problem. Look beneath the surface differences in the stories. Can you see the relevance of the general's strategy for the surgeon? The radiation solution is to use a low-intensity ray that can be aimed at the tumor from several directions. When all the rays reach the tumor, their effects will add up to that of a single high-intensity beam at the site of the tumor, and healthy tissue will not be destroyed. Demonstrating the usefulness of problem solving by analogy, Gick and Holyoak (1980) found that only 8 percent of naive subjects solved the radiation problem on their own, but among those who had first read the general-and-fortress story, the solution rate increased to 76 percent.

Analogical thinking plays a central role in science, where the heart has been likened to a pump, the brain to a computer, the eye to a camera, molecules to billiard balls, the telephone to an ear, and the spinning earth to a slowing toy top. Indeed, research shows that people are quicker to grasp and use new scientific concepts when

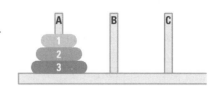

FIGURE 12.5 Tower of Hanoi Problem
Your mission is to move three rings from peg A to peg C. You may move only the top ring on a peg and may not place a larger ring above a smaller one. See solution on page 150.

analogy A problem-solving heuristic that involves using an old solution as a model for a new, similar problem.

"Now I see your problem—linear thought."

Solution to the Tower of Hanoi Problem: To complete this mission, it helps to break the task into subgoals. The first is to get ring 3 to the bottom of peg C (move ring 1 to peg C, ring 2 to peg B, and ring 1 from peg C to peg B; then put ring 3 at the bottom of peg C). Your second subgoal is to get ring 2 to peg C (move ring 1 to peg A and ring 2 to C). The third subgoal is now easy: just move ring 1 over to peg C—and you're finished.

insight A form of problem solving in which the solution seems to pop to mind all of a sudden.

these concepts are taught by analogy than when they are explained in literal terms (Donnelly & McDaniel, 1993). In general, the shorter the "mental leap" is between problems, the more effective is the analogy (Holyoak & Thagard, 1997).

Insight When people struggle with a problem, they usually try to monitor their progress to evaluate whether they're closing in on a solution (Kotovsky et al., 1985). But have you ever puzzled over something, felt as if you were stumped, and then come up with the answer abruptly, out of the blue, as if a lightbulb flashed inside your head? Aha! If so, then you have experienced problem solving by **insight,** a process in which the solution pops to mind all of a sudden—and in which the problem solver doesn't realize the solution is coming and cannot describe what he or she was thinking at the time (Kaplan & Simon, 1990; Sternberg & Davidson, 1995).

Insight is an experience that seems to arise whenever people switch from one strategy to another, reframe the problem, remove a mental block, or identify an analogy from a prior experience (Simon, 1989). Some researchers claim that these apparent flashes of insight actually result from a gradual, step-by-step process—that sometimes we're just not aware of the progress we are making (Weisberg, 1992). Others find that certain types of tasks do seem to promote a special form of problem solving that has a sudden, all-or-none quality (Smith & Kounios, 1996). Is insight gradual but nonconscious, or is it truly sudden? It's hard to know for sure. Janet Metcalfe and David Wiebe (1987) had subjects work on different types of problems and periodically rate how "warm" they were getting on a seven-point scale. On multistep algebra problems, the ratings increased steadily as subjects neared a solution. On insight problems, however, the warmth ratings remained flat and low, then rose at the moment subjects encountered a solution. It's interesting that when people working on insight problems are asked to describe their thinking along the way, which brings the process into consciousness, their performance deteriorates (Schooler et al., 1993).

People often report that they tried unsuccessfully for hours to solve a problem and then, after taking a break, came back and it "clicked": An insight quickly converted into a solution. The improved ability to solve a problem after taking a break from it is called the incubation effect. One puzzle that psychologists have used to investigate incubation effects in the laboratory is the "cheap-necklace problem," shown in Figure 12.6. Try it for five minutes before reading on. Using this problem, J. Silveira (1971) tested three groups of subjects. All groups worked on the same task for a total of thirty minutes. One group worked without a break. After fifteen minutes, however, the second group took a half-hour break and the third group took a four-hour break. During these rest periods, subjects were kept busy with other activities that kept them from continuing to work on the necklace problem. The results provided strong evidence for incubation: Subjects who took a break were more likely to solve the problem than those who did not. In fact, the longer the interlude was, the better the performance. The practical implication of this effect is clear. Sometimes it helps to take a break while trying to solve problems that require a single critical insight—as in the cheap-necklace problem, where the key is to realize that you can't link all four chains (Anderson, 1990).

The history of science is filled with stories of discovery by insight. But is insight necessarily the product of great minds? Many psychologists believe that other animals too are capable of insight, not just of trial-and-error problem solving. Many years ago, Wolfgang Köhler (1925) claimed that a chimpanzee named Sultan displayed insight in problem solving. Köhler put bananas and a long stick outside the chimp's cage, both out of reach, and put a short stick inside the cage. Sultan poked at the banana with the short stick, but it was too short to reach the fruit. After trying repeatedly, he gave up, dropped the stick, and walked away. Then all of a sudden, Sultan jumped up, picked up the short stick, and used it to get the longer stick—which he used to get the banana. Did this episode reveal insight? Many researchers are skeptical of such a claim and suggest that the apparent insight may be no more than an accumulation of learned behaviors (Epstein et al., 1984). Yet others agree with Köhler. Sociobiologist Edward O. Wilson tells a Sultan-like story of a chimp trying to reach some leaves: "He sat and looked at the tree for a long time, and went over to a log. He dragged it over to the tree, propped it against the trunk, then stood back and charged his ramp. It's extremely difficult to explain that, other than to say the chimp was consciously thinking" (Begley & Ramo, 1993).

This brings us back to questions about animal cognition and whether problem solving is uniquely human. Do other animals have insight or use heuristics? Are they capable of conscious thought? Many comparative psychologists (researchers who study and compare different species) are convinced that those who study thought and language have long underestimated the cognitive capabilities of nonhuman animals (Vauclair, 1996)—particularly the great apes (Russon et al., 1996). This issue is difficult to resolve and is currently the source of lively debate (Timberlake, 1993). As we'll see later in this chapter, there is tantalizing evidence to suggest that chimpanzees and other apes can learn to solve problems that require the use of abstract symbols. We will take a closer look at this research when we discuss attempts to teach language to nonhuman primates.

Making Judgments

What is syllogistic reasoning, what's conditional reasoning, and how good are we at using these formal rules of logic? What are judgmental heuristics, and how do they illustrate that we often sacrifice accuracy in making speedy decisions? Why do so many people gamble against the odds, an irrational activity, and then persist in the face of defeat?

People have to make decisions every day. Occasionally we are faced with choices that have a major impact on the rest of our lives. Where should I go to school? Should I get married? Should I save my money, spend it, or invest it in stocks? We all like to think of ourselves as thoughtful and logical decision makers who weigh costs and benefits, calculate the probabilities, and act accordingly. But are we that logical, really? Researchers study human decision making in tasks ranging from formal logic to everyday reasoning. The results have given rise to some rather surprising discoveries about *Homo sapiens*, the "rational animal."

The Rules of Formal Logic

Throughout history, philosophers, psychologists, economists, and others have assumed that our natural way of thinking followed the laws of formal logic. One way to test this assumption is to examine the ways in which people solve strictly logical problems.

" 'Jeopardy!' is on."

Off duty metamorphosis

Syllogistic Reasoning One aspect of formal logic that is studied extensively in psychology is syllogistic reasoning. A **syllogism** is a logical problem in which you are given premises that you must assume are true, then decide whether a certain conclusion can be drawn from these premises. For example, given the premises "All *A*s are *B*s" and "All *B*s are *C*s," is the conclusion "All *A*s are *C*s" a valid one? The answer is *yes*—given the premises, the conclusion must be true. Try the syllogisms in Table 12.1, and try to figure out why some seem so much harder to solve than others. For each set of premises, decide if the conclusion is valid. The answers appear below.

As a general rule, most people find syllogisms easier when they are stated concretely rather than in the abstract "All *A*s are *B*s" format. In fact, one strategy that people naturally use to solve abstract syllogisms is to rephrase them as concrete problems. The problem with this strategy is that it can lead us to make mistakes when we fail to see that there can be more than one way to represent a given premise. Consider the proposition that "Some *A*s are *B*s." The diagrams in Figure 12.7 can be used to

syllogism A logical problem in which the goal is to determine the validity of a conclusion given two or more premises.

make this syllogism more concrete. But note that although the left diagram seems more natural, the right one is also a valid way to show the premise because whenever it's true that "All *A*s are *B*s," it's also true that "Some *A*s are *B*s." After drawing conclusions, people often don't double-check to see if their conclusions would be valid for *all* the different ways of representing the premises (Johnson-Laird, 1983).

A second disadvantage of making syllogisms more concrete is illustrated by the last item in Table 12.1. It's easy to make a logical mistake on this type of problem precisely because the conclusion is true based on general world knowledge. But the actual truth of the matter has nothing to do with whether the conclusion follows logically from the premises. To be sure, some bananas are yellow, as stated in the sample item, but that conclusion does not follow logically from the premises that are provided.

Table 12.1 Syllogism Problems	
1. Some *A*s are *B*s All *B*s are *C*s. Therefore, some *A*s are *C*s.	3. All robins are birds. All birds are animals. Therefore, all robins are animals.
2. All *A*s are *B*s. Some *B*s are *C*s. Therefore, some *A*s are *C*s.	4. All bananas are fruit. Some fruits are yellow. Therefore, some bananas are yellow.

Answers: (1) valid, (2) invalid, (3) valid, (4) invalid

Conditional Reasoning   Another common type of problem derived from formal logic is that of *conditional reasoning,* which takes the form of "if-then" statements. To see what's involved in conditional reasoning, look at the problem shown in Figure 12.8. You're told that each of the four cards has a number on one side and a letter on the other. Your goal is to test the hypothesis that *"if* a card has a vowel on one side, *then* it has an even number on the other side." Using as few cards as necessary, which cards would you need to turn over in order to adequately test this hypothesis? Think about it. What's your answer? Most people realize that the E has to be turned over. But another card is needed as well. Is it the one with the 4 showing? No, this card doesn't really help. If there's a vowel on the other side, the rule could still be invalidated by another card. If there's a consonant, the rule is not invalidated (the rule does not state that a card with a consonant cannot have an even number on the other side). The correct choices are E and 7. A vowel on the other side of the 7 would invalidate the rule. In studies with college students, only 4 percent got the right answer. Most picked the E and the 4, probing only for evidence that was consistent with their hypothesis (Wason, 1960). So if you missed it, you are not alone.

This manifestation of the confirmation bias appears in a wide range of reasoning problems. For example, Deanna Kuhn (1991) interviewed people as to how they would evaluate their beliefs on important real issues (such as the causes of criminal behavior and school failure) and found that very few subjects realized that to truly evaluate their beliefs, they would need to consider disconfirming evidence. Everyone is vulnerable—sometimes even motivated—to confirm their initial beliefs. Indeed, case studies in "pathological science" reveal that scientists have been known to test their pet theories in ways that do not allow for disconfirmation (Rousseau, 1992).

Is the confirmation bias an inevitable, fatal flaw in the way human beings reason? Patricia Cheng and her colleagues (1986) found that, compared to people with no formal training in logic, those who had completed a full-semester course in this discipline performed only 3 percent better. There is hope, however. Research shows that people perform well on conditional-reasoning tests using more familiar content. For instance, suppose you're trying to test this rule: "If a person is drinking beer, then he or she must be over twenty-one." In front of you are four cards, each with an age written on one side and what he or she is drinking written on the other. The four cards read *16, 25, cola,* and *beer.* Look at the problem presented in Figure 12.9. Now which cards would you turn over? In an actual experiment, 74 percent of the subjects chose *16* and *beer*—which is correct (Griggs & Cox, 1982). Why was there such vast improvement compared to the last experiment? It may be that because subjects are accustomed to thinking about drinking-age violations they were reminded in this case to search for disconfirming evidence.

What are the educational implications of this result? Can people be trained in the logic of conditional reasoning? To some extent, yes. But the key may be to teach this form of reasoning through the use of concrete problems, the way psychologists do—not through the presentation of abstract rules, as in philosophy. To test this hypothesis, Michael Morris and Richard Nisbett (1993) assessed the conditional-reasoning performance of first- and third-year graduate students enrolled in psychology or philosophy at Michigan, Chicago, and Brown universities. The results were quite striking. As shown in Figure 12.10, philosophy students did not improve from the first year to the third. But the psychology students performed 33 percent better in their third year of study than in their first. After being trained to conduct experiments that test causal hypotheses, the psychology students had learned how to reason in "if-then" terms.

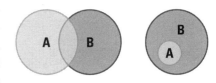

FIGURE 12.7 Different representations of the same premise "Some *A*s are *B*s."

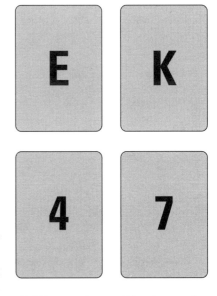

FIGURE   12.8 A   conditional-reasoning problem Each of the four cards has a number on one side and a letter on the other. Using as few cards as necessary, test the hypothesis that if a card has a vowel on one side, then it has an even number on the other side (Wason, 1960).

FIGURE 12.9 **A conditional-reasoning problem with familiar context** Each of the four cards has an age on one side and a drink on the other. Using as few cards as necessary, test the hypothesis that if a person is drinking beer, then he or she must be over twenty-one.

representativeness heuristic A tendency to estimate the likelihood of an event in terms of how typical it seems.

availability heuristic A tendency to estimate the likelihood of an event in terms of how easily instances of it can be recalled.

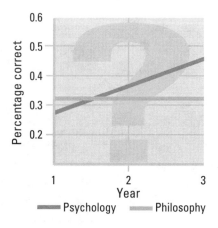

FIGURE 12.10 **Can conditional reasoning be taught?** In this study, graduate students in psychology and philosophy were tested for conditional reasoning. As shown, psychology students improved from their first to their third year but those in philosophy did not (Morris & Nisbett, 1993).

Biases in Judgment

Should I buy a Toyota 4-Runner or a Ford Taurus, an IBM PC or a Mac? Should women over forty have routine mammograms? Should you pour money into the stock market, or is it due for a fall? These are the kinds of decisions that people make every day—decisions that are based on intuitive judgments of probability, estimates we make of the likelihood of good and bad outcomes. How do we go about making these judgments? Do the decisions we make match those we *should* have made based on the actual, objective probabilities? In a series of studies, Daniel Kahneman, Amos Tversky, and others (1982) have found that people consistently use two heuristics in making various judgments: representativeness and availability.

The Representativeness Heuristic A rule of thumb that people often use to make probability estimates is the **representativeness heuristic**—the tendency to judge the likelihood of an event's occurring by how typical it seems (Kahneman & Tversky, 1973). Like other heuristics, this one enables us to make quick judgments. With speed, however, comes bias and a possible loss of accuracy. For example, which sequence of boys (B) and girls (G) would you say is more likely to occur in a family with six children: (1) B,G,B,G,B,G; (2) B,B,B,G,G,G; or (3) G,B,B,G,G,B? In actuality, these sequences are all equally likely. Yet most people say that the third is more likely than the others because it looks typical of a random sequence. As we'll soon discuss (see the Intersection on irrational thinking in the gambling casino, pages 155–157), this use of the representativeness heuristic gives rise to a "gambler's fallacy" in games of chance.

The problem with this heuristic is that it often leads us to ignore numerical probabilities, or "base rates." Suppose I tell you that there's a group of thirty engineers and seventy lawyers. In that group, I randomly select a conservative man named Jack, who enjoys mathematical puzzles and has no interest in social or political issues. Question: Is Jack a lawyer or an engineer? When Kahneman and Tversky (1973) presented this item to subjects, most guessed that Jack was an engineer (because he seemed to fit the stereotyped image of an engineer)—even though he came from a group containing a 70 percent majority of lawyers. In this instance, representativeness overwhelmed the more predictive base rate.

The Availability Heuristic A second mental shortcut that people use is the **availability heuristic,** the tendency to estimate the likelihood of an event based on how easily instances of that event come to mind. To demonstrate, Tversky and Kahneman (1973) asked subjects to judge whether there are more words in English that begin with the letter *K* or the letter *T*. To answer this question, subjects tried to think of words that started with each letter. More words came to mind that started with *T*, so most subjects correctly chose *T* as the answer. In this case, the availability heuristic was useful. It sure beat counting up all the relevant words in the dictionary.

As demonstrated, the availability heuristic enables us to make judgments that are quick and easy. But often, these judgments are in error. For example, Tversky and Kahneman asked some subjects the following question: Which is more common, words that start with the letter *K* or words that contain *K* as the third letter? In actuality, the English language contains many more words with *K* as the third letter than as the first. Yet out of 152 subjects, 105 guessed it to be the other way around. The reason for this disparity is that it's easier to bring to mind words that start with *K*, so these are judged more common.

The letter-estimation bias may seem cute and harmless, but the availability heuristic can lead us astray in important ways—as when uncommon events pop easily to mind because they are very recent or highly emotional. One possible consequence concerns the perception of risk. Which is a more likely cause of death in the United States: being killed by falling airplane parts or being attacked by a shark? Shark attacks get more publicity, and most people say it is a more likely cause of death. Yet the odds of being struck by falling airplane parts are thirty times greater ("Death Odds," 1990). People who are asked to guess the major causes of death thus tend to overestimate the number of those who die in shootings, fires, floods, terrorist bombings, accidents, and other dramatic events—and to underestimate the number of deaths caused by strokes, heart attacks, diabetes, and other mundane and less memorable events (Slovic et al., 1982). Similarly, research shows that the more often a foreign country is in the news, the more people say they know about it—and the higher are their estimates of its population (Brown & Siegler, 1992).

Another consequence of the availability heuristic is that people are influenced more by one vivid life story than by hard statistical facts. Have you ever wondered why so many people buy lottery tickets despite the low odds, or why so many travelers are afraid to fly even though they're more likely to perish in a car accident? These behaviors are symptomatic of the fact that people are relatively insensitive to numerical probabilities and, instead, are overly influenced by graphic and memorable events—such as the sight of a multimillion-dollar lottery winner rejoicing on TV or a photograph of bodies being pulled from the wreckage of a plane crash (Bar-Hillel, 1980). It may not be logical, but one memorable image is worth a thousand numbers.

Intersection

Thought and Language and Business
Irrational Thinking in the Gambling Casino

"I hope to break even today," said one gambler to another. "Why is that?" "I really need the money." Anyone who has played poker for money, dropped coins into a slot machine, bet on a sports event, or bought lottery tickets knows how seductive gambling can be. Every year, people from all walks of life spend hard-earned money at casinos, racetracks, and off-track betting parlors and in state lotteries and numbers games. Americans spend hundreds of billions of dollars a year in legal and illegal gambling activities, and they predictably lose between 5 and 20 percent of that figure (Popkin, 1994).

Gambling is a truly puzzling phenomenon. Ordinarily, people do not like to take large financial risks. Offered a hypothetical choice between receiving a certain $1,000 or a 50:50 shot at $2,500, most people choose the smaller, guaranteed alternative (Kahneman & Tversky, 1984). So why do so many people gamble and persist in the face of defeat? There are different theories. From a cognitive perspective, there are three problems: (1) people harbor the illusion that they can exert control over chance events, (2) they do not completely understand the laws of probability, and (3) they come up with biased explanations for their wins and losses.

In a series of experiments on the **illusion of control,** Ellen Langer (1975) found that people delude themselves into believing they can control the outcome in games of chance that mimic skill situations. When subjects cut cards against a competitor in a game of high-card, they bet more money when their opponent seemed nervous

illusion of control The tendency for people to believe that they can control chance events that mimics skill situations.

With the odds always favoring the house, casinos want to keep you gambling for long periods of time—and at a fast rate. Thus, the lighting is good, the air is cool, the stools have back supports, the drinks are free, beautiful women called "starters" are hired to attract the "high rollers," and blackjack dealers are required to deal 60–75 hands per hour.

rather than confident. When subjects played a lottery, they were more reluctant to sell their tickets after choosing a number themselves than after getting an assigned number. This hardly seems rational. But don't many of us fall prey to these same illusions? Watch people playing slot machines, and you'll see that they try to influence their luck by moving from one machine to another with coins in hand. Or watch players throwing dice in craps, backgammon, or Monopoly, and you'll notice that they often roll hard for high numbers and soft for low numbers (Henslin, 1967).

The effects on gambling are clear. To exploit our tendency to infuse games of chance with an illusion of control, states provide an element of choice in their lotteries by having players pick number combinations themselves. Go to the racetrack, and you will find bettors sizing up the horses and studying the racing forms. In casinos, the dealers are instructed not to intimidate players by shuffling the cards in fancy ways. Why are people so easily fooled? According to Langer, we need to feel that we can control the important events in our lives. Additional research suggests that the more people need to win, the more deluded they become. In one study, for example, subjects took part in a random card drawing with a chance to win a McDonald's Big Mac hamburger. Those who were food-deprived and hungry at the time saw the task as more skill-based and were more confident of success than those who had just eaten (Biner et al., 1995). Thankfully, people think more critically and are less vulnerable when the stakes are high (Dunn & Wilson, 1990).

Gambling also stems from misguided notions about *probability* and the predictions people make about chance events (Wagenaar, 1988). Suppose you flipped a coin six times. Which sequence of heads (H) and tails (T) would you be most likely to get: HHHTTT or HTTHTH? When asked this question, most subjects pick the second alternative. In fact, the two patterns are equally likely. Now suppose you could purchase a lottery ticket containing six numbers out of forty. Would you rather have the numbers *4-33-29-10-2-16,* or *2-2-2-3-3-3?* Given a choice, most people prefer the first ticket over the second (Holtgraves & Skeel, 1992). Yet out of the 3,838,380 possible winning combinations, both are equally likely. In the Pennsylvania Daily Number game, a number between *000* and *999* is randomly drawn every day, and the payoff is always 500 to 1—regardless of how many winners there are. It is not possible to strategically influence one's chances. Yet a study of number selections showed that ticket purchasers shy away from numbers that have won in the recent past (Halpern & Deveraux, 1989). Why?

Kahneman and Tversky (1972) find that the *representativeness heuristic* leads people to falsely assume that any sequence of events, if the result of a truly random process, should "look" random. Since a large number of coin flips will produce roughly a 50:50 split, people expect this ratio to emerge even in a small sample of flips. This assumption gives rise to the *gambler's fallacy*—the belief that random processes are self-correcting so that temporary deviations in one direction will be matched by later deviations in the opposite direction. That's why, after a string of heads, people are likely to predict that the next coin will land on its tail or why, after a long run of red numbers on the roulette wheel, people rush to bet on black numbers. The gambler's fallacy is also the reason many slot-machine addicts say that a machine is "hot" if it has not surrendered a jackpot for a long period of time.

Another problem with the way we judge probabilities stems from the *availability heuristic,* the tendency to overestimate the likelihood of dramatic, memorable events (Tversky & Kahneman, 1973). Think about it. One reason people buy lottery tickets despite the dreadfully low odds of winning is that they are so influenced by the sight of multimillion-dollar winners on TV. The same is true of casinos. The last time I visited one, I had to fight the sense that everyone was coming up a winner. All around me, people were shrieking with joy, bells and sirens were blaring, lights were flashing, and coins were jingling loudly into metal coin trays. What about all those who were losing? They were invisible, a silent majority, nowhere to be seen or heard. If I didn't know any better, I would have thought that everyone was lucky except me. Winning was "available" and easy to overestimate.

The fact that we often bet money on the basis of defective prediction strategies explains part of hte gambler's dilemma. But it doesn't explain why people persist after losing. To understand this problem, it is important to know that gamblers generate *biased explanations* for outcomes. Research shows tht people are quick to take credit for success and to explain away failure. For example, Thomas Gilovich (1983) questioned subjects one week after they had bet on a series of pro football games. He found that although they accepted winning without scrutiny, they tended to cite fluke events to explain away losses—a fumble on the goal line, an injury to a key player, or a close call by the referee—all to suggest that victory was otherwise close at hand. Can this bias inspire persistent gambling? In basketball, the shot that circles the rim and falls out may bolster the belief that a player is hot, but it may also be used to maintain the belief that another player is cold. Likewise, according to Gilovich, the gambler's ace in the hole is to recall a point in time when he or she was winning and should have quit. We have all heard those regretful last words: "I was close; I could have won if . . ." Well, maybe next time.

Dramatic airline disasters, such as the 1996 midair explosion of TWA Flight 800, are so memorable that people overestimate the risks of flying. In fact, mile for mile, travelers are far more likely to die in a car crash than on a commercial flight.

anchoring effect The tendency to use an initial value as an "anchor," or reference point, in making a new numerical estimate.

framing effect The biasing effects on decision making of the way in which a choice is worded, or "framed."

Anchoring Effects   Using the availability heuristic, people are heavily influenced in their judgments by the facts that are most available in memory—and they fail to make adjustments to compensate for that bias. A related phenomenon is the **anchoring effect,** the tendency to use one stimulus as an "anchor," or reference point, in judging a second stimulus. Imagine being asked, "What proportion of African nations are in the United Nations?" Think about it. What would be your estimate? Now suppose that before answering this question, the experimenter spun a roulette wheel marked with numbers from *1* to *100.* You think the outcome of the spin is random, but actually the wheel is rigged to stop either at *10* or at *65.* At that point, the experimenter asks, "Is the proportion of African nations in the United Nations above or below the wheel number? Then what, specifically, is your estimate?" The result of this procedure is that subjects vary their estimates according to the numerical reference point provided by the wheel number. Those for whom *10* was the initial anchor estimated that 25 percent of African nations were in the UN. Among those given *65* as an anchor, the estimate was 45 percent. Even though subjects assumed

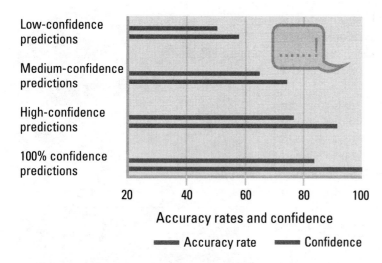

Low-confidence predictions

Medium-confidence predictions

High-confidence predictions

100% confidence predictions

Accuracy rates and confidence

▬▬ Accuracy rate ▬▬ Confidence

FIGURE 12.11 The overconfidence effect Students made 2,760 predictions about others that were later verified. Regardless of whether confidence was low, medium, high, or 100 percent, confidence levels consistently exceeded accuracy rates.

the wheel number to be arbitrary, it served as a starting point for their numerical estimates (Kahneman et al., 1982).

Additional studies have confirmed that anchoring effects are common and that numerical reference points can bias judgments of new events even when subjects are offered a prize to be accurate and even when they say afterward that they were not influenced by the anchor (Wilson et al., 1996). It's no wonder that fund-raisers typically precede their request for a donation by stating a high initial figure.

Framing Effects   Overall, research shows that human beings have some powerful reasoning tools but that the process is flawed in serious ways. This theme repeats itself as we explore a topic that bridges thought and language. In a classic series of studies, Tversky and Kahneman (1981) found that decisions are shaped by the language used to describe a dilemma. This tendency to be influenced by the way an issue is worded, or "framed," is called the **framing effect.** To test for this effect, researchers present two versions of the same problem that are worded differently but are logically equivalent. According to reason, preferences should be unaffected by wording. But that's not what happens.

In one study, a vast majority of subjects thought condoms were effective in stopping AIDS when condoms were said to have a "95 percent success rate" but not when they were presented as having a "5 percent failure rate" (Linville et al., 1992). In a second study, consumers preferred ground beef that was labeled "75 percent lean" rather than "25 percent fat" (Levin & Gaeth, 1988). Framing effects such as these seem to indicate that human judgments are not always well reasoned—which is why we often make poor decisions that we later come to regret. But with people often having to make quick judgments on the basis of very little information, psychologists disagree on the extent of the problem (Payne et al., 1992). It's also helpful to know that people can be taught in college and other educational settings to reason in more logical ways (Kosonen & Winne, 1995; Lehman & Nisbett, 1990; Nisbett et al., 1987).

There is, finally, another lesson to be drawn from framing effects. At the beginning of this chapter, we briefly considered the relationship between thought and language. In that context, framing effects suggest that thinking may be shaped by language. We'll take up this issue again, after surveying what is known about the nature of language.

Overconfidence   Sometimes our judgments are correct; sometimes they are subject to bias. Nobody's perfect. But are we sufficiently aware of our own limitations? Many years ago, Baruch Fischhoff and his colleagues (1977) had people answer hundreds of general-knowledge questions and estimate the odds that each answer was correct. Consistently, the subjects were overly confident. Other studies soon revealed the same pattern. Regardless of whether people are given factual questions ("Which river is longer, the Amazon or the Nile?") or asked to predict future world events

("Who will win the Super Bowl?"), confidence exceeds performance (Kahneman & Tversky, 1996).

In a study that illustrates this point, David Dunning and others (1990) asked students to make judgments of a more social nature—to predict how a target person would react in different situations. Some of the subjects made predictions about a fellow student whom they had just met and interviewed, and others made predictions about their roommates. In both cases, the subjects reported their confidence in each prediction, and accuracy was determined by the responses of the target persons themselves. The results were clear: Regardless of whether they judged a stranger or their own roommate, subjects consistently overestimated the accuracy of their predictions. These results are illustrated in Figure 12.11.

People even overestimate their ability to predict their own future behavior. When ninety-eight first-year students made 3,800 self-predictions about the upcoming academic year—predictions that were later verified ("Will you decide on a major?" "Will you have a steady boy/girlfriend?")—they estimated that they would be accurate 82 percent of the time but actually had an accuracy rate of only 68 percent (Vallone et al., 1990). In later chapters, we will see that, as a general rule, self-confidence is a virtue that promotes health, happiness, and success. The key is to avoid becoming so overconfident that we take foolish risks and make hasty decisions—as people often do when they place bets in the gambling casino.

13 How We Remember— Information Processing and Storage

Objectives

1. Describe the nature and function of short-term memory and how to enhance its effectiveness.

2. Define long-term memory and explain how information is stored in it.

3. Explain the four processes that can produce forgetting or memory failure and provide strategies for reducing memory failure.

Short-Term Memory

What's the limit in the amount of information that can be stored in short-term memory? Is there also a time limit? What functions are served by short-term memory, and can this memory be expanded? What is the serial-position curve and why does it occur?

I recently traveled by Amtrak to New York City. As I climbed the stairs of Penn Station onto Eighth Avenue, I was bombarded by sensations: the vibration under my feet from a train rumbling into the station; the sound of horns honking, a siren blaring, and a bus screeching to a stop; a faint aroma of freshly brewed coffee being overwhelmed by the smell of exhaust fumes; and the sight of skyscrapers, traffic lights, street vendors, cars bouncing over bumps in the road, and white steam billowing through a hole in the ground.

I'm sure more stimuli reached my sensory registers than I can write about, but most never reached consciousness and were quickly "forgotten." The key is *attention*. As noted earlier, sensations that do not capture our attention quickly tend to evaporate, while those we notice are transferred to short-term memory—a somewhat more lasting but limited storage facility. As we have seen, people are selective in their perceptions and can instantly direct their attention to stimuli that are interesting, adaptive, or important. During my visit to New York, I was so busy searching for a taxicab going uptown that I zoomed in on moving yellow objects to the exclusion of everything else.

From the sensory register, information is encoded—that is, converted into a form that can be stored in short-term memory. A stimulus may be encoded in different ways. After you read this sentence, for example, you might recall a picture of the letters and their placement on the page (visual encoding), the sounds of the words themselves (acoustic encoding), or the meaning of the sentence as a whole (semantic encoding). Research shows that people typically encode this type of information in acoustic terms. Thus, when subjects are presented a string of letters and immediately asked to recall them, they make more "sound-alike" errors than "look-alike" errors. For example, subjects misrecall an *F* as an *S* or *X*, but not as an *E* or *B* (Conrad, 1964). Subjects are also more likely to confuse words that sound alike (*man, can*) than words that are similar in meaning (*big, huge*)—further indicating that we tend to encode verbal information in acoustic terms rather than in semantic terms (Baddeley, 1966).

The information-processing model of memory regards attention as a necessary first step. In tennis and other tasks, people selectively tune in to stimuli that are adaptive, interesting, and important.

Capacity

Attention limits what information comes under the spotlight of STM at any given time. To the extent that one stimulus captures our attention, others may be ignored—sometimes with startling effects on memory. For example, research on eye-

155

witness testimony shows that when a criminal displays a weapon, witnesses are less able to identify that culprit than if no weapon is present (Steblay, 1992). Why? One reason is that the witness's eyes fixate on the weapon, thereby drawing attention away from the face. To demonstrate, Elizabeth Loftus and her colleagues (1987) showed subjects slides of a customer who walked up to a bank teller and pulled out either a gun or a checkbook. By recording eye movements, these researchers found that subjects spent more time looking at the gun than at the checkbook. The result: an impairment in their ability to identify the criminal in a lineup.

Limited by attentional resources, short-term memory can hold only a small number of items. How small a number? To appreciate the limited capacity of STM, try the *memory-span task* in Figure 13.1, or test a friend. By presenting increasingly long lists of items, researchers seek to identify the point at which subjects can no longer recall without error. In tasks like this one, the average person can store seven or so list items (usually between five and nine)—regardless of whether they are numbers, letters, words, or names. This limit is so consistent that George Miller (1956) described the human STM capacity by the phrase "the magical number seven, plus or minus two."

Once short-term memory is filled to capacity, the storage of new information requires that existing contents be discarded or "displaced." Thus, if you're trying to memorize historical dates, chemical elements, or a list of vocabulary words, you may find that the eighth or ninth item pushes out those earlier on the list. It's like the view you get on a computer screen. As you fill the screen with more and more new information, old material scrolls out of view. This limited capacity seems awfully disabling. But is it absolutely fixed, or can we overcome the magical number seven?

According to Miller, STM can accommodate only seven items, but there's a hitch: Although an item may consist of one letter or digit, these can be grouped into chunks of words, sentences, and large numbers—thus enabling us to use our storage capacity more efficiently. To see the effects of chunking on short-term memory, read the following letters, pausing at each space; then look up and name as many of the letters as you can in correct order: *CN NIB MMT VU SA*. Since this list contains twelve discrete letters, you probably found the task quite frustrating. Now try this next list, again pausing between spaces: *CNN IBM MTV USA*. Better, right? This list contains the same twelve letters. But because the letters are "repackaged" in familiar groups, you had to store only four chunks, not twelve—well within the "magical" capacity (Bower, 1970).

Chunking enables us to improve our short-term-memory span by using our capacity in a more efficient manner. You may be limited to seven or so chunks, but you can learn to increase the size of those chunks. To demonstrate, a group of researchers trained two male college students, both long-distance runners and of average intelligence, for several months. For an hour a day, three or four days a week, these students were asked to recall random strings of numbers. If they recalled a sequence correctly, another digit was added to the next sequence and the task was repeated. If they made a mis-

5	7	3									
9	0	7	6								
8	5	4	0	2							
0	9	1	3	5	6						
8	6	0	4	8	7	2					
1	7	5	4	2	4	1	9				
9	6	5	8	3	0	8	0	1			
5	7	3	5	1	2	0	2	8	5		
3	1	7	9	2	1	5	0	6	4	2	
2	1	0	1	6	7	4	1	9	8	3	5

FIGURE 13.1 **Memory-span test** Try this memory-span test. Read the top row of digits, one per second, then look away and repeat them back in order. Next, try the second row, the third row, and so on, until you make a mistake. The average person's memory span can hold seven items of information.

take, the number of digits in the next sequence was reduced by one. As shown in Figure 13.2, the improvement was astonishing. Before practicing, their memory span was the usual seven digits. After six months, they were up to eighty items (Ericsson & Chase, 1982; Ericsson et al., 1980). In one session, for example, the experimenter read the following numbers in order:

89319443492502157841668506120948888568
77273 1418610546297480129497496 59228

After two minutes of concentration, the subject repeated all seventy-three digits, in groups of three and four. How did he do it? Given no special instruction, the subject developed his own elaborate strategy: He converted the random numbers into ages ("89.3 years, a very old person"), dates (1944 was "near the end of World War II"), and cross-country racing times for various distances (3492 was "3 minutes and 49.2 seconds, nearly a world's record for the mile").

The value of chunking is evidenced by the way people retain information in their areas of expertise. Study the arrangement of pieces on the chessboard shown in Figure 13.3, and in five seconds memorize as much of it as you can. Chances are, you'll be able to reproduce approximately seven items. Yet after looking at the same arrangement for five seconds, chess masters can reproduce all the pieces and their row-and-column positions almost without error. It's not that chess masters are born with computer-like minds. When chess pieces are placed randomly on the board, they are no more proficient than the rest of us. But when the arrangement is taken from an actual game between good players, they naturally chunk the configurations of individual pieces into familiar patterns such as the "Romanian Pawn Defense" and "Casablanca Bishop's Gambit" (De Groot, 1965; Chase & Simon, 1973). Remarkably, researchers estimate that chess masters store up to 50,000 such chunks in memory (Gobet & Simon, 1996). Indeed, from years of experience, experts in all domains—including computer programmers, sports fans, waiters, bartenders, and professional actors—chunk information to boost their short-term-memory capacity (Cohen, 1989).

Duration

It has happened to me, and I'll bet it has happened to you too. You look up a telephone number, repeat it to yourself, put away the directory, and start dialing. Then you stop. You hit the first three numbers without a hitch, but then you go blank, get confused (was that a 5 or a 9?), and hang up in frustration. After just a few seconds, the phone number is gone, like it evaporated, and is no longer in memory. Then there is the matter of names. I'll be at a party or social gathering and meet someone for the first time. We'll talk for a while, then I'll turn to introduce my wife—only to realize with embarrassment that I have already forgotten the name of my new acquaintance.

These types of experiences are common because short-term memory is limited not only in the *amount* of information it can store but also in the length of *time* it can hold that information. What is the duration of short-term memory? That is, how

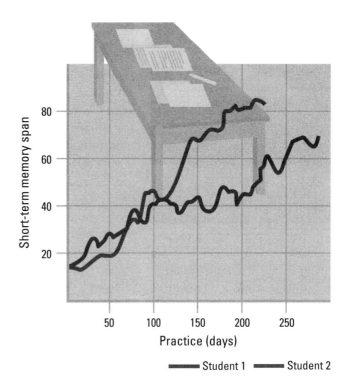

FIGURE 13.2 **Increased memory span** Two students practiced memory-span tasks for an hour a day, three to four days a week, for six months. Remarkably, their short-term memory span increased from seven digits to eighty (Ericsson & Chase 1982). One subject soon had a memory span that exceeded one hundred digits (Staszewski 1988).

FIGURE 13.3 **The value of chunking** Study this arrangement of chess pieces for five seconds. Then turn to the empty board on page 164 and try to reproduce the arrangement as best you can. Unless you are a highly experienced chess player, the number of pieces you can place in the correct squares should approximate the magical number seven.

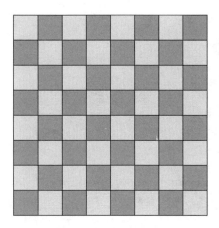

maintenance rehearsal The use of sheer repetition to keep information in short-term memory.

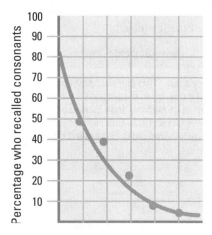

FIGURE 13.4 Duration of short-term memory What is the duration of short-term memory? When subjects are kept from rehearsing material they are trying to recall, their short-term memory vanishes within twenty seconds (Peterson & Peterson, 1959).

"Hi. I'm, I'm, I'm . . .
You'll have to forgive me,
I'm terrible with names.

long does a memory trace last if a person does not actively rehearse or repeat it? To measure how rapidly information is forgotten, Lloyd and Margaret Peterson (1959) asked subjects to recall a set of unrelated consonants such as *MJK*. So that subjects could not rehearse the material, they were given a number and instructed to count backward from that number by 3s: *564, 561, 558, 555,* and so on. After varying lengths of time, subjects were cued to recall the consonants. After eighteen seconds, performance plummeted to below 10 percent (see Figure 13.4).

Knowing the fleeting nature of short-term memory, one can prevent forgetting by repeating information silently or aloud. That's why, if I do not have a pen and paper handy, I will repeat a phone number over and over again until I have dialed it. And that's why I try to silently repeat the person's name while being introduced. Repetition extends the twenty-second duration of STM in the same way that chunking expands its seven-item capacity.

The retention benefits of sheer repetition, or **maintenance rehearsal,** were first demonstrated by Hermann Ebbinghaus (1885; reprinted in 1913), a German philosopher who was a pioneer in memory research. Using himself as a subject, Ebbinghaus created a list of all possible nonsense syllables consisting of a vowel inserted between two consonants. Syllables that formed words were then eliminated—which left a list of unfamiliar items (*RUX, VOM, QEL, MIF*), each written on a separate card. To study the effects of rehearsal, Ebbinghaus would turn over the cards, one at a time, and say each syllable aloud to the ticking rhythm of a metronome. Then, after reading the items once, he would start again and go through the cards in the same order. This procedure was repeated until he could anticipate each syllable before turning over the card. Ebbinghaus found that he could recall a list of seven syllables after a single reading (there's that magical number again) but that he needed more practice for longer lists. The more often he repeated the items, the more he could recall. Numerous other studies confirm the point: "Rehearsal" can be used to "maintain" an item in short-term memory for an indefinite period of time.

In a neighborhood park in Geneva, Switzerland, residents socialize over a giant outdoor chessboard. Do you think chess masters could recall the configurations on this giant board as they can from their perspective on a table? This question has never been put to test.

Long-Term Memory

What input is transferred from short-term memory into long-term memory? Where in the brain are these memories stored, how are they retrieved, and why are they often forgotten? Who is H.M., and why is this amnesia patient so important? Why is it said that memory is reconstructive, and what are the implications?

Do you remember your fourth birthday, the name of your first-grade teacher, or the smell of floor wax in the corridors of your elementary school? Can you describe a dream you had last night or recite the words of the national anthem? To answer these questions, you would have to retrieve information from the mental warehouse of long-term memory. Long-term memory is a relatively enduring storage system that has the capacity to retain vast amounts of information for long periods of time. This section examines long-term memories of the recent and remote past—how they are encoded, stored, retrieved, forgotten, and even reconstructed in the course of a lifetime.

Encoding

Information can be kept alive in STM by rote repetition, or maintenance rehearsal. But to transfer something into long-term memory, you would find it much more effective to use **elaborative rehearsal**—a strategy that involves thinking about the material in a more meaningful way and associating it with other knowledge that is already in long-term memory. The more deeply you process something, the more likely you are to recall it at a later time.

To demonstrate, Fergus Craik and Endel Tulving (1975) showed subjects a list of words, one at a time, and for each asked them for (1) a simple visual judgment that required no thought about the words themselves ("Is ___ printed in capital letters?"); (2) an acoustic judgment that required subjects to at least pronounce the letters as words ("Does ___ rhyme with *small?*"); or (3) a more complex semantic judgment that compelled subjects to think about the meaning of the words ("Does the word fit the sentence 'I saw a ___ in the pond'?"). Subjects did not realize that their memory would be tested later. Yet words that were processed at a "deep" level, in terms of meaning, were more easily recognized than those processed at a "shallow" level (see Figure 13.5). Deep processing can also enhance our ability to recognize faces. Lance Bloom and Samuel Mudd (1991) displayed a series of faces and asked subjects to make judgments that were superficial ("Is the face male or female?") or more complex ("Is the face honest or dishonest?"). Those who had to process the pictures at a deep level spent more time looking, made more eye movements, and were more likely to recognize the faces later.

Does making complex semantic judgments, compared to simple perceptual judgments, activate different regions of the brain? Is it possible to see the physical traces of deep processing? Using functional MRI technology, John

elaborative rehearsal A technique for transferring information into long-term memory by thinking about it in a deeper way.

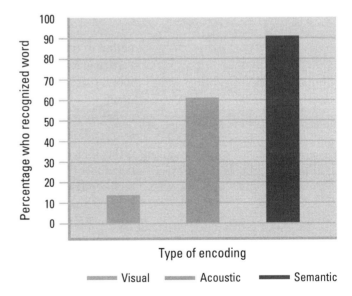

FIGURE 13.5 **Elaborative rehearsal** Subjects read a long list of words and for each one judged how it was printed (visual), how it sounded (acoustic), or what it meant (semantic). The more thought required to process the words, the easier they were to recognize later (Craik & Tulving, 1975).

Gabrieli and others (1996) devised a study similar to Craik and Tulving's in which subjects were shown stimulus words on a computer and were instructed to determine whether the words were concrete or abstract (a semantic judgment) or simply whether they were printed in uppercase or lowercase letters (a perceptual judgment). As in past research, subjects later recalled more words for which they had made semantic rather than perceptual judgments. In addition, however, the brain-imaging measures showed that processing the words in semantic terms triggered more activity in a part of the frontal cortex of the language-dominant left hemisphere.

Perhaps the most effective form of elaborative rehearsal is the linking of new information to the self. In one study, subjects sat in front of a microcomputer and looked at forty trait words (for example, *shy, friendly, ambitious*). In some cases, they were told to judge whether the words were self-descriptive; in others, they judged the words' length, sound, or meaning. When asked to list as many of the words as they could, the subjects remembered more when they had thought about the words in reference to themselves than for other purposes (Rogers et al., 1977). Apparently, the self can be used as a memory aid: By viewing new information as relevant to our own experience, we consider that information more fully and organize it around common themes. The result is an improvement in recall (Greenwald & Banaji, 1989).

Memorizing—definitions, mathematical formulas, poems, or historical dates— usually requires conscious effort. When I teach a large class, I pass out index cards on the first day and ask students to write down their names and a vivid personal detail that will help me remember who they are. Then I locate each student's photograph in the college "face book," match the face to the name, and run through the cards until I can identify each student. With tasks like this one, practice makes perfect. In 1885, Ebbinghaus read through a list of nonsense syllables 0, 8, 16, 24, 32, 42, 53, or 64 times and checked his memory for the items twenty-four hours later. As predicted, the more learning time he spent the first day, the better his memory was on the second day.

But there's more. Ebbinghaus and others found that retention is increased through "overlearning"—that is, continued rehearsal even after the material seems to have been mastered (Driskell et al., 1992; Semb et al., 1993). Researchers also discovered that long-term memory is better when the practice is spread over a long period of time than when it is crammed in all at once, a phenomenon known as the "spacing effect" (Dempster, 1988). Harry Bahrick and Lynda Hall (1991) thus found that adults retained more of their high-school math skills when they had later practiced the math in college—and when that practice was extended over semesters rather than condensed into a single year. When you think about it, this spacing effect makes adaptive sense. Names, faces, and events that recur over long intervals of time rather than in concentrated brief periods are probably, in real life, more important to remember (Anderson & Schooler, 1991).

Although the transfer of information to LTM often requires a great deal of thought and effort, certain types of information are encoded automatically and without conscious control. When I meet someone for the first time, I always have to work on recalling that person's name but I can easily and without rehearsal remember the face. It just happens. Similarly, we encode information about time, spatial locations, and event frequencies. In a study that provides evidence of this automatic processing, Lynn Hasher and Rose Zacks (1984) showed subjects a long list of words. Some subjects were warned in advance that they would be asked to recall how many times a certain word was presented. Yet others who were not similarly prepared were still just as accurate in their later estimates. Evidently, numerical frequencies are encoded without conscious effort.

🔁 Forgetting

Before we celebrate the virtues of memory and outline the techniques that we can use to improve it, let's stop for a moment and ponder the wisdom of William James (1890), who said, "If we remembered everything, we should on most occasions be as ill off as if we remembered nothing" (p. 680). James was right. Many years ago, Russian psychologist Alexander Luria (1968) described his observations of Solomon Shereshevskii, a man he called S., who had a truly exceptional memory. After one brief presentation, S. would remember lists containing dozens of items, recite them forward or backward, and still retain the information fifteen years later. But there was a drawback: No matter how hard S. tried, he could not forget. Images of letters, numbers, and other items of trivia were so distracting that he had to quit his job and support himself by entertaining audiences with his feats of memory. Sometimes it is better to forget.

The Forgetting Curve Memory failure is a common experience in everyday life (see Table 13.1). I wish I had a dollar for every time I left something I needed at home, neglected to bring up a point in conversation, or forgot the name of someone I met. To measure the rate at which information is forgotten, Ebbinghaus (1885; reprinted in 1913) tested his own memory for nonsense syllables after intervals ranging from twenty minutes to thirty-one days. As shown in the **forgetting curve** plotted in Figure 13.6, Ebbinghaus found that there was a steep loss of retention within the first hour, that he forgot more than 60 percent of the items within nine hours, and that the rate of forgetting leveled off after that. How quickly we forget.

The Ebbinghaus forgetting curve shows a rapid loss of memory for meaningless nonsense syllables. Does it apply to real-life memories as well? Bahrick (1984) tested nearly 800 English-speaking adults who took Spanish in high school. Depending on the subject, the interval between learning and being tested ranged from zero to fifty years. Compared to students who had just taken the course, those who were tested two to three years later had forgotten much of what they learned. After that, however, scores on vocabulary, grammar, and reading-comprehension tests stabilized—even among people who had not used Spanish for forty or fifty years (see Figure 13.7 on page 169). A similar pattern was also found for the retention, for up to twelve years, of material learned in a college psychology course (Conway et al., 1991). These impressive results have led Bahrick to argue that such knowledge may enter a *permastore*—a term he coined to describe permanent, very-long-term memory for well-learned material. It's interesting that although this very-long-term curve is not identical to that reported by Ebbinghaus, there are similarities. Based on a summary analysis of 210 post-Ebbinghaus studies, David Rubin and Amy Wenzel (1996) concluded that his classic forgetting curve describes a consistent and lawful pattern of human retention and forgetting.

Why Do People Forget? Knowing the rate at which information is lost is just the first step. The next important question is: Why? Do memory traces fade with time?

Naval Academy photo courtesy of United States Naval Academy Photographic Laboratory.

forgetting curve A consistent pattern in which the rate of memory loss for input is steepest right after it is received and levels off over time.

> *"Memory is the thing you forget with."*
>
> —ALEXANDER CHASE

Table 13.1 Forgetting in Everyday Life

How's your memory? Read the statements below and think about how often you've had each experience. The numbers in parentheses are the ratings given by the average person (Baddeley, 1990).

____ 1. Forgetting where you have put something; losing things around the house (5)

____ 2. Having to go back to check whether you have done something that you meant to do (4)

____ 3. Failing to recognize, by sight, close relatives or friends that you meet frequently (1)

____ 4. Telling friends a story or joke that you have told them once already (2)

____ 5. Forgetting where things are normally kept, or looking for them in the wrong place (2)

____ 6. Finding that a word is on the "tip of your tongue"; you know what it is but cannot quite find it (4)

____ 7. Forgetting important details of what you did or what happened to you the day before (1)

____ 8. Forgetting important details about yourself, such as your birthday or where you live (1)

____ 9. Completely forgetting to take things with you, or leaving things behind and having to go back and fetch them (3)

____ 10. Finding that the faces of famous people, seen on TV or in photographs, look unfamiliar (2)

Note: Subjects responded on the following scale: 1 = never in the last six months, 2 = once in six months, 4 = once a month, 5 = more than once a month, . . . 9 = more than once a day.

Are they displaced by new memories? Or do memories get buried, perhaps blocked by unconscious forces? As we'll see, forgetting can result from one of four processes: a lack of encoding, decay, interference, or repression. In the first two, the forgotten information is simply not in long-term-memory storage. In the second two, the memory may exist, but it is difficult, if not impossible, to retrieve.

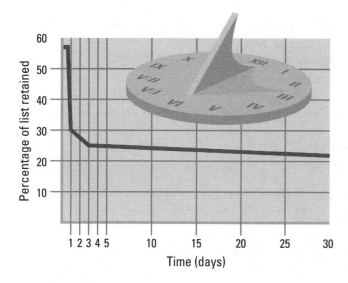

FIGURE 13.6 The Ebbinghaus forgetting curve Ebbinghaus's forgetting curve indicates the rate at which nonsense syllables were forgotten. You can see that there was a steep decline in performance within the first day and that the rate of forgetting leveled off over time.

Encoding Do you know what a penny looks like? Would you recognize one if you saw it? If you live in the United States, you have undoubtedly looked at, held, and counted thousands of copper pennies in your life. Yet many people cannot accurately draw one from memory, name its features, or distinguish between a real penny and a fake. Look at the coins in Figure 13.8. Do you know which is the real one? Raymond Nickerson and Marilyn Adams (1979) presented this task to college students and found that 58 percent did *not* identify the right coin. The reason for this result is not that the subjects forgot what a penny looks like—it's that the features were never encoded into long-term memory in the first place. And why should they be? So long as you can tell the difference between pennies and other objects, there is no need to attend to the fine details. Similarly, you may have difficulty recalling the features of a dollar bill, a telephone dial, the front-page layout of your favorite newspaper, and other common objects.

Decay The oldest theory of forgetting is that memory traces erode with the passage of time. But there are two problems with this simple explanation. One is that there is no physiological evidence of decay that corresponds to the fading of memory. The second is that time alone is not the most critical factor. As we saw earlier, memory for newly learned nonsense syllables fades in a matter of hours, but the foreign language learned in high school is retained for many years.

The key blow to the decay theory of forgetting was landed in 1924 by John Jenkins and Karl Dallenbach. Day after day, these researchers presented nonsense syllables to two subjects and then tested their memory after one, two, four, or eight hours. On some days, the subjects went to sleep between learning and testing; on other days, they stayed awake and kept busy. As shown in Figure 13.9, the subjects recalled more items after they had slept than when they were awake and involved in other activities. Jenkins and Dallenbach concluded that "forgetting is not so much a matter of the decay of old impressions and associations as it is a matter of interference, inhibition, or obliteration of the old by the new" (p. 612). To minimize forgetting, students may find it helpful to go to sleep shortly after studying, thus avoiding "new information" (Fowler et al., 1973).

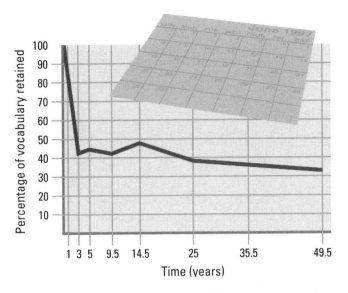

FIGURE 13.7 Long-term forgetting curve This forgetting curve indicates the rate at which adults forgot the Spanish they took in high school. Compared to new graduates, those tested two to three years later forgot much of what they learned. After that, however, test scores stabilized (Bahrick, 1984).

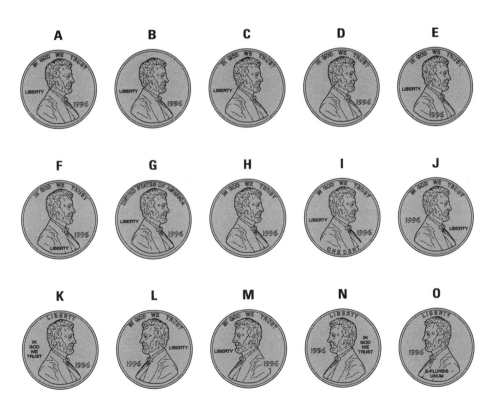

FIGURE 13.8 Can you recognize a penny? Which of these pennies is the real thing? The answer appears on page 164 (Nickerson & Adams, 1979).

Chapter 13 *How We Remember—Information Processing and Storage* 163

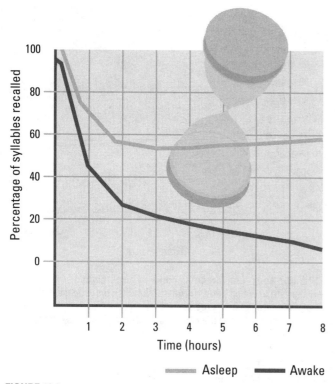

FIGURE 13.9

Using sleep to minimize forgetting Subjects who studied nonsense syllables recalled more items after one, two, four, or eight hours when they slept than when they stayed awake between the learning and test sessions. This result suggests that forgetting is caused by retroactive interference, not by the mere passage of time (Jenkins & Dallenbach, 1924).

Interference By showing that memory loss may be caused by mental activity that takes place when we are awake, Jenkins and Dallenbach's study suggested a third explanation of forgetting—that something learned may be forgotten due to interference from other information. As summarized in Figure 13.10, there are two kinds of interference. In **proactive interference,** prior information inhibits one's ability to recall something new. If you try to learn a set of names, formulas, phone numbers, or vocabulary words, you will find it more difficult if you had earlier studied a similar set of items. Many years ago, Benton Underwood (1957) found that the more nonsense-syllable experiments subjects had taken part in, the more forgetting they exhibited in a brand-new study. A related problem is **retroactive interference,** whereby new material disrupts memory for previously learned information. Thus, subjects in various experiments were at least temporarily less likely to recognize previously seen pictures of nature scenes, faces, and common objects if they were then exposed to similar photographs before being tested (Chandler, 1991; Wheeler, 1995; Windschitl, 1996). Clearly, one learning experience can displace—or at least inhibit—the retrieval of another.

Repression In 1990, a young woman jogging in New York City's Central Park was raped, beaten unconscious, and left for dead by a gang of teenagers. After many months of recovery, the victim said she remembered running that day but could not recall anything about the attack itself. Her amnesia for the event may well have been caused by head injuries she had sustained—or it may have been due to repression, a form of motivated forgetting.

proactive interference The tendency for previously learned material to disrupt the recall of new information.

retroactive interference The tendency for new information to disrupt the memory of previously learned material.

		Time 1	Time 2	Retrieval
Proactive interference		**A disrupts B**		
Experimental		Study A	Study B	Test B
Control			Study B	Test B
Retroactive interference		**B disrupts A**		
Experimental		Study A	Study B	Test A
Control		Study A		Test A

FIGURE 13.10

Interference and forgetting As shown, proactive interference occurs when information acquired at Time 1 inhibits memory for material learned later. Retroactive interference occurs when information learned at Time 2 inhibits memory for material learned earlier. The more similar the two sets of items are, the greater is the interference.

The correctly drawn penny is shown in (A).

Many years ago, Sigmund Freud, the founder of psychoanalysis, observed that his patients often could not recall unpleasant past events in their own lives. In fact, they would sometimes stop, pull back, and lose their train of thought just as they seemed on the brink of an insight. Freud called this repression, and he said it was an unconscious defense mechanism that keeps painful personal memories under lock and key—and out of awareness. We'll see that people who suffer through childhood traumas such as war, abuse, and rape sometimes develop "dissociative disorders" characterized by large gaps in their explicit memory. Although repression is not easily demonstrated in the laboratory, clinical case studies suggest that repressed memories can be recovered in psychotherapy. As we'll see later in this chapter, it can be difficult in cases such as these to distinguish between dormant memories of actual past events and falsely constructed memories of experiences that never occurred (Loftus, 1993a).

Ways to Prevent Forgetting   Before taking office, President Clinton invited 500 business leaders to an economic summit in Little Rock. When it was over, many of the guests marveled at Clinton's ability to address them all by name. I have always been impressed by stories like this one—by stories of stage actors who memorize hundreds of lines in a week of rehearsal, of people who fluently speak five languages, and of waiters who take large dinner orders without a note pad. How can these accomplishments be explained?

Over the years, psychologists have stumbled upon a few rare individuals who seemed equipped with extraordinary "hardware" for memory. But often the actors, waiters, multilinguists, and others we encounter use memory tricks called **mnemonics**—in other words, they vary their memory's "software." Can you boost your recall capacity through the use of mnemonics? Can you improve your study skills as a result? At this point, let's step back, consider the educational implications, and draw concrete advice from this chapter.

Practice Time   To learn names, dates, vocabulary words, formulas, or the concepts in a textbook, you'll find that practice makes perfect. In general, the more time spent studying, the better. Skimming or speedreading will not promote long-term retention. In fact, it pays to *over*learn—that is, to review the material even after you think you have it mastered. It also helps to distribute your studying over time rather than cram all at once. You will retain more information from four two-hour sessions than from one eight-hour marathon.

Depth of Processing   The sheer amount of practice time is important, but only if it's "quality time." Mindless drills may help maintain information in short-term memory, but, as noted in our discussion of elaborative rehearsal, long-term retention requires that you think actively and deeply about material—about what it means and how it is linked to what you already know. There are many ways to increase your depth of processing. Ask yourself critical questions about the material. Think about it in ways that relate to your own experiences. Talk about the material to a friend, thus forcing yourself to organize it in terms that can be understood.

Hierarchical Organization   When you have information to be learned, organize it hierarchically—as in an outline. Start with a few broad categories, then divide them into subcategories and subsubcategories. This is how many experts chunk new information, and it works. When Andrea Halpern (1986) presented subjects with fifty-four popular song titles, she found that recall was greater when the titles were

mnemonics Memory aids designed to facilitate the recall of new information.

"As I get older, I find I rely more and more on these sticky notes to remind me."

organized hierarchically than when they were scrambled. The implication for studying is clear: Organize the material in your notes, preferably in the form of an outline—and be sure to review these notes later (Kiewra et al., 1991).

Verbal Mnemonics   Sometimes the easiest way to remember a list of items is to use verbal mnemonics, or "memory tricks." Chances are that you have already used popular methods such as *rhymes* ("*I* before *E* except after *C*" is my favorite; "Thirty days hath September, April, June, and November" is another) and *acronyms* that reduce the amount of information to be stored (for example, *ROY G BIV* can be used to recall the colors of the light spectrum: *Red, Orange, Yellow, Green, Blue, Indigo,* and *Violet*). Relying on verbal mnemonics, advertisers create slogans, such as those shown in Table 13.2, to make their products memorable. How many of the slogans can you correctly match to the advertised products?

Method of Loci   Virtually all books on how to improve memory recommend that verbal information be represented as visual images, and research shows that this advice is well founded. One popular use of imagery is the method of loci, in which items to be recalled are mentally placed in familiar locations. This method is easy to use. First you memorize a series of objects along a familiar route. For example, you might imagine your morning walk from the bedroom, to the bathroom, to the kitchen, and out the door. As you follow this path, visualize some of the objects you pass: your bed, then the bathroom door, shower, stairs, kitchen counter, and so on. These places become pigeonholes for items to be recalled. To memorize a shopping list, for example, you could picture a dozen eggs splattered on the bed, a bag of red apples hanging on the bathroom door, and butter in the soap dish of the shower. When you take a mental stroll through the house, the items on this list should pop to mind. The trick is to link new items to others already in memory.

Peg-Word Method   Another powerful imagery mnemonic is the peg-word method, in which a list of words serves as memory "pegs" for the material to be recalled. The first step is to learn a list of peg words that correspond to numbers. An example you may have heard of is this: "one is a bun, two is a shoe, three is a tree," and so on. Next you hang each item to be recalled on each of the pegs by forming a mental image of the two interacting. As illustrated in Table 13.3, the images of an egg being laid on a hamburger bun, a shoe stuffed with apples, and trees made from sticks of butter are easier to recall than words on a page. The more bizarre and inter-

Table 13.2 Advertising Slogans		
MATCH **SLOGAN TO**		**ADVERTISED PRODUCT**
___ 1.	Like a good neighbor	(a) General Electric
___ 2.	Be all that you can be	(b) State Farm
___ 3.	You deserve a break today	(c) Busch Beer
___ 4.	Head for the mountains	(d) Allstate
___ 5.	We bring good things to life	(e) McDonald's
___ 6.	You've got the right one, baby	(f) Diet Pepsi
___ 7.	You're in good hands	(g) U.S. Army

Answers: 1(b), 2(g), 3(e), 4(c), 5(a), 6(f), 7(d)

Table 13.3 The Peg-Word Mnemonic

STEP 1 MEMORIZE THESE PEG WORDS IN ORDER.	STEP 2 HANG NEW ITEMS ON THE PEG WORDS.	STEP 3 FORM A BIZARRE, INTERACTIVE IMAGE.
One is a bun	Bun—egg	
Two is a shoe	Shoe—apple	
Three is a tree	Tree—butter	
Four is a door	Door—cola	
Five is a hive	Hive—pasta	
Six is sticks	Sticks—tuna	
Seven is heaven	Heaven—steak	
Eight is a gate	Gate—sugar	
Nine is wine	Wine—chips	
Ten is a hen	Hen—lettuce	

active the image, the better. Try it and you'll see how easily it works. Most people are able to memorize ten new items in order with the peg-word mnemonic.

Interference   Because one learning experience can disrupt memory for another, it is wise to guard against the effects of interference. This problem is particularly common among students, as material learned in one course can make it harder to retain that learned in another. To minimize the problem, follow two simple suggestions. First, study right before sleeping and review all the material right before the exam. Second, allocate an uninterrupted chunk of time to one course, then do the same for the others. If you study psychology for a while, then move to biology, then go on to math and back to psychology, each course will disrupt your memory of the others—especially if the material is similar.

Context Reinstatement   Information is easier to recall when people are in the physical setting in which it was acquired—and in the same frame of mind. The setting and the mood it evokes can serve as cues that trigger the retrieval of the to-be-remembered information. That's why actors like to rehearse on the stage where they will later perform. So the next time you have an important exam to take, it may help to study in the room where the test will be administered.

14 *Setting and Attaining Goals*

Objectives

1. Describe the research-validated approaches to managing time and reducing procrastination.

2. Explain the results of your time-management self-assessment and present a plan for increasing your time management effectiveness.

3. Explain the importance of time management to your success as a naval officer.

Time Management

*Ordinary people think merely how they will spend their time;
a person of intellect tries to use it.*

—ARTHUR SCHOPENHAUER

Doing more things is no substitute for doing the right things.

—ANONYMOUS

Case Study in Time Management

Alarms, Demands, Warning Signs, and CNN

Mornings would be great if weren't for alarms, Rory thought, reaching up and tapping the snooze alarm for ten more minutes of rack time, but already the old worries were invading the brain. I've really dug myself a deep hole to crawl out of this semester. How did I get in this position? I'm in trouble with my housemates, classes look terrible, people at work aren't even excited to see me come in, and I need to start looking for a permanent job when (or if) I graduate next semester.

Rory rationalized: Okay, so my roommates don't get it. I never cleaned up after myself and really don't plan on doing it. Somebody else can put my dirty dishes in the dishwasher and as long as I can find a clean towel, who really cares? I can't believe some of my housemates are such neat-niks they don't want to have friends over just because the place looks like a pit. They need to lighten up!

Now classes—unfortunately this was to have been a no-brainer semester, Rory thought. Only one science course scheduled, meaning only one lab and some extra time that hadn't been available in past semesters, but where did it go? Rory studied once in a while, but surely you didn't have to read all those assignments. And some of the professors were sticklers on attending class.

Maybe I would be doing better in my classes if I had gone to more classes, Rory reflected, but a couple of them cut into some prime television time, and who wants to miss *The Young and the Restless*? And the assignments. In past semesters professors could be persuaded to lower the grade only one letter for turning assignments in late. This semester a couple of profs were unreasonable: It was in on time or forget it. Zeros really sink your grade fast and literally hammer your GPA!

Then there was work. The first year Rory used a work-study grant to work for a department on campus about ten hours a week. The next year, work-study didn't come through, so the department paid a straight hourly salary. The money was okay and the work wasn't too hard. Then one of the secretaries quit and the department was slow about hiring somebody. Because of budget cuts they didn't replace the secretary and asked Rory to work more hours—which led to working some nights and weekends trying to keep up. Rory kept hearing Mom's constant question: "Rory, are you an employee or are you a student?" Maybe a different job was the answer; some people at the department were beginning to get upset because Rory refused to continue to work so many hours.

Even worse than all this was the thought of looking for a position to begin after graduation. Maybe Rory just didn't want to admit that the GPA was going to be a stumbling block to even applying for some of the positions at the Placement Office on campus and showing those recruiters the old "Rory-fied" enthusiasm and drive. Their loss, right? Two close friends had already been through senior check and had started interviewing. One had a second interview already. Yeah, but Jamie's borderline retentive, Rory thought. I'll get over there eventually. But Rory was nagged by the memory of the poster in the Placement Office that said: "Coming to see us after you graduate is like studying after finals." Okay, I'll get there before I graduate, Rory promised, but not today.

The snooze buzzer sounded again and Rory finally decided to get up, feeling more tired than the night before. In the harsh light of the bathroom, Rory looked in the mirror. Wow, what a mess. Rory went through the morning routine: Brush the teeth, stumble out to the kitchenette, grab some cereal from the cupboard. There were no clean bowls to be found, so Rory retrieved one from the living room, rinsed it out, and filled it with cereal and milk.

Wandering into the living room, Rory turned on the television to CNN and soon became engrossed in some interesting news sequences they were running. When Rory looked at the clock again, the bad news sunk in: I just missed my science lecture. Oh well, I can get the notes from somebody. Sometimes life is just overwhelming, Rory mused, settling in to watch a morning of television.

Introduction to Theories of Time Management

We have tried to capture time on calendars, measure it by the clock, extend it by daylight savings time, speed it up, and slow it down. But the simple key to good time management is to work smarter, not harder, in every phase of your life. Determine what is important in your life through visioning, writing goal statements, and taking action steps that will focus in on the goals.

There are three possible approaches to time management. First, you can increase the amount of your available time. This approach means you must stretch the hours of each day as much as possible, a strategy that could result in fatigue, lack of efficiency, and sometimes depression. A second approach is to do more work in the available time. This approach assumes that if you can pack more work into your day, everything will work out great. Likely results, however, include high stress and burnout. The third strategy is to do only the important work in the available time. This approach suggests that a scale of priority be assigned to the use of your time. It also reflects a commitment toward only essential matters. This approach necessitates an action-oriented strategy, and is clearly the best way to manage your time.

Each of us has a clear sense of the importance of various demands on our time. What is important for one person may not be as important for another. But the first rule of effective time management is for you to decide where your priorities lie. If you could save five hours per week or month, how would you use the time? What important activities and tasks would you wish to accomplish? Assigning your own value to tasks and actually completing them will allow you to feel less stressed and more satisfied that you have done something worthwhile.

Researchers into time management identify ten keys to managing time that will give you more focus, less stress, and more control of the important things in your life:

1. Run a time log to help you pinpoint and eliminate one time-consumer each month.
2. Identify priorities each day.
3. Set realistic goals.
4. Use some system for planning.
5. Establish deadlines for yourself.
6. Delegate, when feasible.
7. Plan meetings carefully.
8. Develop procedures for gathering data.
9. Group similar work tasks during uninterrupted time blocks.
10. Schedule some personal time each day.

Let's look at each of these strategies individually. All of them may not work for you, but practicing even one or two can make a significant difference in the way you manage time—and can prevent time from managing you.

1. Run a Time Log

A time log identifies your current use of time to help you discover where you are spending time, both wisely and unwisely, so you can become more effective in completing tasks. A time log is the foundation for building sound time management habits. You cannot begin to improve the ways you budget time until you know where you currently spend it.

Your time log should record all activities you perform, including sharpening pencils, chatting with friends or classmates, studying, using the telephone, etc. To keep a useful time log, you need to make notes as you go through the day. Do not allow more than 15 minutes to pass before adding to your time log record. It is amazing how many things we do, many of them so unconsciously that we forget about them literally moments after we have completed them.

No one needs to see your time log except you, so it can take any form you wish. A basic time log has two columns, one to list the times of the day and another for descriptions of the activities you engage in at those times. It's best to keep a time log for five days in a row, to give you a feel for your habit patterns.

After five days, trace your habit patterns to find your most obvious time-consumers. Make a concentrated effort to eliminate or modify your top three major time-consumers. Don't try to deal with all negative patterns at once. After you feel you have effectively improved your time management skills for your top three concerns, focus on the next group of three time-consumers and try to eliminate them, and so on.

Even though keeping a time log may appear to be time-consuming in itself, you must be willing to give it the effort it deserves and complete it honestly. Time spent at this point is time saved later.

Naval Academy photo courtesy of United States Naval Academy Photographic Laboratory.

2. Identify Priorities Each Day

We all use different criteria to establish priorities for tasks we must accomplish each day. Some of these criteria are:

- personal feelings toward the project or individuals with whom we must work to complete it;
- our degree of interest in the task and our sense of how much fun it will be;
- its importance for us and others it may affect; and
- our sense of the task's urgency in relation to ourselves or to others.

Bliss (1991) prefers to set priorities in terms of importance. You must examine each item on your list of things to do in light of the question. "Does this task clearly contribute to the achievement of my lifetime goals or my short-range objectives?" If it does, put a star by it. Continue until you reach the end of your To Do list. Then number the starred items in the order in which you would like to do them. After you have ranked your starred items by priorities, do the same thing with your less important items. You now have a game plan.

Lakein (1973) says, "No list is complete until it shows priorities. Whenever you make a list, finish the list by setting priorities." Lakein suggests using the ABC priority system. Write a capital letter A to the left of those items on the list that have a high value; a B for those items on the list that have a medium value; and C for those with low value. By comparing the items to one another, you will come up with the

ABC priority choices for every entry on your list. You will get the most out of your time by doing the A's first, and saving the B's and C's for later. You can break down your A's, B's, and C's further so that they become A1, A2, A3, B1, B2, C1, etc.

3. Set Goals

One common thread running through all self-help literature is the idea of the power of goals. We've been told to set long-term goals, short-term goals, daily goals, monthly goals, personal goals, organizational goals, ten-year goals, and lifetime goals. Covey (1994) says "goal-setting is obviously a powerful process. It's based on the same principle of focus that allows us to concentrate rays of diffused sunlight into a force powerful enough to start a fire. It's the manifestation of creative imagination and independent will. It's the transformation of vision into achievable, actionable doing. It's the common denominator of successful individuals and organizations."

When writing your goals be sure that they are realistic, specific, comprehensive, and understandable.

4. Use a System for Planning

Each individual has a system for planning that works for her or him. A plan is an orderly means to establish effective control over your own future. A good plan is logical, comprehensive, flexible, action-oriented, future-driven, formal, and people-focused. According to McGee-Cooper (1993), "One important element in sticking with the plan is to stay refreshed with daily fun and renewal. When you are joy-starved, you become unmanageable. When you stay balanced with ample fun, exercise, and relaxation, you look forward to your daily planning."

The 10/10 Rule is a simple one to follow: If you spend 10 minutes per day planning you will become 10 percent more effective in your life.

5. Establish Deadlines

Remember Parkinson's Law: "Work expands to fill the time available for its completion." You can greatly increase your effectiveness if you simply give yourself a deadline for each task and do your best to stick to it. Bliss (1991) indicates that most people work better under pressure, and a self-imposed deadline can provide the pressure you need to keep at your task until it is completed.

Until you set a deadline for a project, it isn't really an action program; it is more like a vague wish, something you intend to do someday. The problem, however, is that someday is not a day of the week. It will never arrive and the task will never get done.

6. Delegate

To delegate is to appoint someone else to act on your behalf. In other words, delegation means asking someone else to do something that falls within your area of responsibility. There are many advantages to delegating: spreading the workload, taking advantage of someone else's expertise, building the capabilities and responsibilities of the other person, motivating the other person, and freeing yourself for other important tasks.

Remember, however, that delegation has some associated risks, as well, many of which revolve around the capability and commitment levels of the persons to whom

Two F/A-18 Hornets of VMFA-323 prepare for launch aboard USS Constellation (CV 64).

Official U.S. Navy photo.

we delegate. Key questions delegators need to ask are: Does this person have the ability to learn the skills needed to complete the task? Does this person have the commitment to be propelled through to task completion?

Delegating to someone who is not capable or who does not share the delegator's commitment level can lead to unmet expectations on the part of one or both. When we delegate, we are asking someone to do something on our behalf; a lackluster performance, therefore, can have a negative effect on others' perceptions of the delegator. The key to delegation, then, is to be objective about the talents and shortcomings of others and to use that knowledge to delegate wisely.

7. Plan Meetings Carefully

For meetings to be effective, an agenda must be developed and shared before the meeting so participants can be prepared. The meeting needs to always start and end on time; everyone attending the meeting should participate in the problem-solving and decision-making processes; and there needs to be a follow-up of action taken.

Bliss (1991) gives us insight into meetings as we plan before, during, and after. The most important part of a meeting happens before it even starts—the preliminary planning that too often is done haphazardly or not at all. Before scheduling a meeting, ask yourself if a meeting is really needed. If the answer is yes, plan the meeting carefully and prepare a clear agenda. Start the meeting on time, stay on track (according to the agenda you have made), and summarize. After the meeting, record what was decided, what assignments were made, and the deadlines for action.

8. Develop Procedures for Gathering Data

Because so many resources (books, people, magazines, professional associations, seminars, computers, etc.) are available to us, we can easily become confused about what information is really necessary to help us carry out our important tasks. Each one of us has a method we rely on to gather data. Good time management demands that we become aware of our personal information gathering process and evaluate it critically so we can increase the effectiveness of our daily lives.

There are a number of systematic approaches to help you gather data and manage. Examples of these systems include Day-Timer, the Franklin Planner, and Day Runner.

9. Group Similar Tasks during Uninterrupted Time Blocks

You can't eliminate interruptions. Still, you can minimize the number of interruptions you have to deal with. Indeed, you must keep interruptions to a minimum if you wish to operate effectively, because one hour of concentrated effort is worth more than two hours of interrupted segments.

Start by identifying your most productive times during your day. This is the time when you need to do your most important tasks, your highest priorities on your To Do list, those things that you must do. Next, find an area where you can work without interruption and stick to the most important tasks you have to complete at this moment. You can implement this plan for studying, researching, being alone, making telephone calls, or being with friends.

10. Schedule Personal Time Each Day

"Most timelocked schedules need loosening, not tightening. What conventional time management too often does is make us more clock-conscious than ever, more wedded to the notion that our schedules can be sub-divided and re-organized" (Keyes, 1991). Such techniques seldom invite us to reflect, to question the categories themselves, and to remain flexible enough to move as the future demands. We need to set aside one hour each day for ourselves. This gives time for relaxing, meditating, creating, and restoring the energy so vital to our future.

Conclusion

We all know people who seem to get more "life out of their time." These people are wise time managers who have learned to use the skills of prioritizing, goal setting, planning, setting and adhering to timelines, effectively delegating, and scheduling personal time. Through practice, these skills can become part of our daily lives. We, too, can share the quality and quantity of life that wise time managers enjoy.

Time management at its best

Discover Your Time Management I.Q.

▣ Purpose

To help you discover how bright you are when it comes to managing your time.

▣ Activity

Read the following statements and respond to each with often, sometimes, or rarely.

1. I hold planning sessions with myself every day to draft the next day's To Do lists.	Often	~~Sometimes~~	Rarely
2. I tackle the biggest, most important tasks first.	~~Often~~	Sometimes	Rarely
3. I regularly finish all the things on my daily To Do list.	~~Often~~	Sometimes	Rarely
4. I meet deadlines with plenty of time to spare.	~~Often~~	Sometimes	Rarely
5. My room and desk are well organized.	Often	~~Sometimes~~	Rarely
6. I can quickly and easily find items that I put away long ago.	Often	~~Sometimes~~	Rarely
7. I know when and how to cut short unexpected interruptions, such as drop-in visitors.	~~Often~~	Sometimes	Rarely
8. Following interruptions, I am able to resume my work right away.	~~Often~~	Sometimes	Rarely
9. I am able to delegate tasks with ease.	~~Often~~	Sometimes	Rarely
10. I regularly critique my time management techniques.	~~Often~~	Sometimes	Rarely

▣ How to Arrive at Your Time Management I.Q.

Score your answers as follows:

3 points for "often"

2 points for "sometimes"

1 point for "rarely"

Add your total points = ___

28–30	You're doing a great job.
25–27	Keep up the good work, but apply your timesaving techniques more consistently.
19–24	There's room for improvement. Start by analyzing weaknesses in your technique and work to eliminate them one by one.
16–18	Discipline yourself to avoid overcommitment.
Below 16	Get back to basics. Organize yourself and learn to plan ahead.

15

Mid-Term Exam

16 Beating Fatigue— Understanding Sleep and Sleep Deprivation

Objectives

1. Describe the sleep-wake cycle and the stages of sleep.

2. Describe the relationship among the sleep-wake cycle, disruptions to that cycle and health.

3. Describe the implications of sleep deprivation in operational environments,

4. Explain why being able to assess the effects of sleep deprivation on both your own level of performance and that of your troops can lead to better performance and lower the risk of accidents.

The Sleep-Wake Cycle

Many birds migrate south for the winter. Bears and raccoons hibernate. Certain plants open their leaves during the day and close them at night—even if kept in a dark closet. As biological organisms, humans are also sensitive to seasonal changes, the twenty-eight-day lunar cycle, the twenty-four-hour day, and the ninety-minute activity-rest cycle that is linked to variations in alertness and daydreaming. These and other regular fluctuations are forms of **biological rhythms** (Aschoff, 1981).

From a psychological standpoint, there is one particularly important internal clock: Every twenty-four hours, we undergo a single sleep-wake cycle. This cycle and others that take roughly a day to complete are referred to as a **circadian rhythm.** Humans tend to be most active and alert during the middle of the day, when body temperature peaks, and least active and alert at night, when body temperature drops to its low point. The circadian rhythm is also evident in fluctuations in blood pressure, pulse rate, blood-sugar level, potassium level, growth-hormone secretions, cell growth, and other physiological functions.

Everyone is influenced by circadian rhythms, but everyone's inner clock is set somewhat differently. Think about yourself. Are you a morning person or a night person, a lark or an owl? If you had a choice, would you rather wake up at 6, 8, or 10 o'clock in the morning? How easy is it for you to work late into the night? During what time of day are you most productive? These kinds of questions can be used to determine your circadian rhythm (Smith et al., 1989). Although research shows that morning types fall asleep eighty-eight minutes earlier at night and awaken seventy-two minutes earlier in the morning (Kerkhof, 1985), very few people are extreme in their preference. Most fall somewhere in the middle and adapt as needed to the schedules they must keep. Still, it helps to know when you're likely to be at your best. When subjects were tested for memory at 9 AM, 2 PM, and 8 PM, the larks performed worse as the day wore on, while the owls performed better (Anderson et al., 1991). In a study of college students, larks were more likely than owls to take early morning classes—and they earned higher grades in those classes (Guthrie et al., 1995).

Is the circadian rhythm endogenous (set by an inner clock), or is the human body responsive to outside patterns of lightness and darkness? Ask Stefania Follini, an Italian interior designer. In January 1989, she descended into a Plexiglas bunker buried in a cave in New Mexico. Sealed off from sunlight, outside noises, changes in temperature, schedules, and clocks, she lived alone in this underground home for 131 days—a "free-running" period of time that allowed her body to establish its own rhythm. Her only link to the world was a personal computer. When Follini emerged from her isolation in May, she thought it was only March. Her "day" had extended to twenty-five hours, then to forty-eight. As time went on, she slept and woke up later and later. She stopped menstruating, ate fewer meals, and lost seventeen pounds.

Other volunteers have similarly been isolated for extended periods of time. Some naturally settled into a "short" day, but most free-ran on a longer cycle that averaged

biological rhythm Any periodic, more or less regular, fluctuation in a biological organism.

circadian rhythm A biological cycle, such as sleeping and waking, that occurs approximately every twenty-four hours.

"Larks see owls as lazy; owls see larks as party poopers."

—RICHARD M. COLEMAN

twenty-five hours. With each successive cycle, these subjects tended to go to sleep a little later and to wake up a little later (see Figure 16.1). Body temperature and hormone levels tended to follow the same rhythm. Like Follini, these subjects drifted toward a longer day—and then underestimated the amount of time they had been isolated. When reexposed to sunlight, the subjects readjusted their biological clocks.

So where is this timing device? Animal experiments have shown that the circadian rhythm is controlled in the brain by a cluster of neurons in the suprachiasmatic nucleus (SCN) of the hypothalamus. How does the SCN function? Light passing through the eye is converted to neural signals and sent to the cortex through the optic nerve. Apparently, some of these optic nerve axons—and the information they convey about light—are diverted to the SCN (Ginty et al., 1993; Ralph et al., 1990). Nestled in the center of the brain, the pea-shape pineal gland also plays an important role. As darkness falls, the pineal gland produces melatonin—a hormone that facilitates sleep. When light strikes the retina, melatonin secretion is slowed down. Spurred by a rash of books with titles like *The Melatonin Miracle* and *Melatonin: Nature's Sleeping Pill*, melatonin has been in the news a lot lately. As we'll see later, it is currently being used to treat people who suffer from chronic insomnia.

The circadian rhythm is synchronized like a fine watch by interactions between environmental cues and the brain. But what happens when one's rhythm is disrupted?

Stefani Follini emerges into daylight after 131 days in an underground Plexiglas bunker in New Mexico.

One common source of disruption is air travel—specifically, flying across time zones, which throws your body out of sync with the new time of day and causes you to sleep at the wrong time. If you've ever flown from one coast to the other or overseas, then you may have suffered jet lag, a condition that makes you feel tired, sluggish, and grumpy. Most people find it easier to fly west, which lengthens the day, than to fly east, which shortens it. Because the body naturally drifts to a longer day, this makes sense. Flying westward goes "with the flow" rather than against it. Consistent with this analysis, research shows that long-distance travel within a time zone does not cause jet lag (Coleman, 1986).

In recent years, researchers have tested various strategies that long-distance travelers can use to combat jet lag (Czeisler et al., 1989). In *How to Beat Jet Lag,* Dan Oren and others (1995) offer a number of behavioral tips for the weary long-distance traveler (the book comes plastic-wrapped with an eye mask and dark glasses). Always get a full night's sleep before a long trip. Anticipate your new time zone. Drink lots of liquids to avoid dehydration, but avoid alcohol, which disrupts later sleep. If you plan to travel east—say, from Los Angeles to New York—you can facilitate the adjustment process by sleeping earlier than normal before you leave so that you more closely "fit" the light-dark cycle of the new time zone. As soon as you board the plane, set your watch to your destination's time zone and eat and sleep accordingly. Based on studies indicating that bright-light exposure at night speeds the resetting of the inner clock, researchers also advise that, upon arrival, you spend the first day outdoors.

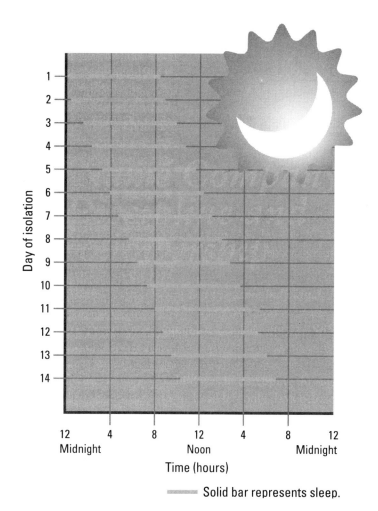

FIGURE 16.1 **The inner clock** When people are placed in a "free-running" environment, isolated from all day and night cues, they typically drift toward a twenty-five-hour day. With each cycle, subjects sleep and wake up a little later.

Night Work, Sleeping, and Health

We humans are diurnal creatures—active during the day and asleep at night. Thus, we like to work from 9 to 5 and then play, sleep, and awaken to the light of a new day. Yet an estimated 25 percent of all Americans—including emergency-room doctors and nurses, police officers, telephone operators, security guards, factory workers, and truckers—are often forced to work late-night shifts. The question is, What is the effect? Do people adapt over time to shift work and other late-night activity, or does it compromise their health and safety?

Both biological and social clocks set the body for activity during the daytime and sleep at night, so it's no surprise that many shift workers struggle to stay alert. People who choose night work fare better than those assigned on a rotating-shift basis (Barton, 1994). Still, shift workers in general get fewer hours of sleep per week than day workers, complain that their sleep is disrupted, and report being drowsy on the job. Often they blame their lack of sleep on ringing phones, crying babies, honking horns, and other daytime noises. But part of the problem too is that the body's internal alarm clock tries to awaken the day sleeper. Either way, the adverse effects can be seen at work, where night-time energy levels are low, reaction times are slow, and productivity is diminished. In a survey of 1,000 locomotive engineers, 59 percent admitted to having dozed off at the controls on several night trips (Akerstedt, 1988). About 75 percent of other workers as well complain of sleepiness during the night shift (Leger, 1994).

As measured by the amount of time it takes to fall asleep, research shows that people are the sleepiest between 1 and 4 A.M.—and then again, twelve hours later, between 1 and 4 P.M. If you find yourself getting drowsy in midafternoon, you're not alone. This circadian low point—not daytime heat or a full lunch—may be the reason why people in many countries take a siesta, or afternoon nap.

Can anything be done to lessen the dangers posed by shift work? Richard Coleman (1986) recommends that when rotating shifts are necessary, employers should maximize the number of days between shift *changes* (adjustment is easier in three-week cycles than in one-week cycles) and assign workers to successively later shifts rather than earlier shifts (a person who is rotated from the 4 PM shift to the midnight shift will adjust more quickly than one who is rotated in the opposite direction). In addition, it seems to take two days of rest, not one, for workers to fully recover from their nocturnal routine (Totterdell et al., 1995). Charles Czeisler and his colleagues (1990) have found that the realignment of the circadian rhythm can also be speeded up by exposing shift workers to bright levels of light in the workplace and to eight hours of total darkness at home during the day. Within a week, the body's biological clock can be reset and the health risks of night work reduced. It takes only four hours of bright-light exposure one night to improve performance the next night (Thessing et al., 1994).

microsleep A brief episode of sleep that occurs in the midst of a wakeful activity.

The National Highway Transportation Safety Administration estimates that up to 200,000 traffic accidents a year are sleep related—and that 20 percent of all drivers have dozed off at least once while behind the wheel. To avoid rush-hour traffic, interstate truckers often drive late at night. As shown in Figure 16.2, however, drivers are five to ten times more likely to have an accident late at night than during the daytime hours (Mitler et al., 1988). Indeed, monitoring of their EEG activity levels showed that those who drove in the middle of the night often took quick, two- to three-second **microsleeps,** which increases the risk of accident (Kecklund & Akerstedt, 1993). There are times when a person just can't avoid the situation. Often when I'm out of town and have to return for an early-morning class, I'll find myself driving late at night and fighting to keep my eyes open. I've also had the jolting—and scary—experience of realizing that I'm nodding off and drifting off the road. Is there any way to counteract this tendency?

James Horne and L. Reyner (1996) recently evaluated the possible benefits of two coping strategies: a brief nap and a cup of coffee. Ten subjects, tested in the afternoon, were restricted to five hours of sleep the nights before the study and then placed into a simulated car. On the windshield was an interactive computer-generated screen that projected a four-lane highway, with a shoulder to the side and two audible "rumble strips" between lanes. The route itself was monotonous, but subjects had to steer along gentle curves and occasionally pass a slow-

"Damn! I keep waking up in the middle of the day."

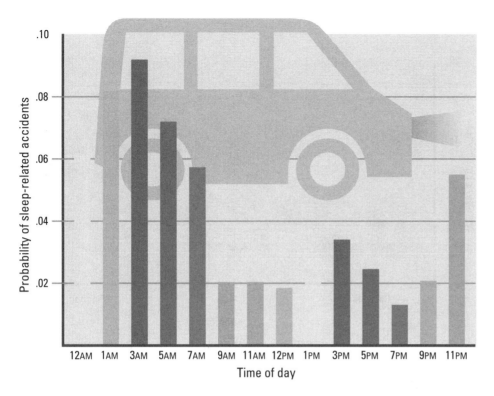

FIGURE 16.2 Probability of sleep-related accidents throughout the day By looking at traffic statistics, researchers have found that sleep-related accidents are unequally distributed across the day. Such accidents are most likely to occur between 1 and 4 AM. Note also that there's a second "mini-peak" between 1 and 4 PM.—which is a time when alertness levels decline (Mitler et al., 1988).

moving car. To measure subjects' driving performance, a computer kept track of the number of incidents in which they drifted from their lane or went off the side of the road. On three separate occasions, subjects drove for an hour, took a thirty-minute break, and then drove for another hour. Would subjects become sleepy—and sloppy—during the second hour? It depended on whether they were assigned, during the break, to drink a regular cup of coffee, to drink a placebo (decaffeinated) cup of coffee, or to take a fifteen-minute nap. Look at the results in Figure 16.3, and you'll see that although the incident rate rose in the placebo group, it dropped in the coffee and nap conditions. Horne and Reyner thus concluded that "many vehicle accidents due to the driver falling asleep at the wheel could be avoided if the driver recognized the dangers beforehand and used the countermeasures investigated here" (p. 309).

The Stages of Sleep

Just as activity levels follow a rhythm, so too does sleep. Every night, humans cycle through five distinct stages of sleep. Much of what is known about these stages first came to light in the 1950s, thanks to the pioneering collaborative work of Nathaniel Kleitman, Eugene Aserinksy, and William Dement.

To avoid traffic, many truckers drive at night. Due to drowsiness, however, they are more likely to have an accident during these hours than in the daytime.

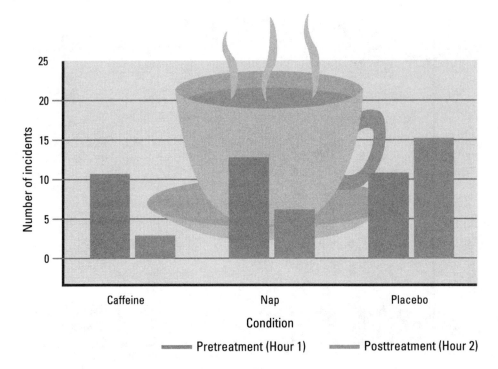

FIGURE 16.3 **How to keep from falling asleep at the wheel** Subjects drove for two hours in a simulated car, with a break during which they drank a regular cup of coffee or a placebo cup of decaffeinated coffee, or took a fifteen-minute nap. As measured by the number of traffic incidents they had in the second hour compared to the first, the incident rate increased in the placebo group but was reduced in the coffee and nap conditions (Horne & Reyner, 1996).

To appreciate how these discoveries were made, imagine that you're a subject in a sleep study. As you enter the sleep lab, you meet an experimenter, who gives you some questionnaires to fill out, prepares you for the experience, and takes you to a carpeted, tastefully decorated, soundproof "bedroom." Electrodes are then taped to your scalp to record brain-wave activity, near your eyes to measure eye movements, and under your neck and chin to record muscle tension (see Figure 16.4). Other devices may also be used to measure your breathing, heart rate, and even genital arousal. The pillow is fluffy, the bed is okay, and the blanket is warm. But you know you're being watched, and you can feel the electrodes and wires on your skin, so you wonder how you'll ever manage to fall asleep. The experimenter reassures you that it may take a couple of nights to adapt to the situation.

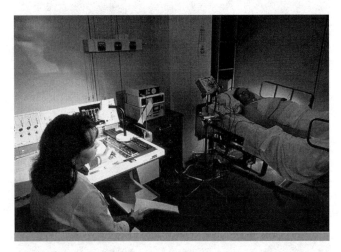

When a subject spends the night in the "bedroom" of a sleep lab, an experimenter in an adjacent room records brain-wave activity, eye movements, muscle tension, and other physiological functions.

Presleep The experimenter departs, shuts off the lights, and leaves you alone. As you try to settle down, EEG recordings reveal that all is well (see Figure 16.5). Typical of a person who is awake and alert, your EEG shows short, quick *beta waves*. This pattern indicates that different parts of your brain are producing small bursts of electrical activity at different times—a sure sign of mental activity. Your eyes move rapidly up and down and from side to side, and there is tension in many of your muscles.

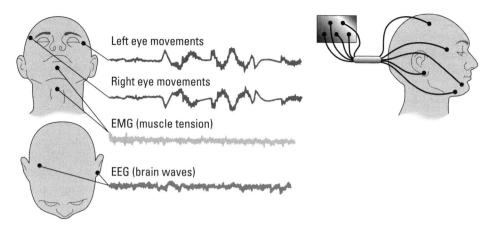

FIGURE 16.4 **Measuring sleep** In sleep laboratories, researchers record brain-wave activity, eye movements, and muscle tension by taping electrodes to the scalp, near the eyes, and elsewhere on the face (Dement, 1978).

Stages 1 to 4 You start to become drowsy. Your breathing slows down, your mind stops racing, your muscles relax, your eyes move less, and EEG recordings show a slower, larger, and somewhat more regular pattern of *alpha waves* (alpha waves appear to occur when people are relaxed but not focused on something specific). For a minute or two, you drift into a "hypnogogic state" in which you may imagine seeing flashes of color or light, and perhaps you jerk your leg abruptly as you sense yourself falling. You are entering stage 1 sleep. Electrical activity in the brain slows down some more. Your breathing becomes more regular, your heart rate slows, and your blood pressure drops. This is a period of very light sleep. No one makes a sound or calls your name, however, so you do not wake up.

After about ten minutes in stage 1 sleep, your EEG pattern shows waves that are even slower and larger. As you slip into stage 2 sleep, you become progressively more relaxed, the rolling eye movements stop, and you become less easily disturbed. On the EEG, stage 2 is marked by periodic short bursts of activity called sleep spindles. If the experimenter in the next room makes a noise, your brain will register a response—but you probably will not wake up.

After about twenty minutes in stage 2, you fall into the deepest stages of sleep. Stages 3 and 4 are hard to distinguish because they differ only in degree. Both are marked by the onset of very slow waves with large peaks, called *delta waves*, which last for about thirty minutes (delta waves seem to indicate that increasing numbers of neurons are firing together, in synchrony). At this point, you are "out like a light" or "sleeping like a rock." If the phone rings, you may not hear it. If you do answer the call, you'll sound dazed and confused. It is during the very deep sleep of stages 3 and 4 when young children may wet the bed or when you may walk or talk in your sleep. It's this stage that Mark Twain had in mind when he said, "There ain't no way to find out why a snorer can't hear himself snore." Yet, in keeping with the adaptive and selective nature of attention, certain noises will penetrate consciousness. New parents may be oblivious to the sounds of traffic outside, for example, but they're quick to hear the baby cry.

REM Sleep After an hour of deepening sleep, something odd happens—something first discovered in Kleitman's lab (Aserinksy & Kleitman, 1953; Dement &

Presleep

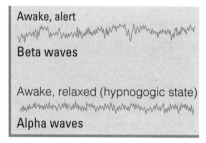

Awake, alert

Beta waves

Awake, relaxed (hypnogogic state)

Alpha waves

Non-REM

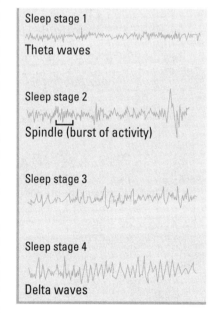

Sleep stage 1

Theta waves

Sleep stage 2

Spindle (burst of activity)

Sleep stage 3

Sleep stage 4

Delta waves

REM

REM stage

FIGURE 16.5 **The stages of sleep** As recorded by the EEG, brain waves get larger and slower as sleep deepens from stages 1 to 4. You can see that REM sleep waves closely resemble those of the presleep stage.

Kleitman, 1957; Kleitman, 1963). Rather than maintain your deep sleep, you begin to cycle backward to stage 3, then to stage 2. But then instead of returning to stage 1, you enter a new, fifth stage, marked by two dramatic types of changes. On the one hand, the EEG reveals a surge of short, high-frequency beta waves like those found when you were awake. Also indicating an increased level of activity, blood flow to the brain increases, your breathing and pulse rates speed up, and your genitals become aroused—even without sexual thoughts or dreams. On the other hand, you have lost skeletal muscle tone throughout the body. In fact, your arms, legs, and trunk are so totally relaxed that, except for an occasional twitch, you are completely paralyzed. You're also hard to awaken at this stage. This odd combination—of being internally active but externally immobile—has led some researchers to refer to this stage of sleep as paradoxical.

The most prominent change occurs in the eyes. The eyelids are shut, but underneath, your eyeballs are darting frantically back and forth as if you were watching a world-class ping-pong match. These *rapid eye movements* are so pronounced that this stage has been named **REM sleep**—and it is contrasted with stages 1 through 4, which are lumped together as non-REM or **NREM sleep.** What makes rapid eye movements so special is what they betray about the state of your mind. When experimenters awaken sleeping subjects during non-REM stages, the subjects report on dreams 14 percent of the time. Yet when subjects are awakened during REM, they report on dreams 78 percent of the time—and that includes those subjects who came into the lab saying they don't ever dream (Dement, 1992). Compared to the fleeting thoughts and images reported during stages 1 through 4, REM dreams are more visual, vivid, detailed, and storylike. In the mind's late-night theater, the production of dreams can be seen in the resurgence of activity within the eyes and brain.

From the time you fall asleep, it takes about ninety minutes to complete one cycle. The contrasts within this cycle are striking. Richard Coleman (1986) describes NREM sleep as "an idling brain in a moveable body" and REM as "an active brain in a paralyzed body." In a full night's sleep, you are likely to recycle through the stages four to six times. The first time through the cycle, you spend only about ten minutes in REM sleep. As the night wears on, however, you spend less time in the deeper NREM periods and more time in REM sleep. During the last hour before you awaken in the morning, the REM period is thirty to sixty minutes long. This explains why people are so often in the middle of a dream when the mechanical tyrant we call an alarm clock rings.

In all cultures of the world, beds are designed for sleep in a horizontal position. This universal aspect of human behavior is highly adaptive. EEG recordings show that when people sleep in an upright position (even if in a comfortable chair), they get very little of the slow-wave sleep needed to feel refreshed.

REM sleep The rapid-eye-movement stage of sleep associated with dreaming.

NREM sleep The stages of sleep not accompanied by rapid eye movements.

Sleep Disturbances

At some point in life, nearly everyone suffers from a sleep-related problem. You lie in bed, tossing and turning, brooding over something that happened or worrying about something that might. Or you keep nodding off in class or at work or in other embarrassing situations. Or you leap up in a cold sweat, with your heart pounding, from a realistic and terrifying nightmare. In general, there are three types of disturbances: sleeping too little (insomnia), sleeping too much (hypersomnia), and having disturbed or troubled sleep (parasomnia).

insomnia An inability to fall asleep, stay asleep, or get the amount of sleep needed to function during the day.

Insomnia   The sleep disturbance known as **insomnia** is characterized by a recurring inability to fall asleep, stay asleep, or get the amount of sleep needed to function during the day. Very few of us adhere to the daily "ideal" of eight hours for work, eight for play, and eight for sleep. On the contrary, people differ in the amount of sleep they want. Some are at their most alert after six hours a night, while others need nine or ten hours to get along. How much time is sufficient depends on who you are.

About 30 percent of the population complain of insomnia—and half of these people consider the problem to be serious (American Psychiatric Association, 1994). It's not that easy to know when someone has insomnia based on self-report, however. In a study that illustrates the point, Mary Carskadon brought 122 insomniacs into the laboratory and compared their self-perceptions to EEG measures of sleep. The next morning, the subjects estimated that it took them an hour to fall asleep and that they slept for 4½ hours. But EEG tracings revealed that it took them only 15 minutes to fall asleep, which is average, and that they slept for 6½ hours. More than 10 percent of all complaints are from "pseudoinsomniacs" who sleep normally but don't realize it (Kelly, 1991).

"It is extremely rare to find an animal with insomnia. . . . Insomnia is a human disorder."

—RICHARD M. COLEMAN

Among people who do have trouble falling or staying asleep, insomnia is not a disease but a symptom with many causes. Studies show that psychiatric patients get less sleep than do people without mental disorders (Benca et al., 1992). Medical ailments, pain, life stresses, depression, jet lag, night work, shifting work schedules, old age, and alcohol and drug abuse are also linked to insomnia. In some cases, the only "problem" is that people who think they should sleep eight hours a night go to bed before they're really tired. The use of medications poses a particularly ironic danger. Over-the-counter sleeping pills such as Sominex and Sleep-eze are not effective. Prescription drugs will, at first, put the insomniac to sleep and prevent rude awakenings during the night. But these sedatives will also inhibit certain stages of sleep and cause restlessness after the drug is terminated—if it is terminated. The habit of popping sleeping pills can be addictive and should be avoided. Numerous studies have shown that most people can successfully overcome insomnia by altering their behavior—but that the benefits are smaller for those who take sleeping pills (Morin et al., 1994; Murtagh & Greenwood, 1995). Some helpful tips are presented in Table 16.1.

"The only thing wrong with insomniacs is that they don't get enough sleep."

—W. C. FIELDS

Table 16.1 How to Overcome Insomnia

- Record how much sleep you *actually* get in a night, and set that total as a goal. If you sleep four or five hours, aim for a four-hour schedule.
- Do not take naps during the day.
- Avoid all alcohol, caffeine, and cigarettes within five hours of bedtime; avoid exercise within two hours of bedtime; relax.
- Make sure the bedroom is completely dark when you go to bed. When you awaken, turn on the lights and raise the shades.
- Keep a rigid schedule. Get into bed at 1 AM, not earlier. Set the alarm for 5 AM—and get out of bed no matter what.
- If you're awake but relaxed, stay in bed.
- If you're awake and anxious, get out of bed and return when you are sleepy. Keep the alarm set, and get up when it rings.
- If you stick to this schedule, you should see results in three to five weeks. If you want, you can then add thirty to sixty minutes to your schedule.
- Rest assured that you can get by on less sleep than you want and that a temporary loss of sleep will not cause harm.

narcolepsy A sleep disorder characterized by irresistible and sudden attacks of REM sleep during the day.

Hypersomnia   Studies in different countries show that about 5 percent of people complain of hypersomnia—being sleepy during the day and sleeping too much at night (Guilleminault & Roth, 1993). The most profound and most dangerous problem of this type is **narcolepsy** (which means "sleep seizure"), an uncommon disorder characterized by sudden, irresistible attacks of drowsiness and REM sleep during the day (American Psychiatric Association, 1994).

A narcolepsy attack may strike without warning at any time—while playing basketball, eating a meal, having a conversation, working in an office, or having sex. The attack lasts from five to thirty minutes and plunges its victim into REM sleep. The narcoleptic's jaw will sag, the head will fall forward, the arms will drop, and the knees will buckle. This collapse is often accompanied by the hypnogogic hallucinations that usher in the onset of sleep. As you might imagine, people with narcolepsy have problems at work and in their social lives. They are often unfairly perceived as lazy and disinterested. Narcolepsy can also be life-threatening. In one study, 40 percent of the narcoleptics who were questioned admitted they had fallen asleep while driving (Siegel et al., 1991). Although there is no cure, daytime sleep attacks can be minimized through the use of stimulant drugs (Mitler et al., 1994) and regularly scheduled naps (Mullington & Broughton, 1993).

Parasomnias   For some people, falling asleep at night and staying awake during the day are not a problem—but too often their sleep is disturbed. There are several specific disorders of this type. One particularly troublesome disturbance is **sleep apnea** (*apnea* means "to stop breathing"), which afflicts between 1 and 4 percent of Americans—mostly obese men. A person with sleep apnea will fall asleep normally but then stop breathing and awaken snorting like a buzz saw, choking, and gasping for air. Sleep-laboratory studies show that a person with sleep apnea will fall asleep again right away, but these partial awakenings can recur 400 times during the night, thus preventing slow-wave sleep and making the person excessively tired and irritable during the day (Langevin et al., 1992). With some success, the problem can be treated with continuous positive airways pressure (CPAP), a plastic mask that gently pumps air into the nose. The air holds the person's throat open and prevents snoring (Sullivan et al., 1981; Wittig, 1993). Of course, many people without apnea also snore while they sleep—much to the chagrin of roommates and bed partners.

There is an old saying, "Laugh and the world laughs with you, snore and you sleep alone!"

Nightmares are vivid, anxiety-provoking dreams that sometimes haunt us during REM sleep. They are common and should seldom be a source of concern. Children are more likely than adults to have nightmares, and it becomes a problem only if they persist for long periods of time. Nightmares are not dangerous, except for people who have **REM sleep behavior disorder (RBD)**—a very rare condition in which the skeletal muscles do not become paralyzed, as they should, during REM sleep. People with RBD have mobility to act on their nightmares and often do so in violent ways. As a result, 85 percent of sufferers have injured themselves and 44 percent have hurt their bed partners, sometimes seriously (Mahowald & Schenck, 1989; Schenck, 1993).

There are also NREM sleep disruptions. In *night terrors,* the person jolts abruptly from a deep sleep, in a state of panic, and gives off a loud, bloodcurdling scream. As with nightmares, this problem is more common among children than adults. It's also more frightening, particularly for others in the household. Because it occurs during NREM sleep, however, the night-terror victim will usually not recall a dream and by morning will have forgotten the whole episode. Another NREM experience is *sleep-walking,* in which the sleeper quietly sits up, climbs out of bed, and walks about

sleep apnea A disorder in which a person repeatedly stops breathing during sleep and awakens gasping for air.

REM sleep behavior disorder (RBD) A condition in which the skeletal muscles are not paralyzed during REM sleep, enabling a sleeper to act upon his or her nightmares, often violently.

with eyes open and a blank expression. Sleepwalkers may start slowly, but soon they're going to the bathroom, dressing, eating, and opening doors. They are prone to accidents such as falling down stairs, so it is safer to gently awaken a sleepwalker than to allow the person to wander about. People used to think that sleepwalkers were acting out dreams. But that's not the case. These episodes occur early in the night, during the deep, slow-wave stages of sleep. Sometimes sleepwalkers will wake up and be disoriented, but most often they just go back to bed. As with night-terror victims, sleepwalkers seldom recall their travels in the morning. This finding reinforces the point that the brain is active even during sleep—and that consciousness is complex and multilayered (Kelly, 1991).

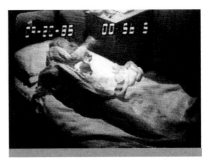

Taken in a sleep lab, this photograph shows a man with REM sleep behavior disorder. While dreaming, he throws a punch at the bed—one of twelve punches he throws in this particular sequence. Fortunately, at this time, he is sleeping alone.

Sleep and Sleep Deprivation

C. DiGiovanni, M.D.

(N.B.: The author is indebted to Col Gregory Belenky, MC, USA, of the Walter Reed Army Institute of Research, for the following material and for the figures that accompany this article.)

Sleep deprivation produces fatigue of the mind and contributes to a sense of fear in the person who faces uncertainty or danger.

Decision-making may be aided by a growing variety of electronic information-processing technology, but it is ultimately a human brain that makes a decision. The more sleep-deprived that brain is, the more likely any decision it makes will be bad, perhaps disastrously bad. Because we all rely on our brains, each of us needs to know how much sleep we need, ways to increase sleep during periods of continuous operations, and what happens when we don't get enough sleep.

The process of sleeping progresses in stages, from stage one (very light sleep) to stage four (the deepest sleep stage). A typical sleep cycle consists of several minutes spent in passing through stages one and two, a lengthier period at stages three and four, and then a few minutes of dream (or rapid eye movement [REM]). sleep. Each cycle lasts 60–90 minutes and repeats itself throughout the course of time spent sleeping. Over a typical eight-hour period of sleep, the amount of time spent in stages three and four progressively diminishes, and the amount of dream sleep progressively increases.

All sleep, regardless of stage, is good and contributes to our daily sleep requirement (The daily sleep requirement is the amount of sleep we need in each 24-hour period. It can be met through one lengthy period of sleep at night or by shorter periods of sleep, including napping, when the opportunity presents itself.) Stages three and four of the sleep cycle are the times of least stimulation to the brain and, thus, are the stages of deepest sleep. The brain emits a different electrical signal at each stage of the cycle, and it is this signal that defines the characteristics of each stage. Figure 1 shows the electrical signals at each sleep stage, as recorded by an electroencephalogram (EEG). You will note the markedly different pattern of stages three and four of sleep.

Awake - low voltage - random, fast

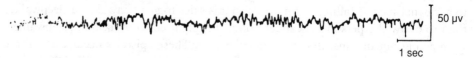

50 µv

1 sec

Drowsy - 8 to 12 cps - alpha waves

Stage 1 - 3 to 7 cps - theta waves

Theta waves

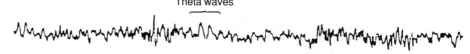

Stage 2 - 12 to 14 cps - sleep spindles and K-complexes

sleep spindles

K-complexes

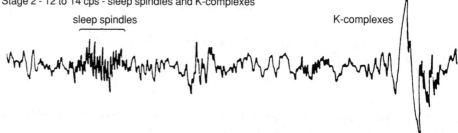

Delta Sleep - 1/2 to 2 cps - delta waves 75 µv

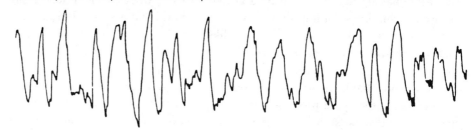

REM Sleep - low voltage - random fast with sawtooth waves

sawtooth waves sawtooth waves

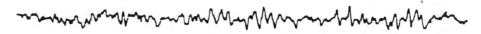

Figure 1

Another factor that influences sleep is Circadian rhythm, which is the biological clock that we all have that regulates the release of hormones in our bodies throughout each 24–25 hour period. One of the results of this biological clock is that our level of alertness varies throughout the 24-hour day. Most of us, who prefer to sleep at night and work during the day, are at our lowest levels of alertness and intellectual ability between the hours of 0200 and 0600. Our level of alertness then begins to increase until noon, when it dips a bit, then resumes rising until around 2000, when

Captain Chris Ames, Commanding Officer of USS Tarawa (LHA 1), briefs his Operations Officer.
Official U.S. Navy photo.

it begins its final decline of the day. Planning raids to begin between 0200 and 0600 gives the attackers an advantage because the enemy is least alert. (For those among us who prefer to work during the night and sleep during daylight hours, the Circadian rhythm just described is reversed.)

The amount of sleep we need in each 24-hour period may differ from person to person, but not by much. The average time is between seven and eight hours, and most of us will fall somewhere in the six to ten hour range. Just as you know the number of miles you can travel in your car on a gallon of gas, you should also know how much sleep you need in each 24-hour period. Without that knowledge, you will not know in advance what your limits are. You can determine the amount of sleep you need by going to bed at night under normal circumstances (not already sleep deprived, and not inebriated), and allowing yourself to wake up naturally (without an alarm clock) the following morning. If you do that for a few nights and take the average of the amount of time you slept, you will have a good idea of your daily sleep requirement. Knowing that requirement will enable you to know when you are beginning to acquire a sleep deficit.

A "Yellow Shirt" lines up an EA-6B Prowler from VAG-137 on the flight deck of USS George Washington (CVN 73).

Official U.S. Navy photo.

You cannot condition yourself to get by with significantly less sleep, and the more sleep debt you acquire, the worse will be your performance. Sleep debt, however, does not produce deterioration in all activities. For example, in static and repetitive tasks, accuracy is generally maintained, but the time it takes to perform those tasks progressively lengthens. Also, many forms of physical activity are not affected, at least initially, by sleep debt. What is affected by sleep debt is the ability of the brain to perform its higher functions, such as learning new information, recalling previously learned information, reacting to information, and analyzing information and making decisions. This deterioration in higher brain functioning has been documented numerous times through neuropsychological testing and from specialized studies of brain metabolism in sleep-deprived persons; their brains show altered

72 Hours of Sleep Deprivation:
Performance on Serial Addition/Subtraction

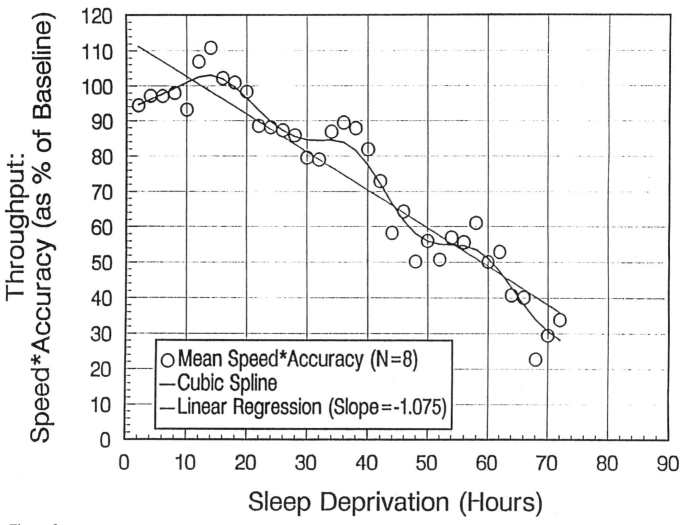

Figure 2

metabolism in those very parts of the brain that are responsible for these higher brain functions.

Figure 2 shows the results of 72 hours of sleep deprivation on the ability of a group of volunteers to perform a task that requires sustained attention. For each 24 hours of sleep deprivation, their performance deteriorated by 25%. Figure 3 illustrates a point made earlier, namely, that in repetitive tasks, it is efficiency, not accuracy, that is hurt by sleep deprivation. In this study, the number of rounds loaded and fired by an artillery battery markedly fell as sleep debt increased.

As a leader of Sailors or Marines who face danger, you have an obligation to make the best decisions you can. You cannot make that quality of decision if your brain is fatigued. Furthermore, you also have an obligation to set a good example for those you lead. If you ignore your own sleep requirements, those whom you lead may ignore theirs. Unfortunately, studies (figure 4) have shown that those who have

Artillery Battery Productivity
During Continuous Operations with 4-9 Hours of Sleep/Day
Army Unit Resiliency Analysis (AURA) Model

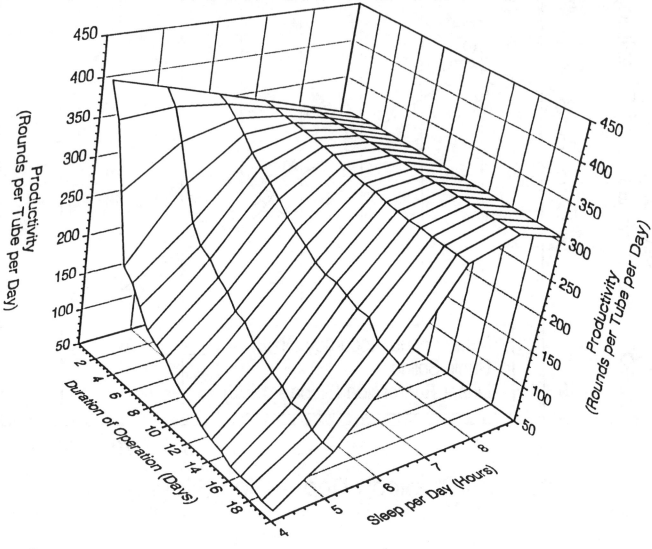

Figure 3

the greatest leadership and decision-making responsibilities during military exercises are the ones who get the least amount of sleep.

Obviously, in the real world of warfighting and continuous operations, loss of sleep is a fact of life. What tactics can one employ to compensate for this reduced opportunity for sleep? One is to begin a period of continuous operations already well rested. You cannot store sleep, but if you begin an operation well-rested, even though your performance will deteriorate with increasing sleep debt, your performance at each point along that time-line will be better than if you were sleep-deprived at the outset. A second ploy is to consume caffeine, in the form of beverage, tablet, or caffeinated chewing gum. If you normally drink several cups of coffee

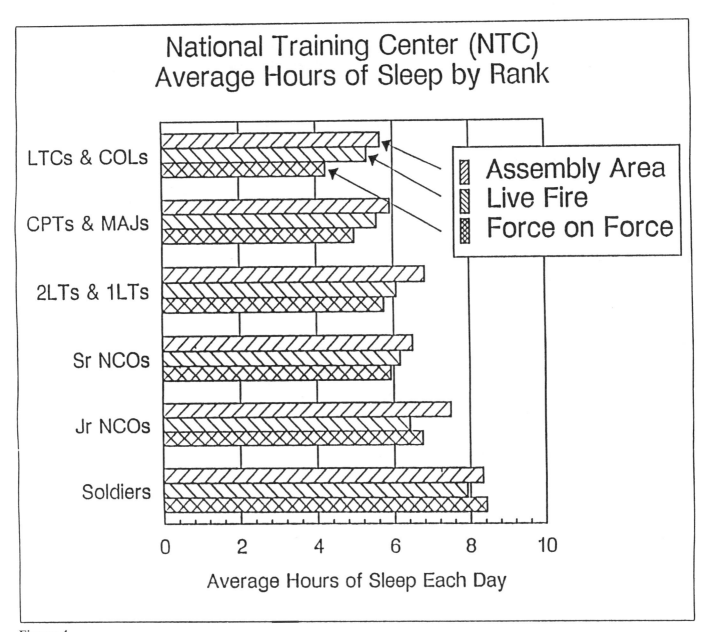

National Training Center (NTC)
Average Hours of Sleep by Rank

Assembly Area
Live Fire
Force on Force

LTCs & COLs

CPTs & MAJs

2LTs & 1LTs

Sr NCOs

Jr NCOs

Soldiers

0   2   4   6   8   10

Average Hours of Sleep Each Day

Figure 4

daily, another cup will not do you much good, but if you are not much of a coffee drinker, a cup's worth of caffeine will give you a brief boost in alertness.

Probably the best tactic to use, however, is to nap. Even one 30-minute nap in each 24-hour period of otherwise sleep deprivation can result in significant, although short-lived, improvement in your ability to use your brain (see figures 5 and 6). Although not ideal, napping can get you through a period of continuous operations, where opportunities for sleep are greatly reduced and fragmented. But if you plan to survive on naps, pay attention to the quality of your naps. Take them under conditions that will allow your brain not to be stimulated by ambient noise, light, or other disturbances. And plan your nap to be of sufficient length to do you some good, the "15 minute power nap" will work, but 30 minutes would be better.

85 Hours of Sleep Deprivation: Performance on Serial Addition/Subtraction

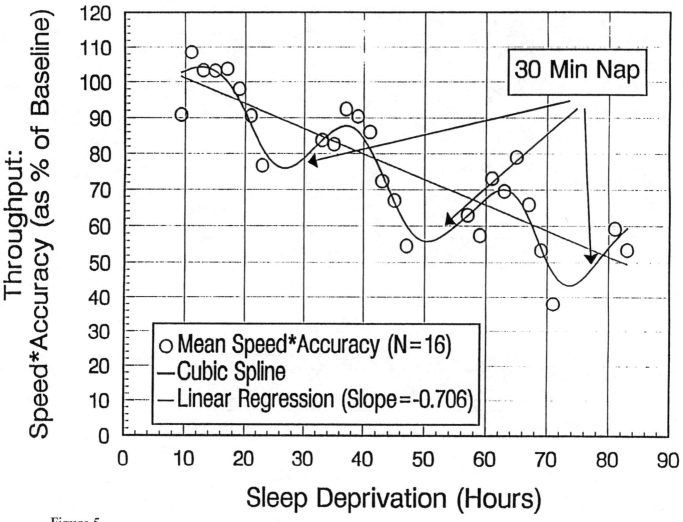

Figure 5

Sleeping medications, acquired by prescription or over the counter, may help promote sleep and improve sleep efficiency. If you take them, however, make sure that you will be able to sleep for an adequate length of time to allow the effects of the drug to wear off. If not, you may be worse off because you will be both sleep-deprived and under the influence of a sleep medication. Check with medical personnel before you take such medication. If in doubt, don't take it.

If you deploy to an area that has a significant time-zone shift from your home base, remember that major Circadian rhythm shifts require 3–5 days to occur. You can help this adjustment process by immediately scheduling your new work, sleep, and off-duty activities by the new local time. Also, if shift work is required, make its

Cognitive Performance in Sleep Deprivation With and Without Daily Nap (30 minutes)

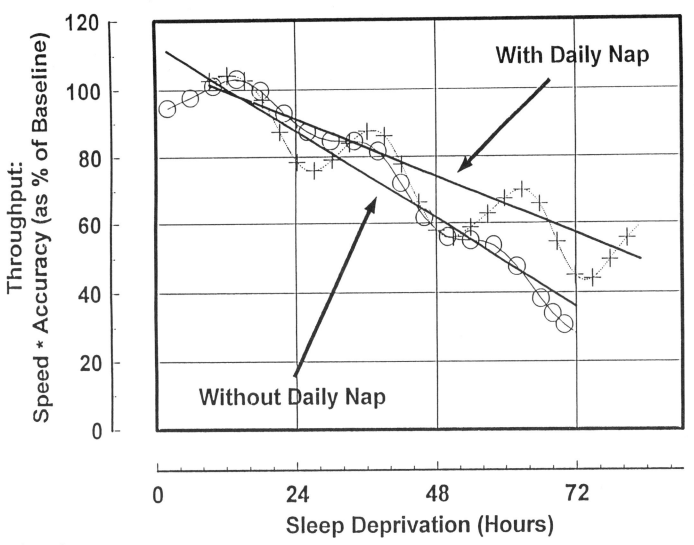

Figure 6

hours and personnel rosters consistent from day to day; do not assign someone to work form 0600 to 1400 hours one day, and from 1400 to 2200 the next day.

Finally, when you work with people who are sleep deprived, remember that they will have deficits in their understanding of what you tell them and in their ability to think, learn, recall, and react. Therefore, speak in simple sentences, limit to a minimum anything unusually complex, don't expect them to remember everything you tell them, repeat often the essential items, have them repeat back to you these essential items to make sure they have registered, and check their performance after the briefing to ensure they are doing what you told them.

17 "No Sweat"—Effective Performance in a High Stress Environment

Objectives

1. Describe the primary sources of stress and the implications of stress for health.

2. Define combat-related Post-traumatic Stress Disorder, its causes and prevention.

3. Assess and discuss your current stress level and vulnerabilities to stress.

4. Describe how proper training enables individuals to cope with extreme stressors like combat or disasters.

5. Classify a stressful experience as a catastrophe, major life event, or microstressor.

6. Explain why it is important for a leader to be able to gauge the amount of stress both they and their personnel are under and determine the effect of this stress on performance.

Stress and Health

What are the main sources of stress in our lives? What are the effects of stress on the body? What is the Type A personality, and why is it bad for your heart? How does the immune system work, and how is it affected by stress and other psychological states?

The reason psychologists are interested in mental health is obvious. But the field has also had a long-standing interest in physical health, a domain normally associated with medicine. Influenced by psychoanalysis, clinical psychologists used to study *psychosomatic* ailments such as asthma, ulcers, headaches, and constipation—conditions thought to result from unconscious conflicts. Working from a behavioral perspective, others later referred to these same ailments as *psychophysiological* disorders. Either way, it's clear that psychological states can influence physical well-being (Gatchel & Blanchard, 1993).

Over the past few years, increasing numbers of researchers have become interested in the emerging area of **health psychology**, the application of psychology to the promotion of physical health and the prevention and treatment of illness. You may wonder, what does psychology have to do with catching a cold, having a heart attack, or being afflicted by cancer? If you could turn the clock back a few years and ask your family doctor, his or her answer would be "very little." In the past, illness was considered a purely biological event. But this strict medical perspective has given way to a broader model that holds that health is a joint product of biological and psychological factors.

Part of the reason for this broadened view is that illness patterns over the years have changed in significant ways. Before the twentieth century, the principal causes of death were contagious diseases—polio, smallpox, tuberculosis, typhoid fever, malaria, influenza, pneumonia, and the like. In the United States, none of these infectious illnesses is currently a leading killer. Instead, Americans are most likely to die, in order of risk, from heart disease, cancer, strokes, and accidents (AIDS is eighth on the list)—problems that are often preventable through changes in mind and behavior (see Figure 17.1).

Although it's not possible to quantify the extent of the problem, psychological stress is known to be a potent killer. Regardless of who you are, when you were born, or where you live, you have no doubt experienced stress. Sitting in a rush-hour traffic jam, getting married or divorced, losing hours of work to a computer crash, getting into an argument with a close friend, worrying about an unwanted pregnancy or the health of your child, living in a noisy neighborhood, struggling to make financial ends meet, and caring for a loved one who is sick—these are the kinds of stresses and strains we all must learn to live with. Whether they are short-term or long-term, serious or mild, no one is immune and there is no escape. But there are ways to cope.

health psychology The study of the links between psychological factors and physical health and illness.

199

On slow days, the captain liked to have SA Sampson give the 1200 reports.

In this section, we examine three interrelated questions of relevance to your health and well-being: (1) What are some of the primary sources of stress? (2) What are the effects of stress on the body? (3) What are the most adaptive ways of coping with stress? Together, the answers to these questions provide a useful model of the stress-and-coping process (see Figure 17.2).

The Sources of Stress

Stress is an unpleasant state of arousal that arises when we perceive that an event threatens our ability to cope effectively. There are many different sources of stress, or *stressors*. Try writing down the stressors in your own life, and you'll probably find that the items in your list can be divided into three major categories: catastrophes, major life events, and daily hassles.

Catastrophes It was the spring of 1997. As water levels rose, many North Dakota families removed whatever valuables they could from their homes. Many stayed to the bitter end, hoping that the river would not engulf their homes. The flood dealt a devastating blow to many people. Other events that have similarly traumatic effects are car accidents, plane crashes, terrorist bombings, hurricanes, tornadoes, earthquakes, and violent crime.

The harmful effects of catastrophic stressors on health are well documented. Paul and Gerald Adams (1984) examined the public records in Othello, Washington, before and after the 1980 eruption of the Mount Saint Helens volcano, which spewed thick layers of ash all over the community. They discovered that there were posteruption increases in calls made to a mental-health crisis line, police reports of domestic violence, referrals to the alcohol treatment center, and visits to the local hospital emergency room. Based on a review of fifty-two additional studies, Anthony Rubonis and Leonard Bickman (1991) concluded that high rates of psychological disorders are common after large-scale environmental disasters.

It has long been known that war in particular leaves deep and permanent psychological scars. Soldiers who experience combat see horrifying injuries, death, and destruction on a routine basis, leaving them with images and emotions that do not fade. In World War I, the problem was called shell shock. In World War II, it was called combat fatigue. It's now called **posttraumatic stress disorder (PTSD)** and is identified by such symptoms as recurring anxiety, sleeplessness, nightmares, vivid flashbacks, intrusive thoughts, attentional problems, and social withdrawal. To evaluate the extent of the problem, researchers at the Centers for Disease Control (1988)

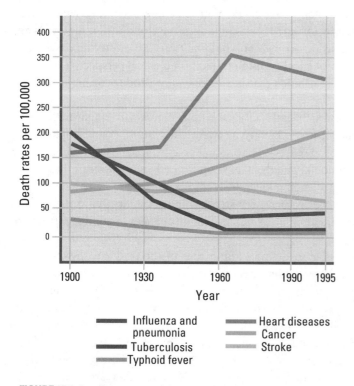

FIGURE 17.1 Leading causes of death, 1900–1995 As shown, heart disease, cancer, and strokes have replaced infectious diseases as the major causes of death in the United States.

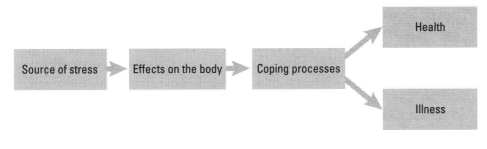

FIGURE 17.2 Stress and coping Advances in health psychology show that although stressful events have effects on the body, the way we cope with stress can promote health or illness.

Tornadoes have such devastating power that those who survive often exhibit posttraumatic stress disorder.

compared 7,000 Vietnam combat veterans with 7,000 noncombat veterans who served in the military at the same time, that is, more than twenty years before the study. They found that although the Vietnam War was a distant memory to most Americans, 15 percent of those who saw combat—twice as many as were in the comparison group—reported lingering symptoms of posttraumatic stress disorder. Those who had the most traumatic of experiences (crossing enemy lines, being ambushed or shot at, handling dead bodies) were five times more likely to suffer from nightmares, flashbacks, startle reactions, and other problems (Goldberg et al., 1990). Similar results have been found among older veterans of World War II and the Korean War (Fontana & Rosenheck, 1994; Spiro et al., 1994).

PTSD, a form of anxiety disorder, can be caused by traumas off the battlefield as well. Based on a nationwide survey of nearly 6,000 Americans, fifteen to fifty-four years old, Ronald Kessler and his colleagues (1995) estimated that 8 percent of the population (5 percent among men, 10 percent among women) have posttraumatic stress disorder in the course of a lifetime—and that the symptoms often persist for many years. Figure 17.3 indicates that different types of experiences produce these

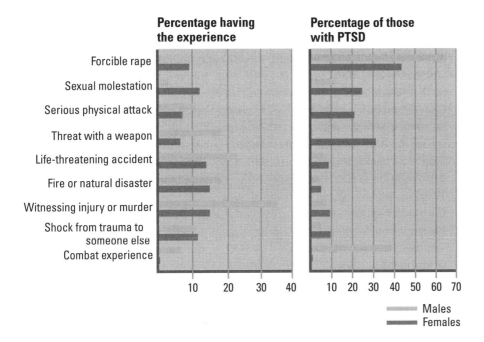

FIGURE 17.3 Lifetime rates of traumas and PTSD

stress An aversive state of arousal triggered by the perception that an event threatens our ability to cope effectively.

posttraumatic stress disorder (PTSD) An anxiety disorder triggered by an extremely stressful event, such as combat.

It has long been recognized that combat leaves psychological scars and the symptoms of posttraumatic stress disorder.

traumas (shown on the left are the percentages of men and women who had various experiences; shown on the right are the percentages of those for whom the experience was likely to have resulted in PTSD). In a study of Miami residents caught in a major hurricane, Gail Ironson and others (1997) found that after a few months, one-third exhibited symptoms of PTSD—and that the more injury, property damage, and loss they suffered from the storm, the more severe their symptoms were.

Major Life Events   Some people are lucky enough to avoid major catastrophes. But nobody can avoid stress. The reason, say some psychologists, is that change of any kind causes stress because it forces us to adapt to new circumstances. This hypothesis was first proposed by Thomas Holmes and Richard Rahe (1967), who interviewed hospital patients and found that their illnesses were often preceded by major changes in some aspect of their lives. Some of the changes were negative (being injured, divorced, or fired from a job), but others were positive (getting married, being promoted, or having a baby). To measure life stress, Holmes and Rahe thus devised the Social Readjustment Rating Scale (SRRS)—a checklist of forty-three major life changes, each assigned a numerical value based on the amount of readjustment it requires (see Table 17.1). The events listed, in order of stressfulness, can be

Table 17.1 Sample Items from the Social Readjustment Rating Scale

LIFE EVENT	VALUE
1. Death of spouse	100
2. Divorce	73
3. Jail term or imprisonment	63
4. Death of a close family member	63
5. Major personal injury or illness	53
6. Marriage	50
7. Losing one's job	47
8. Pregnancy	40
9. Sexual difficulties	39
10. Addition of a new family member	39
11. Change in financial state	37
12. Death of a close friend	36
13. Change to a different line of work	36
14. Taking out a large mortgage	31
15. Change in status at work	29
16. Son or daughter leaving home	29
17. Outstanding personal achievement	28
18. Major change in work hours or conditions	20
19. Move to a new residence	20
20. Transfer to a new school	20
21. Taking out a loan (e.g., for a new car)	17
22. Change in sleeping habits	16
23. Change in eating habits	15
24. Vacation	13
25. Minor law violations (traffic tickets, etc.)	11

Source: T. H. Holmes & R. H. Rahe (1967). The social readjustment rating scale. *Journal of Psychosomatic Research,* 11, 213–218.

used to estimate the amount of recent stress in your life (this scale does not include many events common among college students—such as changes in grades, graduation, and relationships with friends and lovers).

You may have seen the SRRS, or other questionnaires like it, in a book or magazine. The claim made is that the number of stress points or "life-change units" you accumulate in a recent period of time indicates the amount of stress you are under. I recall filling out such a questionnaire the year I finished graduate school. I received my Ph.D. One week later, my wife and I got married, moved 1,500 miles to a new state, rented a new apartment, and started new jobs. For the first and only time in her life, my wife developed an ulcer. Her doctor's first question: "Has anything changed in your life?"

The simple notion that change is inherently stressful has an intuitive ring about it. Indeed, research shows that people with high scores on the SRRS are more likely to come down with various physical illnesses (Dohrenwend & Dohrenwend, 1978; Maddi et al., 1987). But is change per se necessarily harmful? There are two problems with this notion. First, although there is a statistical link between negative events and illness, research does not similarly support the claim that positive "stressors"—taking a vacation, graduating, winning a lottery, starting a new career, or getting married—are similarly harmful (Stewart et al., 1986). Look carefully at the SRRS items in Table 17.1, and you'll see that most events on the list are negative. The second complicating factor is that the impact of any change depends on who the person is and how the change is interpreted. For example, moving to a new country is less stressful to immigrants who know their new language and culture (Berry et al., 1992), and having an abortion is less stressful to women who have the support of their family, partners, and friends (Major et al., 1990). The amount of change in a person's life may provide crude estimates of stress and future health, but the predictive equation is more complex.

Microstressors   Think again about the sources of stress in your life, and catastrophes or exceptional events spring to mind. Researchers have found, however, that the most significant source of stress arises from the hassles that irritate us on a daily basis. Environmental factors such as population density, loud noise, extreme heat or cold, and cigarette smoke are all possible sources of stress. Car problems, waiting in lines, losing keys, arguments with friends, nosy neighbors, bad workdays, money troubles, and other "microstressors" also place a constant strain on us. Table 17.2 shows the events that most routinely stress children, college students, and adults (Kanner et al., 1981; Kanner et al., 1991; Kohn et al., 1990). Unfortunately, there is nothing "micro" about the impact of these stressors on our health and well-being. Studies show that the accumulation of daily hassles contributes more to illness than do major life events (DeLongis et al., 1982; Weinberger et al., 1987; Kohn et al., 1991).

There is one source of stress that plagues many people on a routine basis. At work, relentless job pressures can grind away at a person over time and cause *burnout*—a state of emotional exhaustion characterized by a feeling of distance from others and a diminished sense of personal accomplishment. Schoolteachers, doctors, nurses, police officers, social workers, and others in human-service professions are particularly at risk for burnout. Research shows that people who are burned out describe themselves as used up, drained, frustrated, hardened, apathetic, lack-

Waiting helplessly in traffic is one of the most common microstressors in daily life.

Table 17.2 Common Daily Hassles

CHILDREN AND EARLY ADOLESCENTS

- Having to clean up your room
- Being bored and having nothing to do
- Seeing that another kid can do something better
- Getting punished for doing something wrong
- Having to go to bed when you don't want to
- Being teased at school.

COLLEGE STUDENTS

- Conflicts with a boyfriend or girlfriend
- Dissatisfaction with your athletic skills
- Having your trust betrayed by a friend
- Struggling to meet your own academic standards
- Not having enough leisure time
- Gossip concerning someone you care about
- Dissatisfaction with your physical appearance

MIDDLE-AGE ADULTS

- Concerns about weight
- Health of a family member
- Social obligations
- Inconsiderate smokers
- Concerns about money
- Misplacing or losing things
- Home maintenance
- Job security

---

ing in energy, and without motivation (Maslach, 1982; Cordes & Dougherty, 1993). Research also shows that people are most likely to experience burnout when there are not enough resources at work (such as support from supervisors, friendly relationships with coworkers, autonomy, and opportunities for advancement) to meet the demands of the job (Lee & Ashforth, 1996).

From *Bravo Two Zero:*
The True Story of an SAS Patrol Behind Enemy Lines in Iraq

Andy McNab

During the Gulf War in early 1991, a team of British Special Air Service (SAS) troops was dropped behind enemy lines in Iraq. Their mission was to infiltrate and destroy the supply and communication lines for SCUD missile sites, as well as destroy the missile sites themselves. These long-range missiles were being fired at Israel by the Iraqi army and had already inflicted significant damage and taken several civilian lives.

The SAS team was compromised from the start of the mission. Due to poor intelligence and outdated maps, they were inserted in a heavily populated area which had a large concentration of Iraqi troops. Almost immediately, their intended mission was compromised and their main mission became that of escape and evasion. The team lost its radio in a firefight, and had no contact with friendly forces other than a chance TACBE (Tactical Beacon) transmission that was picked up by a U.S. plane on its way to a strike near Baghdad. Since the team moved so rapidly on its retreat out of Iraq and communications were so limited, no rescue mission was possible and they were on their own in their survival efforts.

In the end, three members of the eight-man team were killed, four were captured by Iraqi troops and survived severe beatings in a prison camp, and one hiked over 300 kilometers alone to safety in Syria after being separated from the rest of the team. He did so over an eight-day period, surviving only on dirty river water and a couple day's supply of crackers.

The following excerpt highlights the beginning of the team's escape and evasion, and outlines how their superior training and knowledge of the body's ability to handle physical and mental stress led to the survival of five members of the team despite the extreme conditions.

All I heard was abuse directed at the manufacturers of TACBE. We would not use it again now unless we got a fast jet flying over. We didn't know whether the Iraqis had aircraft up or not, but we'd just have to take the chance. We were in the shit, and freezing cold shit it was, too.

We got Dinger and Bob back in, gave them the good news, and off we tabbed. We'd only stopped for a minute or two but it was good to get moving again. It was bitterly cold and a strong wind blasted the chill deep into our bones. There was dense cloud cover and we were in pitch darkness. We couldn't see our footing correctly. The only plus was that at least it made it a lot harder for them to find us. There was still the odd vehicle, but in the far distance. We had left them well behind. I was almost feeling confident.

We pushed west for 15Ks, moving fast on a bearing. The ground was so flat that we'd be warned well in advance of any Iraqi presence. It was a balance between speed and observation.

We stopped every hour to rest for five minutes, which is the patrolling SOP. If you go on and on, all you do is run yourself down and you'll end up not being able to achieve what you set out to do. So you stop, get down, get some rest, drink some water, sort yourself out, get yourself comfy again, and off you go. It was freezing cold and I shivered uncontrollably when we stopped.

We had one of our five-minute rests at the 15K mark and did a Magellan check. I made the decision that because of the time factor we'd have to turn north now to get over the MSR before first light.

'Let's just get over that road,' I said, 'then we can go north-west to Syria.'

We'd gone about another 10Ks when I noticed gaps appearing in the line. We were definitely moving more slowly than we had in the beginning. There was a problem. I stopped the patrol and everybody closed up.

Vince was limping.

'You all right, mate?' I said.

'Yeah, I hurt my leg on the way out in that contact, and it's really fucking starting to give me gyp.'

Naval Academy photo courtesy of United States Naval Academy Photographic Laboratory.

The whole aim of the game was to get everybody over the border. Vince clearly had an injury. We'd have to do all our planning and considerations around the fact that he was in trouble. None of this 'No, it's OK, skipper, I can go on' bollocks, because if you try to play the he-man and don't inform people of your injuries, you're endangering the whole patrol. If they're not aware of your problem, they can't adjust the plan or cater for future eventualities. If you make sure people know that you're injured, they can plan around it.

'What's the injury like?' Dinger said.

'It just fucking hurts. I don't think it's fractured. It's not bleeding or anything, but it's swollen. It's going to slow me down.'

'Right, we'll stop here and sort ourselves out,' I said.

I pulled my woollen bobble hat from my smock and put it on my head. I watched Vince massage his leg. He was clearly annoyed with himself for sustaining an injury.

'Stan's in shit state,' Bob said to me.

Dinger and Mark had been helping him along. They laid him down on the ground. He was in a bad way. He knew it and he was pissed off about it.

'What the hell's the matter?' I said, sticking my hat on his head.

'I'm on my chinstrap, mate. I'm just dying here.'

Chris was the most experienced medic on the patrol. He examined Stan and it was obvious to him that he was dangerously dehydrated.

'We've got to get some rehydrate down him, and quick.'

Chris ripped open two sachets of electrolyte from Stan's belt kit and tipped them into his water bottle. Stan took several big gulps.

'Look Stan,' I said, 'you realize that we've got to go on?'

'Yeah, I know that. Just give us a minute, let's get some more of this shit down my neck and I'll sort myself out. It's this fucking Helly Hansen underwear. I was sleeping with it on when we got compromised.'

Dehydration is no respecter of climates. You can become dehydrated in the depths of an Arctic winter just the same as in the middle of the day in the Sahara. Physical exertion produces sweat, even in the cold. And the vapour clouds we see when we exhale are yet more precious moisture leaking from our bodies. Thirst is an unreliable indicator of dehydration. The problem is that just a few sips of liquid might quench your thirst without improving your internal water deficit. Or you might not even notice your thirst because there is too much else going on that needs your attention. After losing 5 per cent of your body weight through dehydration you will be struck by waves of nausea. If you vomit, you'll lose even more precious fluid. Your movements will slow down dramatically, your speech will slur and you'll become unable to walk. Dehydration to this degree can be fatal. Stan had been wearing his thermals ever since we left the LUP. He must have lost pints of sweat.

I started to shake.

'What do we do—take his kit off?' I asked Chris.

'No, it's all he's got on, apart from his trousers, shirt and smock. If we take it off he'll be in a worse state.'

Stan got up and started moving around. We gave him another ten minutes to get himself organized; then it became too cold to stand still any longer and we had to get moving.

We had to do our planning around the two slowest and move at their speed. I changed the order of the march. I put Chris up front, with Stan and Vince behind him. I followed them, with the others behind me.

As scout, Chris moved on the compass bearing and used the nightsight to make sure that we weren't going to walk into anything nasty. We stopped every half-hour instead of every hour. Each time, we had to get more water into Stan. The situation was not desperate, but he did seem to be getting worse.

The weather had become diabolical. We weren't tabbing as hard as we had been because the cold was sapping our strength. The wind was driving into our faces and we were all moving with our heads turned at half-cock to try and protect ourselves.

We pushed on, our pace dictated by the two injured men in front. At one stop Vince sat down and gripped his leg.

'It's getting worse, mate,' he said. It was so out of character for him to complain. The injured leg must have been agony. He apologized for the hassle he was causing us.

We had two enemies now—time, and the physical condition of the two slowest men. By now the rest of us were starting to feel the effects of the night's march as well. My feet and legs were aching, and I had to keep reminding myself that it was what I got paid for.

There was total cloud cover. It was jet-black. I checked the navigation and the rest of the patrol covered the arcs to the sides and the rear. Chris was having trouble with the NVA because there was no ambient light. This was now slowing us down as much as the two injured men.

The wind bit into every inch of exposed skin. I kept my arms tight against my sides to preserve warmth. My head was down, my shoulders shrugged. If I had to move my head I'd turn my whole body. I didn't want the slightest bit of wind down my neck.

We started to hear aircraft coming from the north. I couldn't see a thing because of the cloud cover but I had to make a decision. Was I going to get on the TACBE, only to find they were Iraqi?

'Fucking yeah,' Mark said, reading my thoughts. 'Let's do it.'

I put my hand on Vince's shoulder and said, 'We're going to stop and try TACBE.'

He nodded and said, 'Yep, OK, yep.'

I tried to open my pouch. It was easier said than done. My hands were frozen and so numb that I couldn't get my fingers to work. Mark started fumbling with my belt kit as well but he couldn't unclench his fingers enough to undo the pouch. Finally, somehow, I had the TACBE in my hand. The last couple of jets were still going over.

'Hello any callsign, this is Bravo Two Zero, Bravo Two Zero. We are a ground callsign and we're in the shit. Over.'

Nothing. I called again. And again.

'Hello any callsign, this is Bravo Two Zero, Bravo Two Zero. We are a ground callsign and we're in the shit. We have a fix for you. Over.'

If they did nothing else other than inform somebody of our position, we'd be laughing. Mark got out Magellan and pressed the fix button to give us longitude and latitude.

It was then that I heard the wonderful sound of an American voice and it suddenly registered with me that these would be jets coming from Turkey to do raids around Baghdad.

'Say again, Bravo Two Zero, Bravo Two Zero. You're very weak. Try again.'

The signal was weak because he was screaming out of range.

'Turn back north,' I said. 'Turn back north. Over.'

No reply.

'Hello any callsign, this is Bravo Two Zero. Over.'

Nothing.

They'd gone. They wouldn't come back. Bastards!

Five minutes later, the horizon was lit by bright flashes and tracer. The jets were obviously hosing something down near Baghdad. Their run-ins are crucial, timed to the split second. They couldn't have turned back for us even if they'd wanted to. At least he had repeated our callsign. Presumably this would get filtered through the system and the FOB would know we were still on the ground, but in the shit—or at least, that one of us with a TACBE was.

It was all over within twenty or thirty seconds. I hunched with my back to the wind as I replaced the TACBE in my pouch. I looked at Legs and he shrugged. He was right—so what? We'd made the contact.

'Maybe they'll fly back this way and things will be good,' I said to Bob.

'Let's hope.'

I turned into the wind to tell Chris and the other two that we'd better press on.

'For fuck's sake,' I whispered, 'where's everybody else gone?'

I had told Vince we were going to try TACBE. The correct response is for the message to get passed along the line, but it can't have registered in his numbed brain. He must have just kept on walking without telling Chris and Stan.

It's each man's responsibility in the line to make sure that messages go up or down, and if you stop you make sure that the bloke in front knows that you've stopped. You should know who's in front of you and who's behind you. It's your responsibility to make sure they're always there. So it was my fault and Vince's that they didn't stop. We both failed in our responsibilities—Vince in not passing it on, me in not making sure that he stopped.

We couldn't do anything about it. We couldn't do a visual search because Chris was the only person with a night-viewing aid. We couldn't shout because we didn't know what was ahead of us or to either side. And we couldn't use white light—that's a big no-no. So we'd just have to keep on the bearing and hope that they'd stop at some stage and wait for us. There was a good chance that we'd meet up.

13th Marine Expeditionary Unit (MEU) Human Intelligence Exploitation Team (HET) Interrogator Translator Sgt. Billy Montgomery uses his secondary language, Arabic, to speak with a Bedouin shepherd during daily range sweeps in the desert south of Iraq.

Official U.S. Navy photo.

I felt terrible. We had failed, more or less, in our contact with the aircraft. And now, even worse, we'd lost three members of the patrol—two of whom were injured. I was annoyed with myself, and annoyed with the situation. How the hell had I allowed it to happen?

Bob must have guessed what I was thinking because he said, 'It's done now, let's just carry on. Hopefully we'll RV.'

That helped me a lot. He was right. At the end of the day they were big boys, they could sort themselves out.

We headed north again on the bearing. The freezing wind pierced our flimsy desert camouflage. After two hours of hard tabbing we came to our MSR and crossed over. The next objective now was a metalled road further to the north.

We encountered a couple of inhabited areas, but boxed around without incident. Soon after midnight we heard noise in the distance. We started our routine to box around whatever it was and came across some armoured vehicles, laagered up, then a forest of antennas. The face of a squaddy was briefly illuminated as he lit a cigarette. He probably should have been on stag, but he was dossing in the cab of a truck. It was either a military installation or a temporary position. Whatever, we had to box around again.

Chris and the others can't have gone into it, or we would have heard the contact.

We carried on for about twenty minutes. All of us were on our chinstraps. We'd had eight hours of head down and go for it. The stress on the legs had been immense. My feet hurt. I felt completely knackered.

I had been thinking about the aircraft. It was hours ago that we'd heard them, so the pilots would be back in their hotels now enjoying their coffee and doughnuts while the engineers sorted their aircraft out. Such a lovely way to go to war. They climb into their nice, warm cockpits and ride over to their target. Down below, as far as they are concerned, is jet-black nothingness. Then what should they hear but the old Brit voice gobbing off, moaning about being in the shit. It must have been a bit of a surprise. I hoped so much that they were concerned for us, and were doing something. I wondered if they would have reported the incident by radio as soon as it had happened, or if they'd wait until they returned to base. Probably the latter. Hours ago, and no other fast jets had come over. I didn't know what the American system was for initiating a search and rescue package. I just hoped they knew that it was really important.

I blamed myself for the split. I felt a complete knobber and wondered if everybody else held the same opinion. I remembered a speech I had read by Field Marshal Slim. Talking about leadership, he had said something to the effect of, 'When I'm in charge of a battle and everything's going well and to plan and I'm winning—I'm a great leader, a real good lad. But you find out whether you can really lead or not when everything's going to rat-shit and you are to blame.' I knew exactly how he felt. I could have kicked myself for not confirming that Vince had registered that we were stopping. In my mind, everything was my fault. As we tabbed north I kept thinking, what the hell did I do wrong? The E&E must go right from here on. I mustn't make any more mistakes.

It was time to think about finding somewhere to hide. We'd been going over shale and rock, and had come to an area of solid sand. Our boots were hardly making any imprint. This was fine from the point of view of leaving sign, but the ground was so hard there was no way we could scrape a hiding place. It was nearly first light and we were still running around. Things were just starting to took a bit wriggly when Legs spotted some sand dunes a K to our west. We found ourselves in an area where the constant wind had made ripples and small mounds about 5–10 metres high. We looked for the tallest one. We wanted to be above eye-level.

We did what we should never do by going for isolated cover. But there was only this small knoll on an otherwise flat surface . On top of it was a small cairn of stones. Maybe somebody was buried there.

There was a small stone wall about a foot high around the cairn. We built it up slightly and lay down behind. It was icy cold as the wind whistled through the gaps in the stones, but at least it was a relief to stop tabbing. In the course of the last twelve hours, in total darkness and atrocious weather conditions, we had travelled 85Ks, the length of two marathons. My legs were aching. Lying down and being still was wonderful, but then cramp would start. As you moved, other areas were exposed to the cold. It was incredibly uncomfortable.

Looking to our south, we saw pylons running east–west. We used them to fix our position on the map. If we followed them, we would eventually hit the border. But if we used the pylons for navigation, who was to say that other people wouldn't as well?

We lay there for about half an hour, getting more and more uncomfortable. To our east about 2Ks away was a corrugated-iron building which was probably a water-boring station. It looked very inviting but it was even worse isolated cover. There was nothing to the north. There was no alternative but to stay where we were.

We had to keep really low. We cuddled up and tried to share body warmth. Dark clouds raced across the sky. The wind howled through the stones; I could feel it bite into me. I had known cold before, in the Arctic, but nothing like this. This was lying in a freezer cabinet, feeling your body heat slowly slip away. And we would have to stay there for the rest of the day, restricting our movement to what was possible below the height of the wall. When we got cramp, a common problem after a major tab, we had to help each other.

Legs got out the signals info from his map pocket and destroyed all the sensitive codes and other odds and bods. We lit the code sheets and burnt them one at a time to ensure that everything was destroyed, then crushed the ashes and spread them into the ground.

'I'll have a fag on while you've got your bonfire going,' said Dinger. 'Got to have a gasper before the fun starts.'

We resterilized ourselves, going through all our pockets to make doubly sure we had nothing left on us that would compromise the mission, ourselves, or anybody else. You might have something on you that would mean nothing to them unless you told them, but it could be something they could use as a starting point for the interrogation. 'What is this? What does it do?' You can go through a lot of pain for something that's totally irrelevant.

Naval Academy photo courtesy of United States Naval Academy Photographic Laboratory.

18 Factors that Influence Performance

Objectives

1. List and describe the primary strategies for coping with stress.

2. Discuss those personal traits which have been shown to moderate the effects of stress.

3. Formulate a personal plan for stress management.

4. Describe the impact of "social support" on performance under extreme stress.

Coping with Stress

@ Is it adaptive to block unwanted thoughts and emotions from awareness? Are relaxation and exercise truly healthful? What is the role played by feelings of control and optimism? Why is it said that friendships and other forms of social support are vital to our health and well-being?

Stress is inevitable. No one can prevent it. But we can try to minimize its harmful effects on our health. To understand how some people keep their composure while others crumble under the pressure, it is useful to examine the *coping* process and ask the question: What are some adaptive ways to cope with stress?

Coping Strategies

Leaving home. Taking exams. Breaking up with my college sweetheart. Working long nights on my thesis. Seeking employment in a competitive job market. Having children. Raising children. Facing academic pressures to publish or perish. Struggling to meet the deadline to complete this text. I could have coped with these sources of stress in any number of ways. In each case, I might have focused on solving the problem, talked to friends, invited distractions to pass the time, drunk myself silly, smiled and pretended that all was well—or I could have just freaked out.

Richard Lazarus and Susan Folkman (1984) distinguished two general types of coping strategies. The first is *problem-focused coping*, designed to reduce stress by overcoming the source of the problem. Difficulties in school? Study harder, hire a tutor, or reduce your workload. Marriage on the rocks? Talk it out or see a counselor. Problems at work? Consult with your boss or look for another job. The goal is to attack the source of your stress. A second approach is *emotion-focused coping*, in which one tries to manage the emotional turmoil, perhaps by learning to live with the problem rather than changing it. If you're struggling at school, at work, or in a relationship, you can keep a stiff upper lip and ignore the situation or make the best of it. According to Lazarus and Folkman, people take an active problem-focused approach when they think they can overcome the stressor, but they fall back on an emotion-focused approach when they see the problem as out of their control.

Thought Suppression One emotion-focused strategy people often use is to block stressful thoughts and feelings from awareness. I have used this strategy myself. As I recline in the dentist's chair with my mouth wide open and a bright light blinding my eyes, the sound of the drill and the grinding on my teeth send chills up my spine. To cope, I try to lock eyes with a gigantic toothbrush hanging on the wall or imagine that I'm lying on a warm, sunny beach. Ignore the noise and the pain, I say to myself. Think about something else.

Try not to think of a white bear, and this image is likely to intrude upon consciousness with remarkable frequency.

This strategy, which is a form of *thought suppression*, can have a peculiar, paradoxical effect. Daniel Wegner (1994) conducted a series of experiments in which he had subjects say whatever came to mind into a microphone—and told half of them not to think about a white bear. Wegner found that subjects could not keep the image from popping to mind. What's more, he found that when subjects were permitted later to think about a white bear, those who had earlier tried to suppress the image were unusually preoccupied with it, providing evidence of a "rebound" effect. It is difficult to follow the command "Don't think about it"—and the harder you try, the less likely you are to succeed. The solution: focused self-distraction. In one study, Wegner told subjects to imagine a tiny red Volkswagen whenever the forbidden white bear intruded into consciousness, and the rebound effect vanished.

What do white bears and red cars have to do with coping? Lots. When people try to force stressful thoughts or painful sensations out of awareness, they are doomed to fail. In fact, the problem may worsen. That's where focused self-distraction comes in. In a study of pain tolerance, Delia Cioffi and James Holloway (1993) had subjects put a hand into a bucket of ice-cold water and keep it there until they could no longer bear the pain. One group was instructed to avoid thinking about the sensation. A second group was told to form a mental picture of their room at home. Afterward, subjects who had coped through suppression were slower to recover from the pain than were those who used focused self-distraction. To manage stress—whether it's caused by physical pain, a strained romance, final exams, or problems at work—distraction ("think about lying on the beach") is a better coping strategy than mere suppression ("don't think about the dentist's drill").

It may be particularly maladaptive to keep secrets and hold in strong emotions. More than 100 years ago, Breuer and Freud (1895) theorized that emotional inhibition, or what they called strangulated affect, can cause mental illness. Current studies suggest it may be physically taxing as well. In the laboratory, James Gross and Robert Levenson (1997) showed female students funny, sad, and neutral films. Half the time, they instructed subjects to not let their feelings show. From a hidden camera, videotapes confirmed that when asked to conceal their feelings, subjects were less expressive. But physiological recordings revealed that as they watched the funny and sad films, subjects had a greater cardiovascular response when they tried to inhibit their feelings than when they did not. Physiologically, the effort to suppress the display of emotion backfired.

A recent study by Steve Cole and others (1996) pushes this point a suggestive but profound step further. These investigators identified eighty gay men in the Los Angeles area who were newly infected with the HIV virus but had no symptoms, administered various psychological tests, and monitored their progress every six months for nine years. They found that in men who were partly "in the closet"—compared to those who were completely open about their homosexuality—the infection spread more rapidly, causing them to die sooner. This correlation does not *prove* that "coming out" is healthier than "staying in," but it is consistent with other studies demonstrating the harmful effects of actively concealing one's thoughts and feelings.

Relaxation There are also ways to manage the physical symptoms of stress. One popular technique is *relaxation*. Years ago, cardiologist Herbert Benson (1975) recruited experienced meditators for a study and fitted them with various physiological measurement devices—including catheters in the veins and arteries. Subjects spent twenty minutes in a quiet resting state, then meditated, then returned to a normal state. There were no observable changes in their posture or level of physical activity. But the physiological results were striking. While meditating, subjects consumed 17 percent less oxygen—and also produced less carbon dioxide. Breathing slowed from fourteen or fifteen breaths per minute to ten or eleven breaths per minute. Blood tests showed there was a marked drop in the amount of lactate, a chemical typically associated with anxiety. Finally, brain-wave patterns were slower than those normally found in the waking state.

According to Benson, who went on to establish the Mind/Body Medical Institute at Harvard Medical School, anyone can be taught this "relaxation response." Try it. Sit quietly and comfortably, close your eyes, and relax all the muscles from your feet to your face. Then breathe deeply through the nose, and each time you exhale, silently utter some word (such as "one . . . one . . . one . . . "). As you proceed, let your mind drift freely. If anxiety-provoking thoughts pop into mind, refocus your attention on the word you are chanting and stay calm. Repeat this exercise once or twice a day, for ten to twenty minutes. Says Benson (1993), "By practicing two basic steps—the repetition of a sound, word, phrase, prayer, or muscular activity; and a passive return to the repetition whenever distracting thoughts recur—you can trigger a series of physiological changes that offer protection against stress."

Meditative relaxation can be powerfully effective. In one study, Friedman and Ulmer (1984) randomly assigned hundreds of heart attack patients to one of two treatment groups. In one group, they received standard medical advice on drugs, exercise, work, and diet. In the second group, they were also counseled on how to relax, slow down their pace, smile more, and take time to enjoy the moment. After three years, the relaxation patients had suffered only half as many repeat heart attacks as those in the control group (see Figure 18.1). In another study, Janice Kiecolt-Glaser and others (1985) found that relaxation can also fortify the immune system. Among a group of senior citizens, those who were trained in relaxation three times a week for one month felt better—and exhibited an increase in natural-killer-cell activity—compared to others in a no-treatment control group.

Aerobic Exercise   A second way to manage stress is through *aerobic exercise*—sustained, vigorous physical activity designed to build heart and lung capacity and to enhance the body's use of oxygen. Walking, running, swimming, bicycling, cross-country skiing, and dancing are ideal forms of aerobic exercise. The health benefits seem clear. One large-scale study showed that men who burned at least 2,000 calories a week through exercise lived longer than those who were less active (Paffenbarger et al., 1986). Another study of both men and women showed that even a moderate amount of exercise is associated with increased longevity (Blair et al., 1989).

Don't jump from these correlations to the causal conclusion that if you start running you'll live longer. It is possible, for example, that people who exercise regularly are also more health-conscious about eating, smoking, wearing seat belts, and other factors that contribute to longevity. Still, the effects of exercise on physical health are extensive. Research shows that exercise strengthens the heart, lowers blood pressure, aids in the metabolism of fats and carbohydrates, boosts self-esteem, elevates mood, and improves cognitive functioning (Simon,

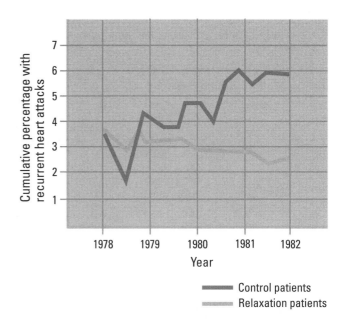

Control patients
Relaxation patients

FIGURE 18.1 **Relaxation and the heart**   After three years, heart-attack victims who were taught to relax their pace suffered fewer recurrences than did those who received only standard medical advice (Friedman & Ulmer, 1984).

"Those who think they have not time for bodily exercise will sooner or later have to find time for illness."

—EDWARD STANLEY

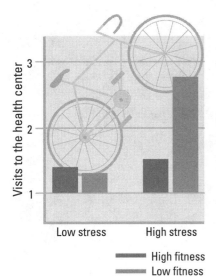

Visits to the health center

3

2

1

Low stress   High stress

High fitness
Low fitness

FIGURE 18.2 Fitness, strength, and health
In a study of college students, life stress was associated with more visits to the health center among students low in aerobic fitness. Those who were high in fitness absorbed the stress with less illness (Brown, 1991).

hardiness A personality style that is characterized by commitment, challenge, and control and acts as a buffer against stress.

1991). In a study involving mildly depressed female students, Lisa McCann and David Holmes (1984) randomly assigned some to take part in a ten-week aerobic-exercise program and others to a ten-week program of relaxation exercises. A third group received no treatment. Afterward, those who exercised were the most improved, scoring lowest on a measure of depression.

Physical fitness can also soften the toxic effects of stress on health. To demonstrate, Jonathon Brown (1991) brought college students into the laboratory, tested their aerobic fitness on an exercise bicycle, inquired about recent stressful events, and counted the number of illness visits they made to the university health center that year. The result: Life stress was linked to illness only among students who were out of shape. Those who were more physically fit absorbed more stress without an increase in illness (see Figure 18.2).

The "Self-healing Personality"

For years, psychologists have speculated about very specific correlations between personality traits and illness. People who are anxious are doomed to get ulcers, we're told, just as angry types are prone to headaches, depressives are prone to cancer, weak and dependent types suffer from asthma, and workaholics die of heart attacks. In light of recent work on psychology and the immune system, others have considered the alternative possibility that there's a generic "disease-prone personality" consisting of a cluster of negative emotional states. According to this view, anger, anxiety, hostility, and depression all lead us to complain of bodily ailments (Watson & Pennebaker, 1989) and perhaps put us at risk for a whole range of illnesses (Friedman & Booth-Kewley, 1987). Whether the links are specific or general is a matter of dispute. However, most health researchers believe that certain traits are healthier and more adaptive than others (Adler & Matthews, 1994)—and that there is, in essence, a "self-healing personality" (Friedman, 1991).

Hardiness Stress affects people differently, an observation that led Suzanne Kobasa (1979) to wonder why some of us are more resilient than others. Kobasa studied 200 business executives who were under stress. Many said they were frequently sick, affirming the link between stress and illness; others had managed to stay healthy. The two groups were similar in terms of age, education, job status, income, and ethnic and religious background. But from various tests, it was clear that they differed in their attitudes toward themselves, their jobs, and the people in their lives. Based on these differences, Kobasa identified a personality style she called **hardiness** and concluded that hardy people have three characteristics: (1) *commitment*, a sense of purpose with regard to work, family, and other domains; (2) *challenge*, an openness to new experiences and a desire to embrace change; and (3) *control*, the belief that one has the power to influence important future outcomes.

In general, research supports the point that hardiness acts as a buffer against stress (Funk, 1992)—and that control is the active ingredient. Studies have shown that the harmful effects of noise, crowding, heat, and other stressors are reduced when people think they can exert control over these aspects of their environment. Thus, rats exposed to electric shock are less likely to develop ulcers if they are trained to know they can avoid it; children awaiting a doctor's injection cope better when they're prepared with a pain-reducing cognitive strategy; nursing-home residents become healthier and more active when they're given more control over daily events; and patients with cancer, AIDS, and coronary heart disease are better adjusted, emotionally, when they think that they can influence the course of their illness (Rodin, 1986; Helgeson, 1992; Reed et al., 1993; Thompson et al., 1993).

Optimism and Hope A second important trait in the self-healing personality is *optimism,* defined as a generalized tendency to expect positive outcomes. Are *you* an optimist or a pessimist? Do you look on the bright side and expect good things to happen, or do you tend to believe in Murphy's Law, that if something can go wrong, it will? By asking questions like these, Michael Scheier and Charles Carver (1985) categorized college students along this dimension and found that dispositional optimists reported fewer illness symptoms during the semester than did pessimists. Correlations between optimism and health are common. Other studies have shown that optimists are more likely to take a problem-focused approach to coping with stress; complete a rehabilitation program for alcoholics; make a quicker, fuller recovery from coronary-artery bypass surgery; and, among gay men concerned about AIDS, take a more active, less avoidant approach to the threat (Scheier & Carver, 1992).

"Cheerfulness is the very flower of health."

—JAPANESE PROVERB

In a book entitled *Learned Optimism,* Martin Seligman (1991) argues that optimism and pessimism are rooted in our "explanatory styles"—in the ways we explain good and bad events. Based on a large number of studies (Sweeney et al., 1986; Abramson et al., 1989), Seligman described the typical pessimist as someone who attributes failure to factors that are internal ("It was my fault"), permanent ("I'm all washed up"), and global ("I'm bad at everything")—and success to factors that are external ("I lucked out"), temporary ("The task was easy"), and specific ("It was my strength"). This explanatory style breeds despair and low self-esteem. In contrast, the typical optimist is someone who makes the opposite attributions. According to Seligman, optimists blame failure on factors that are external, temporary, and specific, while crediting success to factors that are internal, permanent, and global—an explanatory style that fosters hope, effort, and a high regard for oneself. Do *you* interpret events as an optimist or as a pessimist? Imagine the situations described in Table 18.1 and circle cause A or B—whichever you think is most likely. When you've finished, count the number of points you earned (in parentheses). A score of 0 indicates a high degree of pessimism; a score of 8 indicates a high degree of optimism (Seligman, 1991).

In the course of a lifetime, everyone has setbacks. Do optimists weather the storms better? Are they happier, healthier, and more successful? Do they have, in the words of Alan McGinnis (1987, p. 16), "the gift for turning stumbling blocks into stepping stones"? To find out, Christopher Peterson and others (1988) collected personal essays that were written in the 1940s by ninety-nine men who had just graduated from Harvard, and they analyzed these materials to determine what each subject's explanatory style was in his youth. Were these men optimists or pessimists? What eventually happened to them? Their health at age sixty was predictable from their explanatory styles thirty-five years earlier. Young optimists were healthier than young pessimists later in life. Why? A later study by Leslie Kamen-Siegel and colleagues (1991) provides a clue. These researchers measured explanatory style, took blood samples, and found that pessimists had a weaker immune response than optimists.

There's an old saying "While there's life, there's hope." It's possible that the opposite is also true: "While there's hope, there's life." In a remarkable illustration of this point, Susan Everson and others (1996) studied 2,428 middle-age men in Finland. Based on the extent to which they agreed with two simple statements ("I feel that it is impossible to reach the goals I would like to strive for" and "The future seems hopeless, and I can't

Table 18.1 Explanatory-Styles Test

1. You forget your boyfriend's (girlfriend's) birthday:
   - A. I'm not good at remembering birthdays. (0)
   - B. I was preoccupied with other things. (1)
2. You stop a crime by calling the police:
   - A. A strange noise caught my attention. (0)
   - B. I was alert that day. (1)
3. You were extremely healthy all year:
   - A. Few people around me were sick, so I wasn't exposed. (0)
   - B. I made sure I ate well and got enough rest. (1)
4. You fail an important examination:
   - A. I wasn't as smart as the others taking the exam. (0)
   - B. I didn't prepare for it well. (1)
5. You ask someone to dance, and he (she) says no:
   - A. I am not a good enough dancer. (0)
   - B. He (she) doesn't like to dance. (1)
6. You gain weight over the holidays and you can't lose it:
   - A. Diets don't work in the long run. (0)
   - B. The diet I tried didn't work. (1)
7. You win the lottery:
   - A. It was pure chance. (0)
   - B. I picked the right numbers. (1)
8. You do extremely well in a job interview:
   - A. I felt extremely confident during the interview. (0)
   - B. I interview well. (1)

Source: M. E. P. Seligman (1991). Learned optimism. New York: Knopf.

believe that things are changing for the better"), the men were initially classified as having a high, medium, or low sense of hopelessness. When the investigators checked the death records roughly six years later, they found that the more hopeless the men were at the start, the more likely they were to have died of various causes—even when the men were otherwise equated for their age and prior health status. Compared to those who were low in hopelessness, the highs were more than twice as likely to die from cancer and four times more likely to die of cardiovascular disease (see Figure 18.3).

As usual, we should be cautious in interpreting correlations—in this case, between optimism, pessimism, and longevity. Assuming that optimism is adaptive, however, and that it's better to be safe than sorry, Seligman (1991) believes that pessimists can be retrained—not through "mindless devices like whistling a happy tune" but by learning a new set of cognitive skills. According to Seligman, people can train themselves to make optimistic explanations by following three steps: (1) think about situations of adversity (losing in a sports competition, having a friend not return your calls); (2) consider the way you normally explain these events, and if it is pessimistic ("I always choke under pressure," "My friend does not really care about me"); then (3) dispute these explanations by looking closely at the facts ("My opponent played a great game," "My friend has been very busy"). Practice this exercise over and over again. You may find that changing a pessimistic outlook is like breaking a bad habit.

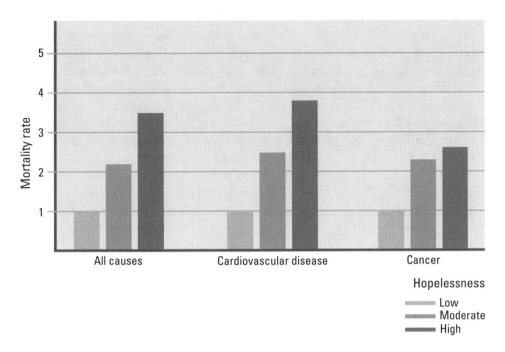

FIGURE 18.3 **Hopelessness and the risk of death**   Among middle-age men in Finland, those who were initially high rather than low in hopelessness were more likely to die within six years—overall, from cancer, and from cardiovascular disease. On these same measures of mortality, those who were moderate in hopelessness fell between the two extremes.

Social Support

We hear it all the time: No man (or woman) is an island, human beings are social animals, people need people, and to get by you need a little help from your friends. Is all this true? Do close family ties, lovers, buddies, community support groups, and relationships at work serve as a buffer against stress? The truth is: yes. An overwhelming amount of evidence now shows that **social support** has therapeutic effects on our psychological and physical health (Wills, 1990; Uchino et al., 1996).

Psychiatrist David Spiegel, of the Stanford University School of Medicine, came to appreciate the value of social connections several years ago when he organized support groups for women with advanced breast cancer. The groups met weekly in ninety-minute sessions to laugh, cry, share stories, and discuss ways of coping. Spiegel had fully expected the women to benefit, emotionally, from the experience. But he found something else he did not expect: These women lived an average of eighteen months longer than did similar others who did not attend these groups. According to Spiegel (1993), "The added survival time was longer than any medication or other known medical treatment could be expected to provide for women with breast cancer so far advanced" (pp. 331–332).

Similar discoveries were also made by other researchers. In one study, Lisa Berkman and Leonard Syme (1979) surveyed 7,000 residents of Alameda County, California, conducted a nine-year follow-up of mortality rates, and found that the more social contacts people had, the longer they lived. In fact, those who lived alone, had very few close friends or relatives, and did not participate in community groups died at a rate two to five times greater than those with more extensive social networks. This was true of both men and women, young and old, rich and poor, and people from all racial and ethnic backgrounds. James House and his colleagues (1988) then

social support The healthful coping resources provided by friends and other people.

Human beings are inherently social creatures. Close and intimate relationships provide us with a buffer against stress and illness.

(Brancusi, Constantin (Rumanian, 1876–1957), "The Kiss," 1916. H: 23 inches, W: 13 inches, D: 10 inches. Limestone. Philadelphia Museum of Art: The Louise and Walter Arensberg Collection. Photo by Graydon Wood, 1994.)

studied 2,754 adults interviewed during visits to their doctors. He found that the most socially active men were two to three times less likely to die within nine to twelve years than those of similar age who were more isolated. Socially active women were almost two times less likely to die. According to House, social isolation, statistically, is as predictive of early death as smoking or high cholesterol.

Research findings like these are now common. Married people are more likely than unmarried people to survive cancer for five years (Taylor, 1990), gay men infected with HIV are less likely to contemplate suicide if they have close ties than if they do not (Schneider et al., 1991), and people who have a heart attack are less likely to have a second one if they're living with someone than if they live alone (Case et al., 1992). Among students stressed by schoolwork and among the spouses of cancer patients, more social support is also associated with a stronger immune response (Baron et al., 1990; Jemmott & Magloire, 1988). Based on their review of eighty-one studies, Bert Uchino, John Cacioppo, and Janice Kiecolt-Glaser (1996) concluded that in times of stress, social support lowers blood pressure, lessens the secretion of stress hormones, and strengthens immune responses. There's no doubt about it: Being isolated from other people is hazardous to your health.

Our social connections can be therapeutic for many reasons. Friends encourage us to get out, exercise, eat regularly, or seek professional help. Emotionally, friends offer sympathy and reassurance in times of stress. Perhaps having a good friend around boosts our confidence, self-esteem, and sense of security. On an intellectual level, having someone to talk to provides a sounding board, new perspectives, and advice as we struggle for solutions to problems. Communicating helps us sort things out in our own minds (Clark, 1993).

It's important to talk about upsetting experiences. James Pennebaker (1990) conducted a number of studies in which he had college students talk to a hidden experimenter or into a tape recorder, or else simply write about a trauma they had experienced. While speaking, subjects were physiologically aroused and upset. Many tearfully recounted accidents, failures, instances of sex abuse, loneliness, rape, the divorce of their parents, shattered relationships, death, and their fears about the future. Soon, however, the subjects were feeling better than ever. Blood samples taken after the experiment revealed a heightened immune response relative to their baseline level, and in the ensuing months subjects who had "opened up" made 50 percent fewer visits to the campus health center. A comparison group of students who talked only about trivial matters did not similarly benefit from the experience.

The value of social support may be so basic that *any* bond formed with another living being—even the companionship of a pet—promotes health and survival (Beck & Katcher, 1983). In one study, heart-attack victims who owned pets were more likely to survive the year than those without pets (Friedmann et al., 1980). In a second study, elderly men and women made fewer visits to the doctor in times of stress if they had pet dogs than if they did not (Siegel, 1990). It may be that animals have a calming influence on us and provide a source of comfort. Karen Allen and others (1991) found that when female subjects (all of whom owned pet dogs) worked on a stressful laboratory task, those who had their pets with them became less physiologically aroused (as measured by changes in blood pressure, perspiration, and pulse rate) than those who were alone or had a human friend present. As companions, pets are wonderfully nonjudgmental.

Four Brave Chaplains

Victor M Parachin

When the U.S.A.T. Dorchester sank, four ordinary chaplains showed extraordinary faith and personal sacrifice.

"It is courage, courage, courage, that raises the blood of life to crimson splendor."

—GEORGE BERNARD SHAW

It was the evening of February 2, 1943, and the U.S.A.T. Dorchester was crowded to capacity, carrying 902 servicemen, merchant seamen and civilian workers. Once a luxury coastal liner, the 5,649-ton vessel had been converted into an Army transport ship. The Dorchester, one of three ships in the SG-19 convoy, was moving steadily across the icy waters from Newfoundland toward an American base in Greenland.

Hans J. Danielsen, the ship's captain, was concerned and cautious. Earlier the *Tampa,* one of the three Coast Guard cutters escorting the convoy, detected a submarine with its sonar. Captain Danielsen knew he was in dangerous waters even before he got the alarming information. German U-boats were constantly prowling these vital sea lanes, and several ships had already been blasted and sunk.

The *Dorchester* was now only 150 miles from its destination, but the captain ordered the men to sleep in their clothing and keep life jackets on. Many soldiers sleeping deep in the ship's hold disregarded the order because of the engine's heat. Others ignored it because the life jackets were uncomfortable.

Naval Academy photo courtesy of United States Naval Academy Photographic Laboratory.

On February 3, at 12:55 A.M., a periscope broke the chilly Atlantic waters. Through the cross hairs, an officer on board the German submarine U-223 spotted the *Dorchester.* After identifying and targeting the ship, he gave orders to fire the torpedoes. The hit was decisive—and deadly—striking the starboard side, amidship, far below the water line.

Danielsen, alerted that the *Dorchester* was taking water rapidly and sinking, gave the order to abandon ship. In less than 27 minutes, the *Dorchester* would slip beneath the Atlantic's icy waters.

Tragically, the hit had knocked out power and radio contact with the three escort ships. One of the cutters, however, saw the flash of the explosion. Two of the three cutters then circled the *Dorchester* rescuing survivors. The third Coast Guard cutter continued on, escorting the remaining two ships to safety.

Aboard the *Dorchester,* panic and chaos had set in. The blast had killed scores of men and many more were seriously wounded. Others, stunned by the explosion, were groping in darkness. Those sleeping without clothing rushed topside where they were confronted first by a blast of icy Arctic air and then by the knowledge that death awaited.

Men jumped from the ship into lifeboats, overcrowding them to the point of capsizing, according to eyewitnesses. Other rafts, tossed into the Atlantic, drifted away before soldiers could get in them.

Through the pandemonium, according to those present, four Army chaplains brought hope in despair and light in darkness. Those chaplains were Lieutenant George L. Fox, Methodist; Lieutenant Alexander D. Goode, Jewish; Lieutenant John P. Washington, Roman Catholic; and Lieutenant Clark V. Poling, Reformed.

Quickly and quietly the four chaplains spread out among the soldiers. There they tried to calm the frightened, tend the wounded and guide the disoriented toward safety.

"Witnesses of that terrible night remember hearing the four men offer prayers for the dying and encouragement for those who would live," says Wyatt P. Fox, son of Reverend Fox.

One witness, Private William B. Bednar, found himself floating in oil-smeared water surrounded by dead bodies and debris. "I could hear men crying, pleading, praying," Bednar recalls. "I could also hear the chaplains preaching courage. Their voices were the only thing that kept me going."

Another sailor, Petty Officer John J. Mahoney, tried to re-enter his cabin but was stopped by Rabbi Goode. Mahoney, concerned about the cold Arctic air, explained he had forgotten his gloves.

"Never mind," Goode responded. "I have two pairs." The rabbi then gave the petty officer his own gloves. In retrospect, Mahoney realized that Rabbi Goode was not conveniently carrying two pairs of gloves, and that the rabbi had decided not to leave the *Dorchester.*

By this time, most of the men were topside, and the chaplains opened a storage locker and began distributing life jackets. It was then that Engineer Grady Clark witnessed an astonishing sight.

When there were no more life jackets in the storage room, the chaplains removed theirs and gave them to four frightened young men.

"It was the finest thing I have ever seen or hope to see this side of heaven," said John Ladd, another survivor who saw the chaplains' selfless act.

Ladd's response is understandable. The altruistic action of the four chaplains constitutes one of the purest spiritual and ethical acts a person can make. When giving their life jackets, Rabbi Goode did not call out for a Jew; Father Washington did not call out for a Catholic; nor did the Reverends Fox and Poling call out for a Protestant. They simply gave their life jackets to the next man in line.

As the ship went down, survivors in nearby rafts could see the four chaplains—arms linked and braced against the slanting deck. Their voices could also be heard offering prayers.

While their words could not be distinguished, it is not too far-fetched to think the chaplains might have recited the Twenty-third Psalm, a passage of scripture revered by Jews and Christians alike. Then, perhaps, each chaplain offered a personal prayer, one in Hebrew, another in Latin and two in English.

Of the 902 men aboard the *U.S.A.T. Dorchester,* 672 died, leaving 230 survivors. When the news reached American shores, the nation was stunned by the magnitude of the tragedy and heroic conduct of the four chaplains.

"Valor is a gift," Carl Sandburg once said. "Those having it never know for sure whether they have it till the test comes."

That night Reverend Fox, Rabbi Goode, Reverend Poling and Father Washington passed life's ultimate test. In doing so, they became an enduring example of extraordinary faith, courage and selflessness.

In Honor and Faith

In February 1951, the Chapel of the Four Chaplains, an inter-faith memorial chapel, was dedicated in Philadelphia. Reverend Daniel A. Poling, Chaplain Clark Poling's father, presided over the ceremony, which was attended by former President Harry S. Truman.

The four chaplains themselves have been awarded the Distinguished Service Cross and the Purple Heart posthumously. The chaplains also received a special Congressional Medal for Valor on July 14, 1990.

Victor M. Parachin is an ordained minister, counselor and freelance writer.

19 Learned Behaviors— Stimuli and Consequences

Objectives

1. Outline the process of classical conditioning.

2. Discuss the primary principles of classical conditioning, including response acquisition, extinction, stimulus generalization and discrimination.

3. Describe the use of classical conditioning techniques to enhance leadership effectiveness.

Classical Conditioning

What did Pavlov learn from his experiments with salivating dogs? What is classical conditioning, and does it have any relevance to human behavior? Is it possible to condition people to develop new fears or attitudes? Can bodily functions similarly be "trained"?

I will always remember the summer of 1969 on the beach—the body surfing, bikinis, Frisbees, rock 'n' roll, the feel of hot sand between the toes, low-flying gulls, and warm air blowing the scent of salt water and coconut-oil suntan lotion. To this day, these memories flood my mind whenever I hear a song that was a radio hit at the time.

In stark contrast, I will never forget a cold, dark night in January 1976. I was in graduate school and had eaten dinner with a friend. Driving back to campus, I hit a patch of ice and skidded. Before I knew it, the car had scraped the wall of a brick building, turned on its side, and stalled. My friend and I were shaken but not hurt. Yet I vividly recall the red lights flashing on the dashboard, the smell of burned rubber, and the blast of cold air that hit my face when we climbed out through the door. I can also recall the song that played on the radio as we tried to escape. I still flinch whenever I hear it.

Following Aristotle, modern philosophers and psychologists have long believed that the key to learning is *association,* a tendency to connect events that occur together in space or time. Can learning by association be studied in a scientific manner? With the arrival of the twentieth century, psychology was poised and ready for one of its most important discoveries.

Pavlov's Discovery

Enter Ivan Pavlov, a Russian physiologist. After receiving his medical degree in 1882, he spent twenty years studying the digestive system and won a Nobel prize for that research in 1904. Pavlov was the complete dedicated scientist. Rumor has it that he once reprimanded a lab assistant who was ten minutes late for an experiment because of street riots stemming from the Russian Revolution: "Next time there's a revolution," he said, "get up earlier!" (Hothersall, 1990).

Ironically, Pavlov's most important contribution was the result of an incidental discovery. In studying the digestive system, he strapped dogs in a harness, placed different types of food in their mouths, and measured the flow of saliva through a tube surgically inserted in the cheek (see Figure 19.1). But there was a "problem": After repeated sessions, the dogs would begin to salivate *before* the food was actually put in their mouths. In fact, they would drool at the mere sight of food, the dish it was placed in,

Ivan Pavlov and some of the 200 other scientists who worked with him during his illustrious career.

classical conditioning A type of learning in which an organism comes to associate one stimulus with another (also called Pavlovian conditioning).

unconditioned response (UR) An unlearned response (salivation) to an unconditioned stimulus (food).

the assistant who brought it, or even the sound of the assistant's approaching footsteps. Pavlov saw these "psychic secretions" as a nuisance, so he tried to eliminate the problem by sneaking up on the dogs without warning. He soon realized, however, that he had stumbled on a very basic form of learning. This phenomenon was **classical conditioning,** and Pavlov devoted the rest of his life to studying it.

To examine the classical conditioning systematically, Pavlov needed to control the delivery of food, often a dry meat powder, as well as the events that preceded it. The animals did not have to be trained or "conditioned" to salivate. The salivary reflex is

FIGURE 19.1 Pavlov's classical-conditioning apparatus Strapped into an apparatus like the one shown here, Pavlov's dogs were conditioned to salivate. Through a tube surgically inserted into each dog's cheek, saliva was recorded by a pen attached to a slowly rotating cylinder of paper.

an innate **unconditioned response** (**UR**) that is naturally set off by food in the mouth, an **unconditioned stimulus** (**US**). There are numerous unconditioned stimulus-response connections. Tap your knee with a rubber mallet and your leg will jerk. Blow a puff of air into your eye and you'll blink. Turn the volume up on an alarm clock and, when it rings, your muscles will tighten. In each case, the stimulus automatically elicits the response. No experience is necessary.

Using the salivary reflex as a starting point, Pavlov (1927) sought to determine whether dogs could be trained by association to respond to a "neutral" stimulus—one that does not naturally elicit a response. To find out, he conducted an experiment in which he repeatedly rang a bell before placing food in the dog's mouth. Bell, food. Bell, food. After a series of these paired events, the dog started to salivate to the sound alone. Because the bell, which was initially a neutral stimulus, came to elicit the response through its association with food, it became a **conditioned stimulus** (**CS**), and salivation, a **conditioned response** (**CR**). With this experiment as a model, Pavlov and others trained dogs to salivate in response to buzzers, ticking metronomes, tuning forks, odors, lights, colored objects, and a touch on the leg. Similarly, researchers have trained animals to react with fear to such stimuli when they are paired with an unpleasant US, such as an electric shock or bright light. In one study, rhesus monkeys reacted with an accelerated heart rate to a simple tone that had been paired with a loud noise and a blast of air to the face (Kalin et al., 1996). In another study, rats froze and did not move whenever they were put into a cage in which they had previously been exposed to high concentrations of carbon dioxide (Mongeluzi et al., 1996). The basic classical conditioning procedure is diagrammed in Figure 19.2.

As we'll see, classical conditioning affects us all in ways that we're often not aware of. We learn to salivate (CR) to lunch bells, menus, the smell of food cooking, and the sight of a refrigerator (CS) because these stimuli are often followed by eating (US). Similarly, we cringe at the screeching sound of a dentist's drill because of past associations between that sound and pain. And we tremble at the sight of a flashing blue light in the rearview mirror because of its association with speeding tickets. For me, the beach—which was the site of so many good times of the past—is a conditioned stimulus that fills me with peaceful, easy feelings.

Basic Principles

Inspired by his initial discovery, Pavlov spent more than thirty years examining the factors that influence classical conditioning. Other researchers throughout the world also became involved. As a result, we now know that various species can be conditioned to blink when they hear a click that is paired with a puff of air to the eye, to fear colored lights that signal the onset of painful electric shocks, and to develop a distaste for foods they ate before becoming sick to the stomach (Schwartz & Reisberg, 1991). We also know that there are four very basic principles of learning: acquisition, extinction, generalization, and discrimination.

unconditioned stimulus (US) A stimulus (food) that triggers an unconditioned response (salivation).

conditioned stimulus (CS) A neutral stimulus (bell) that comes to evoke a classically conditioned response (salivation).

conditioned response (CR) A learned response (salivation) to a classically conditioned stimulus (bell).

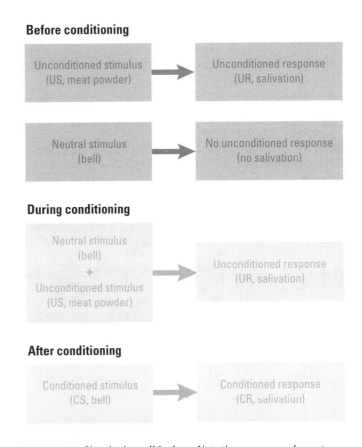

FIGURE 19.2 **Classical conditioning** Note the sequence of events before, during, and after Pavlov's study. At first, only the US (meat) elicits a UR (salivation). After a neutral stimulus (bell) repeatedly precedes the US, however, it becomes a CS and can elicit a CR (salivation) on its own.

Acquisition

Classical conditioning seldom springs full blown after a single pairing of the CS and US. Usually, it takes some number of paired trials for the initial learning, or **acquisition,** of a CR. In Pavlov's experiments, the dogs did not salivate the first time they heard the bell. As shown in the left panel of Figure 19.3, however, the CR increases rapidly over the next few pairings—until the "learning curve" peaks and levels off.

The acquisition of a classically conditioned response is influenced by various factors. The most critical are the order and timing of the presentation. In general, conditioning is quickest when the CS (the bell) precedes the onset of the US (food)—a procedure known as *forward* conditioning. Ideally, the CS should precede the US by about half a second and the two should overlap somewhat in time. When the onset of the US is delayed, conditioning takes longer and the conditioned response is weaker. When the CS and US are *simultaneous,* it takes even longer. And when the US is presented before the CS (a procedure referred to as *backward* conditioning), learning often does not occur at all (see Figure 19.4).

Once a buzzer, light, or other neutral stimulus gains the power to elicit a conditioned response, it becomes a CS—and can serve as though it were the US for yet another neutral stimulus. In one experiment, for example, Pavlov trained a dog to salivate to the sound of a bell, using meat powder as the US. After the CS–US link was established, he presented a second neutral stimulus, a black square, followed by the bell—but no food. The result: After repeated pairings, the black square on its own elicited small amounts of salivation. Through a process of "higher-order" conditioning, as illustrated in Figure 19.5, one CS was used to create another CS. In effect, the black square came to signal the bell, which, in turn, signaled the appearance of food (Rescorla, 1980).

acquisition The formation of a learned response to a stimulus through the presentation of an unconditioned stimulus (classical conditioning) or reinforcement (operant conditioning).

Extinction

In the acquisition phase of classical conditioning, a conditioned response is elicited by a neutral stimulus that is paired with a US. But what happens to the CR when the US is removed? Would a dog continue to salivate to a bell if the

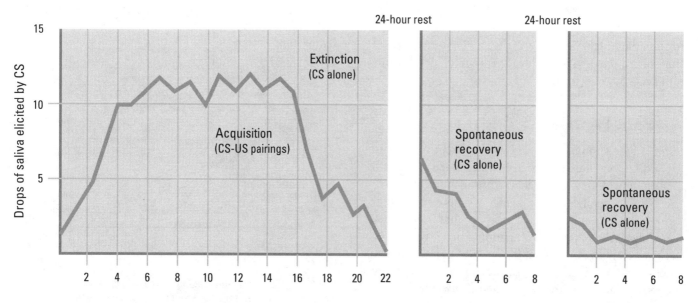

FIGURE 19.3 The rise and fall of a conditioned response In classical conditioning, the CS does not evoke a CR on the first trial, but over time it increases rapidly until leveling off. During extinction, the CR gradually declines. After a brief delay, however, there is usually a spontaneous recovery, or "rebounding," of the CR—until it is completely extinguished.

bell is no longer followed by food? Would the screeching of the dentist's drill continue to send chills up the spine if it is no longer followed by pain? No. If the CS is presented often enough without the US, it eventually loses its response-eliciting power. This apparent reversal of learning is called **extinction** (look again at the middle panel of Figure 19.3).

Extinction is a gradual process. Indeed, Pavlov found that when the same dog was returned for testing a day or two after extinction, it once again salivated to the bell—a rebound effect known as **spontaneous recovery** (depicted in the right panel of Figure 19.3). Often the dogs were easily reconditioned after just one repairing of the CS and US. Apparently, extinction does not *erase* what was previously learned—it only *suppresses* it.

Generalization   After an animal is conditioned to respond to a particular CS, other similar stimuli will often evoke the same response. In Pavlov's experiments, the dogs salivated not only to the original tone but also to other tones that were similar but not identical to the CS. Other researchers have made the same observation. In one study, for example, rabbits were conditioned to blink to a tone of 1,200 Hz (a pitch that is roughly two octaves higher than middle C) that was followed by a puff of air to the eye. Later, they blinked to other tones ranging from 400 Hz to 2,000 Hz. The result: The more similar the tone was to the CS, the more likely it was to evoke a conditioned response. This tendency to respond to stimuli other than the original CS is called **stimulus generalization** (Pearce, 1987).

Discrimination   Stimulus generalization can be useful because it enables us to apply what we learn to new, similar situations. But there are drawbacks. As illustrated by the child who is terrified of all animals because of one bad encounter with a barking dog, or the racist who assumes that "they" are all alike, generalization is not always adaptive. Sometimes we need to distinguish between objects that are similar—a process of **discrimination**. Again, Pavlov was the first to demonstrate this process. He conditioned a dog to salivate in the presence of a black square (a CS) and then noticed that the response generalized to a gray-colored square. Next, he conducted a series of conditioning trials in which the black square was followed by food while the gray one was not. The result: The dog continued to salivate only to the original CS. In a similar manner, the dog eventually learned to discriminate between the color black and darker shades of gray.

Pavlov's Legacy

Classical conditioning is so powerful and so basic that it occurs in animals as primitive as the sea slug, the fruitfly, and even the flatworm (the body of the flatworm contracts in response to electric shock; if the shock is repeatedly paired with light, the flatworm's body eventually contracts to the light alone) and as sophisticated as us humans (Turkkan, 1989; Krasne & Glanzman, 1995). In recent years, psychologists have taken classical conditioning in two directions: Some want to better *understand* the phenomenon—how, when, and why it works—while others are eager to *apply* it to different aspects of the human experience.

Theoretical Advances   Inspired by their initial successes and by the Darwinian assumption that all animals share a common evolutionary past, Pavlov and other early behaviorists made a bold claim: That any organism can be conditioned to any stimulus. It does not matter if the subject is a dog, cat, rat, pigeon, or person. Nor

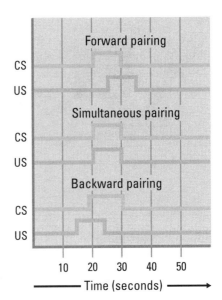

FIGURE 19.4 Temporal relations in classical conditioning A key factor in classical conditioning is the timing of the CS and US. The three temporal patterns illustrated here are presented in order—from the most to least effective.

extinction The elimination of a learned response by removal of the unconditioned stimulus (classical conditioning) or reinforcement (operant conditioning).

spontaneous recovery The reemergence of an extinguished conditioned response after a rest period.

stimulus generation The tendency to respond to a stimulus that is similar to the conditioned stimulus.

discrimination In classical and operant conditioning, the ability to distinguish between different stimuli.

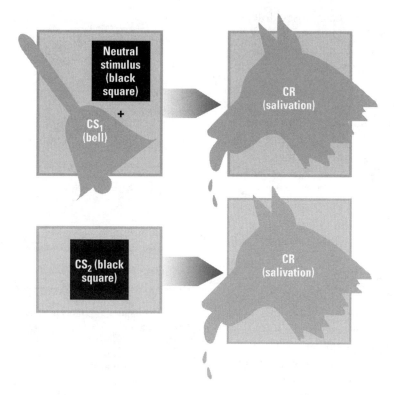

FIGURE 19.5 Higher-order conditioning After Pavlov trained a dog to salivate (CR) to a bell (CS), he preceded the bell with another neutral stimulus, a black square. After repeated pairings, the dog would salivate to the square itself. In effect, one CS was used to create another CS.

does it matter if the conditioned stimulus is a bell, light, buzzer, or odor. Whenever an initially neutral stimulus is paired with an unconditioned stimulus, the result is classical conditioning.

The early behaviorists also insisted that a science of human behavior must focus only on external, objective, quantifiable events. A *stimulus* can be observed and measured. So can its effect on an overt *response*. Together, these form the basis for what is known as S–R psychology. As far as the organism itself is concerned—its instincts, drives, perceptions, thoughts, and feelings—the behaviorists refused to speculate. In fact, Pavlov was said to have fined laboratory assistants who slipped into using soft "mentalistic" language. So where does the *organism* fit in? In recent years, researchers have come to appreciate some of the ways in which the "O" bridges the S and R—giving rise to a more flexible S–O–R brand of behaviorism. Two factors within the organism are particularly important: biological preparedness and cognitive representations.

Biological Preparedness All animals are biologically programmed, for survival purposes, to learn some associations more easily than others. This phenomenon was first discovered by John Garcia and Robert Koelling (1966). While studying the effects of radiation exposure on laboratory rats, they noticed that the animals would not drink from the plastic water bottles inside the radiation chambers. Since the radiation (US) was causing nausea (UR), they reasoned, perhaps the rats had acquired an aversion (CR) to the "plastic" taste of the water (CS).

To test this hypothesis, these investigators rigged an apparatus that worked as follows: When a rat licked a plastic drinking tube, it tasted sweetened water, saw a flash of light, and heard a loud clicking noise—all at the same time. The rats were then exposed to a high dose of X rays, which caused poisoning and nausea. The result: The rats later came to avoid the sweetened water after radiation poisoning, but they did not also learn to avoid the light or noise. The link between taste (CS) and poison (US) was so easily learned that it took only one pairing—even though the rats did not get sick until hours later (a far cry from the split-second CS–US interval that is usually necessary). Garcia and Koelling (1966) next found that when the US was a painful electric shock to the feet instead of X-ray poisoning, the rats continued to drink the water, but this time they avoided the audiovisual stimuli instead. In other words, although the rats were exposed to all stimuli, they proceeded to avoid only the flavored water after X-ray poisoning and only the light and noise after shock. Why was taste such a powerful CS when it was paired with poison but not with shock? And why were light and noise conditioned to the shock but not to the poison? Think about these associations for a moment, and one word will come to mind: *adaptiveness*. In nature, food is more likely to produce stomach poisoning than a pain in the foot, and an external stimulus is more likely to cause a pain in the foot than stomach illness. If you get sick after eating dinner in a new restaurant, you are likely to blame your illness on something you ate, not on the decor or the music that played. Clearly, we are "prepared" by nature to learn some CS–US associations more easily than others.

It is important to note that people acquire taste aversions, too—often with important practical implications. Consider, for example, an unfortunate side effect of chemotherapy treatments for cancer. These drugs tend to cause nausea and vomiting. As a result, patients often become conditioned to react with disgust and a loss of appetite to foods they had eaten hours before the treatment (Bovbjerg et al., 1992). Thankfully, the principles of classical conditioning offer a solution to this problem. When cancer patients are fed a distinctive maple-flavored ice cream before each treatment, they acquire a taste aversion to that ice cream—which becomes a "scapegoat" and protects the other foods in the patient's diet (Bernstein & Borson, 1986).

Research on the classical conditioning of fear reactions also illustrates the point that organisms are biologically predisposed to learn certain stimulus-response connections more than others. People all over the world share many of the same fears. Particularly common are fears of darkness, height, snakes, and insects—relatively harmless objects, some of which are never encountered. Yet very few of us are as terrified of automobiles, electrical outlets, appliances, and other objects that can be dangerous. Why? Martin Seligman (1971) speculated that the reason for this disparity is that humans are predisposed by evolution to be wary of stimuli and situations that posed a threat to our prehistoric ancestors.

Not everyone agrees with this analysis (Davey, 1995). However, it is supported by various strands of research. Susan Mineka and Michael Cook (1993) found that when laboratory-raised rhesus monkeys saw a wild-reared monkey of the same species exhibit fear in the presence of a toy snake, they acquired an intense fear of snakes. But when they saw the other monkey show fear in the presence of a toy rabbit, they did not similarly acquire a fear of rabbits (Cook & Mineka, 1990). Similar results are found in research with humans. When subjects are conditioned to fear an object that is paired with electric shock, their reaction—as measured by physiological arousal—is acquired faster and lasts longer when the object is a snake, a spider, or an angry face than when it is a "neutral" stimulus such as a flower, a house, or a happy face (Ohman, 1986; McNally, 1987). This differential response to fear-relevant objects is so basic that it occurs even when they are presented subliminally, outside of conscious awareness (Esteves et al., 1994).

Cognitive Representations   According to Pavlov, classical conditioning occurs whenever a neutral stimulus is paired with an unconditioned stimulus. With dogs salivating to bells, it all seemed passive, mindless, and automatic—a mechanical process in which the control of a reflex is simply passed from one stimulus to another. But is the process really that passive? Laboratory animals do not have to be geniuses to acquire a conditioned response, but they may be cognitively more active than Pavlov was willing to admit. Perhaps Pavlov's dogs salivated to his bells and tones because prior experience led them to *expect* food.

Based on years of research, Robert Rescorla (1988) concluded that classical conditioning is the process by which an organism learns that one event (CS) *predicts* another event (US). In other words, says Rescorla, a simple pairing of two stimuli is often not sufficient for conditioning. Rather, the organism must also learn that one event signals the coming onset of another. To demonstrate, Rescorla (1968) exposed rats to an electric shock (US) that was always paired with a tone (CS). In one condition, every shock was accompanied by the tone—so the CS reliably predicted the US. In a second condition, the rat experienced the same tone-shock pairs but was occasionally shocked without the tone as well. In other words, although the two events were paired, the CS did not reliably predict the US (see Figure 19.6). As Rescorla expected, the rats acquired a fear of the tone in the first-condition but not in the second. Apparently, classical conditioning requires more than a simple pairing of a CS and US. It requires that there be a reliable predictive relationship.

There is a great deal of research support for Rescorla's cognitive redefinition of the process of classical conditioning (Miller et al., 1995). This point of view is significant because it helps to explain various aspects of classical conditioning. For example, it explains why a conditioned response is hard to produce through a backward conditioning procedure in which the CS *follows* the US. The two stimuli co-occur, as in forward and simultaneous conditioning, but the CS cannot predict the US when it comes second in the sequence of events. Rescorla's model also explains why certain associations are learned more easily than others. You may recall that in the taste-aversion study described earlier, rats quickly learned to avoid food that was paired with stomach poisoning, and lights and noise that were paired with electric shock. But they did not similarly link food to external pain, or lights and noise to stomach poisoning. Why? As Rescorla (1988) put it, "Conditioning is not a stupid process by

Condition 1: Contiguity *with* predictive relationship

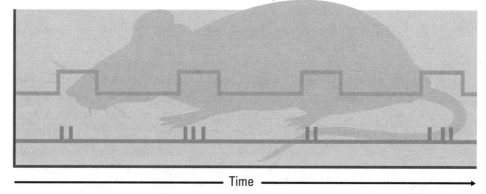

Time

Condition 2 : Contiguity *without* predictive relationship

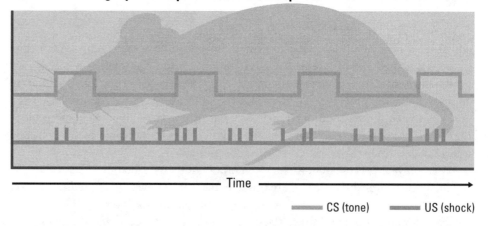

Time

━━━ CS (tone)   ━━━ US (shock)

FIGURE 19.6 **Classical conditioning: when the CS predicts the US** Rescorla (1968) exposed rats to a shock (US) paired with a tone (CS). In one condition, every US was paired by the CS (*top*). In a second condition, shocks were sometimes administered without a tone—so the CS did not predict the US (*bottom*). Indicating that a predictive relationship is required, rats learned to fear the tone in the first condition but not in the second

which an organism willy-nilly forms associations between any two stimuli that happen to co-occur. Rather the organism is better seen as an information seeker using logical and perceptual relations among events and its own preconceptions to form a sophisticated representation of its world" (p. 154).

Practical Applications   When Pavlov first found that he could train Russian dogs to drool to the sound of a dinner bell, nobody cared. In fact, E. B. Twitmyer, an American graduate student, had reported similar results at a psychology conference in 1904—the same year that Pavlov won the Nobel prize. At the time, Twitmyer was studying the knee-jerk reflex in humans. Before each trial, he would ring a bell to warn subjects that a hammer was about to strike the knee. Like Pavlov, he found that the subject's leg would soon twitch in response to the bell—even before the knee was hit. Was this a profound development? You might think so, but Twitmyer's presentation attracted little interest.

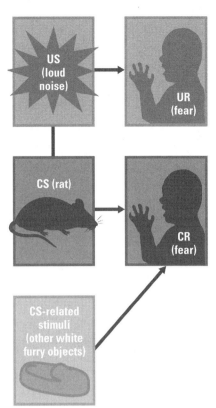

FIGURE 19.7 **The conditioning of Little Albert**   By linking a harmless white rat to an aversive loud noise, Watson conditioned a baby boy to react with terror to the rat. In fact, the fear spread, or "generalized," to other, superficially similar objects.

Conditioned Fears   Psychologists finally took notice of classical conditioning in 1914, when behaviorist John Watson described Pavlov's research to a group of American psychologists. To demonstrate the relevance of the phenomenon to humans, Watson and his assistant Rosalie Rayner (1920) conditioned an eleven-month-old boy named Albert to fear a white laboratory rat. "Little Albert" was a normal, healthy, well-developed infant. Like others his age, he was scared by loud noises but enjoyed playing with furry little animals. Enter John Watson. Modeled after Pavlov's research, Watson presented Albert with a harmless white rat. Then just as the boy reached for the animal, Watson made a loud, crashing sound by banging a steel bar with a hammer, which caused the startled boy to jump and fall forward, burying his head in the mattress he was lying on. After seven repetitions of this event, the boy was terrified of the animal. What's worse, his fear generalized, leading him to burst into tears at the sight of a rabbit, a dog, a Santa Claus mask, and even a white fur coat (see Figure 19.7).

From an ethical standpoint, Watson and Rayner's study was shameful. They infected an innocent baby with a fear that seemed to spread like a contagious disease from one white and furry stimulus to the next—and they did not "decondition" him (in case you're wondering, ethics committees would not approve this study today). Watson said that the boy was taken away before he had a chance to do so, but others believe that he may have known in advance that Albert's mother was going to remove her son from the research project (Harris, 1979). On the positive side, Little Albert's fear is a legend in the history of psychology because it established for the first time a link between Pavlov's dogs and an important aspect of the human experience. We now know that people can come to fear objects or places because they happened to be associated with aversive experiences. Classical conditioning spawned a revolutionary and effective method of treating these irrational fears and other anxiety-related disorders.

It is also important to note that babies can be conditioned to form positive *preferences* as well—for example, toward stimuli that are associated with maternal care. In one study, Regina Sullivan and her associates (1991) exposed newborns to a neutral odor. After each presentation, some were gently touched, an inherently pleasurable experience, while others were not. The next day, all the infants were returned to the lab and tested. As predicted, those for whom the odor was paired with the tactile stimulation were more likely to turn their heads toward that odor rather than away from it. This effect occurs not only in human infants but also in young rats, mice, hamsters, deer, guinea pigs, squirrel monkeys, and other species (Leon, 1992).

Social Attitudes and Behavior   Not everyone was happy about the possible uses of classical conditioning. In *Brave New World,* novelist Aldous Huxley (1932) warned us of a future in which diabolical leaders use Pavlov's methods to control followers. These concerns are unfounded. However, classical conditioning does affect our lives in many ways. Think about the movie *Jaws.* Early in the film, pulsating bass music is followed by the sight of a shark's fin and the bloody underwater mutilation of a young swimmer. Then it happens again. And again. Before you know it, the music alone (CS)—even without the great white shark (US)—has the audience trembling and ducking for cover. Many other examples illustrate this point. Based on powerful associations, American politicians wrap themselves in stars and stripes, the swastika strikes terror in the hearts of Jewish people, and the burning cross arouses fear among African Americans. In the words of Shelby Steele (1990), a black English professor, "there are objective correlatives everywhere that evoke a painful thicket of emotions . . . covering everything from Confederate flags and pickup trucks with gun racks to black lawn jockeys" (p. 154).

These examples suggest that people form strong positive and negative *attitudes* toward neutral objects by virtue of their links to emotionally charged stimuli. Arthur and Carolyn Staats (1958) thus presented college students with a list of national names (German, Swedish, Dutch, Italian, French, and Greek), each repeatedly paired with words that had pleasant (*happy, gift, sacred*) or unpleasant (*bitter, ugly, failure*) connotations. When subjects later evaluated the nationalities by name, they were more positive in their ratings of those that had been paired with pleasant words rather than with unpleasant words. Other researchers have altered people's reactions to neutral strings of letters by pairing their presentation with electric shock (Cacioppo et al., 1992). Recognizing the power of this effect, advertisers try to link their products to positive emotional symbols: sexy models, happy tunes, and nostalgic images—a strategy that seems to work by drawing attention to the product (Janiszewski & Warlop, 1993).

Through classical conditioning, people often react with strong emotions to once neutral objects such as national flags, yellow ribbons, and other symbols.

It's also possible to influence social *behavior* through classical conditioning. Consider the blue-and-yellow stripes on a VISA card, or the orange-and-yellow circles on a MasterCard. Through past associations, these logos may serve as visual cues that lead us to spend money. In one study, college students who were asked to estimate how much money they would be willing to spend on various consumer products gave higher estimates when there was a credit card lying on a table in the testing room than when there was not (Feinberg, 1986). In a second study, which was conducted in a restaurant, diners were randomly given tip trays for payment that were either blank or had a major credit card logo on it. With sixty-six cash-paying customers in the sample, the credit-card tray elicited an increase in tipping from 15.6 percent of the bill to 20.2 percent (McCall & Belmont, 1996).

Naval Academy photo courtesy of United States Naval Academy Photographic Laboratory.

The Immune System   One of the most exciting new research developments is the finding that just as animal reflexes and human emotional reactions can be classically conditioned, so can the body's immune system (Ader & Cohen, 1993). Consisting of more than a trillion white blood cells, the immune system guards our health by warding off bacteria, viruses, and other foreign substances that invade the body. When this system fails, as it does when it is ravaged by the AIDS virus, disease and death are the certain outcome. With that in mind, you can appreciate the following striking discovery. Psychologist Robert Ader had been using classical-conditioning procedures with rats in which he paired sweetened water with cyclophosphamide, a drug that causes nausea. Water, drug. Water, drug. As expected, the rats developed a taste aversion to the sweetened water. Unexpectedly, however, many of the animals died because the drug Ader used weakened the immune system by destroying certain types of white blood cells. To further explore this phenomenon, Ader joined with immunologist Nicholas Cohen (1985) in a series of experiments. They repeatedly fed the rats sweetened water, which is harmless, followed by the cyclophosphamide (US), which weakens the immune response (UR). The result: After several pairings, the sweetened water on its own (CS) caused a weakening of the immune response, followed by sickness and sometimes death (CR).

In light of this result, Dana Bovjberg and others (1990) wondered about cancer patients who take chemotherapy drugs. These drugs are designed to inhibit the growth of new cancer cells, but they also inhibit the growth of immune cells. With chemotherapy drugs always being given in the same room in the same hospital, is it possible, over time, that a patient's immune system would be conditioned to react in advance to cues in the surrounding environment? Yes. In a study of women who had undergone a number of chemotherapy treatments for ovarian cancer, these researchers found that their immune systems were weakened as soon as they were brought to the hospital—before they were treated. As with Pavlov's bell, the hospital setting had become a conditioned stimulus, thus triggering a maladaptive change in cellular activity.

These discoveries raise an exciting question: If the immune system can be weakened by conditioning, can it similarly be strengthened? Might it be possible some day to use classical conditioning to help people fight AIDS? Research on this question is still in its early stages, but positive results with animals have been reported (MacQueen et al., 1989; Shurin et al., 1995; Alvarez-Borda et al., 1995). And in recent studies with humans, researchers found that after repeatedly pairing sweet sherbet or other neutral stimuli with shots of adrenaline (which has the unconditioned effect of increasing activity in certain types of immune cells), the sherbet flavor alone eventually triggered an increase in the immune response (Buske-Kirschbaum et al., 1992, 1994).

20 Managing Behavior—Conditioning and Modeling

Objectives

1. Outline the process of operant conditioning.

2. Distinguish between reinforcement and punishment and provide examples of both.

3. Describe use of operant conditioning techniques to enhance leadership effectiveness.

4. Apply the concepts of operant conditioning to the processes used to shape the behavior of military personnel.

5. Give examples of how consistent application of the Navy's core values can reinforce and encourage favorable behavior in the Navy and Marine Corps.

Operant Conditioning

What is operant conditioning? How does it differ from classical conditioning? What is a reinforcement, and how does it differ from punishment? How do behaviorists explain the persistence of such maladaptive behaviors as gambling? Why are biological and cognitive perspectives on operant conditioning important?

I 'll never forget the first time I took my children to Sea World. After watching a dazzling show that featured killer whales jumping through hoops, sea lions playing volleyball, and dolphins dancing on the water, my son, who was only three years old at the time, asked, "How did the animals learn to do these tricks? . . . Did they go to college?"

Classical conditioning may explain why people salivate at the smell of food, cringe at the sound of a dentist's drill, run when someone yells, "Fire," or tremble at the sight of a flashing blue light in the rearview mirror. But it cannot explain how animals learn to perform complex acrobatics. Nor can it explain how we learn to solve equations, make people laugh, or behave in ways that earn love, praise, sympathy, or the respect of others. As we will see, the acquisition of voluntary, complex, and goal-directed behaviors such as these involves a second form of learning.

The Law of Effect

Before Pavlov had begun his research, an American psychology student named Edward L. Thorndike (1898) was blazing another trail. Interested in animal intelligence, Thorndike built a "puzzle box" from wooden shipping crates so he could observe how different animals learn to solve problems. In one study, he put hungry cats into a cage, one at a time, with a door that could be lifted by stepping on a lever. He then placed a tantalizing chunk of raw fish outside the cage—and beyond reach. You can imagine what happened next. After sniffing around the box, the cat tried to escape by reaching with its paws, scratching the bars, and pushing at the ceiling. At one point, the cat accidentally banged on the lever. The door opened and the cat scampered out to devour the food. Thorndike repeated the procedure again. The cat went through its previous sequence of movements and eventually found the one that caused the latch to open. After a series of trials, Thorndike's cats became more efficient: They went straight to the latch, stepped on the lever, and ate the food (see Figure 20.1).

Based on studies like this one, Thorndike (1911) proposed the **law of effect:** Behaviors that are followed closely in time by a satisfying outcome are "stamped in" or repeated, while those followed by a negative outcome or none at all are extinguished. In the puzzle box, cats spent progressively more time stepping on the latch and less time poking at the bars and ceiling. In the case of humans, Thorndike's law

law of effect A law stating that responses followed by positive outcomes are repeated while those followed by negative outcomes are not.

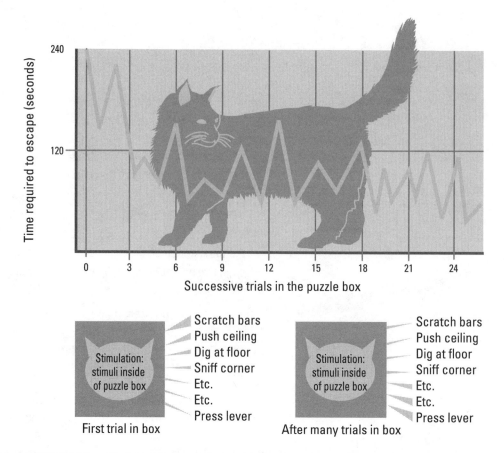

FIGURE 20.1 Thorndike's law of effect Thorndike's hungry cats initially engaged in various behaviors—sniffing, pawing, scratching the bars, pushing the ceiling, and pressing the lever that opened the escape hatch. Over a series of trials, the cats took less and less time to press the lever (*top*). Accordingly, Thorndike proposed that behaviors followed by a reward are "stamped in," while others fade away (*bottom*).

of effect was used to describe the process of socialization. By using rewards and punishments, parents train their children to eat with a utensil, and not to fling their mashed potatoes across the table. To the extent that we learn how to produce desirable outcomes, the process is adaptive.

The Principles of Reinforcement

Following in Thorndike's footsteps, behaviorist B. F. Skinner transformed the landscape of modern psychology. But first things first. To study learning systematically, Skinner knew that he had to design an environment in which he controlled the organism's response-outcome contingencies. So as a graduate student in 1930, he used an old ice chest to build a soundproof chamber equipped with a stimulus light, a response bar (for rats) or pecking key (for pigeons), a device that dispenses dry food pellets or water, metal floor grids for the delivery of electric shock, and an instrument outside the chamber that automatically records and tabulates the responses. This apparatus came to be known as the **Skinner box** (see Figure 20.2).

Next, Skinner introduced a new vocabulary. To distinguish between the active type of learning that Thorndike had studied (whereby the organism operates on the environment) and Pavlov's classical conditioning (whereby the organism is a more

Skinner box An apparatus, invented by B. F. Skinner, used to study the effects of reinforcement on the behavior of laboratory animals.

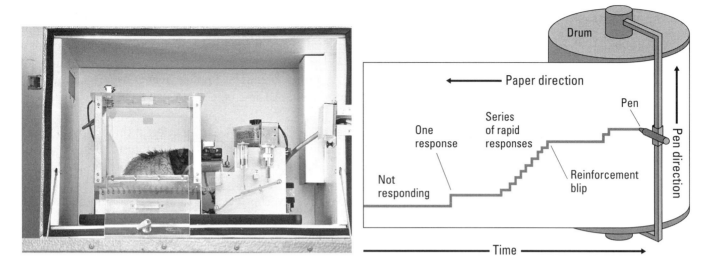

FIGURE 20.2 **The Skinner Box**

passive respondent), Skinner coined the term *operant conditioning*. **Operant conditioning** is the process by which organisms learn to behave in ways that produce desirable outcomes. The behavior itself is called an "operant" because it is designed to operate on the environment. In other words, in contrast to classical conditioning—which involves the learning of associations between stimuli, resulting in a passive response—operant conditioning involves the learning of an association between a spontaneously emitted action and its consequences (Rescorla, 1987).

To avoid speculating about an organism's internal state, Skinner also used the term **reinforcement** instead of *reward* or *satisfaction*. Objectively defined, a reinforcer is any stimulus that increases the likelihood of a prior response. There are two types of reinforcers: positive and negative. A *positive reinforcer* strengthens a prior response through the presentation of a positive stimulus. In the Skinner box, the food that follows a bar press is a positive reinforcer. For humans, so are money, grades, hugs, kisses, and a pat on the back. Even mild electrical stimulation to certain "pleasure centers" of the brain, which releases the neurotransmitter dopamine, has a satisfying effect and serves as a positive reinforcer (Olds & Milner, 1954; White & Milner, 1992; Wise & Rompre, 1989). In contrast, a *negative reinforcer* strengthens a response through the removal of an aversive stimulus. In a Skinner box, the termination of a painful electric shock is a negative reinforcer. Similarly, we learn to take aspirins to soften a headache, fasten our seatbelts to turn off the seatbelt buzzer, and rock babies to sleep to stop them from crying.

It is important to keep straight the fact that positive and negative reinforcers both have the same effect: to strengthen a prior response. Skinner was quick to point out that punishment is not a form of negative reinforcement. Although the two are often confused, **punishment** has the opposite effect: It decreases, not increases, the likelihood of a prior response. There are two types of punishment. A *positive punisher* weakens a response through the presentation of an aversive stimulus. Shocking a lab rat for pressing the response lever, scolding a child, locking a criminal behind bars, and boycotting a product are examples of this form of punishment designed to weaken specific behaviors. In contrast, a *negative punisher* weakens behavior by the removal of a stimulus typically characterized as positive. Taking food away from

operant conditioning The process by which organisms learn to behave in ways that produce reinforcement.

reinforcement In operant conditioning, any stimulus that increases the likelihood of a prior response.

punishment In operant conditioning, any stimulus that decreases the likelihood of a prior response.

"Boy, do we have this guy conditioned. Every time I press the bar down he drops a pellet in."

shaping A procedure in which reinforcements are used to gradually guide an animal or person toward a specific behavior.

a hungry rat and grounding a teenager by suspending driving privileges are two examples. The different types of reinforcement and punishment are summarized in Table 20.1. Notice that a reinforcement is a stimulus that strengthens a response through (1) the presentation of a positive stimulus, or (2) the removal of a negative stimulus. In contrast, punishment is a stimulus that weakens a response through (1) the presentation of a negative stimulus, or (2) the removal of a positive stimulus.

Shaping and Extinction   Modeled after the law of effect, Skinner's basic principle seemed straightforward. Responses that produce a reinforcement are repeated. But wait—if organisms learn by the consequences of their behavior, where does the very first response come from? Before the first food pellet, how does the animal come to press the bar? As demonstrated by Thorndike, one possibility is that the response occurs naturally as the animal explores the cage. Skinner pointed to a second possibility: that the behavior is gradually **shaped,** or guided, by the reinforcement of responses that come closer and closer to the desired behavior.

Imagine that you are trying to get a hungry white rat to press the bar in a Skinner box. Where do you begin? The rat has never been in this situation before, so it sniffs around, pokes its nose through the air holes, grooms itself, rears its hind legs, and so on. At this point, you can wait for the target behavior to appear on its own, or you can speed up the process. If the rat turns toward the bar, you drop a food pellet into the cage. Reinforcement. If it steps toward the bar, you deliver another pellet. Reinforcement. If the rat moves closer or touches the bar, you deliver yet another one. Once the rat is hovering near the bar and pawing at it, you withhold the next pellet until it presses down, which triggers the feeder. Before long, your subject is pressing the bar at a rapid pace. By reinforcing "successive approximations" of the target response, you will have shaped a whole new behavior.

Shaping is the procedure that animal trainers use to get circus elephants to walk on their hind legs, bears to ride bicycles, chickens to play a piano, squirrels to water-ski, and dolphins to jump through hoops—which brings me back to Sea World. The dolphin trainer begins by throwing the dolphin a fish for turning toward a hoop, then for swimming toward it, swimming through it underwater, and finally jumping through a hoop that is many feet up in the air. The process applies to people as well. Young children are toilet trained, socialized to behave properly, and taught to read through step-by-step reinforcement. Similarly, political candidates repeat statements that draw loud applause and abandon those that are met with silence—thereby creating messages that are shaped by what voters want to hear. Rumor has it that a group of college students once conspired to shape the behavior of their good-natured psychology professor. Using eye contact as a reinforcer, the students trained this professor to lecture from a certain corner of the room. Whenever he moved in that direction, they looked up at him; otherwise, they looked down. Before long, he was

Table 20.1 Types of Reinforcement and Punishment

PROCEDURE	EFFECT ON BEHAVIOR	
	INCREASES	*DECREASES*
Presentation of stimulus	Positive reinforcement (feed the rat)	Positive punishment (shock the rat)
Removal of stimulus	Negative reinforcement (stop the shock)	Negative punishment (stop the food)

Using operant conditioning, Sea World animal trainers can get these orca whales to jump on cue.

lecturing from the corner of the classroom, not quite realizing that he had been "shaped."

In classical conditioning, repeated presentation of the CS without the US causes the CR to gradually weaken and disappear. Extinction also occurs in operant conditioning. If you return your newly shaped rat to the Skinner box but disconnect the feeder from the response bar, you'll find that after the rat presses the bar a few times without reinforcement, this behavior will fade and become extinguished. By the same token, people stop smiling at those who don't smile back, stop helping those who never reciprocate, and stop working when their efforts meet with continued failure.

Schedules of Reinforcement   Every now and then, scientists stumble into their greatest discoveries. Pavlov was a classic example. So was Skinner. Early in his research career, Skinner would reinforce his animals on a continuous basis: Every bar press produced a food pellet. Then something happened. At the time, Skinner had to make his own pellets by squeezing food paste through a pill machine and then waiting for them to dry. The process was time consuming. "One pleasant Saturday afternoon," Skinner recalled, "I surveyed my supply of dry pellets and, appealing to certain elemental theorems in arithmetic, deduced that unless I spent the rest of the afternoon and evening at the pill machine, the supply would be exhausted by 10:30 Monday morning" (1959, p. 368). Not wanting to spend the whole weekend in the lab, Skinner rationalized to himself that not *every* response had to be reinforced. He adjusted his apparatus so that the bar-press response would be reinforced on a partial basis—only once per minute. Upon his return the next week, however, he found rolls of graph paper with response patterns that were different from anything he had seen before. From this experience, Skinner came to realize the powerful effects of "partial reinforcement." Indeed, he and others went on to identify four schedules of reinforcement (see Figure 20.3), each having different effects on behavior (Ferster & Skinner, 1957).

Fixed-Interval (FI) Schedule   In the situation just described, reinforcement followed the first response made after a fixed interval of *time* had elapsed. In an FI-1

B. F. Skinner was born in 1904 and received his psychology degree from Harvard in 1931. Skinner's behavioral approach was so influential that it spawned a separate division of the APA, an independent professional organization, and several journals (Latal, 1992). Skinner is consistently ranked by his peers as one of the most important psychologists of all time (Korn et al., 1991).

On August 10, 1990, Skinner made his final public appearance in Boston at the APA's annual convention and he received an award for Outstanding Lifetime Contribution to Psychology. I was there—and so, it seemed, was everyone else I knew. Upon his introduction, Skinner was greeted with a thunderous standing ovation. Everyone in the audience knew they were watching a living legend. They also knew he was dying. The talk itself was vintage Skinner. For twenty minutes, and without notes, he insisted, as always, that psychology could never be a science of the mind, only a science of behavior.

On August 17, 1990, Skinner completed his last article, for the American Psychologist. *He died the next day.*

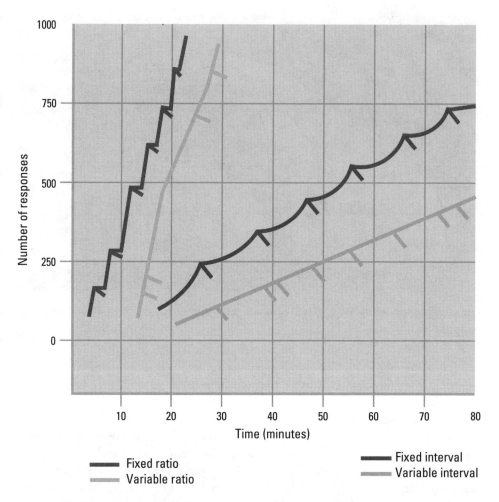

1000

750

Number of responses

500

250

0

10   20   30   40   50   60   70   80

Time (minutes)

Fixed ratio

Variable ratio

Fixed interval

Variable interval

FIGURE 20.3 Schedules of reinforcement   These curves show the response patterns typically produced by different schedules of reinforcement. The steeper the curve, the higher the response rate (the slash marks on each curve indicate the delivery of a reinforcement). As you can see, the rate of responding is higher under ratio than interval schedules.

schedule, the response produces food after each new minute; or it may be made available only after every two (FI-2), ten (FI-10), or fifteen (FI-15) minutes. The schedule is fixed by time, and it tends to produce a slow, "scalloped" response pattern. After the animal learns that a certain amount of time must elapse, it pauses after each reinforcer and then responds at an accelerating rate until it nears the end of the cycle—which signals that the next reinforcement is available. The student whose rate of studying starts slow, increases before midterms, trails off, and picks up again before finals illustrates this reaction to an FI schedule.

Variable-Interval (VI) Schedule   Once animals learn what the fixed pattern is, they press the bar only as they near the end of each interval. To counter this lazy response pattern, Skinner tried varying the interval around an average. In other words, an interval may average one minute in length (a VI-1 schedule), but the actual timing of a reinforcement is unpredictable from one interval to the next—say, after fifty seconds, then two minutes, ten seconds, and one minute. The result is a slow but steady, not scalloped, pattern of responses. In effect, teachers who give pop quizzes are using a VI schedule to ensure that their students keep up with the reading rather than cram at the last minute.

Fixed-Ratio (FR) Schedule   In this situation, a reinforcer is administered after a fixed number of *responses*—say, every third response, or every fifth, tenth, or fiftieth. In an FR-10 schedule, it takes ten bar presses to get food. If thirty responses are needed, it is an FR-30 schedule. The response-to-reinforcement ratio thus remains constant. In a Skinner box, animals on an FR schedule exhibit a burst of bar presses until the food appears, pause briefly, then produce another burst. The result is a fast, steplike response pattern. Frequent-flier programs, where you can earn a free flight after 25,000 miles of air travel, CD clubs that offer a free CD after every fifth purchase, and the employer who pays workers after they produce a certain number of products all operate on a fixed-ratio schedule.

Variable-Ratio (VR) Schedule   In this situation, the reinforcement appears after some average number of responses is made—a number that varies randomly from one reinforcement to the next. On a VR-15 schedule, a rat would have to press the bar an average of fifteen times, but the food may appear on the fifth response, then the twentieth, fourteenth, twenty-first response, and so on. Unable to predict which response will produce a food pellet, animals on a VR schedule respond at a constant high rate. In one case, Skinner trained pigeons to peck a disk 10,000 times for a single food pellet! Slot machines and lotteries are rigged to pay off on a VR schedule, leading gamblers to deposit coins and purchase tickets at a furious, addictive pace. If you've ever tried to access the Internet only to receive a busy signal, chances are you too kept trying with dogged persistence. The reason: When it comes to getting online, our efforts are reinforced, as with slot machines, on a variable-ratio schedule.

Reinforcement schedules affect extinction rates as well as learning. Specifically, the operant response is more enduring and, later, more resistant to extinction when the organism is reinforced on a partial basis rather than on a continuous, 100 percent schedule. This phenomenon is called the **partial-reinforcement effect.** The rat that is fed after every bar press is quick to realize once the feeder is disconnected that the contingency has changed. But the rat that is fed on only an occasional basis persists more before realizing that a reinforcement is no longer forthcoming. If you drop coins into a Coke machine and do not get the drink you ordered, you walk away. Because vending machines are supposed to operate on a continuous-reinforcement basis, it would be immediately apparent that this one is out of order. Deposit coins into a broken slot machine, however, and you may go on to lose hundreds more. After all, you expect slot machines to pay off on an irregular basis. The partial-reinforcement effect has ironic implications. For example, parents who only sometimes give in to a child's temper tantrums and try to tough it out on other occasions create "little monsters" with more tenacious, hard-to-eliminate outbursts than do parents who always give in.

partial-reinforcement effect The tendency for a schedule of partial reinforcement to strengthen later resistance to extinction.

Punishment   In 1948, Skinner wrote *Walden Two*, a novel about a fictional society in which socially adaptive behaviors were maintained by various schedules of reinforcement. The book was a blueprint for the use of "behavioral engineering" to design a happy, healthy, and productive community. Skinner never hesitated to preach the use of reinforcement. Yet he just as adamantly opposed the use of punishment, even though it is a common form of behavior control. Think about it. Parents scold their children, police officers fine motorists for speeding, referees penalize athletes for

"I think I should warn you that the flip side of our generous bonus-incentive program is capital punishment."

committing fouls, and employers fire workers who are lazy. So what's the problem? Aren't these forms of punishment effective?

Research shows that punishment has mixed effects (Axelrod & Apsche, 1983). When it is strong, immediate, consistent, and inescapable, punishment clearly does suppress unwanted behaviors. Shock a rat for pressing the response bar and it will quickly stop making the response. Yell, "No!" at the top of your lungs to a child playing with matches, and it is unlikely to happen again. There is an episode of the old TV show *Cheers* in which Cliff Claivin—an obnoxious, know-it-all postal worker—hires a behaviorist to shape his social skills so that he will be better liked. The two men enter the bar, and each time Claivin makes an offensive or boastful remark, the behaviorist jolts him with a remote-controlled electric-shock device. This scene is hilarious, and it illustrates that punishment can be an effective deterrent.

It is important to know, however, that punishment can also have unwanted side effects. There are four specific problems in this regard. First, a behavior that is met with punishment may be temporarily inhibited or hidden from the punishing agent—but it is not necessarily extinguished. The child who lights matches and the teenager who smokes cigarettes may both continue to do so at school, at a friend's house, or at home when the parent is at work. Second, even when punishment does suppress an unwanted behavior, it does not replace that behavior with one that is more adaptive. It's okay to lock up the convicted criminal, but to change his or her future behavior, some form of rehabilitation program is necessary. Third, punishment can sometimes backfire because a stimulus thought to be aversive may, in fact, prove rewarding. The neglected child who acts up and is scolded by his or her busy parents may actually "enjoy" the attention and make trouble again in the future. Fourth, punishment (especially if it is severe) can arouse fear, anger, frustration, and other negative emotions—leading the person to strike back, retaliate, tune out, or run away.

discriminative stimulus A stimulus that signals the availability of reinforcement.

Properly administered, punishment can be used to suppress an unwanted behavior. As we have seen, however, it can also create more problems than it solves. It is better, advised Skinner, to use a combination of reinforcement (to increase the frequency of alternative desirable behaviors) and extinction (to extinguish the undesirable behaviors) in order to shape a new, more adaptive way of life.

Stimulus Control   In operant conditioning, organisms learn to respond in ways that are reinforced. But there is more to the story. A pigeon trained in a Skinner box learns to peck a key for food, but it may also learn that the response produces reinforcement only in the presence of certain cues. Since reinforcements are often available in one situation but not in another, it is adaptive to learn not only *what* response to make but *when* to make it. If pecking a key produces food only when a green disk is lit, a pigeon may learn to discriminate and to respond on a selective basis. The green light is a **discriminative stimulus** that "sets the occasion" for the behavior to be reinforced (Ross & LoLordo, 1987).

When people learn to respond in some situations and not others, their behavior is said to be under "stimulus control." In human terms, this is often important for treating behavioral disorders. Consider the problem of insomnia. Research shows that insomniacs too often use the bed for nonsleeping activities such as watching TV, listening to the radio, reading magazines, and worrying about personal problems. In other words, the bed is a discriminative stimulus for so many activities that it becomes a source of arousal, not relaxation. To counter this problem, insomniacs are advised, frequently with successful results, to lie in bed only for the purpose of sleeping (Morawetz, 1989).

An operant response may spread from one situation to another through the process of stimulus generalization. As in classical conditioning, the more similar a new stimulus is to the original discriminative stimulus, the more likely it is to trigger the response. In one study, for example, pigeons were reinforced for pecking a key that was illuminated with yellow light. They were then tested with lights of different colors. The more similar the test lights were to the yellow

In recent years, the Chinese government has ordered the execution of hundreds of prisoners—a form of punishment designed to deter crime.

discriminative stimulus—for example, green and orange as opposed to red and blue—the more likely the pigeons were to peck at it (Guttman & Kalish, 1956). In another study, horses were trained to press a lever that was placed in their stalls, a response that released oats and hay into a feed tray. The animals were conditioned in the presence of an illuminated black circle 2.5 inches in diameter. They were then tested in the presence of circles that varied in size from this original. The closer the resemblance, the more likely the horses were to press the lever. The results for two horses, named Lady Bay and Bud Dark, are illustrated in Figure 20.4 (Dougherty & Lewis, 1991).

Discrimination and generalization are important aspects of human operant conditioning. From experience, a child might learn that temper tantrums bring results from busy parents but not from teachers, that studying increases grades in social studies but not math, that lewd remarks elicit laughter in the locker room but not in the classroom, and that aggression wins praise on the football field but not in other settings. As adults, we routinely regulate our behavior according to situational cues.

Practical Applications of Operant Conditioning

From the start, Skinner was interested in the practical applications of operant conditioning. In World War II, he worked for the United States government on a top-secret project in which he shaped pigeons to guide missiles toward enemy ships. Based on this work, the U.S. Navy recently trained dolphins and sea lions to locate explosive mines in the Persian Gulf and perform other dangerous underwater missions (Morrison, 1988). Similarly, the Coast Guard now uses pigeons to search for people lost at sea. The birds are strapped under the belly of a rescue helicopter and trained to spot floating orange objects in the water (orange is the international color of life jackets). In response to this stimulus, the birds are conditioned to peck a key that buzzes the pilot (Simmons, 1981).

Skinner was eager to use operant conditioning in other ways as well, but his efforts were sometimes misunderstood. In 1945, he constructed an "air crib" for his infant daughter, Deborah. This crib, which he called a "baby tender," was a

Skinner's daughter in the air crib he invented. Contrary to popular misconceptions, he did not put her in a Skinner box to shape her behavior.

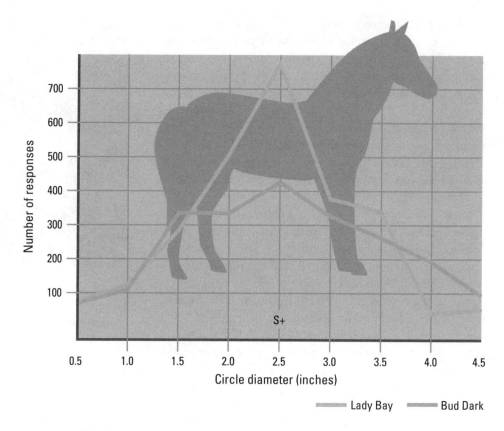

FIGURE 20.4 Stimulus generalization The more similar a new stimulus is to a discriminative stimulus, the more likely it is to trigger the operant response. In this study, two horses trained to press a lever in the presence of a 2.5-inch circle later responded to new circles based on their level of similarity to the original (Dougherty & Lewis, 1991).

temperature-controlled enclosed space equipped with an air filter, sound-absorbing walls, a stretched canvas floor, a safety glass window with a curtain, and a roll of diapers. The goal was to provide the infant with an environment that was comfortable, safe, and stimulating. Skinner tried to market his new invention and wrote about it for *Ladies' Home Journal* in an article he titled "Baby Care Can Be Modernized." Unfortunately, the *Journal* editor changed the title to "Baby in a Box"—which led the public to think that he was experimenting on his daughter the way he did with rats and pigeons. Rumors later spread about his daughter's mental health. Indeed, to this day, many people think that she suffered a nervous breakdown and committed suicide. In fact, she is very much alive and well (Bjork, 1993).

Over the years, Skinner advised parents on how to raise children with the use of reinforcement rather than punishment. He also invented a "teaching machine" that would enable students to learn at their own individualized pace by solving a graded series of problems and receiving immediate feedback on their answers. Today, computer-assisted instruction in schools is based on this early work (Benjamin, 1988). In fact, personal computers are now being used just as Skinner had envisioned to train students to type, play the piano, or practice their academic skills. Inspired by Skinner, other behaviorists have applied the principles of operant conditioning to get people to use safety belts, recycle wastes, conserve energy, or simply help themselves (Martin & Pear, 1992).

"I am not trying to change people. All I want to do is change the world in which they live."

—B. F. SKINNER

The use of operant conditioning is now commonplace in the health clinic, the workplace, the classroom, and other settings. For clinical purposes, it laid an important foundation for the techniques of behavior modification, in which reinforcement is used to change maladaptive thoughts, feelings, and behaviors. It also forms the basis for biofeedback—an operant procedure in which electronic instruments are used to provide people with continuous information, or "feedback," about their own physiological states. With the aid of electronic sensors to the body and an instrument that amplifies the signals, people can monitor—and then learn to regulate—their own heart rate, blood pressure, and muscular tension. Biofeedback can thus be used in the treatment of migraine headaches, chronic back pain, and other health problems (Schwartz et al., 1995).

Operant conditioning has also been extensively used in the workplace. In a study conducted within a large department store, Fred Luthans and his colleagues (1981) observed sales clerks from sixteen departments for a period of four weeks. The employees in half of these departments were then reinforced for productive performance with cash, time off, or a chance to win a company-paid vacation. The other half were not offered added incentives. As shown in Figure 20.5, the two groups were equivalent in their performance during the first phase of the study. In the second phase, however, the reinforced group improved dramatically, even after the reinforcement period, but the control group did not. Similar effects have been produced in work-incentive programs involving waiters and waitresses (George & Hopkins, 1989), electric-utility-company employees (Petty et al., 1992), and others in workplace settings (Pritchard et al., 1988). It is no wonder that so many business organizations now use profit-sharing plans, bonuses, and employee-recognition programs to increase worker satisfaction, motivation, and productivity (Horn, 1987).

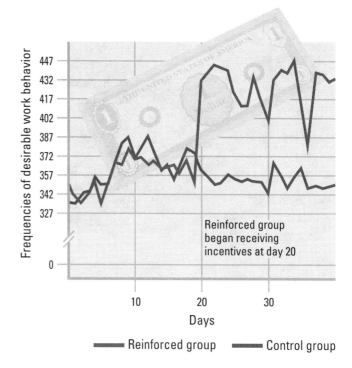

FIGURE 20.5 Using reinforcement to boost job performance As observed in many studies, department-store salesclerks who were offered incentives improved their job performance while those in the control group did not (Luthans et al., 1981).

There are many practical applications of operant conditioning. In the workplace, organizations recognize employees for their performance. In the classroom, computer scenes reward children for correct answers through colorful animated displays.

Finally, operant conditioning is regularly used in the classroom. Skinner's teaching machine was one application, but there are others as well. For example, many teachers establish large-scale reinforcement programs in which children earn gold stars, ribbons, or "tokens" for engaging in desired behaviors—tokens that can be exchanged for toys, extra recess time, and other privileges. Skinner (1988) himself described how a sixth-grade teacher gave her students a card every time they handed in an assignment. The students put their cards into a jar and, at the end of the week, one card was randomly drawn, with the winner receiving a prize—say, a portable radio. The result: a dramatic improvement in the number of assignments completed. Another use of operant techniques is "precision teaching." In this approach, the teacher, serving as a coach, organizes material for students and shows them how to measure and chart their progress to receive immediate feedback. Students are thus trained to teach themselves and each other (Lindsley, 1992).

The Old Horse Soldier

James Hugh Powers

Much of our military and naval tradition passes to succeeding generations by word-of-mouth and family folklore, as well as more formal mechanisms. Seeing the Joint Chiefs of Staff appear in televised excerpts of congressional hearings on the Tailhook investigation and other related issues, this World War II Marine was moved to write to the present Commandant of the Marine Corps, with timeless counsel and advice he had first received as a fresh graduate of boot camp at Parris Island.

As the testimony moved forward, my thoughts wandered back in time to the early weeks of June 1943 and to the Old Horse Soldier, my granduncle, Sergeant Andrew Casey, U.S. Army (Retired). He was a wonderful granduncle for me and my two younger brothers to have had as small boys. He was living history, a reminder that we are the sum of history, and that most valuable of all our treasures—a keeper of the tradition. He was an extraordinary old man.

He had joined the Army as an early teenager in the mid-1870s and had been assigned to the 7th Cavalry out in the Dakota Territory under the command of General George Armstrong Custer. He was fortunate to have been in one of the cavalry units left "back in the fort" when Custer left on his ill-fated march to Little Big Horn. Uncle Andy was a storehouse of information about the Indians, the Indian Wars, and the Wild West in its glory. He had served in the Spanish-American War retiring a little after the turn of the century. He was timeless. He was adventure. And he was ours!

The Old Horse Soldier was tough as nails, yet a good-humored elder, a gentle if firm disciplinarian when his grandnephews got a bit out of line. Even in his 80s, he was lean, proud, and dignified in bearing, standing ramrod straight. Even though partially blind, he kept busy with carpentry at his work bench in the basement of our home and about our premises in Needham, Massachusetts, surrendering nothing to the infirmities of age.

On that day in June 1943, I arrived home from Parris Island, South Carolina, after graduating from Platoon 266, 12th Recruit Battalion, on furlough transfer to New River, North Carolina. I received a joyous welcome from my parents and brothers. And hearing Uncle Andy at work in the basement, I laid below to confront him in all my Marine Corps glory, greens, sharpshooter's medal, and all. Having survived Parris Island, I was a very cocky 20-year-old.

I found the Old Horse Soldier at his bench, his ample white hair reflecting the light from the lamp above. When he heard me, he turned around in his chair to survey this "boot." A slight smile crossed his stern, lined, ancient face. I awaited his verdict. As nearly as I can recall, this is what followed:

"Hmph!" he snorted. "Well, the Marines have done a good job with you."

"Yes sir!" I answered.

"A fine fighting outfit," he observed. "Your chances of coming through are better in such an outfit. A good outfit doesn't have to say that it is good. It just is, and everybody knows it. Just see to it that you measure up!"

Spoken like a true veteran of a good outfit, the 7th Cavalry. In 1943, its horses were gone, and it was mechanized. Its heritage remained, however.

As the Old Horse Soldier chatted, I realized that I was talking to a man who had been alive when the only states west of the Mississippi were those on its west bank, plus Texas, California, Nevada, and Oregon. The rest of the map of the West, divided into territories, was simply inscribed "Indian Country."

Naval Academy photo courtesy of United States Naval Academy Photographic Laboratory.

The Old Horse Soldier now looked me squarely in the eye and said something I was never to forget, something as timely for officers and enlisted personnel of our armed forces today as it was in 1943.

"Young fellah, I have a little advice for you, some things I want you to keep at the top of your agenda."

"You are now wearing the uniform of the United States. You shall, at all times, remember that while you are wearing that uniform you represent the government and the people of the United States. They have entrusted to you the obligation of upholding the honor of that uniform and all that it represents. The whole world will judge you in terms of that uniform and your conduct while wearing it.

"You shall therefore comport yourself at all times, on all occasions and in all circumstances in such a manner as to reflect credit upon your branch of service, our government, and the American people. Your every act shall be such as to encourage confidence in all people and in that uniform and what these things represent.

"You shall be mindful that fine men have died wearing the uniform of the United States Army, Navy, Marine Corps, and Coast Guard. You are accountable to their memory. Be proud of your branch of service, but remember that no branch has a monopoly on courage, conviction, and sacrifice. You best honor all by honoring your own.

A Navy HH-60H helicopter on deck in Glamoc, Bosnia, during a range reconnaissance mission.
Official U.S. Navy photo.

"You shall remember that your rank and uniform do not excuse you from the responsibilities of behaving like a gentleman and a responsible member of society. You were not brought up to act like a pig at home. The Marine Corps has not issued you a license to behave like a pig while you are in that uniform. Use common sense. Discipline is best served by common sense.

"That's it! Do I make myself clear? Is that all understood?"

These two questions were posed with a vigor that showed the Old Horse Soldier still knew how to skin mules and recruits. I was addressing the ultimate Drill Instructor, who had raised these issues in a way they had never been raised by my drill instructors at Parris Island.

"YES SIR!" I replied.

"Good lad," he answered. "You will do just fine. Now, get on upstairs and help your mother. She worries a lot about you."

I left him puttering at his bench after imparting to me a legacy of military tradition and family values that carried me through the rigors of World War II and through later life. He was still training his troops with tough love, the true mark of a caring and competent leader.

The Tailhook events suggest that his values bear some repeating today at our service academies, in officer candidate schools, and armed forces boot camps. It appears that we have here and there in our forces some folks who have lost touch with our country's values and traditions—and with common sense. These deficiencies in their education must be addressed in no uncertain terms, out of respect for the vast majority of our armed forces personnel who are doing their best to live decent lives and to function as real professionals. We cannot abide conduct that undermines discipline or the confidence of our people in our armed forces.

Whatever else happens, of one thing I am certain: That our Corps will not be found wanting in these matters: that the Corps will fall upon one who dishonors it as the Assyrians fell upon the fold; that the word will go out: When we remember that we are family, we do just fine. It is when someone forgets that we are family that trouble enters our tent. "Family" means showing respect, respect of all for one and of one for all. It is that simple. Common sense is surprisingly simple.

Good luck, and God bless your efforts.

Semper Fidelis!

Mr. Powers, Harvard '46, is Secretary of the Marines 8th Defense Anti-aircraft Artillery Battalion Reunion Association.

21 *The Basics of Obedience and Conformity*

Objectives

1. Define conformity and identify the factors that increase or decrease the influence of the majority and minority.

2. Describe Milgram's classic study on obedience and its implications for human nature and leadership.

3. Develop and describe a strategy for inoculation against potentially harmful conformity and obedience.

4. Describe how the strength of conformity can lead men to perform acts of extreme selflessness and heroism.

Social Influence

What's the difference between public and private conformity? Just how far can people be pushed to obey the commands of an authority? What makes for a persuasive communication? Why is it that a change in behavior can elicit a change in attitude? When do groups arouse us, when do they relax us, and why do they sometimes make bad decisions?

Advertisers hire celebrities and supermodels to sell soft drinks, sneakers, and other products. Sports fans spread the "wave" and chant "de-fense" in a spectacular show of unison. Protestors, lost in a sea of anonymous faces, shed inhibitions and become transformed into a mob. Performers with stage fright tremble, turn pale, and freeze before appearing in front of an audience. These examples illustrate that people influence one another in various ways. As we'll see, the source of this influence may be a person or a group, the effect may be a change in behavior or attitude, and the change may be socially destructive (hurting others) or constructive (helping others).

Intersection

Social Influences and Law: Social Perception in Jury Trials

It was called the trial of the century. When O. J. Simpson was tried for the murders of his former wife Nicole Brown and Ronald Goldman, the case involved celebrity, sports, sex, money, racial tension, and violence. As in a live theater, the trial was packed with drama. Outside the courthouse, TV cameras and microphones lined a parking-lot area that was called Camp OJ. Inside the courtroom, the jury struggled to decide whether Simpson stabbed his wife and her friend to death and, if so, whether the act was premeditated. The prosecution presented evidence in the form of pictures, witnesses, blood-soaked socks and a glove, shoeprints, and DNA tests. In turn, the defense argued that Simpson was at home at the time, that he was physically unable to overpower the two victims, and that the physical evidence could not be trusted. The trial lasted for nearly a year, and when it was over, the jury announced its controversial verdict: not guilty. For those who disagreed with it, Simpson was retried in a civil suit filed by the victims' families. In February 1997, that jury found Simpson liable for the murders and ordered him to pay the families more than $30 million.

Regardless of how one felt about the trials of O. J. Simpson, they illustrated the importance of social psychology at work in the legal system. Every day, ordinary people are brought together in a courtroom and empowered to make decisions of utmost importance. The trial consists of three stages. First, members of the community are summoned to court, sworn in, questioned, and selected. Next comes the

Realizing the power of social influence, the photographer who took this picture anticipated that when one schoolgirl climbed the wall at the Tower of London, others would soon follow.

presentation of testimony, arguments, and the judge's instructions. Third, jurors go off to deliberate as a group and strive to reach a common verdict. By law, juries are told to base their decisions only on evidence presented in court—not on extraneous factors. But is this ideal achieved? Over the years, social psychologists have examined some of the possible sources of bias.

Pretrial Publicity When cases are featured in the newspapers and on TV, does the pretrial publicity corrupt the jury? Public opinion surveys have shown that the more people know about a case, the more likely they are to presume the defendant guilty (Moran & Cutler, 1991). This result is not hard to explain. The information appearing in the news tends to come from the district attorney's office, so it typically reveals facts unfavorable to the defense. The real question is whether this exposure overwhelms the evidence—and the jury.

Norbert Kerr and his colleagues (1991) played a videotaped simulation of an armed-robbery trial to hundreds of subjects who took part in 108 mock juries. Before watching the tape, they were exposed to news clippings about the case. Some read material that was neutral, but others received information that implicated the defendant in another crime. As in court, mock jurors were told to base their decisions solely on the evidence. But the pretrial publicity had a marked effect. In groups exposed to the neutral story, 33 percent of the subjects voted guilty after the trial and deliberations. In groups exposed to an incriminating story, that figure increased to 48 percent. Why is pretrial publicity so harmful? Part of the problem is that it is revealed *before* the evidence—bringing primacy effects and first-impression biases into play. Indeed, additional studies have shown that jurors exposed to pretrial publicity later see the prosecutor's evidence as more incriminating (Otto et al., 1994). Clearly, justice demands that prospective jurors with knowledge about a case be excluded or that highly publicized cases be moved, if possible, to less informed communities.

Football Hall-of-Famer O. J. Simpson was charged with the murders of Nicole Brown Simpson and Ron Goldman. In 1996, he was quickly and unanimously acquitted by a criminal jury. Then in 1997, he was found liable for the murders and ordered to pay more than $30 million in damages by a unanimous civil jury. This case has raised many questions about the jury system.

Inadmissible Evidence In his opening statement, Simpson's defense lawyer Johnnie Cochran made reference to witnesses who would not later testify, eliciting objections from prosecuting attorneys. The trial judge sustained the objection and ordered the jury to disregard these references. Similar events from both sides occurred repeatedly. In each case, the jury was instructed to disregard the information.

Jurors often are exposed to extralegal information during a trial. By law, a judge may exclude from evidence any items that are inflammatory, are unreliable, or have been illegally obtained. If such information is disclosed at trial, the judge instructs jurors to disregard it. But can people really strike information from the mind the way a court reporter can strike it from the record? Can jurors resist the forbidden fruit of inadmissible testimony? Common sense suggests not, and so does the research.

In one study, Kassin and Sommers (1997) had mock jurors read a transcript of a double-murder trial based on evidence that was relatively weak, leading only 24 percent to vote guilty. Three other groups read the same case except that the state's evidence included a wiretapped phone conversation in which the defendant had confessed to a friend. In all cases, the defense lawyer objected to this disclosure. When the judge admitted the tape into evidence, the conviction rate rose considerably, to 79 percent. But when the judge excluded the tape and instructed jurors to disregard it, their reaction depended on the reason for the tape being excluded. When told to disregard the tape because it was barely audible and could not be trusted, subjects mentally erased the information, as they should, and delivered the same verdict as in the no-tape control group. But when told to disregard the item because it had been illegally obtained, 55 percent voted guilty. Despite the judge's warning, these subjects were unwilling to ignore testimony they found relevant merely on the basis of a legal "technicality."

Physical Appearances   There is a third possible source of bias that is perhaps the most basic of all. As we saw, social perceivers are influenced by physical appearances. Does this bias extend into the courtroom, or is justice truly blind? Diane Berry and Leslie Zebrowitz (1988) speculated that adults with "baby-face" features (high eyebrows, large eyes, round cheeks, a large forehead, and a round chin) would be seen as naive and honest compared to "mature-face" adults—and that this perception would bias judgments in a legal proceeding. They showed mock jurors two versions of a trial. In one, the defendant was charged with negligence for forgetting to warn a customer about the hazard of a product he was selling. In the other version, the defendant was said to have deliberately misled a customer to make the sale. Interestingly, subjects were more likely to find the baby-face defendant negligent, a crime that "matched" his appearance. But they were less likely to judge him as guilty of the crime of deception. A similar pattern was uncovered in the decisions made by small-claims-court judges (Zebrowitz & McDonald, 1991). And other studies have shown that a defendant's physical attractiveness also plays a role: Among defendants whose appearances were rated from photographs, those seen as more attractive received lighter sentences and smaller fines from state judges (Stewart, 1980; Downs & Lyons, 1991).

The law states that verdicts should be based only on evidence presented in court. But jurors are ordinary people—which means that they are subject to the biases of social perception. Having identified some of the problems, researchers are now seeking ways to minimize these prejudicial effects.

Conformity

As social animals, we are all vulnerable to subtle, reflexlike influences. We yawn when we see others yawning, and laugh when we hear others laughing. In one study, research confederates stopped on a busy street in New York City, looked up, and gawked at a window of a nearby building. A camera stationed behind the window showed that roughly 80 percent of passersby stopped and gazed up when they saw these confederates (Milgram et al., 1969). Knowing that people are quick to imitate others, TV producers infuse situation comedies with canned laughter to make viewers think the shows are funny, political candidates trumpet inflated results from their own public-opinion polls to attract new voters, and bartenders stuff dollar bills into empty tip jars to draw more money from their customers. As they say, "Monkey see, monkey do."

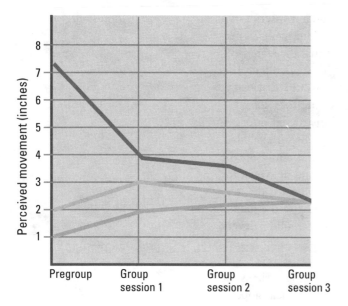

FIGURE 21.1 A classic case of suggestibility This group in Sherif's study illustrates how subjects' estimates of the apparent movement of light converged over time. Gradually, the group established its own set of norms.

conformity A tendency to alter one's opinion or behavior in ways that are consistent with group norms.

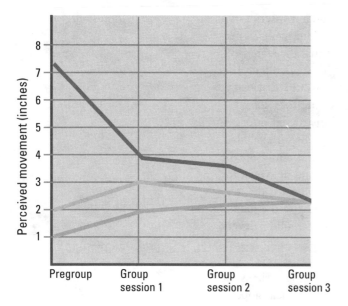

A
Standard line

A B C
Comparison lines

FIGURE 21.2 Line-judgment task in Asch's study Which comparison line—A, B, or C—is the same length as the standard line?

Conformity, the tendency for people to bring their behavior in line with group norms, is a powerful fact of social life. Cast in a positive light, it promotes harmony, group solidarity, and peaceful coexistence—as when people assume their places in a waiting line. Cast in a negative light, conformity has harmful effects—as when people drink too heavily at parties or tell offensive ethnic jokes because others are doing the same. For the social psychologist, the goal is not to make moral judgments but, rather, to determine the factors that promote conformity and the reasons for it.

The Early Classics In 1936, Muzafer Sherif published a classic laboratory experiment on how norms develop in small groups. The subjects in his study, thinking they were in a visual-perception experiment, sat in a dark room, saw a beam of light, and then estimated the distance the light had moved. This procedure was repeated several times. Subjects didn't realize it, but the light never moved. The movement they thought they saw was merely an optical illusion. At first, subjects sat alone and reported their perceptions only to the experimenter (most estimates stabilized in the range of one to ten inches). Then, during the next few days, subjects returned to participate in three-person groups. Each time a beam of light was flashed, subjects stated their estimates one by one. As shown in Figure 21.1, initial estimates varied considerably, but the subjects eventually converged on a common perception, each group establishing its own set of norms.

Fifteen years after Sherif's experiment, Solomon Asch (1951) constructed a different situation. Imagine yourself as a subject in his study. You sign up for a psychology experiment, and when you arrive you find six other students waiting around a table. You take an empty seat, and the experimenter explains that he is measuring people's ability to make visual discriminations. As a warm-up, he asks you and the others to indicate which of three comparison lines is identical in length to a standard line (see Figure 21.2).

That seems easy enough. The experimenter then asks you all to take turns in order of your seating position. Starting on his left, the experimenter asks the first person for a judgment. Seeing that you are in the next-to-last position, you patiently await your turn. The opening moments pass uneventfully. The task is clear and everyone agrees on the answers. On the third set of lines, however, the first subject selects the wrong line. Huh? What happened? Did he suddenly lose his mind, his eyesight, or both? Before you know it, the next four subjects choose the same wrong line. Now it's your turn. Faced with what seems like an easy choice, you rub your eyes and take another look. What do you think? Better yet, what do you do? As you may have guessed by now, the other "subjects" were confederates trained to make incorrect judgments on certain trials. The right answers were clear. In a control group, where subjects made their judgments alone, performance was virtually errorless. Yet subjects in the experimental group went along with the incorrect majority 37 percent of the time. This result may seem surprising, but recent studies too have shown that people conform to the responses of others on a variety of cognitive tasks (Larsen, 1990; Schneider & Watkins, 1996).

Both Sherif and Asch found that people are influenced by the behavior of others. But there is an important difference in the types of conformity exhibited in these studies. Sherif's subjects were literally "in the dark"—uncertain of their own perceptions. Wanting to be correct, they looked to others for guidance and adopted the average of the group's estimates as their own. In Asch's study, however, the task was simple enough for subjects to see the lines with their own eyes. Most knew that the majority was wrong but went along to avoid becoming social outcasts. In short, there are two very different types of social influence: informational and normative (Deutsch & Gerard, 1955; Campbell & Fairey, 1989). **Informational influence** leads people to conform because they assume that the majority is correct. In the case of **normative influence,** people conform because they fear the social rejection that accompanies deviance. For good reason. Research shows that people who stray from the norm are disliked and often are ridiculed and laughed at (Levine, 1989)—especially in groups that need to reach a consensus (Kruglanski & Webster, 1991).

After two uneventful rounds in Asch's line-judgment study the subject (number 6) faces a dilemma. Confederates 1 through 5 all gave the same wrong answer. Should he give his own or conform to theirs?

The distinction between the two types of social influence is important because they produce different types of conformity—private and public. Like beauty, conformity may be skin-deep or may penetrate beneath the surface. In *private conformity,* we change not only our behavior but our opinions as well. To conform at this level is to be genuinely persuaded that the majority is right. In contrast, *public conformity* refers to a temporary and superficial change in which we outwardly comply with the majority in our behavior but privately maintain our own beliefs.

informational influence Conformity motivated by the belief that others are correct.

normative influence Conformity motivated by a fear of social rejection.

In a study that demonstrates both processes, Robert S. Baron and his colleagues (1996) had subjects, in groups of three (the other two were confederates), act as eyewitnesses: First, they would see a picture of a person, then they would try to pick that person out of a lineup. In some groups, the task was difficult, like Sherif's, as they saw each picture only once, for half a second. For other subjects, the task was easier, like Asch's, in that they saw each picture twice for a total of ten seconds. How often did subjects conform when the confederates made the wrong identification? It depended on how motivated the subjects were. When the experimenter downplayed the task as only a "pilot study," the conformity rates were 35 percent when the task was difficult and 33 percent when it was easy. But when subjects were offered a financial incentive to do well, conformity went up to 51 percent when the task was difficult—and down to 16 percent when it was easy (see Figure 21.3). With pride and money on the line, the Sherif-like subjects conformed more, and the Asch-like subjects conformed less.

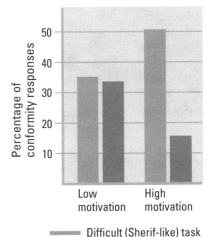

FIGURE 21.3 **Private and public conformity** Regardless of whether the task was difficult or easy, there were moderate levels of conformity when subjects had a low motivation (*left*). But when motivated (*right*), with pride and money on the line, subjects conformed more when the task was difficult, as in Sherif's study, and less when it was easy, as in Asch's study (Baron et al., 1996).

Majority Influence   Realizing that people can be pressured by others is only the first step in understanding the process of social influence. The next step is to identify the situational factors that make us more or less likely to conform. One obvious factor is the size of a group. Common sense suggests that as a majority increases in size, so does its impact. Actually, it is not that simple. Asch (1956) varied the size of his groups—by using one, two, three, four, eight, or fifteen confederates—and found that conformity increased only up to a point. After four confederates, the amount of *additional* influence was negligible, subject to the law of diminishing returns (see Figure 21.4). Bibb Latané (1981) likens this impact on an individual to the way light bulbs illuminate a surface. Add a second bulb in a room, and the effect is dramatic. Add a tenth bulb, and its impact is barely noticed.

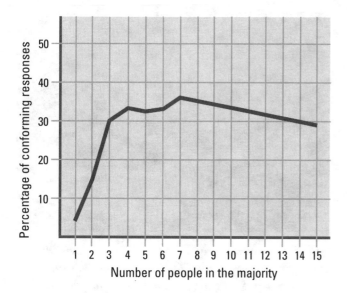

FIGURE 21.4 Group size and conformity By varying the number of confederates, Asch found that conformity increased with the size of the majority, but only up to a point. As you can see, fifteen had no more impact than did four.

In Asch's initial study, subjects were pitted against a unanimous majority. But what if they had an ally, a partner in dissent? Put yourself in this situation: How do you think having an ally would affect *you?* Varying this aspect of his experiment, Asch found that the presence of just one confederate who gave the correct answer reduced conformity by almost 80 percent. In fact, any dissenter—even one whose competence is called into question—can break the spell cast by a unanimous majority and reduce the pressure to conform (Allen & Levine, 1971).

Although the size of a majority and the presence of an ally influence the amount of pressure that is felt, people are most likely to conform when their attention is drawn to social norms (Cialdini et al., 1991). Of course, we must know what the norms are in a group in order to conform. This may sound like an obvious point, yet we often misperceive what is normative—as when others are afraid or embarrassed to publicly present their true views or behaviors. One common example concerns perceptions of alcohol usage. In university-wide surveys, Deborah Prentice and Dale Miller (1996) found that many students overestimated how comfortable their peers were with the drinking level on campus. They also found that the more positive students thought others were at the start of the school year, the more likely they were, eventually, to conform to this misperception in their own attitudes and behavior. The point is that we are influenced not by social norms per se but by our *perceptions* of those norms.

Finally, cultural factors play a key role. In many Western cultures—most notably, the United States, Australia, Great Britain, Canada, and the Netherlands—autonomy and independence are highly valued. In contrast, many cultures of Asia, Africa, and Latin America place a value on social harmony and "fitting in" for the sake of the community. Among the Bantu of Zimbabwe, for example, an African people in which deviance is scorned, 51 percent of the subjects placed in an Asch-like study conformed to the majority's wrong answer—more than the number typically obtained in the West (Triandis, 1994; Bond & Smith, 1996).

Minority Influence It is not easy for individuals who express unpopular views to enlist support from others. Philosopher Bertrand Russell once said that "conventional people are roused to frenzy by departure from convention, largely because they regard such departure as criticism of themselves." Russell may have been right. People who challenge the status quo may be perceived as competent, but they are intensely disliked (Bassili & Provencal, 1988).

Maintaining independence in the face of social pressure to follow is difficult, but it is not impossible. In *The Dissenters,* anthropologist Langston Gwaltney (1986) interviewed "ordinary" nonconformists—an Irish man who befriended black people in a racist community, a New England grandmother who risked arrest to protest nuclear weapons, and a group of nuns who sued their church. Laboratory research also provides relevant evidence. Think about it. Asch's subjects conformed on 37 percent of the trials, but this means that they openly refused to acquiesce in the other 63 percent—a result that bears witness to the human spirit of independence (Friend et al., 1990).

How do nonconformists withstand the pressure to change? Better yet, how do they sometimes manage to sway the majority? According to Serge Moscovici (1985), majorities exert power by sheer numbers, but those in a minority derive their power by sticking to their positions in a persistent, unwavering, and self-confident manner. By holding firm, dissenters can get others to sit up, take notice, and rethink their own positions. Does it work? Yes. Dozens of studies have shown that dissenters who take a position and remain consistent over time are successful at producing minority influence (Wood et al., 1994).

Moscovici and his colleagues (1969) first observed this phenomenon by confronting real subjects with a *minority* of confederates who made incorrect judgments. In groups of six, subjects took part in what was believed to be a study of color perception. They viewed a series of blue slides and, for each, took turns naming the color. The task was simple—until two confederates described the slides as green. When these confederates were *consistent*—that is, when both made incorrect green judgments for all slides— one-third of all subjects incorrectly reported seeing at least one green slide. People can be influenced in important but subtle ways by minority opinion. Because of social pressures, we may be too intimidated to admit or even to recognize the influence. But it is there, and it is especially likely to materialize when subjects give their answers anonymously or in an indirect way (Clark & Maass, 1990; Moscovici & Personnaz, 1991).

It may not be easy, but individuals sometimes resist the social pressure to conform.

Obedience to Authority   Allen Funt, creator of the TV program *Candid Camera,* used to spend as much time observing people as most psychologists do. His conclusion: "The worst thing is how easily people can be led by any kind of authority figure, or even the most minimal signs of authority." Funt went on to describe the time he put up a road sign that read DELAWARE CLOSED TODAY. The reaction? "Motorists didn't question it. Instead they asked, 'Is Jersey open?'" (Zimbardo, 1985, p. 47).

Blind obedience may seem funny, but as the pages of history attest, the implications are sobering. In World War II, Nazi officials participated in the deaths of millions of Jewish men, women, and children. When they came to trial for these crimes, their defense was always the same: "I was just following orders." Was this episode a fluke? A historical aberration? In *Hitler's Willing Executioners,* historian Daniel Goldhagen (1996) argues on the basis of past records that many ordinary German people were willing, anti-Semitic participants in the Holocaust—not just following orders. On the other hand, human crimes of obedience are not unique to Nazi Germany and are committed all over the world, even today (Kelman & Hamilton, 1989). On one most extraordinary occasion, such obedience was carried to its limit: In 1978, 912 men and women of the People's Temple cult obeyed an order from the Reverend Jim Jones to kill themselves.

To study the power of authority, Stanley Milgram conducted the dramatic experiments described at the start of this chapter. In his 1974 book, *Obedience to Authority,* Milgram reported on the results of having put 1,000 subjects into a situation in which they were ordered by an experimenter to administer painful electric shocks to a confederate. Recall that subjects thought they were "teachers" in a study of the effects of punishment on learning and that each time the "learner" made a mistake, they were to deliver a shock of increasing intensity. The subjects could not actually see the learner, but they could hear grunts of pain, objections, loud screams, and eventual silence. Yet at each step, they were ordered to continue up the shock scale. Despite

Taken to extreme, blind obedience can have tragic results. In World War II, Nazi officials killed millions of Jews in the Holocaust. Were these Germans willing participants, as suggested by Daniel Goldhagen in his 1996 book, Hitler's Willing Executioners, *or were they just following orders, as subjects did in Milgram's research?*

Milgram's subjects used the shock generator shown here to seemingly deliver up to 450 volts to a confederate who was strapped into his chair. (Copyright 1965 by Stanley Milgram. From the film Obedience, *distributed by Penn State Media Sales.)*

the pain subjects thought they were inflicting, and despite the guilt and anguish they were experiencing, 65 percent in Milgram's initial study delivered the ultimate punishment of 450 volts.

At first, these grim results led people to conclude that Milgram's subjects were heartless and cruel, not "normal" like you and me. On the contrary. Most subjects were tormented by the experience—and comparable levels of obedience were also then found among men, women, and college students all over the world (Miller, 1986; Blass, 1992), leading one author to ask, *Are We All Nazis?* (Askenasy, 1978). Indeed, high levels of obedience were found just a few years ago in studies much like Milgram's that were conducted in the Netherlands (Meeus & Raaijmakers, 1995).

The lesson of Milgram's research is clear. Although some people are more obedient than others, even decent human beings can be pushed to behave in ways that violate the conscience. Think about it. To me, the most striking aspect of Milgram's findings is that a psychology experimenter, unlike one's boss or military superior, cannot ultimately enforce any commands. Can you imagine the power that is wielded by real-life figures of authority? Not content merely to demonstrate obedience, Milgram altered aspects of his experimental situation in order to identify the factors that affect levels of obedience. Three types of factors were systematically varied:

- *The authority.* When Milgram moved his experiment from the prestigious campus of Yale University to a run-down city office building, arranged for the experimenter to issue his commands by telephone, or replaced the experimenter with an ordinary person, obedience levels dropped.

- *The victim.* In Milgram's main experiment, subjects were physically separated from the learner, so they could distance themselves emotionally from his pain and suffering. When the subject and learner were seated in the same room, however, especially when subjects had to touch the learner, levels of obedience declined.

- *The situation.* Two aspects of the experimental situation fueled the high levels of obedience: (1) The experimenter explicitly assumed responsibility for the victim's welfare, and (2) full obedience was reached gradually, each step requiring only 15 volts more than the last one. As Milgram (1965) said, people become "integrated in a situation that carries its own momentum. The subject's problem . . . is to become disengaged from a situation which is moving in an altogether ugly direction" (p. 73).

1852
The Birken'ead Drill
Women and Children, First!

To take your chance in the thick of a rush, with
  firing all about,
Is nothing so bad when you've cover to 'and, an'
  leave an' likin' to shout;
But to stand an' be still to the Birken'ead drill
  is a damn tough bullet to chew,
An' they done it, the Jollies—'Er Majesty's
  Jollies—soldier an' sailor too!
Their work was done when it 'adn't begun; they
  was younger nor me an' you;
Their choice it was plain between drownin' in
  'eaps an' being mashed by the screw,
So they stood an' was still to the Birken'ead
  drill, soldier an' sailor too!

—RUDYARD KIPLING—*Soldier an' Sailor Too*

The wreck of H.M.S. *Birkenhead* in 1852 was the genesis of Kipling's tribute to the Royal Marines ("'Er Majesty's Jollies—soldier an' sailor too"). But the *Birkenhead*'s loss also helped to establish—or at least to confirm—an Anglo-Saxon tradition of the sea—women and children, first. J. G. Lockhart in his book *Peril of the Sea* declares, "the story of the *Birkenhead* has become a tradition—a tradition of which succeeding generations are justly proud . . . it established a law which has become embodied in the unwritten maritime code . . . that . . . in the moment of danger at sea the weak must not be allowed to go to the wall, nor the fittest claim the right to survive . . . and that . . . women and children must first be saved."

It was Britain's imperial era; never had the jewels of Empire glittered so brightly as in the reign of Victoria, that beloved Queen.

The White Ensign and the Red Duster fluttered from gaffs and flagstaffs to the winds of all the seas; the sun never set upon Her Majesty's ships and armies.

In South Africa, where the Queen's forces under Sir Harry Smith were fighting for dominion and glory against the Kaffirs, Her Majesty's Steam Ship *Birkenhead*, transporting much-needed drafts (replacements) for ten regiments, stood into Simon's Bay on Feb. 23, 1852, forty-seven days out of Cork.

Birkenhead was a 1,400 ton paddle steamer, which carried canvas (as did nearly all steamers in those days). She was laid down in 1845 as the Royal Navy's first iron steamer; she was designed as a frigate but used as a transport. And it was as a transport that she steamed to the Cape of Good Hope in 1852, with men—many of them raw recruits—from ancient British regiments.

Birkenhead lay in Simon's Bay for two days, provisioned, coaled, discharged some fifty of her passengers, embarked a few officers' horses and fodder for them, and stood out at four bells in the "fine and calm" evening of the twenty-fifth. Her

Naval Academy photo courtesy of United States Naval Academy Photographic Laboratory.

master, Commander Robert Salmond, had his orders for Algoa Bay and Buffalo Mouth, where he was to land the drafts of the different regiments. Embarked were 630 souls—130 in the ship's company including a file of Royal Marines; seven women and thirteen children, the families of some of the soldiers; and 480 officers and soldiers from the Queen's Regiment, the 6th Royal Regiment, the 12th Lancers, the 60th Rifles, the 74th Highlanders, and other units serving in the Kaffir War.

At eight bells, as the evening watch was set and the bright stars of the Southern constellations gleamed in the sky, *Birkenhead*'s position was picked off on the chart and the course was set for the night to give Cape Hanglip a "berth of about four miles." John Haines, A.B., relieved the wheel at four bells (10 P.M.) and repeated the course—S.S.E. ½ E. Mr. Spear, who was Second Master, was the Officer of the Watch, and checked the steersman frequently.

"Don't let her go to eastward of the course; keep her a quarter point to windward," he cautioned Haines.

The watch was uneventful and gradually the crowded ship, hot and sultry with its packed humanity, settled down.

The mid-watch started with dragging feet. Mr. Davis, the officer of the watch, checked the course intermittently by the glowing light of the binnacle, as *Birkenhead* logged about 7½ knots, her paddle wheels chunking rhythmically. Captain Salmond and the sailing master, Mr. Brodie, had turned in; no other officer except Mr. Davis, the officer of the watch, kept the deck. Thomas Daly, A.B., and John Butcher, A.B., were lookouts, stationed on either bow of the fo'c'sle, and Able Stone was the leadsman in the chains. Sometime before four bells (2 A.M.), Thomas Cuffin who had the wheel watched Mr. Davis take bearings on a light ashore. At ten minutes of two Able Stone, the leadsman, heaving the lead from the chain on the after sponson of the port paddle box, sang out the sounding:

"By the mark thirteen . . ."

Before he could cast again, the ship struck forward, scrunching aground with a rolling, ripping jar on a pinnacle rock or reef off Danger Point, several miles from shore.

Soundings were made as the ship woke and stirred to slow fright—two fathoms by the impaled bow, seven alongside, and eleven by the stern.

William Culhane, the Assistant Surgeon, rushed to the deck and asked Davis what was the matter.

Davis: "Unfortunately it is my watch and she is gone on shore and I steered the course I was ordered by Mr. Spear at eight bells."

Back in the gunroom, Mr. Culhane, reassured by Mr. Davis' matter-of-fact manner, was horrified when a clerk rushed in:

"Good God! Doctor; all the people who were down in the cockpit in the forward part of the ship are drowned in their hammocks; the water rushed in so fast I barely got out through a hatch ahead of it."

Aft on the poop the captain had come up in his bathrobe to ask what the noise was and where the ship was.

"She's ashore, sir," some of the men said.

"Mr. Davis, what course are you steering?" the captain asked sharply.

"S.S.E. ½ E., sir," Mr. Davis responded.

"That is right," the captain said simply.

And then—

"Let go the bower anchor and call the boats away. . . ."

"Aye, aye, sir."

Men ran about the ship to carry out the command, as John Drake, the *Birkenhead*'s Colour Sergeant, acting on the captain's orders, called all officers up on deck. The officers stood by as Captain Salmond gave a fatal command; he called for a "back turn." The engine was reversed; the paddle wheels chunked backward for a few revolutions; the ship struggled on the rock—the gouge and rent in her hull was opened wide, and she backed off into deep water.

There was not much time after that; *Birkenhead* was gone completely in twenty to thirty minutes after striking.

John Archbold, the gunner, heard the chief engineer report to Captain Salmond that the rising water "was making" three or four feet a minute and had put out his fires. Archbold tried to "fire away" some guns, at the captain's orders, but he could not get to the magazines for powder; the lower decks were flooded to the hatches. The gunner got some "blue lights" and rockets from the passage leading to the captain's cabin and sent them fiery, sizzling, high into the night.

Up from the lower decks, half-dressed, some clad only in thin shirts, the troops streamed as the ship's crew struggled with the boats, and the water rose in the hold and the fires died beneath the boiler.

"Major Seton of the 74th Highlanders called all the officers about him and impressed on them the necessity of preserving order and silence amongst the men."

The troops stood in seried, silent ranks at quarters awaiting orders. Captain Edward R. Wright of the 91st Regiment was directed to receive, transmit, and have executed Captain Salmond's commands.

"Get the men aft on to the poop," the captain ordered hoping to ease the damaged bow.

USS Bunker Hill (CG 52) fires a Standard Missile (SM-2).
Official U.S. Navy photo.

The soldiers moved smartly as ordered, and then Captain Wright sent men to lead the plunging, kicking horses out of the port gangway over the side and into the sea.

As soon as the horses were over and well clear of the wreck, where they could do no damage to the boats, seven soldiers' wives and their thirteen children (all the dependents that were aboard)—some of them tearfully clinging to their husbands and fathers—were passed down into the cutter, manned by a few seamen and in charge of Mr. Richards, Master's Assistant. Mrs. Spruce; Mrs. Nesbit; Mrs. Montgomery and other wives struggled to stay with their soldier-husbands and some of them had to be torn away—sobbing—to be put into the boat. The cutter with its helpless cargo was almost swamped by a large roller as it pulled clear. But the men left on the wreck breathed more freely as the cutter pulled away; "it is hard to describe the sensation of oppression lifted from one's mind on knowing the utterly helpless part of the ship's living cargo had been deposited in comparative safety."

Thirty soldiers were sent atop each paddle box to aid the seamen trying to cant and launch the paddle box boats, and sixty more under two officers were detailed in three shifts to man the chain pumps on the lower afterdeck. This was scarcely done when *Birkenhead*'s flooded bow, to aft of the foremast, broke off with a sharp crack, rose to the perpendicular, with the bowsprit pointing toward the stars and with the foremast jabbing and raking the rest of the hulk. The stays to the funnel parted; the stack fell crashing across the starboard paddle box, crushing some of the men working on the boat; and Mr. Brodie, the Sailing Master, was knocked from the bridge into the sea. But there was no panic; the men carried out orders as if embarking on a routine voyage, instead of facing death; most of them stood silently waiting, "as if on parade."

Ensign Lucas of the 73rd Regiment shared with another officer the duty of supervising the men at the chain pumps. Lucas had dressed carefully in his uniform after the ship struck; his men, some of them only half uniformed, were disciplined, quiet, and obedient. The troops toiled at the pumps, but the futility was obvious now.

There was not much more that could be done; the second cutter with the women and children; the first cutter with seamen and some troops; the gig with about nine men had been lowered and were standing by—filled to virtual capacity—about 100 to 150 yards away. Three boats with 60 to 70 people, and save for those drowned in their hammocks when the ship struck, or killed by the falling stack, the rest of the 630 souls were still aboard. Still drawn up in ordered ranks—most of them; still standing silent facing danger. . . .

There were other boats aboard and crew and soldiers struggled in these last minutes to free them. The starboard paddle box boat was damaged and partly carried away by the falling funnel; the port boat was jammed and ultimately capsized; the long boat, or pinnace, had to be hoisted with a complicated system of tackles—and there was no time. There was another gig, too, and a dinghy (but there were no davits in those days as we know them now), and it took time and backbreaking labor to launch boats—and there was no time.

But still the "orders were implicitly obeyed and perfect discipline maintained," as the stern part of the ship slowly sank.

The men found it hard to hold their footing and to remain in ranks, for the hulk—deep in the water, and lifted by the long swell—was rolling heavily, dipping her yardarms under.

The last moments of *Birkenhead* were distinguished by the same simple courage and "utmost order"; there "was not a cry or murmur from soldiers or sailors."

Under the dark, starlit sky, the three loaded boats lay near by, lifting and falling on the long swells. The dull boom of the surf, breaking on the shore several miles away, the creak of cordage as the hulk lifted heavily, the straining efforts of the men working on the unlaunched boats, and an occasional quiet word from the officers broke the stillness. Wreckage, a few bodies—the horses swimming far away—and men who had been washed overboard clinging to a truss of hay or a hatch cover surrounded *Birkenhead*. But no ship had come in answer to the blue lights and the rockets. . . .

Toward the end, Captain Salmond despairing, as the stern sank deeper and deeper, gave his final order:

"All those who can swim, jump overboard and make for the boats."

But Major Seton, Captain Wright, and other officers, standing in the stern in front of their men, saw the danger instantly:

"Stand fast!"

They "begged the men not to do as the captain said, as the boat with the women must be swamped. Not more than three" jumped overboard; hundreds stood fast in disciplined ranks.

Just before the end, the ship broke in two again—just abaft the engine room, washing large numbers of men into the sea. In the final minute or so before the after portion sank, Ensign Lucas of the 73rd Regiment, saw the dark sea "alive with men"—some drowning, some swimming strongly, some struggling toward bits of wreckage. The shrouds and rigging of the mainmast were lined with men from deck to trucks. The poop and extreme after-portion—still crowded with troops, some fully uniformed, some half-dressed, still in ranks—slowly up-ended until the heel of the rudder was "completely out of water." Lucas, with Major Seton beside him, stood looking out over the up-ending stern in those final seconds.

Lucas "shook hands with Seton and expressed the hope we would meet ashore."

Seton: "I do not think we shall, Lucas, as I cannot swim a stroke."

Those were probably Seton's last words; the final plunge of the wreckage swept the officers apart and Seton was never seen again. Captain Salmond, too, disappeared; he was swimming strongly in the water near Colour Sergeant Drake when something struck the commander, and he went under.

With them died most of the ship's company and most of the soldiers bound for the Kaffir War. About 210 were saved—some were in the boats; thirty to forty exhausted survivors were rescued by the schooner *Lioness* the next day from the main topmast which remained above water when the after part of *Birkenhead* sank. Still others clinging to wreckage, or hanging to a makeshift raft, made it to shore, and four were found alive after thirty-eight hours in the water. But hundreds, stalwart to the last, went down with *Birkenhead;* others died in the pounding surf after almost reaching shore, and many were entangled and drowned in the thick kelp which rimmed Danger Point.

But not one woman or child was lost and the surviving officers were unanimous in their judgments:

"... the resolution and coolness of all hands ... in a moment of extreme peril ... was remarkable. ...

"The order ... that prevailed on board from the time the ship struck until she totally disappeared far exceeded anything that ... could be effected by the best discipline, and is more to be wondered at, seeing that most of the soldiers were but a short time in the service. ... Everyone did as he was directed and there was not a murmur or cry among them until the vessel made her final plunge."

The tragedy of the *Birkenhead* excited the pride of England; Queen Victoria erected a marble memorial to the dead in the colonnade of Chelsea Hospital, London. The King of Prussia had the record of the wreck read to his regiments, as an example of the best meaning of discipline.

And the name *Birkenhead* became a nautical and military tradition, a tradition which has lived brightly in the century since her stranding—a tradition of order and obedience in the face of imminent peril, a tradition of women and children, first.

NOTES

Estimates of the *Birkenhead* dead differ. Lockhart, depending apparently chiefly upon Captain Wright's report and the report from Commodore Wyvil, says 445 were drowned and 193 saved. However, this writer believes there were only 630 souls aboard when *Birkenhead* was wrecked, and figures presented to the Portsmouth courts-martial indicate 210 were saved and 420 lost. Among those saved were Captain Wright, senior surviving military officer, and R. B. Richards, Master's Assistant, senior surviving officer of the ship's company. Fifty-nine of the ship's company, including six officers, forty-two seamen, five boys, and six Marines were saved; of the passengers five army officers, 126 soldiers, seven women, and thirteen children—a total of 151—were rescued.

The courts-martial at Portsmouth exonerated completely all the survivors; the proceedings found "no blame imputable" to any of the survivors, "but on the contrary the court sees reason to admire and applaud the steadiness shown by all in most trying circumstances." It declared, however, that though it might "be unjust to pass censure upon the deceased [Captain Salmond and, presumably, his sailing master, Mr. Brodie], whose motives for keeping so near the shore cannot be explained," nevertheless, the "fatal loss was owing to the course having been calculated to keep the land in close proximity. . . ."

The court added "praise of the departed for the coolness displayed at the moment of extreme peril and for the laudable anxiety shown for the safety of the women and children to the exclusion of all selfish consideration."

The court specifically ignored or rejected inferences by Commodore Wyvil that the failure of Captain Salmond and Sailing Master Brodie to come on deck between 10 P.M. and the time the ship struck inferred "extreme neglect of duty." It also rejected contentions that the boats might have saved more survivors from the water and that the rescue operations were not well organized. It specifically praised the "conduct of those who were first in the boats" and endorsed their judgments.

Read a hundred years later, the eye-witness testimony in the courts-martial and the questions asked leave, however, some room for doubt about the judgment of Captain Salmond and the conduct and judgment of all of those in the boats. And the list of survivors seems to include a disproportionate number of the ship's company and too few troops.

It seems indeed probable that the story of the *Birkenhead* has been embellished somewhat with the years and that the few discreditable events which probably occurred have been forgotten and the general discipline, courage, and steadiness somewhat, though not greatly, magnified. It is almost certain that the imaginative painting "The Wreck of the *Birkenhead*," by Henry (London) represents an heroic generalization of the final scene.

Ensign Lucas, in his letter, suggests that the soldiers did not know the ship was foundering; he states he asked the ship's carpenter after *Birkenhead* struck the reef what the trouble was and was told:

"We have struck a rock and we are going down fast."

Lucas says he asked "the carpenter not to tell the men, fearing panic."

Captain Wright in his letter-report of March 1, 1852, included with the court-martial papers, states that the perfect discipline and excellent conduct of the men "struck me as being one of the most perfect instances of what discipline can effect, and almost led me to believe that not a man on board knew the vessel was likely to go down."

It is indeed possible that many of the young soldiers did not realize their peril until the very end, but many in the ship's company certainly understood the danger, and after the bow broke off few in the *Birkenhead* could have had many illusions. And, in any case, the great majority of the men held steady until the very end—refusing to leap into the water and swamp the boats.

It is curious—in view of Kipling's utilization of the *Birkenhead* incident in his tribute to the Royal Marines—that one of the few criticisms of the conduct of any of the *Birkenhead* personnel to be found in the courts-martial proceedings was directed

Official U.S. Navy photo.

against a Marine survivor in one of the boats, who was alleged to be impudent and surly. Kipling's poem, indeed, leaves a false impression—the impression that the glory of the *Birkenhead* was chiefly the glory of the Royal Marines. There were a handful of Marines aboard attached to the ship's company—(six were saved)—and probably their conduct as well as that of the great majority of all aboard was courageous and disciplined. But the principal glory of the *Birkenhead* must go to the young soldiers and their officers who were passengers in an alien environment, yet who stood "an' [were] still to the *Birken'ead* drill"—the drill of discipline, obedience, and courage.

ACKNOWLEDGMENTS

The principal source for the *Birkenhead* story is the "Sessional Papers"—House of Commons, 1852, Volume 30, pages 219–249. These papers contain the proceedings of two courts-martial of the surviving officers and crew of H.M.S. *Birkenhead* held aboard H.M.S. *Victory* at Portsmouth, England, on 5 and 7 May, 1852, under the

Presidency of Henry Prescott, Esq., C.B., Rear Admiral of the Red and Second Officer in Command of Her Majesty's ships and vessels at Spithead and in Portsmouth Harbor. Included in these papers are eyewitness reports of survivors, official reports, a letter to the Admiralty from Commodore C. Wyvil at Simon's Bay, describing the wreck, and a letter report from Captain Edward R. Wright of the 91st Regiment, dated March 1, 1852. I have drawn liberally upon these documents, and quotations in this account are chiefly from these papers.

J. G. Lockhart, *Peril of the Sea,* Frederick Stokes, 1925, is another important source consulted. Lockhart quotes from a letter written by a survivor, Ensign Lucas, and in turn I have utilized some of the Lucas material in this account.

Other sources of secondary importance are *Notes and Queries, London*—"Loss of Her Majesty's Steamship *Birkenhead,*" Jan.–June, 1921; "The Loss of the *Orion,* the *Amazon* and the *Birkenhead*"—a letter by William S. Lacon to the President of the Board of Trade, London, Parker, Furnival and Parker—Military Library, 1852; and *Ships and South Africa,* by Marischal Murray, Oxford University Press, London, 1933.

22 Rallying Around the Flag— The Fundamentals of Motivation

Objectives

1. Outline Maslow's hierarchy of needs theory of human motivation and describe how it could impact your approach to leading subordinates.

2. Define need for achievement, need for esteem, need for power, equity needs and internal versus external rewards as they relate to building motivation.

3. Assess and describe what motivates you.

4. Describe what motivated VADM Stockdale during his leadership experience as a Prisoner of War in Vietnam. Describe the price of being motivated in this way rather than being motivated to improve your own personal situation.

What Motivates Us?

Are there general principles that explain what motivates us? Are people driven by instincts, a need to achieve a certain level of bodily tension, or a desire for attractive rewards? Do all people want to satisfy the same basic needs, and, if so, what are these needs?

Over the years, psychologists have approached the subject of motivation in two ways. Some have proposed general theories to explain what all human motives have in common. Others have focused on specific motives such as hunger, sex, affiliation and belonging, and achievement. Let's begin with the first approach.

General Theories of Motivation

Early in this century, as Darwin's theory of evolution gained prominence, many psychologists believed that human behavior, like the behavior of animals, was biologically rooted in instincts. An **instinct** is a fixed pattern of behavior that is unlearned, universal within a species, and "released" by a specific set of conditions. Thus, canaries sing, spiders weave webs, and beavers build dams—specific actions that are "hard-wired" by evolution. But is complex human behavior similarly programmed? In 1908, motivation theorist William McDougall argued that a whole range of human behaviors are instinctually based. He went on to compile a long list of human instincts, including those for acquisition, jealousy, mating, parenting, pugnacity, greed, curiosity, cleanliness, and self-assertion.

Instinct theories of human motivation were soon rejected. One problem was that they explained human behavior through a flawed process of circular reasoning: "Why are people aggressive? Because human beings possess a powerful instinct to aggress. How do we know humans have this instinct? Because there is so much aggression." Notice the circularity in the logic: Behavior is attributed to an instinct that, in turn, is inferred from the behavior. A second problem with instinct theory is that many so-called instinctual behaviors are learned, shaped by experience, subject to individual differences, and influenced by culture.

Drive Theory   With the demise of instinct-based accounts, psychologists turned to **drive theory** of human motivation. According to drive theory, physiological needs that arise within the body create an unpleasant state of tension, which motivates or *drives* the organism to behave in ways that reduce the need and return the body to a balanced, less tense state (Hull, 1943). In its original form, drive theory was used to explain various biological functions such as eating, drinking, sleeping, and having sex. The hunger-eating cycle illustrates a presumed chain of events: food deprivation → hunger (drive) → seeking food and eating → drive reduction. Clearly, drive theory

instinct A fixed pattern of behavior that is unlearned, universal in a species, and "released" by specific stimuli.

drive theory The notion that physiological needs arouse tension that motivates people to satisfy the need.

271

"You want only happiness, Douglas. I want fame and happiness."

Individuals differ in the strength of their various motives.

arousal theory The notion that people are motivated to achieve and maintain an optimum level of bodily arousal.

incentive theory The notion that people are motivated to behave in ways that produce a valued inducement.

hierarchy of needs Maslow's list of basic needs that have to be satisfied before people can become self-actualized.

Need for self-actualization

Esteem needs

Belongingness and love needs

Safety needs

Physiological needs

FIGURE 22.1 Maslow's pyramid of needs Maslow theorized that everyone is motivated to fulfill a hierarchy of needs ranging from those most basic to survival up to those that promote self-enhancement.

can be used to explain certain biologically driven behaviors. But today, psychologists agree that it cannot also explain what motivates the compulsive overeater, the late-night workaholic, or the power-starved politician. In particular, drive theory cannot explain why people often engage in activities that *increase* rather than reduce tension—as when we explore new surroundings just to satisfy our curiosity, skip a snack to save our appetite for dinner, or run miles with our hearts pounding in order to stay in shape. Nor can drive theory explain the popularity of ice climbing, extreme skiing, skydiving, bungee jumping, and other high-risk activities.

Arousal Theory   To account for the fact that people often seek to increase rather than reduce tension, many psychologists turned to **arousal theory** of motivation. According to arousal theory, human beings are motivated to achieve and maintain an *optimum* level of bodily arousal—not too little, not too much (Fiske & Maddi, 1961). Studies show that people who are put into a state of sensory restriction (blindfolded, ears plugged, and unable to move) or into a monotonous situation quickly become bored and crave stimulation. Studies also show that when people are bombarded with bright lights, blaring music, and other intense stimuli, they soon withdraw in an effort to lower their level of arousal. Individuals differ in the amount of stimulation they find "optimal" (Eysenck & Eysenck, 1985; Zuckerman, 1979). We'll also see, however, that as a general rule people are happier and more motivated when engaged in activities that are challenging in relation to their ability—not too easy, which is boring, and not too difficult, which triggers anxiety (Csikszentmihalyi, 1990; Moneta & Csikszentmihalyi, 1996).

Incentive Theory   In contrast to the notion that people are "pushed" into action by internal need states, many motivation psychologists believe that people are often "pulled" by external goals, or incentives. According to the **incentive theory** of motivation, any stimulus that people have learned to associate with positive or negative outcomes can serve as an incentive—grades, money, ice cream, respect, a romantic night out, or relief from pain. People are motivated to behave in certain ways when they *expect* that they can gain the incentive through their efforts and when they *value* that incentive. Recognizing that human beings set goals, make plans, and think about the outcomes they produce, motivation theorists today believe that there is a strong cognitive component to many of our aspirations (Atkinson, 1964; McClelland, 1985; Weiner, 1989).

The Pyramid of Human Motivations

Now that we have considered general theories of motivation, let us examine some of the specific motives that direct and energize our behavior. In other words, what is it that we want most in life? In response to this question, Abraham Maslow (1954) proposed that all human beings are motivated to fulfill a **hierarchy of needs,** from those that are basic for survival up to those that promote growth and self-enhancement (see Figure 22.1).

At the base of the hierarchy are the physiological needs for food, water, oxygen, sleep, and sex. Once these needs are met, people seek safety, steady work, financial security, stability at home, and a predictable environment. Next on the ladder are the social needs for affiliation, belongingness and love, affection, close relations, family ties, and group membership (if these needs are not met, we feel lonely and alienated). Next are the esteem needs, which include our desires for status, respect, recognition, achievement, and power (failing to satisfy this need, we feel inferior and unimportant). In short, everyone strives in their own way to satisfy all the needs on the hierarchy. Once these needs are met, said Maslow, we become ready, willing, and able to strive for self-actualization—a distinctly human need to fulfill one's potential. As Maslow (1968) put it, "A musician must make music, an artist must paint, a poet must write, if he is ultimately to be at peace with himself. What a man *can* be, he *must* be" (p. 46).

By arranging human needs in the shape of a pyramid, Maslow was claiming that the needs at the base take priority over those at the top. In other words, the higher needs become important to us only after more basic needs are satisfied. Research generally confirms Maslow's prediction that those motives lower in the pyramid take precedence, though there are occasional exceptions, as when people starve themselves to death in order to make a political statement. Research also shows that not everyone climbs Maslow's hierarchy in the same prescribed order. Some people seek love and romance before fulfilling their esteem motives, but others who are more achievement-oriented may try to establish a career before a family (Goebel & Brown, 1981).

Maslow's theory may not accurately describe the motivational path all people take, but his distinctions and the notion that the various needs form a hierarchy provide a convenient framework for the study of motivation. In the coming pages, we'll begin at the base of Maslow's pyramid with hunger and sexuality, then we'll work our way up to the needs for affiliation, intimacy, achievement, and power. Finally, we'll put the psychology of motivation to work, literally, in a discussion of what motivates people on the job.

Basic Human Motives

How do we regulate eating? Is hunger a strictly biological state, or is it influenced by psychological factors? What causes obesity and eating disorders, and what can be done to correct these problems? Turning to the study of sexual and reproductive behavior, are men and women similarly motivated? What influences sexual orientation?

Hunger and Eating

It has been said that "a hungry stomach has no ears" (Jean de La Fontaine), that "Nobody wants a kiss when they are hungry" (Dorothea Dix), and that "Even God cannot speak to a hungry man except in terms of bread" (Mahatma Gandhi). It seems that when it's time to eat, all other urges, desires, and ambitions fade into the background.

Hunger is a powerful sensation that sets in motion the search for and consumption of food. It's interesting that our commonsense notions about hunger are often incorrect. Sometimes, after working nonstop for several hours, I'll hold my stomach, feel the growling, and just know that I'm hungry. On empty. Time to eat. Breakfast, lunch, dinner, a morning coffee break, an afternoon snack, even a late-night raid on the refrigerator are part of the daily routine. At other times, after a big meal, I'll put my hand over my stomach, feel bloated and stuffed, and complain that I'm full. Time to stop. It's as if sensations from the belly were sending "eat" and "stop" messages straight to the brain. But is this the way hunger works?

When snow falls, children in all parts of the world make snowballs. Instinct theorists of the past would attribute this universal behavior to an instinct for play. In an interesting parallel to humans, young Japanese macaques also make snowballs, carry them around as play objects, and even roll them along the ground. But here's where the similarity ends: No one has ever seen a macaque throw a snowball.

"Your clock may be telling you to get married, but mine's telling me to have lunch."

When it's time to eat, other motives take a back seat.

The Biological Component   The biological mechanisms underlying hunger are complex. Following their common sense, early researchers believed that hunger was triggered by sensations in the stomach. In an initial experiment, researcher A. L. Washburn, working with Walter Cannon, swallowed a long tube with a balloon that was then partially inflated and specially designed to rest in his stomach. Whenever the stomach contracted, the balloon compressed. At the same time, Washburn pressed a key each time he felt hungry. Using this device, and testing other subjects, Cannon and Washburn (1912) observed a link between stomach contractions and reports of hunger. In fact, the subjects reported feeling hungry at the height of a contraction, not at the beginning—thus suggesting that the contractions had caused the hunger and not the other way around (see Figure 22.2). Indeed, more recent research shows that people begin to feel hungry when the stomach is about 60 percent empty (Sepple & Read, 1989).

There may be a correlation between stomach contractions and hunger, but additional observations soon discredited Cannon and Washburn's theory. The fatal blow came when studies revealed that even after people had had cancerous or ulcerated stomachs surgically removed, they continued to feel hungry. Clearly, if hunger can be felt without a stomach, then stomach contractions cannot be the cause of hunger. Confronted with this realization, researchers turned their attention to the brain and central nervous system.

According to one theory, the brain monitors fluctuating levels of glucose (a simple sugar that provides energy) and other nutrients circulating in the bloodstream. When glucose drops below a certain level, people become hungry and eat. When the glucose level in the blood exceeds a certain point, they feel satiated and stop eating (see Figure 22.3). How and where in the body is blood glucose monitored? Although different regions of the brain may be involved in the process, two distinct areas of the *hypothalamus* play a key role (as we saw in Chapter 2, the hypothalamus is a tiny brain structure that regulates body temperature, the autonomic nervous system, and the release of hormones).

Initially, researchers saw the *lateral hypothalamus* (LH) as the "hunger center": when its neurons are stimulated, an animal will eat, and eat, and eat—even if it's full. And when the LH is destroyed, the animal will not eat and may even starve to death unless it is force-fed (Anand & Brobeck, 1951; Teitelbaum & Epstein, 1962). Similarly, researchers identified the *ventromedial hypothalamus* (VH) as a "satiation center": When it is stimulated, an animal will not eat, even if it has been deprived of food. When this area is destroyed, an animal will consume larger quantities than usual and eventually triple its own body weight (Hetherington & Ranson, 1942; Wyrwicka & Dobrzecka, 1960).

At first, these findings suggested that the hypothalamus monitors blood glucose levels and has an on-off switch for eating (Stellar, 1954). But more recent studies show that the mechanism is far more complicated. It turns out, for example, that certain nerves form a tract that runs up from the brainstem through the lateral hypothalamus—and that these nerves are somehow involved. In fact, such areas may be part of a more general motor-activation system that, when stimulated, motivates an animal to "Do something!" This general command triggers eating if food is present, drinking if water is present,

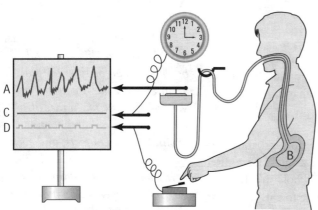

FIGURE 22.2 Cannon and Washburn's hunger experiment   In this study, subjects swallowed a balloon, which rested in the stomach. Recorded over time (A) is the volume of the balloon (B) in minutes (C). Subjects pressed a key whenever they felt hungry (D). Subjects reported feeling hungry at the height of their stomach contractions.

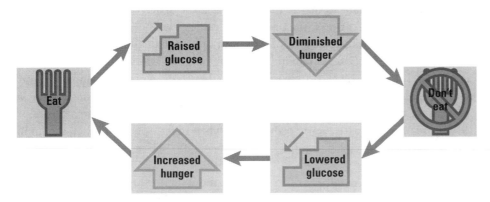

FIGURE 22.3 The hunger-regulation cycle When blood glucose levels are low, people become hungry and eat. The food then raises glucose levels, which lessens hunger and eating. The "thermostat" that monitors glucose levels is in or near the hypothalamus. Other factors as well control hunger and eating.

or running if neither food nor water is present (Berridge et al., 1989). Research also shows that other factors control hunger and eating as well—including levels of protein, fat, and insulin and other hormonal activities associated with the liver, pancreas, and intestines. In short, the body is equipped with a complex biochemical system for the regulation of hunger and eating (Logue, 1991; Stricker, 1990; Winn, 1995).

Psychological Influences Hunger may be biologically driven, but researchers have learned that other factors such as taste, smell, and visual cues also play an important role—and that eating patterns, which are learned, can also be unlearned (Capaldi, 1996). Among the psychological influences on eating is taste. There are four primary tastes: sweet, sour, salty, and bitter. It turns out that infants and adults all over the world seek out sweet-tasting foods such as cookies, ice cream, soda, ripe fruit, and candy, as well as salty foods such as pretzels and potato chips. These preferences are innate and universal. Yet in other ways, our tastes in food are shaped by personal and cultural experience. In China, food is flavored primarily with soy sauce, rice wine, and ginger root; in Greece, olive oil, lemon juice, and oregano are used; Moroccan food is seasoned with coriander, cumin, cinnamon, onion, and fruit; and in Mexico, tomatoes and hot chilies are common ingredients (Rozin, 1983). Consistently, people tend to prefer foods that are familiar rather than exotic, which is why most Americans react with disgust to such culinary "treats" from other parts of the world as sheep's eyes, dog meat, snakes, sea urchins, and grasshoppers. Interestingly, taste preferences and aversions that are learned can also be unlearned through repeated exposure to new foods and food-eating models (Hobden & Pliner, 1995; Pliner et al., 1993).

External food cues can also entice us into eating. If you've ever inhaled the floury aroma of pastries in a bakery, popcorn in a movie theater, or garlic in an Italian restaurant, or if you've ever had a sudden urge for beer and a hot dog while sitting in a ball park, you know that sometimes we're drawn into eating by external cues, or incentives. The time of day is also a powerful food cue. For example, Stanley Schachter and Larry Gross (1968) brought subjects into a laboratory, rigged the clock on the wall so that it ran fast or slow, then offered crackers as a snack. Not wanting to spoil their appetite, most subjects of normal weight ate fewer crackers when they thought it was late than when they thought it was early in the afternoon.

A bilateral lesion of the ventromedial part of the hypothalamus caused this rat to triple its body weight over a short period of time. Think about this result. How much would you weigh if your body weight were to triple?

Finally, it's important to realize that eating is a social activity and is often subject to social influences. At times, the presence of others can inhibit us from eating—as when young women consume less food in front of men than alone in order to present themselves as appropriately "feminine" (Mori et al., 1987; Pliner & Chaiken, 1990). As a general rule, however, people eat more rather than less in the company of others. Eating-diary studies show that the more people we're with, the longer time we spend at the table and the more food we are likely to consume (de Castro & Brewer, 1992). This effect is particularly pronounced when the people we're with are family and friends (de Castro, 1994).

Obesity   With all the talk that surrounds us about dieting and exercise, one would think that Americans are obsessed with their weight. Yet the National Institutes of Health (1992) estimates that one-fourth to one-third of all Americans are overweight, or **obese.** Definitions of obesity vary somewhat, but individuals are generally classified as obese when they carry a surplus of body fat that causes them to exceed their optimum weight by 20 percent.

obesity The state of having a surplus of body fat that causes a person to exceed his or her optimum weight by 20 percent.

Being slightly overweight does not pose a health risk. But statistically, obese individuals are more likely to suffer from diabetes, high blood pressure, heart disease, arthritis, respiratory problems, gallstones, and certain forms of cancer (Bray, 1986). To make matters worse, obese people are also subject to stereotyping, ridicule, and discrimination. Research shows that obese people are assumed to be slow, lazy, sloppy, and lacking in willpower (Ryckman et al., 1989). And in a study of long-term social and economic consequences, researchers followed a group of overweight sixteen- to twenty-four-year-old women and found that those who were still obese after seven years made less money than their peers and were less likely to be married (Gortmaker et al., 1993).

What causes obesity? Why do some people but not others fight a chronic battle against gaining weight? As with other aspects of hunger and eating, both biological and psychological factors play a role. Physiologically speaking, getting fat is easy to explain. People gain weight when they *consume* more calories than their body can *metabolize,* or burn up. The excess calories are stored as fat. Evidence for the role of biological factors begins with the finding that obesity runs in families and is influenced by genetics. In one study, Albert Stunkard and others (1990) compared the "Body Mass Index," or BMI (a measure of obesity that controls for height), of genetically identical twins and fraternal twins who were raised together or apart. As illustrated in Figure 22.4, two results provided strong evidence for the role of genetics: (1) The identical twins were more similar in their BMI than were the fraternal twins, and (2) identical twins were similar in this regard even when raised apart, in separate homes. The same conclusion emerges from adoption studies, which show that, when it comes to body weight, adoptees resemble their biological parents more than their adoptive parents (Grilo & Pogue-Geile, 1991).

So what, specifically, is inherited? Do obese people inherit a tendency to consume large quantities of food, or are they born with a slow metabolism, making it more difficult for them to burn up calories? Research shows

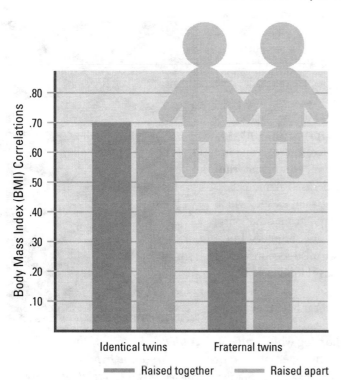

FIGURE 22.4 Body weight of identical and fraternal twins   Indicating the role of genetic factors in body weight, you can see that identical twins (*left*) had more similar body weights than did fraternal twins (*right*). Note also that this same pattern was found regardless of whether the twins were raised together or apart (Stunkard et al., 1990).

that most obese individuals have normal metabolism rates, a finding that suggests that they must eat more than the average person. Why? According to one theory, each of us has a **set point,** a level of weight toward which our body gravitates, and obese people are programmed to maintain a high set-point weight (Keesey, 1995). The set point itself may be genetic or stem from eating habits established early in life. Either way, set points are relatively stable—which explains why it's hard to lose massive quantities of weight and why, after dieting, it's so hard to maintain the loss over time (Garner & Wooley, 1991).

set point A level of weight toward which a person's body gravitates.

Thankfully, it is not impossible to achieve long-term weight loss. Some people resort to high-risk medical procedures such as gastric-restriction surgery to shrink the stomach and diet drugs that suppress appetite or increase energy expenditure. For most, however, weight reduction can be achieved through alterations in behavior. In this regard, the key to success is to realize that a change in diet must be permanent and that it must be accompanied by a steady regimen of physical exercise (Brownell & Wadden, 1992). Two factors must be present for someone to sustain this effort: information and motivation. First, a person must have an accurate sense of his or her caloric intake and exercise. This sounds easy, but Steven Lichtman and his colleagues (1992) had a group of failed dieters keep a diary and discovered that they unwittingly underreported the amount of food they consumed and overestimated their daily exercise. Second, one's motivation for losing weight is also critical. Research shows that people are more likely to succeed in a long-term weight-reduction program when motivated by their own desires than when motivated by external incentives such as the wishes of a spouse (Williams et al., 1996).

Social Motives

After biological needs are satisfied, what do we strive for? Do people actually *need* other people? Is the desire for social relationships a fundamental human motivation? What drives individuals who are highly motivated to achieve? What about the need for power—does it promote good leadership or bad?

Satisfying the body's appetite for food or the urge for sex helps propel the biological human engine. But people are not content merely to survive. Most of us want more out of life, much more. In varying degrees, we want to be part of a community, to love and be loved, and to achieve recognition, status, fame, wealth, and power. Whether one's goal is to raise a family, travel the world, earn a million dollars, climb the highest mountain, care for those in need, or paint a masterpiece, to be human is to strive for more than a mere satisfaction of basic drives. Using Maslow's motivational pyramid as a framework, we'll examine two broad classes of motives: belongingness needs and esteem needs.

Belongingness Motives

Although born helpless, human infants are equipped at birth with reflexes that orient them toward people. They are responsive to faces, turn their head toward voices, and are prepared to mimic certain facial gestures on cue. Much to the delight of parents, the newborn seems an inherently social animal. If you reflect on the amount of time you spend talking to, being with, pining for, or worrying about other people, you'll realize that we all are. People need people.

Recognizing the power of our social impulses, Maslow ranked belongingness and love needs third in his hierarchy. Being part of a family or community, playing on a sports team, joining a social or religious or professional group, making friends, falling in love, and having children—all service this important motive. So just how important is it? Do people really *need* other people?

According to Roy Baumeister and Mark Leary (1996), the need to belong is a fundamental human motivation. As they put it, "human beings have a pervasive drive to form and maintain at least a minimum quantity of lasting, positive, and significant interpersonal relationships" (p. 497). This conclusion is supported by a great deal of research. All over the world, people experience joy when they form new social attachments and react with anxiety, loneliness, and grief when these bonds are broken—as when separated from a loved one by distance, divorce, or death. The need to belong runs deep. People who have a network of close social contacts—in the form of lovers, friends, and relatives—tend to be happier and more satisfied with life than those who are more isolated (Myers and Diener, 1995). In fact, we'll see that people who are more socially connected are also physically healthier and less likely to die a premature death (House et al., 1988; Uchino et al., 1996).

Dan McAdams (1989) notes that Maslow's belongingness motive is actually composed of two distinct needs. The first is the **need for affiliation,** which is defined as a desire to establish and maintain social contacts. The second is the **need for intimacy,** defined as a further desire for close relationships characterized by an openness of communication. Let's consider each of these needs in turn.

need for affiliation The desire to establish and maintain social contacts.

need for intimacy The desire for close relationships characterized by open and intimate communication.

The Need for Affiliation   Do you ever crave the company of others? Do you ever enjoy being alone? Chances are that you answered *yes* to both questions. Research shows that individuals differ in the strength of their need for affiliation. As you might expect, people with a high need for affiliation are socially more active than lows. They prefer to be in contact with others more often and are more likely to visit friends or even make phone calls and write letters as a way to maintain social contact at a distance (McAdams & Constantian, 1983).

Although individuals differ, even the most gregarious among us wants to be alone at times. In fact, it seems that people are motivated to establish and maintain an *optimum* balance of social contact (not too much, not too little) the way the body maintains a certain level of caloric intake. In an interesting study, Bibb Latané and Carol Werner (1978) found that laboratory rats were more likely to approach others of their species after a period of isolation and were less likely after prolonged social contact. These researchers suggested that rats, like many other animals, have a built-in "sociostat" (a social thermostat) to regulate their affiliative tendencies. Is there any evidence of a similar mechanism in humans? Shawn O'Connor and Lorne Rosenblood (1996) recently had college students carry portable beepers for four days. Whenever the beeper went off (on average, every hour), the students wrote down whether, at the time, they were *actually* alone or in the company of other people, and whether, at the time, they *wanted* to be alone or with others. The results showed that the students were in the state they desired two-thirds of the time—and that the situation they wished they were in on one occasion predicted their actual situation the next time they were signaled. Whether it was solitude or social contact that the students were craving, they successfully managed to regulate their own personal needs for affiliation.

People may differ in the strength of their affiliative needs and in the overall amount of social contact they find satisfying, but there are times when we would all rather be with other people. I'll never forget being with my son at Yankee Stadium in October 1996, the night the New York Yankees won the World Series. There were more than 60,000 fans at the game, and when it ended, nobody wanted to go home. Nobody rushed for the parking lot or raced to the subway. For nearly half an hour, nobody even left their seat. Out in the street, jubilant pedestrians exchanged high-fives, slaps on the back, hugs, and kisses. It was clear, even in the big city of strangers, that people wanted to celebrate together rather than alone. Affiliating can be satisfying for other reasons as well. From others, we get energy, attention, stimulation, information, and emotional support (Hill, 1987).

One condition that strongly arouses our need for affiliation is stress. It's always amazing to see how neighbors who otherwise never stop to say hello come together in snowstorms, hurricanes, power failures, and other major crises. Many years ago, Stanley Schachter (1959) theorized that external threat triggers fear and motivates us to affiliate—particularly with others who are facing a similar threat. In a laboratory experiment, Schachter found that subjects expecting to receive painful electric shocks chose to wait with other nervous subjects rather than alone.

Why do we affiliate in times of stress? Recent research suggests that people under stress seek each other out in order to gain *cognitive clarity* about the danger they are in. In one study, James Kulik and Heike Mahler (1989) found that hospital patients awaiting open-heart surgery preferred to have roommates who were postoperative rather than preoperative, presumably because they were in a position to provide information about the experience. Indeed, patients in a second study who were assigned postoperative rather than preoperative roommates became less anxious about the experience and were later quicker to recover from the surgery (Kulik et al., 1996). Even in a laboratory setting, Kulik and his colleagues (1994) found that subjects awaiting the painful task of soaking a hand in ice-cold water (compared to those told that the task would not be painful) also preferred to wait with someone who had completed the task than with one who had not—and they asked more questions of these experienced peers. Under stress, we adaptively become motivated to affiliate—not with just anybody but with others who can help us cope with an impending threat.

The Need for Intimacy Affiliating with other people, even superficially, satisfies part of our need for social contact. But in varying degrees, people also have a need for close and intimate relationships. Research shows that individuals who score high rather than low on measures of the need for intimacy are seen by peers as warm, sincere, and loving. They also look at others more, smile more, laugh more, and confide more in their friends. People who score high rather than low on intimacy may also be happier and healthier (McAdams, 1989).

In looking at close relationships and the deep affection that grows between friends or lovers, psychologists have observed that the key ingredient is **self-disclosure,** the sharing of intimate, often confidential details about oneself with another person (Jourard, 1971; Derlega et al., 1993). Self-disclosure tends to follow three predictable patterns. The first is that we typically reciprocate another person's self-disclosure with one of our own—and at a comparable level of intimacy. Bare your soul to someone, and that person is likely to react by doing the same (Berg, 1987). Second, there are sex differences in openness of communication. Compared to men, women tend to self-disclose more than men *to* others (both male and female), and, in turn, they elicit more self-disclosure *from* others (Dindia & Allen, 1992). Third, individuals reveal more and more to each other as relationships grow over time. In the early stages, people give relatively little of themselves to others and receive comparably little in

"At this point, my privacy needs are interfering with my intimacy goals."

People are motivated to establish and maintain an optimum level of social contact.

self-disclosure The sharing of intimate details about oneself with another person.

On January 1, 1997, Microsoft's Bill Gates was worth $23.9 billion, making him the richest person in the world, by far. What motivates Gates? Looking back on Bill as a child, his father recently said, "The play was serious. Winning mattered" (Isaacson, 1997).

return. If these encounters are rewarding, however, the communication becomes more frequent and more intimate (Altman & Taylor, 1973). Self-disclosure is the glue that binds our most intimate relations. The more of it there is among friends, dating partners, and married couples, the more they like each other, the happier they are in the relationship, and the more inclined they are to stay together (Hendrick, 1981; Collins & Miller, 1994).

Esteem Motives

Have you ever met someone so single-mindedly driven to succeed that you couldn't help but wonder why? One individual who pops to mind is Bill Gates—cofounder and chair of Microsoft. Gates is now the richest man in the world and seems to have an insatiable appetite for more. By his own admission, Gates wants to gain worldwide domination of the computer industry. Other images that come to mind are that of the politician who runs for president, the workaholic scientist who spends weekends in the laboratory, and athletes like Kerri Strug, the 1996 Olympic gymnast. What fuels the drive we often have to succeed, excel, and advance in our work? Over the years, psychologists have examined two motives that play a role in this regard: the need for achievement and the need for power.

The Need for Achievement   In a classic book entitled *The Achievement Motive*, David McClelland and his colleagues (1953) sought to identify people with high levels of **achievement motivation**—defined as a strong desire to accomplish difficult tasks, outperform others, and excel. There was no question that individuals differ in the intensity of their achievement strivings. The question was how this important and perhaps unconscious motive could be measured. Seeking what he would later call a "psychic X ray," McClelland believed that our motives are revealed in our fantasies. To bring these fantasies out, he asked subjects to make up stories about a series of ambiguous pictures. Look at the sample photo in Figure 22.5. What's your interpretation? Who is the boy, what is he thinking about, and what will happen to him? Assuming that subjects will naturally identify with the main character (some are male, others female), pictures like this provide a screen on which people can project their own needs. Based on a scoring system devised by McClelland and his colleagues, you would be classified as high in the need for achievement if you say that the boy in Figure 22.5 is recalling with pride an exam he aced, thinking about how to win a scholarship, or dreaming of becoming a doctor—and if these types of concerns are a recurring theme in your stories.

From the start, this fantasy measure proved intriguing. For example, it proved to be a reasonably sensitive measure of the need for achievement. To demonstrate this, McClelland and his colleagues (1953) had subjects solve word puzzles before responding to the pictures. Some subjects were told that the puzzles were not that important; others were told that the puzzles tested intelligence and leadership ability—an instruction used to arouse performance concerns. Sure enough, subjects who were induced into a heightened state of achievement need told more achievement-relevant stories. Yet research soon showed that scores from this fantasy measure of achievement do not correlate with the way subjects described their own achievement needs on questionnaires. The reason? It appears that the story-based measure uncovers deeply ingrained, enduring, unconscious motives that predict a person's behavior over long periods of time, while questionnaires measure only conscious, self-attributed motives relevant to the way a person is likely to behave in the immediate situation (McClelland et al., 1989).

achievement motivator A strong desire to accomplish difficult tasks, outperform others, and excel.

As you might expect, there are strong links among a person's motivation, behavior, and level of accomplishment. Those who score high rather than low in the need for achievement work harder and are more persistent, innovative, and future-oriented. They also crave success more than they fear failure (Atkinson, 1964) and then credit success to their own abilities and efforts rather than to external factors (Weiner, 1989). One particularly interesting difference between the highs and lows concerns their level of aspiration. You might think that individuals driven by a need to achieve would take on exceedingly difficult tasks. Not so. When college students playing a ring-toss game could choose where to stand, those high rather than low in the need for achievement stood a moderate distance from the peg—not so close that success would come easy but not so far that they would fail (Atkinson & Litwin, 1960). People who are truly motivated to succeed set goals that are challenging but realistic (McClelland & Koestner, 1992). Indeed, they are more interested in mastering a task than they are fearful of failure (Elliot & Church, 1997).

Clearly, hard work and realistic goal setting pay off in life. Individuals high in the need for achievement get better grades in school, are more successful in their careers, and are more upwardly mobile. In fact, McClelland (1985) and others have found that there is often a positive correlation between the achievement orientation of a whole society (which they measure by analyzing magazine articles and other popular writings) and overall levels of economic growth, scientific progress, and productivity. For example, changing levels of achievement motivation in the United States—as derived from children's readers in the years 1800 and 1950—closely paralleled inventiveness as measured by the per capita number of patents issued during those same years (deCharms & Moeller, 1962). Although these correlations are open to interpretation with regard to cause and effect, it's clear that the more achievement-oriented a society is at a given point in time, the more productive it is likely to be.

The Need for Power   Related but not identical to achievement motivation is the **need for power,** a strong desire to acquire prestige and influence over other people (Winter, 1973). As you might expect, men and women who are high rather than low in the need for power are more likely to run for public office and strive for other positions of authority. In a study that followed women for fourteen years after they graduated from college, those who had scored high in the need for power as seniors were later more likely to plan on, enter, and remain in careers that involved the exercise of power (Jenkins, 1994).

The need for power provides the fuel for great leadership. To be effective, however, leaders must also exercise self-control and use their power for social goals rather than for personal gain. William Spangler and Robert House (1991) analyzed the inaugural speeches written by thirty-three U.S. presidents, from George Washington to Ronald Reagan, in order to determine their need for power and other motives. Using complex measures of presidential effectiveness (which took into account their record on war, peaceful solutions to crises, and other decisions made), they discovered that more effective presidents had higher needs for power and more motivation to use that power for social rather than personal objectives. Can a leader's power motivation influence the course of world events? Perhaps. In a series of studies, David Winter (1993) analyzed 400 years of British history, the outbreak of World War I, and the 1962 Cuban Missile Crisis involving the United States and the former Soviet Union. In each study, Winter derived power-motivation scores for the leaders involved by using government documents and speeches given before, during, and after each conflict. The result: The leaders' need for power was statistically predictive of war

FIGURE 22.5 **Fantasy measure of achievement** Who is the boy, what is he thinking about, and what will happen to him? Using ambiguous pictures like this one, researchers get people to tell stories and then code the stories for achievement imagery.

need for power A strong desire to acquire prestige and influence over other people.

and peace. As Winter put it, "When it rises, war is likely; when it falls, war is less likely and ongoing wars are likely to end" (p. 542).

Motivating People at Work

What motivates us on the job? Are we driven by strictly economic costs and benefits? Does offering rewards for performance, as in corporate incentive programs, increase or undermine a worker's intrinsic motivation? How do people react when they feel overpaid or underpaid for their work?

In any organization—from Microsoft and Sony to your school and library—one of the critical challenges for industrial/organizational (I/O) psychologists is to determine what motivates individuals to work hard and to work well. Think about it. What drives *your* on-the-job performance? Are your concerns strictly economic, or do you have other personal needs to fulfill? There is no single answer. At work, as in the rest of life, our behavior often stems from the convergence of multiple motives.

Reward-Based Motivation

Out of necessity, people work for money and other economic benefits such as vacation time, sick leave, health insurance, and retirement pensions (Heneman & Schwab, 1985; Judge & Welbourne, 1994). Some of the rewards people get at work are not monetary but symbolic—for example, titles, large offices, windows, and access to parking (Becker, 1981; Sundstrom, 1986). The most popular theory of worker motivation is Victor Vroom's (1964) expectancy theory. According to Vroom, people are rational decision makers who analyze the benefits and the costs of their possible courses of action. Specifically, he states, people are motivated to work hard whenever they expect that their efforts will improve performance, believe that good performance will be rewarded, and value the rewards they expect to receive. Over the years, expectancy theory has been used with some success to predict worker attendance, productivity, and other job-related behaviors (Mitchell, 1974). In addition, research has shown that people perform better at work and are more productive when they're given specific goals and a clear standard for success and failure than when they're simply told to "do your best" (Locke & Latham, 1990).

Consider a practical application of expectancy theory. In recent years, many corporations have devised and implemented innovative incentive-based programs to motivate workers. A survey of 1,600 American companies revealed that many of them used: (1) individual incentive programs that provide an opportunity to earn time off or extra pay, (2) small-group incentive plans that offer bonuses to members of a work unit for reaching specified goals, (3) profit-sharing plans in which workers earn money from company profits, (4) recognition programs that single out "employees of the month" for trophies and gifts, and (5) pay-for-knowledge plans that raise salaries for workers who are flexible and can perform different jobs within a work unit (Horn, 1987).

Intrinsic Motivation

Although people strive for tangible reward, there's more to money than just economics and more to motivation than just the size of a paycheck. Novelist Mark Twain (1876) seemed to realize this in *The Adventures of Tom Sawyer*, where he quipped,

"There are wealthy gentlemen in England who drive four-horse passenger coaches twenty or thirty miles on a daily line, in the summer, because the privilege costs them considerable money; but if they were offered wages for the service that would turn it into work then they would resign." Twain's hypothesis—that reward for an enjoyable activity can undermine interest in that activity—seems to defy intuition and a great deal of psychological research. After all, aren't we all motivated by reward, as declared by B. F. Skinner and other behaviorists? The answer depends on how "motivation" is defined.

As a keen observer of human behavior, Twain anticipated a key distinction between intrinsic and extrinsic motivation. **Intrinsic motivation** originates in factors within a person. People are said to be intrinsically motivated when they engage in an activity for the sake of their own interest, the challenge, or sheer enjoyment. Eating a fine meal, listening to music, and working on a hobby are among the activities you might find intrinsically motivating. In contrast, **extrinsic motivation** originates in factors outside the person. People are said to be extrinsically motivated when they engage in an activity for money, recognition, or other tangible benefits. As the behaviorists have always said, people do strive for reward. The question is: What happens to *intrinsic* motivation once that reward is no longer available? It's clear that business leaders want their employees to be intrinsically motivated, loyal, satisfied, and committed to their work. So where does money fit in? Is tangible reward the bottom line or not?

Research shows that when people start getting paid for a task they already enjoy, they sometimes lose interest in it. In the first demonstration of this effect, Edward Deci (1971) recruited college students to work for three one-hour sessions on some fun block-building puzzles. During the first and third sessions, all subjects were treated in the same manner. In the second session, however, half the subjects were paid for each puzzle that they completed. To measure intrinsic motivation, Deci left subjects alone during breaks and secretly recorded the amount of free time they spent on the puzzles when other fun activities were available. Compared to subjects in the no-reward group, those paid in the second session later exhibited less interest in the puzzles when the payment was no longer available (see Figure 22.6). The moral: Receive money for a leisure activity, and, before you know it, what used to be "play" comes to feel like "work."

This paradoxical effect—that rewards can undermine intrinsic motivation—has been observed in many studies using rewards and other extrinsic incentives such as deadlines, competition, and evaluation (Deci & Ryan, 1985; Lepper & Greene, 1978; Tang & Hall, 1995). In the long run, rewards may even have adverse effects on performance. In one study, for example, Teresa Amabile found that subjects who were paid for artistic activities, compared to others who were not paid, produced work that was later judged to be less creative by independent raters. To be maximally productive, people should feel internally driven, not compelled by outside forces.

But wait. If money undermines intrinsic motivation, should employers *not* use monetary incentives? Are pay-for-performance programs often used in the workplace doomed to fail, as some have suggested (Kohn, 1993)? Not necessarily.

intrinsic motivation An inner drive that motivates people in the absence of external reward or punishment.

extrinsic motivation The desire to engage in an activity for money, recognition, or other tangible benefits.

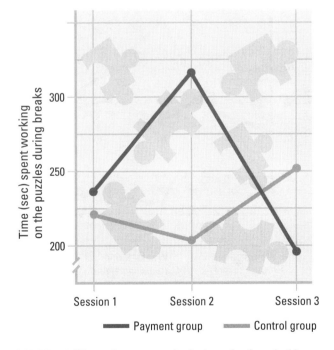

FIGURE 22.6 Effects of payment on intrinsic motivation In this study, subjects worked three times on fun puzzles. Half were paid for completing puzzles during session 2, the others were not. As measured by the amount of free time spent on the puzzles after each session, those who had been paid later had less interest in the puzzles when the money was no longer available (Deci, 1971).

"Productivity is up nine percent since I made everyone a vice president."

equity theory The notion that people want the ratio between input and outcome to be roughly the same for themselves as for others.

To answer this question, it's important to realize that a reward can be interpreted in two ways, depending on how it is presented. On the one hand, being offered payment can make a person feel bribed, bought off, and *controlled,* which can result in the detrimental effects just described. On the other hand, rewards often provide people with positive *information* about the quality of their performance—as when people earn bonuses, scholarships, and verbal praise from others they respect. Research now shows that just as controlling rewards can lower intrinsic motivation, informational rewards can have the opposite, positive effect (Eisenberger, 1992; Eisenberger & Cameron, 1996; Cameron & Pierce, 1994). Studying an office-machine company, Deci and his colleagues (1989) found that the less controlling the managers were, the more satisfied workers were with the company as a whole. Many years ago, Studs Terkel (1972) interviewed secretaries, stockbrokers, baseball players, garbage collectors, and workers in other occupations. Over and over again, he heard two complaints: being too closely watched, or "spied on," and getting too little positive feedback—in other words, too much control and not enough strokes.

🔲 Equity Motivation

A second aspect of payment that influences motivation is the perception that it is *fair.* According to **equity theory,** people want rewards to be equitable, meaning that the ratio between inputs and outcomes should be roughly the same for ourselves as for others. Relative to coworkers, then, the better your performance is, the more money you think you should earn. If you think you're being overpaid or underpaid, however, you'll feel distressed and try to relieve that unhappy state either by restoring actual equity—say, through working less or seeking a raise—or by convincing yourself that equity already exists (Cropanzano, 1993; Greenberg, 1982).

Equity theory has some fascinating implications for behavior in the workplace. Consider Jerald Greenberg's (1988) study of workers in a large insurance firm. To allow for refurbishing, some 200 employees had to be moved temporarily from one office to another. Randomly, they were assigned to offices that belonged to others who were higher, lower, or equal in rank (the higher the rank, the more spacious the office). Would the random assignments influence job performance? By keeping track of the number of cases processed and the quality of the decisions made, Greenberg measured each worker's job performance before, during, and after the office switch. To restore equity, he reasoned, the workers given higher-status offices would feel overcompensated and improve their performance, while those sent to lower-status offices would feel undercompensated and lower their performance. As shown in Figure 22.7, that is exactly what happened. In a later study, Greenberg (1993) found that many subjects who were underpaid for their participation in an experiment went on to restore equity by stealing from the experimenter.

When we stop to reflect on our own motivations, we see just how varied they are. From the constant

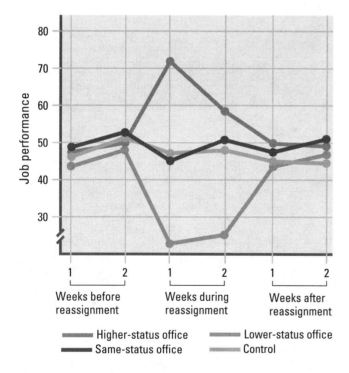

FIGURE 22.7 Equity motivation in the workplace Insurance company workers were moved temporarily to offices that were higher, lower, or equal in status to their rank. Supporting equity theory, those assigned to higher-status offices increased their job performance, while those sent to lower-status offices exhibited a decrease. When the workers were reassigned to their original offices, their productivity levels returned to normal (Greenberg, 1988).

short-term need to stuff our face with food or satisfy the urge to have sex, to the desire to be with others or form close relationships, to the burning ambition to achieve excellence or gain power over others, it's clear that we are energized in many ways and toward many goal objects. Is there any more that we want from life? Is there some "ultimate" motivation? Perhaps. If you've ever met someone who seems to have it all—money, a successful career, good friends, a loving partner, and wonderful children—and yet yearns for more, you'll appreciate what's at the very top of Maslow's pyramid. Maslow theorized that once our biological and social needs are met, we strive to fulfill all of our potential—toward a state he called self-actualization.

From
In Love and War

Vice Admiral James Bond Stockdale

James Bond Stockdale graduated from the United States Naval Academy in 1946 and is one of the most highly decorated officers in the history of the U.S. Navy. Over the course of thirty-three years, he served successively as a destroyerman, carrier aviator, landing signal officer, test pilot, test pilot school instructor, fighter pilot, graduate student, aircraft squadron commander, airwing commander, commander of ASW wing of the Pacific Fleet, and president of the Naval War College.

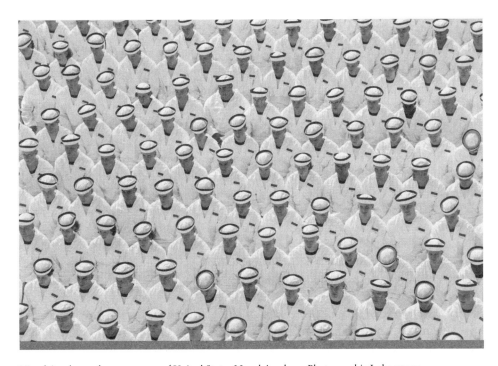

Naval Academy photo courtesy of United States Naval Academy Photographic Laboratory.

He had more flight time in the supersonic F-8 Crusader, a single seat fighter, than any man in the world when he led the initial strikes from a carrier deck in the Tonkin Gulf against North Vietnam in 1964. Deployed to Vietnam waters aboard the USS Oriskany, Air Group Commander Stockdale was shot down in an A-4E Skyhawk attack bomber on September 9, 1965.

For the next seven and a half years he was the senior naval service prisoner of war in North Vietnam. As a result of North Vietnamese reprisal for his leadership of organized resistance, he was kept in solitary confinement for more than four years, was in leg irons for two years, and was tortured fifteen times. Despite the repeated torture and restraint in leg irons and handcuffs, he maintained contact with his fellow prisoners by clandestine means, setting standards and policy for the prisoners' organization and united resistance.

In the purge of his underground organization of 1967, his leg was broken a second time and he was left to hunch around helplessly on a concrete floor, blindfolded, hands cuffed behind him, for a month. Two years later, caught with a note and tortured for information, he broke a window and cut himself up with the glass shards rather than divulge the names of his key organizational cohorts. Revived by the North Vietnamese in a pool of his own blood, they discontinued their line of interrogation. Likely as a result of this action and other factors, a steady improvement of the conditions of all prisoners in North Vietnam commenced.

Repatriated with the rest of the American prisoners in the spring of 1973, he was selected for Rear Admiral. He retired as a Vice Admiral and president of the Naval War College in 1979 to become president of the Citadel, the military college of South Carolina. In 1981 he was named a senior research fellow with Hoover Institution at Stanford University, a position he still holds. His decorations include two Distinguished Flying Crosses, ten Air Medals, the Legion of Merit, three Distinguished Service Medals, four Silver Stars, two Purple Hearts, and the Medal of Honor.

February, 1967

I issued a group of standing orders to all POW's while Dan [LTJG Dan Glenn] was with me. It became obvious to all in Las Vegas (the nickname given to a segment of Hoa Lo prison camp) that our camp was a more or less permanent residence for the senior prisoners, but a holding point between the initial shakedown at Heartbreak and an outlying camp assignment for others. That population in transit through Las Vegas in the spring of 1967 provided a unique courier service for the dissemination of standardized orders all over the North Vietnamese prison system. Dan served as a sounding board and source of advice as I tried to build a foundation of fair and easily understood law. That law could not be vague; to just give the order "Obey the Code of Conduct" would have been the biggest cover-your-ass maneuver of all. The Code, as good as it is, is like a constitution-arguments can go on endlessly about how it should be applied to specific situations. I had to spell out our Hanoi-specific applications, to select out certain of Cat's (the nickname given to the prison camp administrator) key programs that we would likely be able, by corporate effort, to defeat.

For instance, to just issue the order "Do not bow" would have been folly and ultimately destructive of prisoner unity. The Vietnamese had gotten the drop on us with this bowing to every one of them at every meeting, and right now an order to refuse would have meant the beating of most of us into submission. That is, if the offense

Official U.S. Navy photo.

was committed inside the camp. But they couldn't afford to show their viciousness in public, and I learned that ex-post-factor punishments were more often than not half-hearted. It was in public that the real prisoner humiliation came in, so "Don't bow in public" was a good, practical, useful law.

Here in Las Vegas we had just proved that as long as we all stuck together, as long as we provided no exceptions, no deviationists cases off which they could play the weak, we could all "stay off the air"—no broadcasts, no recordings.

It would be the height of ignorance to order sententiously, "Make no confessions"; the toughest of the tough were forced to make them from time to time. But I thought that if everybody applied his post-torture skill and cunning to the problem of avoiding the use of the word *crime* in confessions, we could do it, and thereby take a lot of the emotional steam out of what they published. "Admit no crimes" thus became law.

One of the greatest booby traps I saw on the horizon, one on which they could surely capitalize, given the euphoria all would feel at release time, was the "let bygones be bygones" scene when we left for home. By the time we got to that threshold, I reasoned, all the chips would be in; they wouldn't dare turn people back in public. I felt sure all could hold to the figurative expression "Don't kiss them goodbye."

My whole concept of proper prisoner-of-war behavior was based on sticking together. We were in a situation in which loners could make out. If, after the initial shakedown, you refused to communicate with Americans, there was a tacit agreement that the Vietnamese would leave you alone; there would likely be no more torture, no confessions, no radio broadcasts, maybe not even another tough military information interrogation. One interested only in keeping his own nose clean could score lots of points by remaining a loner. I asked everybody to give up this edge of individual flexibility and get in the swim, communicate, level with your American neighbors on just what-all you compromised, what information you had to give up in the torture room, to freely enter into collusions with Americans, to take your lumps together and, if necessary, all go down the tubes together. In this circumstance our highest value had to be placed on the support of the man next door. To ignore him was to betray him. The bottom line was placing prisoner unity over selfish interests. It was "Unity over Self."

This first set of Hanoi-wide laws was put out in easy-to-remember acronym form—Bow, Air, Crime, Kiss, Unity over Self. BACK US. These orders were absolutely prohibitory—that is, you were required to take torture, forcing the Vietnamese to impose significant pain on you before acceding to these specific demands. In the spring of 1967, the orders were carried to every camp in the Hanoi prison system under my name as the senior American *communicating in* that system.

September, 1967

About ten the next morning, I was marched to the sound-proofed knobby room in the New Guy Village courtyard. An unprecedented array of people and paraphernalia was there to meet me. A long table was against the wall opposite the door; and behind it, arms resting on its "Ho Chi Minh blue" cloth, were at least a half dozen Vietnamese officers I had never seen before. The man in the center was portly and spoke English. I mentally nicknamed him "Mao." Behind me was a semicircle of about ten riflemen, bayonets fixed and pointing toward the floor. Pigeye was up front where I expected to see him, and he had there as his assistant torturer the big kid who had been at the Zoo as a recruit, Big Ugh.

Mao opened the proceedings by stating, "I have not been here long, but I have heard a lot about you and it's all bad. You have incited the other criminals to oppose the Camp Authority."

Then it was Pigeye with a clout to the jaw and into the ropes amid extraordinary shouting from both the table and ring of soldiers behind. Somewhere in this excitement, as my head was forced down into the claustrophobia position for my "submit," Pigeye, I think by mistake, looped the rope under my left (broken) leg and around my neck and took a purchase on forcing my head down to my left knee, rather than to my right knee as he had done before. My leg was bending backward, giving at the knee, when suddenly—pop!—there went that hard-won cartilage.

Pigeye heard it, everybody heard it, but nobody could acknowledge it. I was out of business. I submitted, and told them all they wanted to hear. Yes, I had opposed the Camp Authority and I had incited the other criminals to oppose the Camp Authority. The whole thing ended there sort of self-consciously, with everybody filing out and me sitting there on the floor. I was not able to get up for over a month.

January, 1969

It was midafternoon on a cold but sunny January day when Pigeye escorted me across the main courtyard of Hoa Lo Prison toward Heartbreak Hotel. We wheeled in through the green door of Heartbreak, and I was steered left into cell 8, the old bath-and-dump room. Pigeye gave me the razor and soap, said, "Queekly," and left to attend to some other duties.

I had lived enough years close to Cat's horns to realize that this was no free shave. He had pushed all the buttons to intimidate me, and the stage was set for my imminent personal exploitation in public. I had to use my initiative to do something to derail it. My only hope was to disfigure myself.

Already I had the plan. To hell with washing—work fast! Pigeye will be back in a minute! To look authentic, I stripped. Faucet on, wet the soap and get it sudsing, blade into the razor, now stoop forward over the faucet, direct your bare ass to the peephole. Head under the faucet for a splash, now lather your hair and cut a swath right down the middle of your head, from way back right down to your forehead. Make it a "reverse Cherokee," cut it right down to the skin. Pop! goes the peephole. "Queek!" yells Pigeye, then it pops closed. I'm up to the count of two and the bolt has not been thrown. Good! Pigeye is going about more chores. Cut, cut, cut. God, my old hair is matted and tough from a week of sweat and tears. What's this? Blood! I must be tearing up my scalp trying to rip this hair out! Pop! goes the peephole. Clunk! goes the peephole, and he swings the door open. By this time, there is blood all over my hands and the floor, and in my soapy hair. Pigeye grabs me by the arm, screaming, "Eoow!" Out we rush into the central court, I totally naked, blood running down my shoulders now, civilians all over the courtyard, men and women, standing aghast.

By no means expecting us back so soon, Rabbit had left the door of room 18 ajar. We entered the room at a half-run. Rabbit looked at me, wheeled, and nearly expired of shock. I was slow to realize that, seeing all the blood, he thought I had tried to kill myself. I felt good, felt that I was on the right track. I figured I had the ropes coming, so I sat down in a position for Pigeye to put on the straps and get it over with. Rabbit and Chihuahua both started yelling, "No! No! Get on your feet!" Typical Vietnamese face-savers, I thought. It was my idea to take the ropes, so they say, "No! You are not entitled to the ropes!"

I stood up as Chihuahua was shouting, "Why are you taking your own life? I know you want to kill yourself, but you must not do it. You have things to do. You have an appointment to keep tonight. The general staff officer wants to see you downtown tonight."

Rabbit and Chihuahua knew they had to work fast. Cat would be furious. What to do? Send Pigeye for the hair clippers! When he came back, he sat me in a chair, wiped my soapy head with a towel, and worked away with the clippers while the two Vietnamese officers scowled. This would never do—the hair was irreparable for tonight. Rabbit had an inspiration: "You will make the movie tonight! We will get a hat!" All three of them—Pigeye and the two officers—strode out of room 18 into that late-afternoon sun, locking the door behind them.

Now the ball is in my court again. What can I do to counter the hat move? I had already considered self-destruction with everything in the room. There was a crap bucket with its rusted-out jaggedness. Cut myself up? I don't like the infection risk. The windows in the French doors can be broken (those are just about the only glass panes in Hanoi accessible to prisoners). But why go that far? Why not this heavy mahogany quiz stool I've sat on so many times?

That's it! Get going! Close those eyes! You bruise easily! Mash those cheekbones! You know how swollen-eyed you used to be after playing in the center of that line all game. I picked up the fifty-pound stool and thump! thump! thump! thump! thump!—left cheekbone. Now right—thump! thump! thump! thump! thump! Now left again . . .

I wasn't any more conscious of pain than if I had been running up my imaginary hill evading capture with a leg full of morphine. I kept thumping, and then the

French doors began to shake. There was a crowd outside trying to look in! I could see the faint outlines of their faces against the painted panes in the doors. Now they were starting to talk loudly and to shout. No time to worry about a bunch of civil servants. Thump! Thump! Thump! Thump! These eyes aren't quite closed yet. In the background, I can hear Rabbit's voice above the crowd. Now the key is in the door. The crowd is pushed back by Pigeye at the doorway as Rabbit and Chihuahua stride in with a silly-looking hat. I can hardly see it; my eyes are mere slits. Blood is running down the front of my pajama shirt from cheekbone cuts.

Chihuahua steps forward and shouts, "Now look what you've done. What are we going to do? You tell me what we are going to tell the general staff officer about the trip downtown after the way you behaved."

"You tell the major that the commander decided not to go."

They then sent Pigeye for traveling irons and handcuffs. He locked both on (cuffs in front), and the three of them went over to see Cat while I waddled to the back wall and banged my face against the bricks some more, just in case.

August, 1969

My luck on notes ran out on an afternoon in late August 1969. I had just successfully brought in a note from Hatcher and was answering Dave by way of his toothpaste-on-brown-paper method, when the roving patrol doubled back, and noticed my arm moving. As he opened the door, I thrust my all-but-finished note into the top of my pajama pants. He frisked me hurriedly, searched my cell as he sent me to the far wall at the end to the passageway, frisked me again, and motioned for me to go back into the ransacked cell. As I was walking the six to eight paces back to the safety of my cell, the note fell out of my pant leg right in front of him.

I was devastated as I waited alone in the empty cellblock. I was in the worst kind of trouble. Ever since I had left Alcatraz, the Camp Authority had spent untold energy and manpower trying to keep me "sterilized," away from any form of prisoner contact. They had put me in special cells, they had laid on special guards. I felt sure that before this afternoon they'd been convinced that there was no way I could have been conversant with names, events, or anything to do with the prisoner community in Las Vegas.

But the note was written proof that I had been communicating with so-and-so and so-and-so for some time. Even the note-drop procedures were so intricate that they implied an articulate and precise transfer of words over a long period. That note was full of leads they could exploit in the ropes. There were, literally, long lists of things that logically they now could know that I knew. They had the drawstrings of a web that would suck dozens of my old friends and many I had never directly communicated with into complicity. All my friends would first go into the ropes. In turn, third parties would be involved, and then they would be put in the ropes. I was about to be the cause of another Las Vegas purge, with all the grief and death that this was likely to entail.

Early the next morning, the guards come to get me. I am taken to the Star Chamber, room 18. Bug is behind the single big table; I am summoned over, a guard on either side of me, and charged with grave crimes of an unspecified nature. "Get on your knees!" And that's how we spent the day—me on my right knee, left leg straight out to the side, Bug after information. Bug just stands or sits before me, fires abstract questions about the chain of events that got me into communication with the camp at Las Vegas, and lashes me across the face with a two-foot-long strip of rubber from a truck tire (we prisoners named them "fan belts") whenever he feels like it.

By late afternoon I was worn to a frazzle, but was somewhat mystified. Bug had worked all day, slapped the hell out of me with that fan belt, cut my face, but he didn't seem to be closing in on the subject like Rabbit would. We spent hours arguing about what different words in the note meant. I had not pulled any great coups, but here it was evening and Bug hadn't even got the name of Dave Hatcher out of me.

About dusk, a guard came in with my blanket roll and threw it down by the north wall, opposite the table. A guard came in with traveling irons, put them on me, and bound me with "loose ropes," which partially constrained my arms but did not induce steady pain. Bug had left for the time being. A suddenly enraged Bug was standing in the doorway with a guard with him. "Get on your feet. You are not to rest!" He motioned for the guard to bring his chair from behind the table and put it right in the middle of the floor. "You will sit in that chair all night. You will contemplate your crimes against the Vietnamese people. These are bad days for us. Our beloved president [Ho Chi Minh] is dead. You have seen nothing yet. Tomorrow you will give me details. You will see. Tomorrow is when we start; you will be brought down!"

Darkness fell. I worked myself to my feet, waddled to the chair, and sat facing the table. I was thinking again. Tomorrow is the day. Another purge, more deaths. But I've got to go on the offensive; I can't just wait for the axe to fall and then be sorry about it. I'm right where I was last winter when Rabbit and Chihuahua went for the hat; I've got to do something. I have to stop that interrogation; I have to stop the *flow*. If it costs, it costs.

No stool here tonight. That rusty toilet can is still a loser, but those windows in the French doors . . . I didn't have the guts to break one when Cat was gearing me up for the release movie, but now I do. This is the only cell with an inside light switch in Hanoi. I'll douse it while I do it! These loose ropes can be worked even looser to give me enough arm action. The guard left a few minutes ago; he'll be back in maybe half an hour. It's now or never.

I'm in automatic—I know the motions without thinking. I waddle to the light switch. Light off! Pop the glass pane in the French door with the heel of my hand; dig out those long shards—get the ones with sharp points—don't think—move quickly—light back on—waddle to the chair in the traveling irons—sit down and *go* for it—the artery. No use messing around.

Chop chop chop chop chop on the left wrist. Blood! Running all down my hand and onto the floor! Go at it again . . . and again . . . and again. This is tough, even in the loose ropes; get a good sharp piece in your left hand. Chop chop chop chop chop on the right wrist. Now again . . . and again. How do you get more blood? Squeeze your hand, wring it out. My God, the floor is coming up to meet me . . . The blood . . . I'm lying in it . . .

Lots of talk and footsteps all around me. Somebody is waking me up and taking my arm ropes off. The room is full of people! The old doc with the spectacles who first checked my broken leg is bandaging my arms, very carefully. Bug is here now, shouting alternately, "How *dare* you do this!" and *"Why* did you do this?"

I was taken back to my cell and left to myself for about six weeks while my arm wounds healed. They were dressed every few days by the old doc who didn't speak a word of English. I had stopped the flow! I sat up the night "writing" a braille "note," tying knots in a piece of thread for all in Stardust; I had to get the word out that I had protected all names, that there was no danger of another purge.

23 "Heads I Win, Tails You Lose"—The Power of Perspective

Objectives

1. Describe the process of making attributions.

2. Define and discuss the fundamental attribution error and its implications for leadership.

3. Explain how impressions are formed and how they may be biased.

Social Perception

🔘 How do we come to know other people? What is the fundamental attribution error—and is it "fundamental"? Why are we so slow to revise our first impressions in light of new evidence? In liking, do birds of a feather flock together, or do opposites attract? And is physical beauty an objective characteristic or strictly in the eye of the beholder?

As social beings, humans are drawn to each other. We work together, play together, live together, and often make lifetime commitments to grow old together. In all our interactions, we engage in **social perception,** the process of coming to know and evaluate other persons. People are complex, not transparent, and it's not easy to form accurate impressions of them. So how do we do it? What kinds of evidence do we use? We cannot actually "see" inner dispositions or states of mind any more than a detective can see a crime that has already been committed. So, like the detective who tries to reconstruct events from physical traces, witnesses, and other clues, we observe the way people behave, try to explain that behavior, then put all the pieces together to form an impression.

🔲 Making Attributions

Why did the police officers beat Rodney King senseless—were they angry or sadistic, or had King inflamed them? In trying to make sense of people from their actions, we need to understand what *causes* their behavior. What kinds of explanations do we come up with, and how do we go about making them? In *The Psychology of Interpersonal Relations,* Fritz Heider (1958) proposed that we are all "intuitive scientists" in the way we determine why people behave as they do. According to Heider, the explanations we come up with are called attributions, and the theory that describes the process is called **attribution theory.**

social perception The processes by which we come to know and evaluate other persons.

attribution theory A set of theories that describe how people explain the causes of behavior.

Attribution Theory   Although there are numerous possible explanations for the events of human behavior, Heider found it useful to group our attributions into two major categories: personal and situational. The juries that tried the four police officers in the Rodney King case, for example, had to decide: Was the beating caused by characteristics of the officers (a *personal attribution*), or had King somehow provoked their actions (a *situational attribution*)? For the attribution theorist, the goal is not to determine the true causes of this event but, rather, to study our *perceptions* of the causes.

Following Heider, Harold Kelley (1967) theorized that people often make attributions on the basis of three types of information: consensus, distinctiveness, and consistency. To illustrate these concepts, imagine that you're standing on a street corner one hot, steamy evening, when all of a sudden a stranger bursts out of a cool,

Lt. Venglar tripped and fell on his sword, thus dooming himself to a lifetime of ridicule.

Why were Israeli Prime Minister Netanyahu and Palestinian leader Yasser Arafat shaking hands? Did they really want to, or was the greeting compelled by the situation? In understanding people, we make attributions for their behavior. In this particular meeting, held in 1996, the rival leaders greeted each other—but at a distance. In the past, Netanyahu had said he would never shake Arafat's hand.

air-conditioned movie theater and blurts out, "Great movie!" Looking up, you don't recognize the film title, so you wonder what to make of this candid appraisal. Was the behavior (the rave review) caused by something about the person (the stranger), the stimulus (the film), or the specific circumstances (perhaps the comfortable theater)? Because you're possibly interested in spending an evening at the movies, how do you explain this incident?

Thinking like a scientist, you would probably seek *consensus information* to see how other persons react to the same stimulus. In other words, how do other moviegoers feel about this film? If others also rave about the film, the stranger's behavior is high in consensus and is thus attributed to the stimulus. If others are critical of the same film, the behavior is low in consensus and is attributed to the person.

Still thinking like a scientist, you might want to have *distinctiveness information* to see how the same person reacts to different stimuli. In other words, how does this raving moviegoer react to other films? If this stranger is critical of many other films, then this rave review is highly distinctive and is attributed to the stimulus. If the stranger gushes about everything, then this review is low in distinctiveness and is attributed to the person, not to the film.

Finally, you might seek *consistency information* to see what happens to the behavior at another time when the person and the stimulus both remain the same. How does this moviegoer feel about this same film on other night? If the stranger raves about the film on video as well as in the theater, then the behavior is consistent. But if the stranger does not always enjoy the film, then the behavior is low in consistency. According to Kelley, behavior that is consistent is attributed to the stimulus when consensus and distinctiveness are also high, and to the person when they are low. Behaviors that are low in consistency are attributed to fleeting circumstances, such as the temperature of the movie theater (the theory and the predictions it makes are represented in Figure 23.1).

Kelley's attribution theory is logical, but does it describe the way that you and I analyze the behavior of others? To some extent, yes. Research shows that when people are asked to make attributions for someone's behavior, they often follow this logic and make attributions on the basis of consensus, distinctiveness, and consistency information (McArthur, 1972; Cheng & Novick, 1990; Fosterling, 1992). But as social perceivers, do we really analyze behavior in the way one might expect of a computer? Do we have the time, the desire, or the cognitive capacity for such mindful processes? Not always. With so much to explain and not enough time in a day, we often take mental shortcuts, cross our fingers, and get on with life (Fiske & Taylor, 1991). The problem is that with speed comes bias and perhaps even a loss of accuracy. We now examine two types of biases in attribution.

The Fundamental Attribution Error   By the time you complete this chapter, you will have learned the cardinal lesson of social psychology: People are influenced in profound ways by situations. This point seems obvious, right? So why, then, are parents often astonished to hear that their mischievous child, the family monster, is a perfect angel in school? And why are students often surprised to see that a favorite professor, an eloquent lecturer,

"It's not you, Frank, it's me—I don't like you."

People make attributions all the time in an effort to make sense of their social world.

can be awkward in informal conversation? These reactions are symptoms of a well-documented aspect of social perception. When people explain the behavior of others, they typically overestimate the role of personal factors and underestimate the role of the situation. This bias is so pervasive, and often so misleading, that it has been called the **fundamental attribution error** (Ross, 1977).

The fundamental attribution error was first discovered in a study by Edward Jones and Victor Harris (1967). In that study, subjects read a speech presumably written by a college student that was either for or against Fidel Castro, the communist leader of Cuba. Some subjects were told that the student had freely chosen his or her position; others were told that the student was assigned the position by an instructor. What was the student's true attitude? In response to this question, subjects sensibly judged the student's attitude from the speech when the position was freely chosen. So far, so good. But even when subjects knew that the student had no choice, they still inferred his or her attitude from the speech. Thus, the student who wrote for rather than against

fundamental attribution error A tendency to overestimate the impact of personal causes of behavior and to overlook the role of situations.

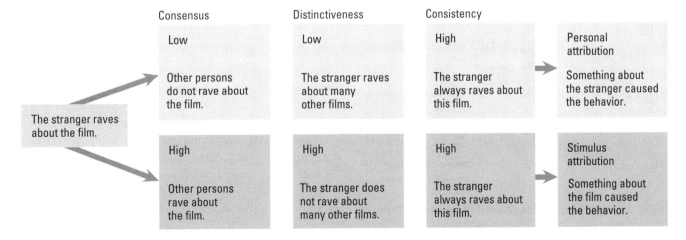

FIGURE 23.1 Kelley's attribution theory For behaviors that are consistent over time, attribution theory predicts that people make personal attributions under conditions of low consensus and distinctiveness (*top row*), and situational attributions under high consensus and distinctiveness (*bottom row*). Behaviors that are low in consistency (not shown) are attributed to passing circumstances.

What are Michael Richards, Jason Alexander, Jerry Seinfeld, and Julia Louise-Dreyfus, really like*? As a consequence of the fundamental attribution error, TV viewers might assume that these actors are, in life, like Kramer, George, Jerry, and Elaine—the bizarre characters they play on* Seinfeld.

Castro was seen as more favorable toward the Cuban leader—whether that essay position was freely chosen or not. This finding has been repeated many times, typically with the same result: Except when subjects are highly motivated to make a careful judgment (Webster, 1993; Fein, 1996), they attribute the speaker's position to his or her attitude—regardless of the situation (Jones, 1990; Gilbert & Malone, 1995).

A fascinating study by Lee Ross and others (1977) exposes the fundamental attribution error in a familiar setting, the TV quiz show. By a flip of a coin, subjects were randomly assigned to play the role of either the questioner or the contestant in a quiz game, while spectators looked on. In front of the contestant and spectators, the experimenter instructed the questioner to write ten challenging questions from his or her own store of general knowledge. If you're a trivia buff, you can imagine how esoteric these questions might have been: Who was the first governor of Idaho? What team won the NHL Stanley Cup in 1968? It's no wonder that contestants correctly answered less than 40 percent of the questions asked. When the game was over, all participants rated the questioner's and contestant's general knowledge on a scale of 0 to 100.

Picture the events that transpired. The questioners appeared more knowledgeable than the contestants—after all, they knew all the answers. But a moment's reflection should remind us that the situation put the questioner at a huge advantage. So did subjects take the situation into account, or did they conclude that the questioners actually had more knowledge? As shown in Figure 23.2, the results were startling. Spectators rated the questioners as above average in their general knowledge and the contestants as below average. The contestants even rated themselves as inferior to their partners. Like the spectators, they too were fooled by the loaded situation.

What's going on here? Why do social perceivers consistently make unwarranted attributions for behavior to persons and fail to appreciate the impact of situations? According to Daniel Gilbert and Patrick Malone (1995), the problem stems primarily from *how* attributions are made. Attribution theorists used to assume that people survey all the evidence and then decide on a personal or situational attribution. Instead, claims Gilbert, there is a two-step process: First, we identify the behavior and make a quick personal attribution; then, we correct or adjust that inference to account for situational influences. The first step is simple, natural, and automatic—like a reflex; the second one requires attention, thought, and effort.

Why is it so natural to attribute behavior to persons rather than to the situations they are in? Is this tendency universal, or is it limited to Western cultures in which individuals are seen as autonomous and responsible for their own actions? Indeed, many non-Western cultures take a more holistic view that focuses on the relationship

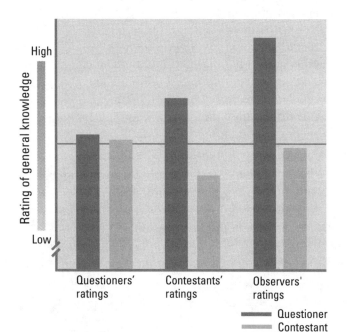

FIGURE 23.2 Fundamental attribution error in a TV quiz show The simulated quiz show put questioners at an advantage over contestants, yet observers still saw the questioners as more knowledgeable (*right*). Although questioners did not overrate their own general knowledge (*left*), contestants, like the observers, rated themselves as inferior (*middle*). These results illustrate the fundamental attribution error.

between persons and their social roles. To see if these differing worldviews are related to attributions, Joan Miller (1984) asked people of varying ages from the United States and from India to describe what caused certain positive and negative behaviors they had observed in their lives. Among the youngest children, there were no cultural differences. With increasing age, however, the American subjects made more personal attributions, while the Indian subjects became more situational. These findings suggest that the fundamental attribution error may be unique to Western cultures (see Figure 23.3).

Self-Serving Attributions   As logical as we try to be, our attributions are sometimes colored by an underlying need to maintain and enhance our self-esteem. Time and again, research has shown that when students receive their exam grades, those who do well take credit for the success; those who do poorly complain about the instructor and the questions. When professors have their articles accepted for publication, they assume it reflects on the high quality of their work; when articles are rejected, they blame the editor or the reviewers. In a whole range of situations, it seems that we are biased in the attributions we make for our own outcomes—taking quick credit for success but distancing ourselves from failure (Schlenker et al., 1990).

Other motives can also influence our attributions for the behavior of others. For example, William Klein and Ziva Kunda (1992) showed subjects the performance on a practice quiz of another subject, a male target, who was later expected to become either their partner or their opponent in a competition. In all cases, the target answered the practice questions correctly. The reason for his success? Hoping he was not too competent, subjects who thought that the target was to be their opponent perceived him as less able than those who thought he was their prospective partner. To justify their wishful thinking, the subjects reasoned that the task was easy and that luck was a contributing factor.

Forming Impressions

In the process of forming an impression of a person, making attributions is only the first step. A second step is to combine and integrate all the evidence into a coherent picture. Research shows that the impressions we form of people are generally based on a "weighting" and "averaging" of all the evidence (Anderson, 1981; Kashima & Kerekes, 1994). This same research also shows, however, that once we do form an impression of someone, we become less and less likely to revise our opinions in light of new, even contradictory evidence. As we'll see, first impressions are powerful.

Cognitive-Confirmation Biases   It is often said that first impressions stick, and social psychologists are inclined to agree. In a classic demonstration of this phenomenon, Solomon Asch (1946) told a group of subjects that a person was "intelligent, industrious, impulsive, critical, stubborn, and envious." He then presented a second group with exactly the same list, but in reverse order. Logically, the two groups should have formed the same impression. Instead, however, subjects who heard the first list—in which the positive traits came first—were more favorable in their evaluations than those who heard the second list. The reason: People are influenced more by information they receive early in an interaction than by information that appears later—a finding known as the **primacy effect.**

The primacy effect occurs for two reasons. The first is that we become somewhat less attentive to later behavioral evidence once we have already formed an impression. Thus, when subjects in one study read a series of statements about someone, the

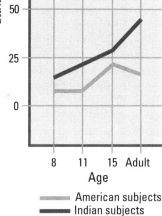

FIGURE 23.3 **Fundamental attribution error: a Western bias?** Subjects from the United States and India described the causes of various behaviors. Among young children, there were no cultural differences. With age, however, the Americans made more personal attributions and Indian subjects made more situational attributions.

primacy effect The tendency for impressions of others to be heavily influenced by information appearing early in an interaction.

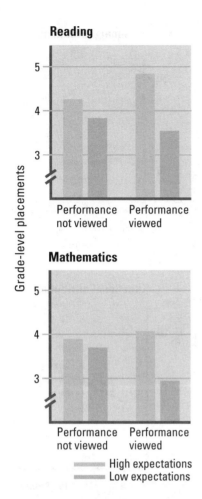

Reading

(bar graph: y-axis "Grade-level placements" with values 3, 4, 5; x-axis groups "Performance not viewed" and "Performance viewed")

Mathematics

(bar graph: y-axis values 3, 4, 5; x-axis groups "Performance not viewed" and "Performance viewed")

High expectations
Low expectations

FIGURE 23.4 Mixed evidence: does it extinguish or fuel first impressions? Subjects rated the potential of a school-girl. Without seeing her test performance, those with high expectations rated her slightly higher than did those with low expectations. Among subjects who watched a tape of the girl taking a test, the expectations effect was even greater.

"It is a capital mistake to theorize before you have all the evidence. It biases the judgment."

—ARTHUR CONAN DOYLE

amount of time they spent reading each statement declined steadily as they proceeded through the list (Belmore, 1987). Does this mean that we are doomed to a life of primacy? No, not necessarily. Tired, or unstimulated, one's attention may wane. Donna Webster and others (1996) found that college students "leaped to conclusions" about a person on the basis of preliminary information when they were mentally fatigued from having just taken a two-hour exam. But when they were alert and sufficiently motivated to keep from tuning out, this bias was diminished.

More unsettling is the second reason for primacy, known as the change-of-meaning hypothesis. Once people form an impression, they later interpret inconsistent information in light of that impression. Asch's research shows just how malleable the meaning of a trait can be. When people are told that a kind person is *calm,* they assume that he or she is gentle, peaceful, and serene. When a cruel person is said to be *calm,* however, the same word is interpreted to mean cool, shrewd, and calculating. There are many examples to illustrate the point. Based on your first impression, the word *proud* can mean self-respecting or conceited; *critical* can mean astute or picky; and *impulsive* can mean spontaneous or reckless (Hamilton & Zanna, 1974; Watkins & Peynircioglu, 1984).

A study by John Darley and Paget Gross (1983) illustrates this point in an important setting. In their study, subjects were asked to evaluate the academic potential of a fourth-grade girl named Hannah. Half of the subjects were led to believe that she was from an upper-middle-class home with educated, professional parents (high expectations). The other half were told that she lived in a run-down neighborhood and had poorly educated working parents (low expectations). As illustrated in Figure 23.4, subjects in the first group were somewhat more positive in their ratings of Hannah's ability than were those in the second group. Within each of these groups, however, half the subjects watched a videotape of Hannah taking a short achievement test. Her performance on the tape was not particularly high or low but was average—she correctly answered some hard questions but missed others that were easy. With all these subjects seeing the same objective-test performance, you would think that the difference between the high- and low-expectation groups would be completely wiped out. Yet among subjects who saw the tape, Hannah received even lower ability ratings from those with low expectations and even higher ratings from those with high expectations. Presenting a body of evidence did not extinguish the first-impression bias; it *fueled* it.

In events that are ambiguous enough to support contrasting interpretations, perceivers see what they expect to see. We are even biased in the way we interpret evidence that plainly disconfirms our opinions. Kari Edwards and Edward Smith (1996) presented both advocates and opponents of various issues—such as abortion, the death penalty, and affirmative action—with arguments that were compatible or incompatible with their own points of view. They found that subjects spent more time scrutinizing the incompatible arguments, saw more flaws in them, and rated them as weaker—particularly when they felt committed to their initial opinions. Additional studies have shown as well that people are quick to discredit evidence that contradicts the conclusions they want to reach (Ditto & Lopez, 1992; Kunda, 1990).

Behavioral-Confirmation Biases As social perceivers, we interpret new information in light of our existing beliefs and preferences. At times, we may even unwittingly *create* support for these beliefs and preferences. In Chapter 12, we saw that teachers who have positive or negative expectations of a student, perhaps based on an IQ score, alter their behavior toward that student, thus setting into motion a self-fulfilling prophecy (Rosenthal & Jacobson, 1968). The same process is at work in other settings as well. In a study of 34 corporate managers and 164 job applicants,

Amanda Phillips and Robert Dipboye (1989) found that when the managers had positive expectations, they spent more interview time trying to impress rather than to evaluate the applicant and were more likely to make a favorable hiring decision. In another study involving actual job interviews, Thomas Dougherty and others (1994) found that interviewers with positive rather than negative expectations were warmer, more outgoing, and more cheerful in their demeanor. They also gave more information and spent more time selling the company.

How does this self-fulfilling prophecy work? How do social perceivers transform beliefs into reality? As shown by research on teacher expectations, the process involves a three-step chain of events (see Figure 23.5). First, a perceiver forms an opinion of a target person—based on the target's physical appearance, reputation, gender, race, or initial interactions. Second, the perceiver behaves in a manner that is consistent with that first impression. Third, the target unwittingly adjusts his or her behavior to the perceiver's actions (Darley & Fazio, 1980). By steering interactions with others along a path narrowed by our beliefs, we engage in a "behavioral-confirmation" bias that keeps us from judging others objectively. Thankfully, this bias is not inevitable. If we conceptualize the problem as a three-step process, it is possible to identify two links in the chain that can be broken to prevent a vicious cycle (Hilton & Darley, 1991; Snyder, 1993).

First, there's the link between the perceiver's expectations and behavior toward the target. When perceivers are highly motivated to seek the truth (as when they evaluate the target as a possible teammate or opponent), when they can attend closely to the interaction, and when they are concerned about the way they are being judged by the target, they become more objective—and often do not confirm prior expectations (Neuberg, 1989; Copeland, 1994; Snyder & Haugen, 1994; Harris & Perkins, 1995). Next is the link between a perceiver's actions and a target's response. Often, the targets of our perceptions are not aware of the expectations that we have of them. But what if they were? How would you react, for example, if *you* knew that you were being cast in a particular light? When it happens to subjects in social-perception studies—especially when they think they are being misjudged—they often make it a point to behave in ways that contradict the perceiver's initial beliefs (Hilton & Darley, 1985; Swann & Ely, 1984). Clearly, the persons we perceive have their own prophecies to fulfill.

FIGURE 23.5 The behavioral-confirmation process People can create false support for their first impressions through this three-step chain of events.

Naval Academy photo courtesy of United States Naval Academy Photographic Laboratory.

24 It Doesn't Take a Hero—Reacting in an Emergency

Objectives

1. Explain the bystander effect and diffusion of responsibility.

2. Describe a strategy for reducing these phenomena in operational environments.

3. Describe some situations in which you, as a future leader in the Navy, may have to confront the bystander effect and diffusion of responsibility.

▣ Altruism

Everyone knows the horrid tales of obedience to authority in Nazi Germany. But, as depicted in the film *Schindler's List,* that same situation also exposed the brightest side of human nature—as Oskar Schindler and several other German citizens risked their lives to hide and protect Jewish friends and neighbors. Why did these heroes try to rescue those in need? And why did others not intervene?

Focusing on prosocial aspects of human interaction, many social psychologists study **altruism,** helping behavior that is motivated primarily by a desire to benefit a person other than oneself. When people are asked to list instances of helping in their own lives, they cite helping a classmate with homework, listening to a friend's problems, giving moral support, lending books or CDs, giving directions to someone who is lost, giving rides, and so on (McGuire, 1994). Everyday examples are not hard to find. Yet psychologists ask: Does altruism really exist, or is helping always selfishly motivated? And why do we sometimes fail to come to the aid of someone who needs it? These are just some of the puzzling questions asked about helping and the factors that influence it.

The Altruism Debate   On the surface, altruism—as an act of self-sacrifice—seems personally maladaptive. The hero who risks life and limb to save a crime victim and the philanthropist who donates large sums of money come out losers in the exchange. Or do they? Evolutionary psychologists claim that in the fight for survival, helpfulness can perpetuate our own "selfish" genes (Dawkins, 1989). One way this may operate is that people of all cultures follow the norm of reciprocity—a moral code that directs us to help, not hurt, those who have helped us. Helping can thus be considered a long-term investment in the future. Evolutionary psychologists also point out that people are quick to help their own offspring, followed by other family members in proportion to their genetic relatedness and strangers who are similar to themselves. The result: self-sacrificing behavior that, paradoxically, promotes one's own genetic immortality (Rushton, 1989; Burnstein et al., 1994).

It is often said that helpfulness serves short-term personal interests as well. According to some theorists, people decide whether to intervene by weighing the costs (time, stress, the risk of injury) against the benefits (financial reward, praise, social approval, a feeling of satisfaction). This decision making may not be conscious, but if the anticipated benefits exceed the anticipated costs, we help; if not, we stay put. In other words, helping is motivated by self-serving goals (such as a desire for a "helper's high" or to avoid feeling guilty for not helping), not by altruism (Cialdini et al., 1973; Piliavin et al., 1981).

Are humans ever truly altruistic, or is our behavior always selfishly motivated? C. Daniel Batson (1991) argues that an act of assistance should be considered altruistic when the helper's main goal is to benefit someone in need—independent of the consequences for the helper. According to Batson's **empathy-altruism hypothesis,**

altruism Helping behavior that is motivated primarily by a desire to benefit others, not oneself.

301

Binti Jua is a gorilla in the Brookfield Zoo, near Chicago. One day, a three-year-old boy fell eighteen feet into her area and was knocked unconscious. He was not a fellow ape. Yet with her baby clinging to her back, Binti scooped him up, cradled him, and took him to the door, where the keepers could reach him. She was a hero. But was her act one of "altruism"? Some say yes, she was motivated by kindness and empathy. Others say she merely acted, as trained, to pick up and fetch objects that fall into her cage. This episode brings the altruism debate to life—even in the animal world.

empathy-altruism hypothesis The proposition that an empathic response to a person in need produces altruistic helping.

diagrammed in Figure 24.1, people have two emotional reactions to someone in need: *personal distress* (guilt, anxiety, and discomfort) and *empathy* (sympathy and compassion for the other person). When the first reaction predominates, we help primarily to relieve our own discomfort—a self-centered, "egoistic" motivation. When the second reaction predominates, however, we help in order to alleviate the other's suffering—an altruistic motivation. In other words, says Batson, helping can satisfy both selfish and noble motives.

If Batson is correct, then empathy—a genuine, gut-level compassion for another person—is the engine that drives pure altruism. Can empathy inspire helping? How can the two helping motives be distinguished? According to Batson, people who come face to face with a needy person—say, a beggar on the street or an accident victim—can relieve their *own* distress by offering help or by escaping the situation (out of sight, out of mind). For people with empathy for the victim, however, there is no mental escape. The *victim's* distress can be reduced only by helping.

To demonstrate, Batson and his coworkers (1981) devised a situation in which subjects watched a female accomplice, posing as another subject, receive electric shocks as part of an experiment. Over closed-circuit TV, they saw that she was upset and heard her say that she had suffered an electrical accident as a child. What next? Given a choice, would subjects leave the experiment, having already completed their part in it (escape), or would they volunteer to trade places with the accomplice (help)? As predicted by Batson, the choice subjects made depended on their feelings of empathy for the woman. Among those low in empathy (because her values were different from theirs), only 18 percent agreed to trade places. But among subjects who were high in empathy (because she shared similar values), 91 percent agreed to the trade. These latter subjects could have made themselves feel better by leaving, but instead they stayed to help the other person. Does this mean that pure altruism exists? Some say *yes* (Batson et al., 1989; Dovidio et al., 1990); others say *no* (Cialdini et al., 1987; Schaller & Cialdini, 1988).

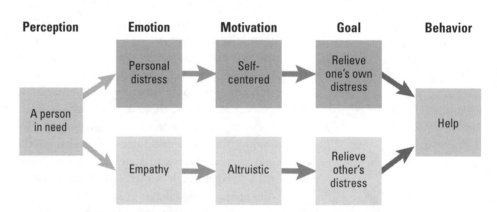

FIGURE 24.1 Two pathways to helping In response to someone needing help, people feel a combination of personal distress and empathy. Accordingly, there are two paths to helping: One is self-centered (aimed at the relief of one's own discomfort), and the other is altruistic (designed to alleviate the other's suffering).

Bystander Intervention   This debate about human nature is fascinating, but what inspired social psychologists to study helping in the first place were hair-raising news stories about bystanders who fail to take action even when someone's life is in danger. The problem first made headlines in March 1964. Kitty Genovese was walking home from work in Queens, New York, at 3:20 in the morning. As she crossed the street from her car to her apartment, a man with a knife appeared. She ran, but he caught up and stabbed her. She cried frantically for help and screamed, "Oh my God, he stabbed me! . . . I'm dying, I'm dying!"—but to no avail. The man fled but then returned, raped her, and stabbed her eight more times, until she was dead. In the still of the night, the attack lasted for over half an hour. Thirty-eight neighbors heard the screams, turned lights on, and came to their windows. One couple even pulled chairs up to the window and turned out the light to see better. Yet nobody came down to help. Until it was over, nobody even called the police.

What happened? How could people have been so heartless and apathetic? How could they have remained passive while a neighbor was being murdered? Rather than blame the bystanders, Bibb Latané and John Darley (1970) focused on the social factors at work in this situation. In a series of important experiments, they staged emergencies, varied the conditions, and observed what happened. In one study, Darley and Latané (1968) took subjects to a cubicle and asked them to discuss the kinds of personal problems that college students face. For confidentiality purposes, they were told, subjects would communicate over an intercom system and the experimenter would not be listening. The subjects were also told to speak one at a time and to take turns. Some were assigned to two-person discussions, others to larger groups. Although the opening moments were uneventful, one subject (an accomplice) mentioned in passing that he had a seizure disorder that was sometimes triggered by pressure. Sure enough, when it came his turn to speak again, this subject struggled and pleaded for help:

> "I could really-er-use some help so if somebody would-er-give me a little h-help-uh-er-er-er c-could somebody-er-er-help-er-uh-uh-uh (choking sounds) . . . I'm gonna die-er-er-I'm . . . gonna die-er-help-er-er-seizure-er."

If you were in this situation, how would you react? Would you stop the experiment, dash out of your cubicle, and seek out the experimenter? As it turned out, the response was strongly influenced by the size of their group. Actually, all subjects participated alone, but they were led to believe that others were present and that there was a real crisis. Almost all subjects who thought they were in a two-person discussion left the room for help immediately. In the larger "groups," however, subjects were less likely to intervene and were slower to do so when they did. In fact, the larger the group was supposed to be, the less helping occurred (see Figure 24.2). This pattern of results was labeled the **bystander effect**: The more bystanders there are, the less likely a victim is to get help. In an emergency, the presence of others inhibits helping.

At first, this pioneering research seemed to defy all common sense. Isn't there safety in numbers? Don't we feel more secure rushing in to help when others are there for support? To fully understand what went wrong, Latané and Darley (1970) provided a careful, step-by-step analysis of the decision-making process in emergency situations. According to their scheme, bystanders help only when they *notice* the incident, *interpret* it as an emergency, *take responsibility* for helping, *decide* to intervene, and then *act* on that decision (see Figure 24.3).

This analysis of the intervention process sheds light on the bystander effect, as the presence of others can inhibit helping at each of the five steps. Consider, for example,

bystander effect The finding that the presence of others inhibits helping in an emergency.

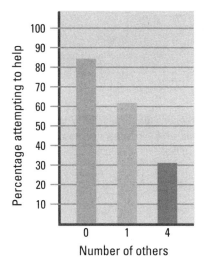

FIGURE 24.2 The bystander effect
When subjects thought that they alone heard a seizure victim in need, the vast majority sought help. As the number of bystanders increased, however, they became less likely to intervene (Darley & Latané, 1968).

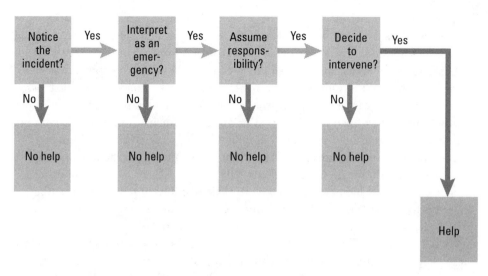

FIGURE 24.3 **A model of bystander intervention** This step-by-step analysis suggests several reasons for the fact that bystanders often do not help in emergencies.

the second requirement, that bystanders interpret an event as an emergency. Have you ever heard screaming from a nearby house and the sound of crashing objects, only to wonder if you were overhearing an assault or just a family quarrel? Cries of pain may sound like shrieks of laughter, and heart-attack victims may be mistaken for drunk. How do other bystanders influence our interpretation? Faced with a sudden, possibly dangerous event, everyone pretends to stay calm. As each person sees that others seem indifferent, they shrug it off. As a result, the event no longer feels like an emergency.

This process was observed in a study in which Latané and Darley (1970) had subjects fill out questionnaires alone or in groups of three. Shortly after the experimenter left, white smoke was pumped into the room through a vent. Alone, most subjects worried that there was a fire and quickly reported the smoke to the experimenter. Yet in the company of others, most subjects did not seek help. In some groups, the smoke was so thick that subjects rubbed their eyes and waved the fumes away from their face as they worked on the questionnaires, but they did not call for help. Why not? In postexperiment interviews, they said they assumed the smoke was harmless steam, air-conditioning vapors, or even "truth gas"—but not a fire.

diffusion of responsibility In groups, a tendency for bystanders to assume that someone else will help.

The presence of others also inhibits helping by causing a **diffusion of responsibility,** a belief that others will intervene. Thirty-eight people watched from their apartments and did nothing while Kitty Genovese was killed. Subjects in the group conditions of the seizure experiment also did not intervene. When subjects thought that they alone could hear the victim, making them solely responsible for his welfare, they took action. Many of those who thought that others were also present, however, behaved like the neighbors of Kitty Genovese: They stayed put because they assumed someone else was helping.

The bystander effect is powerful and scary. Over the years, researchers have observed behavior in different kinds of staged crises. Would subjects report a theft or a possible fire? Would they stop for a stranded motorist, help a woman who faints or sprains an ankle, or try to break up a fight? Would they rush to the aid of a seizure victim, a subway passenger who staggers and falls to the ground, or an experimenter who has an asthma attack? What are the odds that a person in need will actually receive help? Clearly, helping depends in complex ways on characteristics of the vic-

Table 24.1 When Helping Is Most Likely to Occur

1. When the bystander is in a good mood
2. When the bystander feels guilty or needs a self-esteem boost
3. When the bystander observes someone else helping
4. When the bystander is not pressed for time
5. When the bystander is male and the victim female
6. When the victim makes a direct request for help
7. When the victim is physically attractive
8. When the victim appears to deserve help
9. When the victim is similar in some way to the bystander
10. In a small town or rural area, not a large city

tim, the bystanders, and the situation (see Table 24.1). The fact remains, however, that a person is less likely to intervene in a group than when alone. Even more remarkable is that victims are more likely to get help from some*one* when their welfare rests on the shoulders of a single potential helper than when many others are present (Latané & Nida, 1981).

Social psychologists have studied a wide range of important behaviors—and in a wide range of important settings. From the studies of social perception, attraction, conformity, obedience, persuasion, group processes, aggression, and altruism, the research message is clear: We are influenced in profound ways by the words and actions of other people.

1857–
Herndon
of the Central America

All hope had gone. The *Central America* was dying—dying in the darkness of a wild September night, her seams opened to the sea, her top hamper wrecked and broken, her sails shredded bits of canvas ripped from the bolt ropes.

Herndon, her captain, clung to a bridge stanchion as the hulk rolled heavily in the trough of the giant seas. He had seen the sun set—a pale and lusterless glow toward Hatteras—the last sunset he would ever see. He had watched the quick twilight fade as the last boat got away, laboring frightfully in the roar of the waters. He had seen the darkness shut down, the smashing rollers fade into the gloom. The night wore on with dragging weariness, the ship settled deeper, and Herndon knew it was the end. Slowly he turned toward his cabin. . . .

He had commanded her for almost two years—this ship that was now sinking beneath his feet. She was skippered, like all Pacific Mail ships, by a naval officer; Herndon had gone to her, with the rank of commander, from the old *Potomac* of the Home Squadron. For almost two years he had taken her back and forth on the run from New York via Havana to the fever-ridden hole at Aspinwall. He had brought many of the forty-niners home with their bulging sacks of gold; he had taken giddy trollops and scores of adventurous young blades, eager for fame and fortune, down the long seaway to the Isthmus—gateway to California's gold. Two years, and the *Central America* had helped to make history. Now it was all over, and the stout side-wheeler with her lofty masts and reaching yards was to sink into the limbo of the past.

She had stood out of Havana past the old Morro on September 8, 1857, with her crew of 101, a full passenger list of 474—most of them from California—and about two million dollars in gold. Out of Havana in fair weather and high spirits, with Cuba behind them like a cloud on the horizon and ahead of them the well-traveled sea lane to Sandy Hook. Out of Havana she sailed with the northeast trades tautening her canvas and her paddle wheels chunk-chunking on the sea lane to New York.

Midnight of the ninth the wind had freshened; in the midwatch the barometer dropped rapidly, and by dawn a gale was roaring out of the nor'nor'east.

Two days of wind and weather—great seas rolling southward from the pole, spindrift pattering like hail on the storm sails, the paddles churning slowly as the ship labored. The sea made up; the *Central America* strained and groaned. On the forenoon of the eleventh her seams opened; the sea had won. But Herndon did not admit defeat. Red-eyed and tired, he ordered his men to the pumps. The wind shrieked at whole-gale force; the sea lipped eagerly about the opened seams and gurgled into the hold, giving her a starboard list. Huge seas broke aboard; green water fumed about the decks. By two bells of the afternoon watch the strakes had worked so far apart with the straining of the vessel that the inrushing water had extinguished some of the boiler fires, and the engines had soughed to a stop for lack of steam.

Herndon routed out the passengers—all hands to save ship. He organized bailing gangs; buckets, barrels, scoops, pots, and wheezing pumps sucked and dipped at the ocean in the hold. The passengers tailed on to whips, hoisted high the barrels, dumped them overside, dropped them again into the gaining water below decks. Herndon put some of them to shifting freight—from starboard to larboard—while he tried to keep his ship headed up with some wisps of canvas. All passengers not working on the whips were ordered to the windward side; the ship was trimmed; once more, briefly, she rode the combers on an even keel.

But the *Central America*'s seams were wide to the eager sea. Passengers, men and women and even the older children, worked side by side with the exhausted crew at the buckets and the barrels and the pumps. It was no good. The water gained; tired muscles wearied in the endless struggle. Slowly the ship settled. The water crept up into the ashpits, above the grate bars, toward the boiler drums. The storm spencer blew out of its boltropes; the ship's head fell off; she wallowed in the troughs. The night came down as the storm shrieked on and the ship settled. The pumps wheezed; the barrels came up out of the flooded hold at a run—men and women on the whips, urged on to new exertions by Herndon's encouragement. A sailor started an old chantey:

> *"Whiskey is the life of man.*
> *O Whisky Johnny!*
> *I'll drink whisky while I can.*
> *O Whisky Johnny!"*

During the night Herndon had the foreyard sent down; he tried time and again to get the *Central America* before the wind, but there was no canvas strong enough to

E-2C Hawkeyes of VAW-114 fly in formation over the Sea of Japan during a western Pacific deployment.
Official U.S. Navy photo.

hold in the gale. The head sails were blown to tatters. Herndon ordered the clews of the foresail lashed to the deck, hoping to hoist the yard, if only a few feet, show canvas, and get her off; but the yard was scarcely clear of the bulwarks when the wild wind took it entirely out of the boltropes.

Toward dawn axes bit into the foremast. It fell crashing to leeward, and out of the foreyard and bits of timber and canvas were fashioned a rough sea anchor. Aft tattered scraps of canvas were spread in the rigging; but the *Central America*, the water rising toward her main deck, would not answer; she rolled heavily in the troughs. Dawn of the twelfth revealed a drifting hulk, battered and sinking. But the captain still refused to despair. They were in the shipping lanes, help might come. "Rally all," he said. He kept them at the pumps, hoisted the ensign upside down, had minute guns fired.

About noon the wind commenced to abate, but the gale had done its work; the *Central America* was doomed. In early afternoon a ship was sighted; hope rose—but the ship held her course. Later, more yards against the clouded sky: a few wisps of canvas on another vessel, scudding fast.

"A sail! A sail!"

The gun boomed; and the passing ship, the brig *Marine* out of Boston, Captain Burt, hove to—though she herself had been damaged by the storm. Herndon had the boats manned and lowered; the women and children climbed in; the boats commenced their perilous pull to leeward. Flung skyward, then dropped between the waves, they rode the combers, reached the brig, pulled back a long pull to the foundering vessel. A second time they made the dangerous passage with their gunwales awash—one hundred saved. As the last boat was ready to pull away, the sky darkening in the east, Herndon halted a passenger about to embark, and handed him his watch. The captain choked up—he who had stuck to his bridge, encouraged his crew, bravely fought the old fight against great waters. There was everything to live for (he was only forty-four): his wife; his sister, the wife of Commander Matthew Fontaine Maury; his daughter Ellen who later, after he was dead, was to marry Chester A. Arthur, twenty-first President of the United States; his service, and his friends. He thrust the watch at the passenger, spoke of his wife.

"Give it to her, and tell her—tell her—tell her from me . . ."

He could not go on; he shook his head and turned away. The boat pulled off; in a moment Herndon was back on the bridge, composed and awaiting the end.

It was not to be long in coming. The brig *Marine* had drifted several miles to leeward; the *Central America*'s boats were battered, leaking, and half-filled with water—useless; the steamer was settling lower, listing to starboard, her main deck almost awash. But there was no panic; those hundreds left aboard saw their commander on the bridge, cool and quiet, looking out at the faint glow in the west.

The *Central America* foundered that night, carrying down with her the bags of California gold, her commander, and 423 of her passengers and crew. In addition to the hundred taken to the *Marine,* forty-nine passengers were picked out of the water next morning by the Norwegian bark *Ellen,* after clinging for hours to bits of wreckage. Three others were saved, days later, by the English brig *Mary,* after having drifted with the Gulf Stream more than 450 miles from the scene of the sinking. Herndon's last hours had been spent in vain attempts to save more lives. Rockets were sent up every fifteen minutes; life preservers were distributed as the ship settled to her doom, and the commander set the passengers and crew to work chopping away part of the hurricane deck to make an impromptu raft.

Toward the last, through the night, above the waves and wind, a boat's oars had been heard. But it was too late; the ship was going; Herndon had warned the boat off to keep her from being sucked down with the sinking ship.

"Keep off! Keep off!"

Everything had been done that could be done; it was only a question of moments. Herndon called his first officer, Van Rennselaer, and told him he was going below for his uniform. The commander went to his stateroom, and in a few minutes returned to the bridge. He had put on his full-dress uniform and removed the oilskin cover that concealed his naval-cap insignia. He took his stand on the wheelhouse, bracing himself against the ship's list.

A rocket went up—a fiery meteor illuminating briefly the dismasted foundering ship, the wrecked hopes of those who had gone west for gold. The waves seethed against the open strakes; scud and spume and salt rind whitened the top hamper; green water lapped the decks. The *Central America* gave a final lurch. Herndon, clinging to the wheelhouse rail, uncovered, waved his hand. The side-wheel steamer, out of Aspinwall for New York, turned on her side and sank.

NOTES

I am indebted to Mrs. E. S. Lewars of Seminary Ridge, Gettysburg, Pa., for the information that one of those lost with the *Central America* was William Ulrich, a mulatto waiter. Ulrich had a distinguished patron, Thaddeus Stevens, who had procured for him the job which led to Ulrich's death. Ulrich was the son of a former slave—Ephraim Ulrich—who was bought and freed by Thaddeus Stevens of Gettysburg, the fiery figure whose name is forever associated with the stormy period of American history which culminated in the War Between the States.

ACKNOWLEDGMENTS

Republished from the *United States Naval Institute Proceedings* with permission of the editor.

This chapter is based primarily upon documents in the Navy Department library, particularly upon an account of the *Central America*'s loss by Commander Matthew Fontaine Maury, "the pathfinder of the seas," who was Herndon's brother-in-law. I have quoted from these documents and have also drawn upon articles in the *United States Naval Institute Proceedings*.

25 Death and Disaster—Dealing with Traumatic Events

Objectives

1. Describe the range of normal reactions to extreme stress.

2. Describe Post-traumatic Stress Disorder and the Navy's programs for minimizing the negative effects of extremely stressful events.

3. Outline a leadership strategy for helping your people respond to a catastrophic event.

4. Describe aspects of the military lifestyle that can cause stress for military members and for their families as well.

Sources of Extreme Stress

Extreme stress has a variety of sources, ranging from unemployment to wartime combat, from violent natural disaster to rape. We look briefly now at some major stressors, the effects they have on people, and the coping mechanisms people use to deal with them.

1. *Unemployment.* Joblessness is a major source of stress. When the jobless rate rises, so do first admission to psychiatric hospitals, infant mortality, deaths from heart disease, alcohol-related diseases, and suicide (Brenner 1973, 1979; Rayman & Bluestone, 1982). "Things just fell apart," one worker said after both he and his wife lost their jobs.

   People usually react to the stress of unemployment in several stages (Powell & Driscoll, 1973). First comes a period of relaxation and relief, in which they take a vacation of sorts, confident they will find another job. Stage 2, marked by continued optimism, is a time of concentrated job hunting. In Stage 3, a period of vacillation and doubt, jobless people become moody, their relationships with family and friends deteriorate, and they scarcely bother to look for work. By Stage 4, a period of malaise and cynicism, they have simply given up.

   Although these effects are not universal, they are quite common. Moreover, there are indications that joblessness may not so much create new psychological difficulties as bring previously hidden ones to the surface. Two studies have shown that death rates go up and psychiatric symptoms worsen not just during periods of unemployment but also during short, rapid upturns in the economy (Brenner, 1979; Eyer, 1977). This finding lends support to the observation that change, whether good or bad, causes stress.

2. *Divorce and separation.* As Coleman and colleagues (1988) observe, "the deterioration or ending of an intimate relationship is one of the more potent of stressors and one of the more frequent reasons why people seek psychotherapy" (p. 155). After a breakup, both partners often feel they have failed at one of life's most important endeavors. Strong emotional ties frequently continue to bind the pair. If only one spouse wants to end the marriage, the one initiating the divorce may feel sadness and guilt at hurting a once-loved partner, while the rejected spouse may vacillate between anger, humiliation, and self-recrimination over his or her role in the failure. Even if the decision to separate was mutual, ambivalent feelings of love and hate can make life upsetting and turbulent. Thus, people commonly use defensive coping techniques, particularly denial and projection, to cushion the impact of divorce or separation.

3. *Bereavement.* Following the death of a loved one, people generally experience the strong feelings of grief and loss known as *bereavement.* Most people emerge from this experience without suffering permanent psychological harm, but usually not before they pass through a long process that

Freud called the "work of mourning." Janis and his colleagues (1969) have described normal grief as beginning with numbness and progressing through months of distress in which anger, intense grief and yearning, depression, and apathy may all come to the fore. During this phase, people in mourning tend to cope defensively with an inescapable and extremely painful reality. In most cases, denial, displacement, and other defense mechanisms allow the survivor to gather strength for the more direct coping efforts that will be necessary later on—such as, in the case of a spouse's death, selling belongings and moving out of the marital home.

4. *Catastrophes.* Catastrophes include floods, earthquakes, violent storms, fires, and plane crashes. Psychological reactions to all these stressful events have much in common. At first, in the *shock stage,* "the victim is stunned, dazed, and apathetic," and sometimes even "stuporous, disoriented, and amnesic for the traumatic event." Then, in the *suggestible stage,* victims are passive and quite ready to do whatever rescuers tell them to do. In the third phase, the *recovery stage,* victims regain emotional balance, but anxiety often persists, and they may need to recount their experiences over and over again (Morris, 1990). Some investigators report that in later stages survivors may feel irrationally guilty because they lived while others died.

5. *Combat and other threatening personal attacks.* Wartime experiences often cause soldiers intense and disabling combat stress. Similar reactions—including bursting into rage over harmless remarks, sleep disturbances, cringing at sudden loud noises, psychological confusion, uncontrollable crying, and silently staring into space for long periods—are also frequently seen in survivors of serious accidents and violent crimes such as rapes and muggings.

Post-traumatic Stress Disorder

What is post-traumatic stress disorder? What kinds of events are most likely to trigger this disorder?

post-traumatic stress disorder (PTSD) Psychological disorder characterized by episodes of anxiety, sleeplessness, and nightmoares resulting from some disturbing event in the past.

In extreme cases, severely stressful events can cause a psychological disorder known as **post-traumatic stress disorder (PTSD)**. Dramatic nightmares in which the victim reexperiences the terrifying event exactly as it happened are common. So are daytime *flashbacks,* in which the victim relives the trauma. Often, victims of PTSD withdraw from social life and from job and family responsibilities.

Post-traumatic stress disorders can set in right after a traumatic event or within a short time. But sometimes, months or years may go by in which the victim seems to have recovered from the experience, and then, without warning, psychological symptoms appear, then may disappear only to recur repeatedly; some people suffer for years (Kessler et al., 1995). Exposure to events reminiscent of the original trauma intensify symptoms of PTSD (Moyers, 1996).

Combat veterans appear to be especially vulnerable to PTSD. More than one-third of men involved in heavy combat in Vietnam showed signs of serious PTSD. Many veterans of World War II, old men now, still have nightmares from which they awake sweating and shaking. The memories of combat continue to torment them after more than half a century (Gelman, 1994).

Yet not everyone who is exposed to severely stressful events such as heavy combat or childhood sexual abuse develops PTSD. Individual characteristics including gender, personality, a family history of mental disorders, substance abuse among relatives, and even preexisting neurological disorders appear to predispose some people to PTSD more than others (Curle & Williams, 1996; Friedman, Schnurr & McDonagh-Coyle, 1994; Gurvits et al., 1997). For instance, vulnerability to PTSD in Vietnam veterans was associated with specific personality characteristics that existed before their military experience (Schnurr, Rosenberg, & Friedman, 1993). Injury from post-traumatic stress disorder is strongly related to the amount of emotional support survivors receive from family, friends, and community.

The Gulf War

Ann E. Norwood, M.D.
Robert J. Ursano, M.D.

War and the threat of war represent significant psychological trauma. Indeed, much of the literature on posttraumatic stress disorder (PTSD) stems originally from studies of soldiers, sailors, airmen, and Marines who were exposed to war and its attendant horrors. It is important to study the effects of war so that "lessons learned" can be applied in future wars and conflicts and a better understanding of the effects of other human-caused and natural disasters and traumas can be attained. In the case of the Persian Gulf War, because the war was relatively brief and the outcome militarily successful, we run the risk of complacency; it is tempting to rest on our laurels rather than to carefully analyze and record the lessons learned. During the Gulf War, American forces sustained 148 battle deaths and 145 nonbattle deaths (as a result of motor vehicle accidents, etc.); 467 American servicemembers were wounded in action (U.S. Department of Defense 1991). Although the forecasts of Iraqi chemical and biological warfare, which would result in tens of thousands of American dead, did not come to pass, such warfare, the use of which we so feared in the Gulf War, could well be the scenario of the next war. The U.S. military has also found itself increasingly involved in humanitarian missions that, despite their name, still expose our forces to the stress and trauma of combat. It is likely that American servicemembers, their families, and our nation will continue to grapple with the injuries and deaths of its servicemembers operating in these contingencies. The knowledge of psychological and behavioral responses to war—of families, communities, and nations, as well as of individuals—will be needed in the future.

Although many researchers in this field have concentrated on the effects of combat and its sequelae, it is important to recognize that combat is not the only traumatic stressor inherent in war; nor are those persons directly affected by combat its only victims. PTSD is only one of several possible psychological outcomes following trauma. Substance abuse, depression, generalized anxiety disorder, and adjustment disorders are some of the other psychiatric disorders that have been associated with traumatic exposure (Ursano et al. 1994). Moreover, individuals exposed to trauma do not always develop psychiatric illness. In the Gulf War, combat-related stressors included "friendly fire" incidents, tank battles, air strikes, and other potentially lethal events. Fear of capture, injury, and death was a common concern of those sent to the combat theater. In the course of the war and its aftermath, many personnel saw the bodies of dead Iraqis and Kuwaitis. The debilitated condition of the Iraqi enemy prisoners of

"Seal Team on the Move."
Official U.S. Navy photo.

war (POWs) and of ethnic minorities such as the Kurds was also distressing to many. As is true of all wars, witnessing the results of atrocities was especially troublesome.

Increasingly, we appreciate the ever-expanding reverberations of trauma. In studying the effects of war, investigators first explored the direct victims of combat: combatants and civilian casualties. Although these direct victims of trauma are often readily discernible, there are also hidden victims. Trauma impacts the victims' friends and loved ones, rescue workers and medical personnel, colleagues/co-workers, communities, and social groups. Witnesses of traumatic events are also vulnerable to psychological sequelae. Research on terrorism and the effects of conventional war on indirect victims has been of relatively recent origin.

Similarly, the study of war's effects on families has been relatively limited. The first published report on families' reactions to war was Reuben Hill's (1949) observations on families' responses to World War II. His observations led him to develop the ABCX model of family stress crisis. During the Vietnam War era, families of military personnel who were either POWs or missing in action (MIA) were studied (McCubbin and Patterson 1983). Most recently, the effects of soldiers' PTSD on families and spouses have been reported. Solomon (1993) found increased somatic and psychiatric distress in the wives of Israeli veterans with diagnoses of PTSD or combat stress reaction. There is a relative dearth of contemporary work on the longitudinal stressors of war on families. Special populations, such as reserve families, single-parent households, and joint service marriages, may be particularly vulnerable. In one of the few studies on Desert Storm, Rosen and colleagues (1993) reported the results of questionnaires in which parents were asked to rate their children's responses to Operation Desert Storm. Sadness was a common complaint for both girls and boys. From 42% to 64% of children between the ages of 3 and 12 years were described by their parents as being sad or tearful. Discipline problems at home were reported to occur fairly frequently with boys but infrequently with girls. Both boys and girls demanded more attention from the nondeployed parent.

Children of deploying parents were not the only ones who worried about the war. There were reports of children throughout the United States who feared terrorist attacks and/or did not realize that they were geographically distant from where hostilities were taking place. War affects an entire nation, before, during, and after hostilities.

The mobilization of reservists for Desert Storm exerted a substantial burden on many small communities in America. Deployment resulted in some small towns los-

Naval Academy photo courtesy of United States Naval Academy Photographic Laboratory.

ing major figures in their communities such as business and civic leaders, teachers, and health care providers. The burden experienced by these communities was compounded by the ambiguity and uncertainty surrounding when (and if) these individuals would return. The impact of war on these relatively neglected populations is an area that future research must address.

In addition to considering a broader array of populations—both those directly and those indirectly affected by war—it is important to dissect war into its component traumatic stressors. Too often, we focus narrowly on combat-related stressors, forgetting that threat to life and exposure to death, injury, and the grotesque are not the only stressors that cause the pain and suffering of combat. Separation of family members; fear of capture, injury, and death; shifts in family roles; disruption of the normal routine; increased financial pressures; fear of terrorist attacks—all are part of the experience of nations, communities, and families during time of war. It is helpful to conceptualize the stressors of war along the following time line: predeployment, deployment, sustainment, hostilities, reunion, and reintegration (Figure 25-1).

Applying this time line to different populations increases our ability to identify the multitude of war stressors encountered by various individuals and groups. For example, the stressors encountered by active-duty soldiers along this continuum differ substantially from those experienced by family members of reserve units during the same periods. Similarly, the experience for families of active-duty personnel who were being

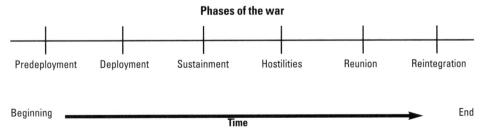

FIGURE 25-1 **Phases of war, which call for different psychological support.**

A safety officer checks the flight deck of USS Constellation (CV 64) as a Carrier On-board Delivery C-2 Greyhound prepares to taxi for launch.
Official U.S. Navy photo.

deployed to the Gulf differs from that of those who were stationed abroad and of those who lived on bases and posts within the U.S. The identification of populations at risk and of the relevant biopsychosocial stressors can further our understanding of the factors that render certain individuals relatively more vulnerable or more resilient to the development of psychological sequelae to war. Specific interventions can then be targeted toward specific individuals and populations, either to inoculate them against the effects of particular stressors, or to increase their ability to cope successfully.

Based on the regularity with which we find ourselves involved in armed conflicts, the psychological legacy of war merits study in its own right. In addition, however, although direct exposure to war is not a common part of most Americans' experience, exposure to significant traumatic stressors is. An estimated 6% to 7% of the American population is exposed to some sort of significant trauma each year (Norris 1988). Thus, although the odds of American civilians being directly impacted by a war seem low, it is possible that they will be subject to, or witness, a natural disaster, motor vehicle accident, physical assault, or other traumatic event. The extent to which findings from research on war can be generalized to other traumatic stressors must always be carefully assessed. But such findings can offer important considerations for all health care providers. The study of psychological reactions to war, then, holds broader implications for the understanding of other types of trauma.

In this volume the authors focus on the stressors associated with the Persian Gulf War and on the populations and time phases of the war that are often overlooked. We do not focus on combat psychiatry. Rather, the psychiatric and psychological effects seen before and after combat—in those about to leave for war and in those returning from war, as well as in their children and families—are highlighted, as are the potential long-term effects as suggested by studies of previous war veterans. Whenever possible, attempts are made to quantify the nature of the stressor and the individual or community response to the trauma.

Stressors of the Persian Gulf War

The pace of the Gulf War buildup was unprecedented in military history. Iraq invaded Kuwait on August 2, 1990. On August 7, the U.S. began moving air forces to the region, the Eighty-Second Airborne Division from Ft. Bragg began deploying, and the first prepositioned ship departed for the Gulf from Diego Garcia. On August 22, President Bush signed an executive order placing 48,000 American reservists on active duty by September 1. By August 18, there were 50,000 Americans in the Gulf theater.

With the addition of reservists, the number of American servicemembers reached 150,000 by September 15, 1990. Within the next month another 60,000 Americans arrived in the theater. On November 14, Secretary of Defense Cheney activated 72,500 reservists and extended the current call-up from 90 to 180 days. Approximately 2 weeks later, Secretary Cheney authorized the call-up of an additional 63,000 reservists and guard members, raising the total to 188,000. By Christmas 1990, there were over a quarter of a million U.S. military personnel in the Gulf. By the beginning of the air war on January 17, 1991, there were over 300,000 American troops deployed. Over half a million Americans were deployed to Southwest Asia when the ground war began on February 24 ("Tracking the Storm" [Chronology] 1991).

The Gulf War brought both old and new threats to American forces (Table 25.1). A number of stressors were unique to living in the desert. As in other areas of military medicine, strong emphasis was placed on prevention through educating soldiers and command about these dangers. High priority was placed on acclimatizing soldiers as rapidly as possible. The first stressor to overcome was jet lag after the long flights to Southwest Asia. Familiar and well-publicized threats included venomous snakes and scorpions indigenous to Southwest Asia. From a medical perspective, however, the largest predictable threat was heat injury. Air temperature in the summer can exceed 115°F. Sand receiving full sun is usually 30 to 45° hotter than the air and can reach temperatures of 150°F. Command emphasis was placed on educating soldiers to force fluids—for example, instructing them to drink even when they were not thirsty, because by the time a person experiences thirst, he or she is 1½ quarts below the optimal physiological level. Television news was filled with images of soldiers carrying bottles of spring water.

Heat is not the only environmental hazard. The desert can also become very cold in the winter; the wind chill at night drops well below freezing. Protection of skin and eyes from sand and dust was imperative. The wearing of contact lenses was prohibited except in areas that were air-conditioned and protected from sand. Sunglasses and goggles were distributed for eye protection. Soldiers were urged to use extra caution in securing tent pegs and other objects that could be turned into missiles by heavy winds.

Medical authorities were educated on the types of problems they might encounter over the course of the deployment. In the first few weeks of deployment, diarrheal diseases were expected. The dusty environment was expected to precipitate acute respiratory illness. Medical authorities were cautioned to be vigilant within the first month for the development of febrile illnesses caused by viral respiratory diseases, arboviruses such as sandfly fevers or dengue, enteric diseases, hepatitis A and E, and rickettsial diseases.

After several weeks of deployment, illnesses in soldiers could herald other diseases such as hepatitis B, leishmaniasis, and parasitic infections. Medical personnel were also instructed to watch for psychological problems; both health problems and the strain of preparing for battle might manifest themselves in acting out of tensions. It

Table 25.1. Major stressors of the Persian Gulf War

Threat of chemical/biological warfare	Desert environment
Threat of mass casualties	Jet lag
(up to 50% losses predicted)	Cultural isolation
	Media

should be remembered, too, that psychological factors can influence the development of physical illness. For example, noncompliance with preventive measures, such as malaria prophylaxis or use of sunscreens and proper clothing to prevent sunburn, generates nonbattle injury casualties that are truly psychological casualties.

The experience of U.S. personnel in Saudi Arabia differed strikingly from that of Vietnam War veterans with regard to the social outlets available to them. Servicemembers in Saudi Arabia were culturally isolated: troops were given orders not to fraternize with local people. In accord with the religious dictates of the host countries, alcohol was prohibited.

Living conditions were harsh for U.S. personnel in Saudi Arabia. Hot showers were an infrequent luxury. Cots were usually lined up side by side in buildings, an arrangement that afforded virtually no privacy or quiet. Although living aboard ship provided a few more amenities, lack of privacy, fear of chemical/biological attack, and other stressors were part of everyday life for naval personnel (Dinneen et al. 1994).

The threat of chemical and biological warfare was a major consideration throughout the war. During the Iran-Iraq War and in attacks on the Kurdish minority in Iraq, Saddam Hussein had used mustard gas, nerve agents, and T-2 toxin. At the time of the war, Iraq was believed to have a 2,000- to 4,000-ton arsenal of chemical weapons, consisting predominantly of mustard gas but also including the nerve agents sarin and tabun. It was estimated that Iraq had the capability of annually producing more than 700 tons of mustard gas and 50 tons each of sarin and tabun. Moreover, Iraqi delivery systems were capable of striking distances up to 530 miles (Knudson 1991). Intelligence agencies reported that Iraq had been conducting research on biological agents, including anthrax, botulism, cholera, typhoid, equine encephalitis, and tularemia (Knudson 1991).

The Persian Gulf War also offered the world glimpses of high-technology warfare in the coming millennium. In addition, the war showcased the ways in which media coverage of warfare has changed. The media not only reports the war but also observes and participates in it. The media has changed not only the way in which the public learns about the war but also the very ways in which wars are fought. For example, the television display of the battered American aviator held as a POW by the Iraqis helped galvanize public support for the war.

The Gulf War: Technological Advances and Their Implications for Future Wars

The Persian Gulf War represented the largest military deployment since World War II (Salomon and Bankirer 1991). It was a new, fast-paced, "high tech" war that differed from past wars both in terms of the armament employed and in the ways in which the news of the war was conveyed to the public back home. The Vietnam War has been characterized as the first "television war"; the Gulf War, then, was the first war that was televised "live." Beginning with the initial reports of a radar blip indicating that U.S. warplanes were headed for Baghdad, television brought the war as it unfolded into the living rooms of America. Many Americans, especially military spouses, became "news junkies." One military spouse noted, "I watch ABC while I tape CBS, then *MacNeil/Lehrer*. I get *Christian Science Monitor* and the *World Monitor*. Also the *Louisville Courier-Journal* and *USA Today*. And I watch CNN" (Kantrowitz 1990, p. 33). Satellite technology also brought closer and more rapid communication from soldiers to their families, allowing soldiers to "phone home" from the combat theater. As in previous wars, mail provided a key link with home. Often, soldiers exchanged audiotapes with their families back home in an effort to bridge the distance.

In many important ways the Gulf War bears a closer resemblance to World War II than it does to either the Korean War or the Vietnam War. The Gulf War, like World War II, was characterized by clear-cut objectives, whereas the objectives in the Korean and Vietnam Wars were not so clear. Other similarities included the massive deployment of multilateral forces in World War II and the Gulf War. In the Gulf War, in contrast to the Korean and Vietnam Wars, the U.S. and the host countries shouldered the vast majority of the personnel commitment (Summers 1992).

As in World War II, large numbers of reservists were activated. The first reservists were called up by Secretary Cheney on August 23, 1990 ("Tracking the Storm" [Chronology] 1991). Between August 1990, the time of Iraq's invasion of Kuwait, and March 1991, approximately 227,000 reservists and National Guard members were called up; an additional 10,700 volunteered for service (see Dunning, Chapter 8, this volume). Approximately 7% of the American forces in the Gulf were women; 43% of the American forces were married, and the average age was 28 (U.S. Department of Defense 1991). The mobilization of reservists permeated the fabric of American society. Involvement of individuals from communities across the nation highlighted the fact that the war was going on. The decision to call up the reserves was considered by some to be a pivotal event in galvanizing public opinion to support the strategy in the Gulf.

Another important distinction was that both the Gulf War and World War II were successful offensive wars. Fear of provoking the Soviet Union and China changed American policy in the 1950s from its historic policy of "rollback and liberation" to a policy of "containment" (Summers 1992). This policy of containment was also used in Vietnam. Under a policy of containment, the most successful outcome is a stalemate; this carries implications for national sentiment and popular support. The move away from containment to a policy that allowed the possibility of victory was made possible by the resolution of the Cold War. Because war with the Soviet Union was no longer an issue, a multinational coalition could be forged (Summers 1992).

The logistical support provided by the military was the largest supply effort since World War II (Salomon and Bankirer 1991). Although airlift played a minor role in World War II, it contributed significantly to the success of the Allied forces. By January 11, 1991, the Military Airlift Command (MAC) had flown more than 10,000 missions, carrying more than 370,000 passengers and more than 346,000 tons of cargo ("Tracking the Storm" [Chronology] 1991). Over the course of the war, the MAC flew more than 15,800 missions and moved more than half a million passengers and almost half a million tons of supplies (Summers 1992). Ships, as they had during World War II, carried the bulk of supplies. The sealift consisted of some 250 ships that carried, in total, 9 million tons of equipment and fuel (Summers 1992). The Allied forces had a combined strength of more than 1,500 combat aircraft (Van Voorst 1991, p. 34); between January 17, 1991, the initiation of the air war, and January 27, 1991, the coalition flew more than 18,500 bombing sorties, losing 23 planes ("Tracking the Storm" [Chronology] 1991). American forces fielded almost 1,000 M1A1 tanks, which were capable of outrunning and outgunning any Iraqi tanks (Van Voorst 1991, p. 35).

Perhaps the most striking feature of the Gulf War in comparison with past wars was the compression of time and space because of the increased pace of battle and the increased accuracy and range of weapons (RisCassi 1993). The speed with which personnel and equipment were moved to Southwest Asia was extraordinary. The impressive logistical support provided during Desert Storm, in comparison with that provided in other recent American wars, is documented in Table 25.2.

Table 25.2 Army deployment in the first 90 days of four wars

	WORLD WAR II	KOREAN WAR	VIETNAM WAR	PERSIAN GULF WAR
Passengers	138,060[a]			
Via ship		—[b]	82,800	1,453
Via air		32,357	85,562	183,030
Supplies and equipment: tons shipped	836,060	979,833	1,300,000	1,071,317
Supplies and equipment: tons airlifted	—[b]	—[b]	38,564	175,668

[a]Mostly by ship.

[b]Not available.

Source. Adapted from "Tracking the Storm" [Chronology] 1991.

It is not just that the pace was fast, but that it was unremitting. Modern military operations are continuous (Peters 1993). A key innovation contributing to the 24-hour waging of war has been night-vision equipment. This advantage was pressed in the Gulf by using nighttime air raids and tank maneuvers in fighting the Iraqis. Interestingly, the only major change in weapons used since World War II "involved space, stealth, and the mating of nuclear power and missiles with submarines" (Bodnar 1993, p. 8). The tremendous advantage we have gained in terms of military capability is in large part a result of the revolution in military sensors and communications. Combat efficiency has increased as a result of our ability to collect, analyze, and respond to sensor data and then, based on these data, to launch "smart" weapons. With the exception of satellites, communications hardware is not better than that used in the Vietnam War (Peters 1993). However, in the Gulf War, satellites were important. They provided critical intelligence, communications, and location data for friendly forces. Although similar numbers of troops had been used in other invasions, their movements had always been programmed ahead of time. In Desert Storm, technological advances allowed close monitoring of the battlefield and continual fine-tuning (Bodnar 1993). However, despite the advances, problems occurred. For example, navigation difficulties, inaccurate target identification, lack of fire discipline, and the confusion of battle contributed to "friendly fire" casualties among tank units (Fontenot 1993).

Changes in Demographics of the Military Since the Vietnam War

There have been several major demographic changes in the military since the Vietnam War and earlier wars as a result of policy changes within the Department of Defense and changes in cultural values. Some of these differences are summarized in Table 25.3. Perhaps the most significant policy changes, which in turn have caused other changes, were the replacement of the draft by an "all volunteer" force and the broadening of fields open to women. Women now account for 11% of active-duty

Table 25.3 Differences in the American military between the Gulf War and the Vietnam War	
VIETNAM WAR	**GULF WAR**
Draftees	All-volunteer force
No reserves	Reserves activated
2% women; limited jobs	10% women; wider variety of jobs
High alcohol/drug use	Lower alcohol/drug use
Ground war	Air war highlighted
Conventional weapons	High-technology weapons (e.g., "smart" bombs)

personnel in the armed forces—up from 2% in 1972. From 1951 to 1975, being a parent, getting married, or becoming pregnant was grounds for terminating service-women's employment. Therefore, the Gulf War represents the military's first experience with the deployment of large numbers of active-duty mothers and wives. More than 33,300 military women were deployed to the Gulf. The Army deployed 26,000 female soldiers to the theater during Desert Storm. These women functioned in varied roles: flying helicopters, commanding air defense batteries and military police, and performing medical, administrative, intelligence, and transportation duties (Maginnis 1992). Over the course of the war, 11 Army women died, 5 of them killed in action (Becraft 1991); 21 female soldiers were wounded in action, and two women were Iraqi POWs (Maginnis 1992).

The Air Force deployed 3,800 women to Southwest Asia; women piloted and crewed aircraft that were involved in aeromedical evacuation, reconnaissance, and transport missions. The Navy deployed 2,500 women who served on a wide variety of ships, worked in construction units, staffed hospitals, and flew aircraft. The Marine Corps sent 1,000 women to the theater in combat support roles. The Coast Guard also was represented by women during Desert Storm; 13 women participated in port security operations (Becraft 1991).

Women lived under the same austere conditions as their male counterparts. Generally, either women had separate showers or special times were set aside for their use of the showers. Hygiene concerns proved inconsequential for the most part (U.S. General Accounting Office 1993), although sanitary napkins and tampons were initially in short supply.

Today's military members are better educated. In the Army, the percentage of recruits who enlisted with at least a high school education rose from 64% in 1979 to 93% by 1988. Another important change has been in the amount of substance use and abuse in today's military compared with the military during the era of the Vietnam War. For example, in 1990 the Army reported that fewer than 1% of drug tests were positive. In compliance with the request of the host countries that alcohol not be used, there was dramatically less alcohol (and other substances) use during the Gulf War than in previous wars.

The reduction in the size of the military and other considerations have also changed military doctrine toward increasing reliance on augmentation from the reserves. This increased involvement of the reserves results in an entire nation's experiencing being engaged in war, as in the Persian Gulf, rather than just a segment of society—the military—being engaged in war. As a result, whether reservist and National Guard troops were more likely to develop PTSD was an important question

Table 25.4 Changes in the military family since the Vietnam War
More single-parent families
More dual-career couples
Higher percentage of married soldiers
More "temporary" military families (because of activation of reserves)

in the Persian Gulf War. Similarly, the chance that their families would be more adversely affected was of concern. Reserve and National Guard units tend to have less well developed family support structures in place, which may place their families at higher risk of psychological sequelae, but they also are very cohesive units that have lived and worked together for years.

Just as today's military members have changed, so too have the members' families (Table 25.4). The military has seen a dramatic increase in the number of single-parent families and dual-career couples since the Korean War and the Vietnam War. Some 75% of officers and 60% of enlisted personnel are married; roughly half of their spouses work outside the home (Brant 1993). During the Gulf War, there were over 32,000 children affected by the deployment of their single parents. These children represent approximately 8.2% of all children (390,283) of deployed active-duty, reserve, and National Guard personnel (U.S. Department of Defense 1992).

Sadly, about 140 American children lost one of their parents during the Persian Gulf War (Dunnigan and Bay 1992, p. 342).

Combat Psychiatry in the Gulf War

The principles of combat psychiatry that were applied during the Gulf War, involving proximity, immediacy, and expectancy, were originally developed during World War I. Nonpathological labels (e.g., "combat fatigue"), simple interventions, and treatment in non-hospital-based facilities were used to promote recovery and return to duty (McDuff and Johnson 1992). The principles had been well tried in the context of previous wars and conflicts, and the Gulf War afforded the Army the opportunity to use its combat stress control (CSC) teams for the first time on a major scale. During the Gulf War, psychiatric care for the Army Seventh Corps (roughly 100,000 soldiers) was provided by the 531st Psychiatric Detachment. Mental health personnel were located at three different sites. One psychiatrist, 1 psychologist, 1 social worker, and 5 to 8 enlisted mental health counselors were assigned to each forward combat division. During the Gulf War, each of the 400-bed evacuation hospitals located at the rear of the corps was also supported by a psychiatrist and nursing personnel. These evacuation hospitals could be augmented by additional psychiatric personnel to create a 20-bed psychiatric unit. Mental health assets at the corps level consisted of a 48-person detachment including 5 psychiatrists, 6 social workers, 2 psychiatric nurses, 1 psychologist, 1 field officer, and 33 enlisted mental health counselors (McDuff and Johnson 1992). These multidisciplinary teams provided education and consultation to commanders and medical staff and performed psychiatric interventions (Hales 1992).

The Army reported extremely low evacuation of psychiatric casualties from the theater, equivalent to only 2.7 per 1,000 evacuations per year (Hales 1992). Follow-up studies by the Department of Veterans Affairs indicate that approximately 9% of Persian Gulf returnees reported symptoms scoring in the PTSD range on the Mississippi Scale for Combat-Related PTSD (Keane et al. 1988) in the first 6 to 9 months after returning. As many as 34% have experienced other forms of psychological distress since their return from Southwest Asia (Rosenheck et al. 1992). In the National Vietnam Veterans Readjustment Study, 31% of the male veterans and 27% of the female veterans were reported to have met criteria for PTSD at some time since their war zone deployment (Kulka et al. 1990), and 14% reported current PTSD symptomatology. The low rate of combat stress in the Gulf War may be a result of the war's brevity and successful outcome; time to train and adapt to hostilities; reduced alcohol or drug use; the no-replacement policy; older, better-educated, and better-trained troops; and favorable public opinion to bolster morale before going and upon return (Hales 1992).

The mental health community has also changed since the Vietnam War era. PTSD is now well recognized as a psychiatric condition. Progress has been made in identifying and treating persons affected by trauma. Finally, advances in telecommunications have enabled satellite broadcasts and conference calls as means of promoting interactive continuing education on PTSD. Mental health professionals can be linked with PTSD experts and have access to the medical literature throughout the world.

REFERENCES

Becraft CH: Women in the U.S. Armed Services: The Persian Gulf War. Washington, DC, Women's Research & Education Institute, March 1991

Bodnar JW: The military technical revolution: from hardware to information. Naval War College Review, Summer 1993, pp 7–21

Brant BA: Vanguard of social change? Military Review, February 1993, pp 12–19

Dinneen MP, Pentzien RJ, Mateczun JM: Stress and coping with the trauma of war in the Persian Gulf. the hospital ship USNS Comfort, in Individual and Community Responses to Trauma and Disaster: The Structure of Human Chaos. Edited by Ursano RJ, McCaughey BG, Fullerton CS. Cambridge, UK, Cambridge University Press, 1994, pp 306–329

Dunnigan JF, Bay A: From Shield to Storm: High-Tech Weapons, Military Strategy, and Coalition Warfare in the Persian Gulf. New York, William Morrow, 1992

Fontenot G: Fright night: Task Force 2/34 Armor. Military Review, January 1993, pp 38–52

Hales RE: Taking issue: psychiatric lessons from the Persian Gulf War. Hosp Community Psychiatry 43:769, 1992

Hill R: Families Under Stress: Adjustment to the Crises of War Separation and Reunion. Westport, CT, Greenwood Press, 1949

26 A Leader Is a Communicator— Getting Your Message Across

Objectives

1. Describe the essential components of active listening and nonverbal communication.

2. Describe your strengths and weaknesses as a communicator and their implications for your leadership effectiveness.

3. Apply active listening to your experience as a follower. Describe how a leader's listening abilities affect you as a follower, and listening techniques you could practice as a leader in order to help your subordinates.

4. Describe how active listening can benefit you as a midshipman and as a student.

5. Identify some psychological barriers to active listening.

Active Listening

Know how to listen and you will profit even from those who talk badly.

—Plutarch

Introduction to Theories of Active Listening

Why should a textbook on interpersonal skills include a lesson on listening? People who study the way humans communicate have found that most people spend 70 percent of their waking day engaged in some form of communication; college students may spend as much as three-fifths of that time listening. That means if you are awake for 16 hours, you're communicating in some way during 11 of those hours, and you spend between six and seven hours listening (Osborn & Osborn, 1994). Studies of student listening habits have shown that good listeners earn better grades. Still, many college students are remarkably inefficient listeners. At any given time, only 20 percent of the students present at a college lecture are paying attention, and only 12 percent are actively listening (Carosso, 1986).

On the job, many employers have discovered that balanced listening skills result in fewer misunderstandings, more innovation, improved morale, and a more pleasant and productive work environment (Hanna, 1995; Yukl, 1994). The national Agribusiness Management Aptitude and Skill Survey (AGRIMASS), conducted by researchers at Texas A&M University (Litzenberg & Schneider, 1988), asked 543 agribusiness managers to rate the relative importance of 74 personal and professional skills and characteristics required for successful agribusiness careers. The general categories of Interpersonal Characteristics and Communication Skills proved to be the highest rated areas. In the Communication Skills category, the ability to "listen and carry out instructions" was rated highest; furthermore, out of all 74 characteristics (including business skills, computer skills, and technical skills), listening ranked fifth.

In spite of the importance of listening in school and in the workplace, "most people make numerous listening mistakes [in family communication, business, government, and international affairs] every week but the costs—financial and otherwise—of poor listening are seldom analyzed. Because of listening mistakes, appointments have to be rescheduled, letters retyped and shipments rerouted. . . . At the least, productivity is affected and profits suffer. . . . Many of the divorces granted annually in the United States are related to the inability or unwillingness of one or both partners to listen to the other" (Nixon & West, 1989, p. 28).

Listening is a crucial element of the communication process that also includes speaking, writing, and reading. Yet very little time (if any) is devoted to teaching

Witty repartee at the USMC officers' club

people the skills they need to become better listeners. We learn in elementary school how to write, read, and speak, but virtually no class time is spent teaching techniques to make listening more effective. While the other three modes of communication are important, listening deserves at least as much attention in the skill-building process. The table below (Nixon & West, 1989) ranks the four basic communication skills in the order in which they are learned, used, and taught. It's clear that listening, our most called-upon communication faculty, receives the least attention.

In the next few pages, we'll look at some of the theories communication specialists have developed to help them understand how people listen. We'll first look at the general nature of listening, then analyze the listening process. Next, we'll consider some common barriers to active listening and present several suggestions for improving listening skills.

▣ What Is Listening?

Just as reading is not merely the sensory perception of words on a page but the act of interpreting those words and making meaning from them, listening is much more than the sensory perception of sounds. It is the act of interpreting those sounds and making meaning from them. Both the speaker and the listener share the responsibility for making meaning—a process Osborn and Osborn (1994) call participative communication.

Think about the way in which you learn best. Do you prefer to listen to information or to read it? Which is easier for you—that is, which requires the least amount of effort? Which is most effective—that is, which mode of taking in data helps you remember the most information? Do you see the difference between ease and effectiveness? Most people say listening is easier than reading, despite the fact that reading is a more effective way for most people to learn.

Readers have more control than listeners do over the process by which information is delivered. They can control the pace of its delivery; they can return to previous information or skip ahead, bypassing information they don't need or rereading

Basic Communication Skills Profile			
COMMUNICATION SKILL	ORDER LEARNED	EXTENT USED	EXTENT TAUGHT
Listening	First	First	Fourth
Speaking	Second	Second	Third
Reading	Third	Third	Second
Writing	Fourth	Fourth	First

information they want to focus on. Listeners, on the other hand, are subject to the whims of the speaker, receiving information at the speaker's own pace, limited to the information they are receiving at the moment, without the freedom to move backward or forward in the message to refresh memory or anticipate later ideas. But to many people, the control that comes with reading requires a significant expenditure of energy to extract the message the words convey. They believe listening is less strenuous, requiring only that they be there for the message to hit its mark. However, most people remember only half of what they hear immediately after listening to someone talk, no matter how carefully they thought they were listening. Two months later, they can remember only 25 percent of what they heard.

Listening may seem to be a passive activity: Just sit there and take in what you hear. But active listening requires the expenditure of much more energy than many people are willing to give. Not only do good listeners help themselves, they also help the person to whom they are listening. It may seem that listening doesn't communicate much to the speaker, but the listener's attitude and responsiveness can say a great deal (Rogers & Farson, 1992).

Think about a time when you tried to have a conversation with someone who was reading a newspaper or watching TV while you were talking. You may have offered to continue the conversation later, but the other person replied, "No, it's okay. I can hear what you're saying." But their attitude—their unwillingness to give you their full attention—probably conveyed the message, "I don't think what you have to say is very important. I'm not all that interested in you or your ideas." Good listening conveys another message altogether. The listener who looks at you, who gives you his or her undivided attention, says, "I'm interested in you as a person. I think what you have to say is important. I think you are worth listening to." The mere behavior of listening conveys the listener's message without the listener having to say a word. It's much harder to convince someone that you respect her and her ideas by telling her you do—but attentive, active listening convinces rather easily.

The Listening Process

Active listening is a process that passes through several stages: hearing, focusing on the message, comprehending and interpreting, analyzing and evaluating, responding, and remembering (Osborn & Osborn, 1994). We don't always move consciously through these stages in a linear sequence, and sometimes we spend more time in one stage than another. Still, if you are a good listener, you'll recognize all these stages. If any seem to be missing from your listening repertoire, something crucial may be missing in your interpersonal communication.

Hear the Message   Hearing is the physiological process in which sound waves stimulate nerve impulses that the brain interprets as sound. Sound travels in waves,

Stages of the Listening Process

- Hearing
- Focusing on the Message
- Comprehending and Interpreting
- Analyzing and Evaluating
- Responding
- Remembering

Naval Academy photo courtesy of United States Naval Academy Photographic Laboratory.

which are captured by the outer ear and directed into the ear canal. There they strike the ear drum, which begins to vibrate at the same frequency as the sound waves. The vibrations of the ear drum pass to the small bones (ossicles) in the middle ear, which themselves start to vibrate. The ossicles transfer the vibrations to the fluid within the cochlea, a seashell-shaped, fluid-filled structure lined with many specialized hair cells. The hairs move in response to the waves the sound vibrations create in the cochlear fluid. Movements of the hair cells stimulate fibers in the eighth cranial nerve to send signals to the brain, which reads those signals and interprets them as distinct sounds (Auditory Pathway, 1994).

You may hear many things, but you don't listen to everything you hear. Listening is a voluntary process that goes beyond mere reaction to sounds.

Focus on the Sounds of the Message   Focusing requires that you block out other distractions that may compete for your attention. Most listening problems occur because we fail to focus adequately. We let other stimuli interfere with our ability to hear the words the other person is saying. Some common listening problems may stem from environmental, physiological, or psychological factors, all of which may impede our ability to listen carefully. You'll find a description of common impediments to listening and how to deal with them in a later section of this chapter.

Comprehend and Interpret What You Hear   Comprehension requires you to attach meaning to combinations of sounds—you must understand both the language and the point of view of the speaker—as well as process visual and tonal cues in combination with the sound cues. Remember that in your attempt to discern the speaker's intention, you sometimes need to look beyond the words. Often you must hear things that aren't said, but are evident in body language, inflection, and tone (Rogers & Farson, 1992; Minninger, 1984). For example, you may hear someone say, "Oh, I couldn't possibly eat dessert. I'm on a diet," or "I'm sure you have better things to do than waste your time playing checkers with your old Grandpa." But in each case, the speaker's intention may not be consistent with the words. As a listener, you must discern the intent before you can respond appropriately.

Analyze and Evaluate What You Hear   A crucial part of the listening process that leads to understanding is to examine the message—not to just accept it at face value. That doesn't mean you should judge whether the message is right or wrong, good or bad. Instead, try to see beneath the message to the speaker's attitudes and emotions. If you disagree with what the speaker says, try to explore the reasons for the person's conclusions or assertions, without challenging his or her honesty or intelligence (Yukl, 1994). Sometimes it's more important to respond to the emotion underlying the speaker's message. If a colleague says, "I'd like to melt this copy machine down and make paper clips out of it," you can't really respond to the content of the message. Instead, you need to respond to the anger or disgust the colleague feels about the machine. You need to be sensitive to the total meaning of the message (Rogers & Farson, 1992).

Offer Feedback (Respond)   Your movements and facial expressions, as well as questions or vocal comments, let the speaker know how you are responding. There are a number of ways a listener can provide feedback—both positive and negative. A good listener responds in ways that signal acceptance and positive regard (Yukl, 1994). Good feedback should be immediate, honest, and supportive. Sources of feedback include (Hanna, 1995):

- *Eye contact.* Have you ever tried to carry on a conversation with someone who doesn't look at you? Or who makes eye contact with the top of your head, your left ear, your feet, but never your eyes? This doesn't mean you have to look the speaker squarely in the eye the entire time she is talking. Eye contact is almost never a direct meeting of the eyes. If you focus anywhere on the speaker's face, you'll achieve the positive effects of good eye contact. As a rule of thumb, look at the speaker's face about 75 percent of the time, in glances lasting from one to seven seconds. (A speaker will look at a listener for less than half that time, and in glances that last no more than a second or two.)

- *Facial expression.* Save the poker face for card games—good listeners let their faces register their responses: they smile, frown, express bewilderment, show surprise.

- *Head movements.* An affirmative nod of the head signals not only understanding, but agreement. Even a negative shake of the head sends a useful signal to the speaker.

- *Touching.* Sometimes, if your relationship with the speaker warrants it, a gentle touch on the arm can be reassuring and signal understanding. The arm is generally considered a non-vulnerable or neutral area, but avoid touching if it seems at all inappropriate. While touching can provide positive feedback, appropriateness is more important.

- *Verbal responses.* Even though you can't listen well when you are talking, some verbal responses can make listening more effective. Simple *words of affirmation* or encouragement ("I see," "That's interesting," "Go on") tell the speaker you continue to be attentive. *Questions* that encourage the speaker to continue also provide good feedback ("How does that make you feel?" "What is it that seems to be frustrating you?"). *Paraphrasing,* or restating in your own words what you think the speaker has said, offers several benefits. It shows the speaker you received the message and it lets you test your understanding (Yukl, 1994). Some effective lead-ins to a paraphrase include: "Let me make sure I understand what you mean," "What I hear you saying is," and "In other words." Here is an example of paraphrasing:

> *Speaker:* "I can't get this assignment done by Monday. Don't teachers know that we take more than one class in a semester? I've got two other projects due next week, too."
> *Listener:* "It sounds like you have more work than you can manage."

Remember   The last stage of the listening process helps you build a storehouse of information you can use in a variety of ways, including future listening tasks. Store what you have heard for future reference. Good listeners may use several devices to help them remember key information—from something as simple as a person's name to a complex process introduced in a college lecture. *Repetition* helps anchor information. When someone tells you his name for the first time, make a point of repeating it or using it again in the conversation. *Mnemonics* (any artificial technique used as a memory aid) let you put information in a form that's easier for you to recognize. At some point in an elementary school geography class, for example, you probably used the acronym HOMES as a mnemonic device to remember the names of the Great Lakes (Huron, Ontario, Michigan, Erie, Superior).

Note-taking, while inappropriate in casual conversations, can be a powerful tool for increasing recall when used in connection with phone calls, briefings, interviews, classes, and business meetings. Notes provide a written record of key ideas. More importantly, some research shows that the act of writing notes is more helpful than the notes themselves—that is, by taking notes, we play a more active role in the listening process (Verderber & Verderber, 1995).

Barriers to Active Listening and How to Overcome Them

To become more active listeners, we need to acknowledge listening problems that could become barriers to good communication. Most problems are one of three types: environmental, physiological, or psychological. You will soon see, however, that most listening problems are psychological in nature.

Environmental Barriers   Many distractions that keep us from listening actively are physical, coming from outside us or from within. External noises (traffic, a radio playing in another room, other conversations) compete with the speaker for our attention. Not only do we have to listen over other sounds, we often have to repress other sensory stimuli that may interfere with our ability to listen attentively. It's harder to give your full attention to the act of listening if you're too hot or too cold, tired, hungry, sitting in an uncomfortable chair, wearing tight-fitting shoes, or suffering from a headache or upset stomach or other physical ailment.

To overcome environmental barriers, you need to do everything you can to minimize physical distractions when it is important for you to listen carefully. Turn off the TV or radio. Consciously screen out other noises you can't so easily control, or move to a quiet place. Get comfortable. Turn your back to visual distractions. Prepare to listen by directing your attention to the speaker. Adjust your physical posture to enable you to listen. Make eye contact.

Physiological Barriers   Another barrier to active listening is caused by the different rates at which we think and speak. A person is capable of thinking at a rate about five times faster than he or she can speak. While the average rate of speech is 125 to 150 words per minute, the brain can think at a rate between 500 and 1000 words per minute (Hanna, 1995). That difference can cause a listener's mind to wander, leading to daydreaming and unconscious self-talk. The speaker's message may have to compete with random, unrelated snippets of thought: "I like her shoes," "I need to remember to turn in that history paper before four o'clock," etc.

It's not easy to eliminate this physiological hurdle altogether, but you can try to reduce it. As you listen, try to keep pace with the speaker. Use your mental energy to think about what the speaker is saying and to analyze and interpret his or her words.

Paraphrase silently if you don't have an immediate opportunity to paraphrase aloud. Try to be aware of intrusive mental noise and block it out. If you find your mind shifting to an unrelated subject, deliberately bring it back to the message.

Mishearing also accounts for some errors in listening (Minninger, 1984). One obvious physiological barrier to active listening arises whenever a physical condition affects the organs of hearing. A cold, an ear infection, or other conditions that prevent the eardrum, ossicles, and cochlea from functioning normally will certainly interfere with your ability to simply hear sounds. At other times we may hear incorrectly because the speaker has used a word that is hard to interpret: homonyms (plain/plane, tied/tide) can cause confusion, as can words that mean more than one thing (bill, check, let). Another source of erroneous interpretation is the speaker's use of slang expressions or incorrect pronunciation (youse/use; grammar/grandma).

If you hear something that seems to make no sense or leads you to an apparently incongruous interpretation of the speaker's message, try to correct what may be a mishearing. (Could Eliza Doolittle possibly have meant the rain in Spain stays mainly in the *plane*? Probably not—she must have meant *plain*.)

Psychological Barriers   Almost everyone comes equipped with a set of psychological filters through which any spoken message must pass. Psychological factors that influence listening include "preconceived ideas, moods, assumptions, labels, stereotypes, past experiences, emotions, hopes, memories, and even degree of self-esteem" (Hanna, 1995, p. 185). We form fast impressions of both speaker and message, and our filters strongly influence those impressions. As a result, we may erect these psychological barriers to active listening: selective listening, negative listening attitudes, personal reactions to words, and poor motivation to listen well.

Selective listening. Selective listening is the process of choosing to hear only what we consider important and disregarding the rest. For example, if you go into your annual review with your supervisor, and, among other things, she tells you that some clients say they think your telephone manner is somewhat stiff and formal, your self-esteem filter may catch only that criticism and you won't hear your supervisor praise your record-keeping skills, your diligence, and your dependability. The only thing that sticks with you is the critical remark—psychological noise has made it impossible for you to hear the positive things that were said.

Be on your guard for selective listening. Practice listening for the whole message, not just those parts that get caught in your psychological filters.

Negative listening attitudes. Attitudes, too, shape our ability to listen. Negative listening attitudes interfere with reception of the entire message and lead to selective listening. In addition, those attitudes go hand in hand with behaviors that are counterproductive to good communication. Your attitude sends both verbal and nonverbal signals to the speaker; negative attitudes may make the speaker feel nervous, uncomfortable, and unappreciated. Your feedback clearly tells the speaker, "I'm bored," "I don't care about what you're saying," "I'm anxious to get out of here," "I

Psychological Barriers to Active Listening

- Selective Listening
- Negative Listening Attitudes
- Personal Reactions
- Poor Motivation

---

don't respect your views," or "My ideas are more valuable than yours." The speaker may decide to stop talking and the communication fails.

Hold your reactions and attitudes in check. If you begin to feel a negative listening attitude creep up on you, force yourself to practice behaviors of the positive opposite. For example, if you feel yourself growing bored, sit up straight, look at the speaker, and analyze what she is saying in terms of its relevance to you. Some people say that "attitude follows behavior"—if you *act* interested, you may soon find that you *are* interested.

Personal reactions to words. We respond to words at two levels of meaning: the denotative and the connotative. Denotative meanings are those literal meanings assigned to words to which we all subscribe. But connotative meanings develop when certain words are used in certain contexts and come to be associated with words beyond the denotative level (Verderber & Verderber, 1995; Osborn & Osborn, 1994). Everyone has a red flag filter that catches words that may cause strong reactions—like *liberal, feminist, income tax,* or *communist.* For example, if you hear a speaker use *girls* in reference to adult females, the rest of the message may get lost in your reaction to the connotation you associate with the term *girls* and the related assumptions you make about persons who would refer to women as *girls.*

A Plane Captain washes an F-14B "Tomcat" from VF-102 on the flight deck of USS George Washington (CVN-73).
Official U.S. Navy photo.

When a speaker uses a word that waves a red flag at you, look past it. Instead of giving in to the emotional deafness such a word is likely to inspire, focus on the entire message and try to see where the word fits in the overall context.

In other cases, connotative meanings may smudge the message with inadvertent humor or ambiguity. Consider this situation: When Marge visited California for the first time several years ago, she rolled up the legs of her jeans and waded into the Pacific Ocean. Unfortunately, she didn't roll them up far enough, and one of the waves she hadn't anticipated doused her to mid-thigh. She called her children that evening to describe her experience and told them, "I wet my pants in the Pacific Ocean." They laughed because the connotation of the phrase "wet my pants" was stronger than the literal meaning Marge had intended.

We also need to beware of chance associations a speaker's words may trigger in us as we listen. The speaker may be telling you about a problem she is trying to resolve with the instructor of her art history class, but the word *art* makes you think of painting and painting makes you think about the garage you are building but haven't been able to finish because it has been too rainy to paint it, and suddenly you are focusing not on your friend's problem, but your own. The message has fallen by the wayside along the path of your free association.

It's important to focus on the denotative meanings of words. Use nonverbal cues to help you determine what the speaker meant. If the connotation was unintended, let it go. If other cues tell you the connotative mix-up was intended, enjoy the resultant humor. If a speaker's word triggers an unrelated association, you may need to make a conscious effort to suppress it. Just attend to the speaker's words extra carefully and intently for a couple of minutes to force the intrusive association away.

Poor motivation. Another psychological impediment to active listening is lack of preparation. You can listen most actively if you know your listening goals. Without goals, you have no point on which to focus, and, consequently, no motivation to stay attuned to the speaker's message. So, while the other person is speaking, you may be thinking your own thoughts or preparing your rebuttal, without giving the speaker's ideas the attention they deserve.

To deal with motivational problems, you must clearly define your reasons for listening. The ladder shown in the box suggests the increasing level of complexity of listening goals. The higher the goal on the ladder, the more intense your listening needs to be. When you know what your goal is, you can identify and practice listening behaviors that will help you achieve your objective.

To Be a Good Listener

Good listening behaviors can be learned, but like any skill, they require practice to be perfected. Here are ten guidelines for good listening that you can practice right away (Sayre, 1989). They work in any listening situation and can lead to more sophisticated and refined listening habits.

1. Stop talking. Listen quietly until the speaker's message is complete.
2. Avoid, reduce, or eliminate distractions.
3. Expend the energy needed to give the speaker the benefit of your attention.
4. Use pauses to reflect on what the speaker is saying.
5. Identify the speaker's main ideas and central themes.
6. Judge the content of the message, not the speaker's delivery style.
7. Use paraphrasing, note-taking, and questions when appropriate to ensure understanding.
8. Interpret loaded emotional words appropriately; don't overreact.
9. Give useful feedback.
10. Listen between the lines and beyond the words: Listen for the speaker's feelings as well as facts.

Listening Goals Ladder

Response/Action

Analysis

Retention

Understanding

Enjoyment

Introduction to Nonverbal Communication

Although we may assume that the words we speak carry significant weight when we communicate with someone else, the fact is the true nature of our communication with other people has little to do with words. We depend instead on a language without words referred to collectively as nonverbal communication.

Various experts in communication estimate that between 75 percent and 90 percent of the information we gather from others is nonverbal in nature. In some cases nonverbal communication is used to either affirm or contradict a verbal message. At other times the nonverbal channel carries the primary message. Audience members listening to a public speaker, for example, communicate their responses, attitudes, and questions almost exclusively through nonverbal signals, without saying a single word. Active listeners look at the speaker and respond honestly with smiles, nods or other forms of body language, which can improve the quality of communication and keep the dynamic circle intact (Osborn & Osborn, 1994).

It is important to remember that we send nonverbal signals all the time, whether we are listening or speaking. The most profound impact of nonverbal communication is the degree to which it reinforces or contradicts other communication channels. The presidential debate between Richard Nixon and John Kennedy in 1960—the first ever televised—is often cited as an example of how nonverbal channels can be more powerful than the verbal message.

After the debate there was considerable disagreement as to which candidate won the contest. Television viewers generally believed that Kennedy had carried the day, while those who listened to the debate on the radio felt Nixon had prevailed. The difference in the perceptions of these groups had to do with the nonverbal messages that were visually apparent on television, but not discernible on radio. Nixon's nonverbal signals made him appear ill at ease and nervous. His stance was closed, his shoulders slightly turned away from the camera. He was a man with heavy facial hair and his five o'clock shadow was not well concealed by his stage makeup, making him look a little "shady." Kennedy, on the other hand, looked relaxed and vibrant. He used open gestures and faced the camera directly. His hands were often open as if ready to embrace. He was clean-cut and he smiled.

The difference in appearances strongly influenced the television viewers, to the point that their impression of the event was significantly different from the impression of radio listeners. Television viewers felt more comfortable with Kennedy because the nonverbal portions of his presentation were complementary to his verbal message. Nixon was the favorite going in to the debate, but Kennedy was in the White House soon afterward.

What are you communicating to others through the signals you send by your movements and gestures? How do you interpret or read the same nonverbal cues from others? Are you communicating honesty, competence, and positive assurance? Are your nonverbal messages consistent with the message contained in the words you say?

Channels of Nonverbal Communication

Nonverbal communication channels play incredibly important roles in communication. The way these channels affect and influence the communication process may vary from culture to culture, but in virtually every situation they carry a significant portion of the communication load, and in many cases the message is dominated by nonverbal symbols. Nonverbal communication channels can include, but are not limited to:

- physical appearance.
- facial expressions.
- eye contact.
- body language (including gestures, posture, and body orientation).
- proxemics (relating to the distance between two communicators) (Marsh, 1988).

Appearance   Appearance is an important channel of nonverbal communication. Most of us, whether we admit it or not, do pick up signals from a person's physical appearance. Within the first two minutes of seeing someone, we make some kind of judgment about them, and appearance is the largest single factor guiding that judgment. Overall appearance is one nonverbal channel over which we have considerable conscious control and it tells others a good deal about how we feel and how we wish to be viewed.

We respond differently, for example, to a young man with neatly combed hair dressed in a business suit and wire-rimmed glasses than we do to the same young man with day-glo orange and green spiked hair, wearing cut-off jeans, tank top, and chrome-plated sunglasses. Our responses are governed by our expectations and the communication context. In a job interview situation, we would respond more positively to the appearance of the young man in a business suit; but at a rock concert we might consider the same young man (dressed in professional attire) extremely out of place. The choices you make about your appearance clearly signal your attitudes and expectations about the communication context you have entered. Personal grooming (cleanliness, hairstyle, use of makeup) also conveys unspoken information to complement verbal messages.

Facial Expressions   Our language is full of expressions reflecting the powerful influence of facial signals. When we say that someone is shifty-eyed, is tight-lipped, has a furrowed brow, flashes bedroom eyes, stares into space, or grins like a Cheshire cat, we are speaking in a kind of shorthand and using a set of stereotypes that enables us to make judgments—consciously or unconsciously—about a person's abilities and qualities. Those judgments may not be accurate, but they are usually difficult to reverse.

It is possible to read emotion and attitude from people's faces. Smiles and frowns are often spontaneous expressions of happiness and anger. Yet we use smiles and frowns for other purposes—to greet someone or to show doubt. Using facial expressions this way does not necessarily mean we have strong feelings, but that we are simply following conventional rules for using the face as a vehicle for expressions.

Researchers have demonstrated that certain clearly distinguishable facial expressions communicate the same emotions in every human culture studied. The six basic emotions (happiness, sadness, anger, surprise, fear, and disgust) are expressed and recognized in pretty much the same way in all parts of the world, using three independently expressive regions of the face—eyebrows, eyes, and lower face (Marsh, 1988).

EMOTION	BROWS	EYES	LOWER FACE
Happiness		Wrinkles around the eyes	Smiling mouth
Sadness	Raised	Lowered upper eyelids	Down-turned mouth
Anger	Lowered or drawn together	Penetrating stare or tensed eyelids	Lips pressed together or opened and pushed forward
Surprise	Raised	Open wide	Dropped jaw, open mouth
Fear	Raised and drawn together	Open and tense, lower lid raised	Mouth open, lips drawn back tightly
Disgust	Lowered	Lower eyelid pushed up	Wrinkled nose, raised upper lip

Humans are capable of blending facial expressions, which explains why it is sometimes difficult to say what emotion someone's face may reveal. For instance, there may be anger or fear in the brows but a smile on the lips. We may be aware of the mixture of feelings we see on the face, but unable to see immediately what the feelings truly are.

The ability to control facial muscles voluntarily means that some people can display as much or as little emotion as they wish. It takes considerable effort to suppress spontaneous facial expressions, and those who can do so have learned the skill because they were taught self-control. Voluntary control of the face allows us to suppress emotional displays and to mask negative feelings with imitations of happiness. It also allows for many other social uses of the face.

The nonverbal signals sent by facial expressions are a constant source of information in a conversation. Many expressions used in conversation are not emotional. For instance, raising the eyebrows may not signal surprise, but instead serves as a question mark or a sign of emphasis. Listeners, too, nod and smile, frown in puzzlement, or widen eyes and raise eyebrows to encourage speakers and show they have understood and are impressed or dismayed at what they heard. People also may yawn deliberately as a signal that they do not want the speaker to go on.

Eye Contact   The eyes are the most important feature of facial expressiveness. Looking at the eyes of another person is such a powerful act of communication that we must control it carefully. We rarely maintain long stretches of eye contact (unless we are gazing lovingly at someone close or fixing someone we dislike with a hostile stare). Instead, we restrict eye contact to brief glances and it is the nature of these glances that determines the impression we make on others. When people are forced into close physical contact, as in subways and elevators, eye contact decreases considerably.

Eye contact helps us know when it is our turn to speak in conversation (through a characteristic pattern of looking, making eye contact, and looking away). Listeners use more eye contact than speakers, looking at the other person's face for three-fourths of the time in glances lasting from one to seven seconds. Speakers look at their listeners for less than half the time and maintain eye contact through intermittent glances that last no more than a second each (Marsh, 1988). We generally maintain eye contact better when we are talking about topics with which we are comfortable and with people in whose ideas we are genuinely interested. Conversely, we avoid eye contact when discussing topics that make us uncomfortable or when we have little interest in the person to whom we are talking.

It should be noted, too, that eye contact behavior differs between sexes and among cultures. Women hold eye contact longer than do men, regardless of the sex of the person with whom they are interacting. Amount of eye contact varies from culture to culture, too, with the highest levels shown in Arab and Latin American cultures and lowest in Indian and northern European cultures (Verderber & Verderber, 1995). In American culture, frequent and sustained eye contact suggests honesty, openness, and respect. People who use eye contact are viewed as confident, credible, and having nothing to hide.

If eyes are windows into the self, then lack of eye contact is like drawing the shades on the windows of communication. It suggests you don't care about the person you are talking to, or that you're afraid of them, or that you're trying to put something over on them. Little eye contact can communicate a desire to hide something (Osborn & Osborn, 1994). In fact, studies have shown quite clearly that when people are required to lie, or have been encouraged to cheat, their deception is accompanied by an averted gaze (Marsh, 1988). Some people, however, have learned to hide their emotions to manipulate others. They are practiced at lying while maintaining eye contact. So the mere fact that someone looks you in the eye is not an unquestioned indicator of honesty or trustworthiness. (Likewise, failure to look you in the eye isn't necessarily a sign of dishonesty, either.)

Body Language Our bodies say a lot about us in many ways as we communicate. Studies have demonstrated the significance of body language to the communication of attitudes. Words are a minor contributor (only about 10%) to one's perception of attitudes. Vocal qualities reveal much more (30%) of what we think and feel. But body language (a combination of gestures, posture, facial expressions, patterns of eye contact, and touch) conveys attitudes more readily (60%) than words and vocal qualities combined (Covey, 1989).

Body language is often called *kinesic code*, a package of behaviors that are classified as emblems, illustrators, regulators, affect displays, and adaptors. They may be displayed through movement of the head, the arms and hands, the torso, or the legs and feet, and serve important communication functions.

Types of Body Movements
Posture. The first important kinesic behavior is posture, which involves positioning and movement of the body. Posture communicates interest, respect, and openness to ideas, and it can change from moment to moment in a social encounter. Changes in posture can send nonverbal messages. For example, if someone stands up suddenly, that movement may signal "I'm done now," while turning one's back says, "I'm no longer interested."

The most common messages conveyed by posture indicate levels of interest or agreement. When we disagree with what is being said, we use closed postures: holding trunk and head straight and folding the arms, or, if sitting, crossing the legs above the knee. A more neutral posture is conveyed by hands folded in the lap and legs crossed at the knee. When we agree, we are more likely to have open postures: leaning head and trunk to one side and leaving the legs uncrossed.

An interested listener typically leans forward (if seated, he or she also will draw his or her legs back). When interest fades, the head begins to turn while the trunk and legs straighten. When a listener is bored, the head may begin to lean and require

Common Postural Cues and Their Interpretation

Slumped posture	Low spirits
Erect posture	High spirits, energy, and confidence
Lean forward	Open and interested
Lean away	Defensive or disinterested
Crossed arms	Defensive
Uncrossed arms	Willingness to listen

support from a hand. Complete boredom is signaled by letting the head drop and leaning the body backward with legs outstretched.

Transition from one body position to another carries the most significant meaning. If a person spends the entire conversation leaning forward, that may be just a matter of comfort. But if the same person starts out leaning back and then gradually leans forward as the conversation progresses, that's nonverbal communication.

Most people can more easily read postural cues than they can consciously produce them. Being aware of them can help overcome the gap between reactions you *want* to communicate and those you *can* communicate on the occasions you need them (as in a job interview, for example, or trying to give encouragement to a respected but boring speaker).

Hand Gestures. Gestures, or movements of hands, arms, and fingers, are used to describe or emphasize. One type of hand movement, called the baton gesture, actually beats time to what you or someone else is saying. Baton gestures put emphasis on what is being said, add punctuation to verbal communication, and remove ambiguities. Some people use gestures, or talk with their hands, much more freely than others, but speech and gesture are closely bound together for almost everyone. One way to see the strong connection between the two is to watch someone speaking on the telephone. Even though the person on the other end of the line cannot see body movements and gestures, it is almost impossible to talk without them (Marsh, 1988).

Some gestures, however, can be an obstacle to successful interaction. Watch out for hands and fingers that take on a life of their own, fidgeting with themselves or other objects such as pens, paper, or your hair. Pen tapping is interpreted as the action of an impatient person. Rubbing the palms together or clasping hands are signs of nervousness or anxiety.

Body Gestures. Nonverbal signals communicated by moving your body are called body gestures. We may move the entire body to change the mood or pace of a conversation, to draw attention, or to reinforce an idea. Here are some examples of body gestures:

Rapidly nodding your head can leave the impression that you are impatient and eager to add something to the conversation. Slower nodding emphasizes interest, shows that you are validating the comments of your conversation partner, and subtly encourages him or her to continue. Tilting the head slightly, when combined with eye contact and a natural smile, demonstrates friendliness and approachability.

Smiling is one of the most powerful positive body signals in your arsenal. Offer an unforced, confident smile as frequently as opportunity and circumstances dictate. But avoid grinning idiotically; this will only communicate that you are either insincere or not quite on the right track.

It's worth noting that the mouth provides a seemingly limitless supply of opportunities to convey weakness. This may be done by touching the mouth frequently and unconsciously; faking a cough when confused with a difficult question; or gnawing on the lips absentmindedly. Employing any of these insincerity signs will confirm or instill suspicions about your honesty and effectiveness.

Some foot signals can have negative connotations. Women and men wearing slip-on shoes should beware of dangling the loose shoe from the toes; this can be quite distracting and, as it is a gesture often used to signal physical attraction, has no place in most communication situations. Likewise, avoid compulsive jabbing of the floor, desk, or chair with your foot; this can be perceived as a hostile and angry motion, and is likely to annoy your conversation partner. Rapid tapping of the foot may signal impatience.

Uses of Body Language   Although movements of the body may seem random and not clearly connected to a verbal message, they do serve important communication functions that can be classified as emblems, illustrators, affect displays, regulators, and adaptors (Verderber & Verderber, 1994).

Emblems are body motions that supplement or replace words. Some emblems we know and use daily; others we may not use ourselves but can recognize if others use them; still others require us to discover their meaning. For example, almost all Americans use a nod of the head to signify "yes," or a shrug of the shoulders to signify "I don't care." Some people recognize or understand certain obscene gestures but wouldn't use them themselves. Finally, we may encounter emblems we don't understand because they are gestures that have meaning only for members of a specific group.

Illustrators are movements or gestures that accent or emphasize what is being said. We may emphasize by pounding the table to make a point. We may show the path or direction of thought by moving our hands from one point to another to show the range of ideas we are discussing, We may indicate position by pointing. We may describe by using hands to imitate shape or size ("The fish that got away was this big."). We may use gesture to mimic (waving as we say, "Did you see how she waved at me?").

Affect Displays are movements (usually facial expressions or body responses) that display the nature of a pronounced physical sensation. For instance, when you stub your toe, you not only say "Ouch!," you also make a face that displays the pain you feel. Affect displays are generally unconscious and will take place whether you are with someone else or alone.

Different people have adapted different patterns of affect display (just as some people have mastered control of facial expressions). They may be able to deintensify the display (attempt to look less afraid, less happy, less hurt than they actually are); over-intensify or amplify the display; take neutral positions (or display a poker face—that is, whether they are experiencing joy, fear, or sadness, their displays tend not to vary); and mask displays by showing a reaction that is the opposite of what would be expected (smiling, for example, when one is hurt).

Regulators are nonverbal communication cues that regulate the flow of conversation. They include such movements as shifting eye contact, changes in posture, raised eyebrows, and slight head motions. (Try holding your hand up in a stop gesture the next time someone starts to interrupt you and you'll easily see the regulating effect of body language.) Some nonverbal cues serve more than one function. For example, nodding the head can be an emblem for "yes," but also can be a regulator that means "go on, continue."

Most people are aware of regulators only on the periphery of consciousness—unless they become exaggerated to the point of rudeness. Someone who puts on a coat, picks up things, and heads toward the door is regulating the conversation, but

Naval Academy photo courtesy of United States Naval Academy Photographic Laboratory.

in a fairly noticeable and emphatic way. Usually regulators are not so obvious; we do not know we are using them and don't necessarily notice when others do so.

Adaptors are nonverbal efforts to satisfy personal needs that arise as people relate to each other. They are difficult to define because they change from person to person and situation to situation. We employ adaptors based on previous experience with someone, by changing body posture, gestures, facial expression, and amount of eye contact to suit our perception of the other's degree of comfort. Some researchers believe that we are attracted or repelled by others based on their adaptive behaviors.

Proxemics   Proxemics is the study of informal space—the amount of space around or between us and others. How closely people position themselves to each other during a discussion communicates the type of relationship that exists between the two people. This space and meaning differ from culture to culture, but in American culture the following standards generally apply:

DISTANCE	TYPE OF SPACE	USES
0–18 inches	intimate space	interactions with family and close friends
18 inches to 4 feet	personal space	most interpersonal interactions
4–12 feet	social-consultative space	more formal interactions
more than 12 feet	public space	large audience interactions

Intimate distance is the one that should be of greatest concern. People become uncomfortable if an outsider violates the 18-inch circle reserved for family or intimate friends.

A number of factors influence the way people use space, as well as the ways they defend it. Here are some examples of the effect of power, gender, and culture on space:

- In almost all cultures, high-status people are given more space than low-status people.
- Aggressive people tend to take up—and are granted—more space than less dominant people.
- Men generally occupy more personal space than women.
- A woman's intimate space tends to be violated more frequently than a man's.
- Extroverts take up more space than introverts.

As these examples suggest, not only do more powerful people take up more space and freely invade the intimate space of others, but less powerful people actually yield space to them. You can give an impression of personal power if you simply occupy more space than someone else when you sit or stand and if you do not move out of the way or allow someone else to enter your personal space. You also are more likely to sit or stand closer to someone you feel positive about (Elsea, 1984).

Touching, too, can be a very powerful communicator, especially for establishing a link to a receiver or conveying emotion. A strong handshake may acknowledge equality, while a limp handshake may signal lack of interest or timidity. One of the dangers of communicating via touch, however, is the fact that it invades a person's intimate space and may be perceived as an unwanted intrusion. Because power, gender, and status play such significant roles in the use and perception of tactile communication, it is important to pay attention to the other person's nonverbal cues before deciding to initiate a touch. In most cases, it is best to limit tactile communication to a firm handshake when meeting someone you have not met before or do not know well.

Using Nonverbal Communication to Your Advantage

Body language is more meaningful when several expressions take place at the same time. For example, the combination of leaning forward, nodding, and smiling is a strong indication of agreement and openness. Most meaningful is a matched set of gestures that also agree with what the person is saying.

The main problem with interpreting nonverbal language, however, is that it is dangerous to draw conclusions from single actions. For example, crossed arms are said to indicate distance or defensiveness, but they could also mean that the person is chilly or just striking a comfortable pose. Interpreting an isolated action is a little like taking a word or sentence out of context; it changes the meaning. In order to read body language accurately, it is necessary to consider all of the evidence: eye contact, body positioning, facial expression, and appearance.

Here are some things to keep in mind as you pay greater attention to nonverbal signals—both those you receive from others and those you convey yourself. Also see the chapters on active listening and cross-cultural communication for more information on how to monitor and interpret nonverbal communication behaviors.

1. Become aware. Pay attention to what others communicate nonverbally. Examine what you convey with your own facial expressions, posture, and gestures. Note when someone misinterprets what you have said and look for ways in which nonverbal communication might have affected your message (Carter & Kravitz, 1996).

2. Don't contradict your words with body language. Watch out for saying things with your body that run counter to what you speak. The mixed message can confuse your listener and may make you appear to be dishonest (Carter & Kravitz, 1996).

3. Know what your face says. Facial expression may be the most controllable nonverbal cue, but it is also the one others use to gauge your attitude, feelings and emotional state. You may be able to fool yourself into feeling better than you do simply by smiling (Elsea, 1984).

4. Smiling and head nodding are the most powerful nonverbal cues in social attraction. A blank expression ranks lowest in terms of attractiveness, power, and credibility.

5. Direct eye contact is more powerful than averting the eyes. If you're uncomfortable about making direct eye contact, look at the other person's forehead or hairline.

6. Gesture with purpose.

7. Establish your intimate space and deal assertively with those who violate it.

8. Touch appropriately and deal assertively with those who touch you inappropriately.

9. Note cultural differences. Certain aspects of body language are interpreted differently from culture to culture. In some cultures, casual acquaintances stand very close to each other when speaking; in others only intimate, personal relationships would allow such closeness. American culture encourages eye contact as a sign of honesty and openness; other cultures may interpret too much eye contact as a sign of dominance or disrespect. Let the context of the conversation help you determine what type and degree of body language is appropriate. Take your cues from the person you are talking to (Carter & Kravitz, 1996).

10. Occasionally monitor your nonverbal cues. Look at yourself in a mirror, on videotape, or in photographs to examine your body language. Or ask a close friend to give you feedback about the nonverbal signals you send.

The Vocabulary of Body Language

This list provides you with some common body language terms and their generally accepted meanings:

Nonverbal Behavior	Interpretation
Brisk, erect walk	Confidence
Standing with hands on hips	Readiness, aggression
Sitting with legs crossed, foot kicking slightly	Boredom
Arms crossed on chest	Defensiveness
Walking with hands in pockets, shoulders hunched	Dejection
Hand to cheek	Evaluation, thinking
Touching, slightly rubbing nose	Rejection, doubt, lying
Rubbing the eye	Doubt, disbelief
Hands clasped behind back	Anger, frustration, apprehension
Locked ankles	Apprehension
Head resting in hand, eyes downcast	Boredom
Rubbing hands	Anticipation
Sitting with hands clasped behind head, legs crossed	Confidence, superiority
Open palm	Sincerity, openness, innocence
Pinching bridge of nose, eyes closed	Negative evaluation
Tapping or drumming fingers	Impatience
Steepling fingers	Authoritative
Patting or fondling hair	Lack of self-confidence; insecurity
Tilted head, lean forward	Interest
Stroking chin	Trying to make a decision
Looking down, face turned away	Disbelief
Biting nails	Insecurity, nervousness
Pulling or tugging at ear	Indecision

(Seitz, 1996)

27 *Getting Things Done—Negotiating and Winning Support*

Objectives

1. Describe the major components of persuasive communication and give examples of how you might use this information to heighten your effectiveness.

2. Define cognitive dissonance and describe how it could be used to change the attitudes and behavior of those you lead. Identify situations you may encounter as a midshipman that could lead to cognitive dissonance.

⊡ Attitudes and Attitude Change

People often change their behavior in response to social pressure from a group or figure of authority. These changes, however, are typically limited to one act in one situation at a fleeting moment in time. For the effects to endure, it is better to change attitudes, not just behavior. An **attitude** is a positive or negative reaction toward any person, object, or idea. People hold quite passionate attitudes about a whole range of issues—from abortion and political correctness to whether they prefer using a PC or a Mac. Thus, whether the goal is to win votes on election day, get consumers to buy a product, raise funds for a worthy cause, or combat sexual harassment in the military, attitude change is the key to a deeper, more lasting form of social influence (Eagly & Chaiken, 1993; Petty et al., 1997).

Persuasive Communications   Persuasion, the process of changing attitudes, is a part of everyday life. The most common approach is to make a persuasive communication. Appeals made in person and through the mass media rely on the spoken word, the written word, and the picture that is worth a thousand words. What determines whether an appeal succeeds or fails? To understand why some approaches work and others do not, we need a road map of the persuasion process.

It's a familiar scene in American politics: Every four years, presidential candidates launch extensive campaigns for office. In a way, if you've seen one election, you've seen them all. The names and dates may change, but over and over again opposing candidates accuse each other of ducking the issues and turning the election into a popularity contest. Whether or not the accusations are true, they illustrate that politicians are keenly aware that votes can be won through two very different methods. They can stick to the issues, or they can base their appeal on other grounds.

To account for these varying approaches, Richard Petty and John Cacioppo (1986) proposed a two-track model of persuasion. When people have the ability and motivation to think critically about the contents of a message, they take the **central route to persuasion.** In these instances, people are influenced by the strength and quality of the arguments. When people do not have the ability or motivation to pay close attention to the issues, however, they take mental shortcuts along the **peripheral route to persuasion.** In this case, people may be influenced by a speaker's appearance, slogans, one-liners, emotions, audience reactions, and other superficial cues. This two-track model of persuasion—and others like it (Chaiken et al., 1989)—help to explain how voters, consumers, juries, and other targets of persuasion can seem so logical on some occasions, yet so illogical on others.

To understand the conditions that produce change on one route or the other, it's helpful to view persuasion as the outcome of three factors: a *source* (who), a *message* (says what, and how), and an *audience* (to whom). If a speaker is clear, if the message is relevant and important, if there is a bright and captive audience that cares deeply about the issues, then that audience will take the effortful central route. But if the

attitude A positive or negative reaction to any person, object, or idea.

central route to persuasion A process in which people think carefully about a message and are influenced by its arguments.

peripheral route to persuasion A process in which people do not think carefully about a message and are influenced by superficial cues.

source speaks too fast to comprehend, if the message is trivial, or if the audience is distracted, pressed for time, or uninterested, then the less strenuous peripheral route is taken. Particularly important is whether the target audience is personally involved in the issue under consideration. High involvement leads us to take the central route; low involvement, the peripheral route (Johnson & Eagly, 1989; Petty & Cacioppo, 1990). This model is illustrated in Figure 27.1.

The Source   The communicator, or source of a message, is the first important consideration in changing attitudes. What makes some communicators more persuasive than others? There are two key characteristics: credibility and likability. To have credibility, a communicator must be perceived as both an *expert* and as one who can be *trusted* to tell the truth. Doctors, scientists, film critics, and other experts can have a disarming effect on us. To engender trust, however, they must also be seen as willing to state a position honestly and without compromise. If a source has been bought and paid for, has an ax to grind, or has something else to gain, then he or she will lose credibility. Using both expertise and trustworthiness to create high- and low-credibility sources, Shelly Chaiken and Durairaj Maheswaran (1994) thus found that subjects were more impressed by, and willing to purchase, a consumer product (a telephone answering machine) when they read a favorable review attributed to *Consumer Reports* rather than to a K-mart promotional pamphlet.

A second important characteristic is likability. As Dale Carnegie (1936) implied in the title of his classic, *How to Win Friends and Influence People,* being well liked and being persuasive go hand in hand. Thus, the speaker who is similar to us or is physically appealing has a unique advantage. In one study, Diane Mackie and others (1990) found that college students were more influenced by a speech on the SATs when the speaker was said to be from their own university than from another school. In another study, Chaiken (1979) had male and female assistants try to get students on campus to sign a petition and found that the more attractive the assistants were, the more signatures they were able to collect. It's no wonder that advertisers spend millions of dollars a year on celebrity endorsements from Cindy Crawford, Michael Jordan, Jerry Seinfeld, Tiger Woods, and other popular stars.

The Message   Does the source hold the key to success? Are we so impressed by experts and so drawn to beautiful models that we uncritically embrace whatever they have to say? In light of what we know about the central and peripheral routes to persuasion, the answer is that it depends. When the target audience has a low level of involvement, superficial source characteristics make a difference. Under high

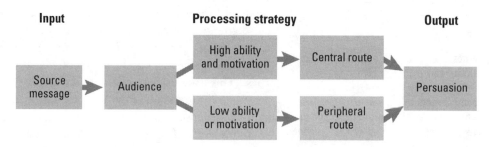

FIGURE 27.1 Two routes to persuasion   Based on aspects of the source, message, and audience, people take either a "central" or a "peripheral" route to persuasion. On the central route, we are influenced by strong arguments and evidence. On the peripheral route, we are influenced more by superficial cues.

involvement, however, a lack of substance cannot so easily be masked by style (Petty et al., 1997). So how can a message be constructed for maximum impact? Should it be crammed with facts or short and to the point? What about using one-sided versus two-sided arguments, and visual versus auditory media? Despite many years of research, there are no specific formulas—but there are answers. To illustrate, let us consider two strategic questions that confront all communicators.

Before making an appeal, the astute communicator knows that audience members are not blank slates but human beings endowed with preexisting attitudes and values. Knowing this, how discrepant a position should one advocate from that of an audience? Is it better to stake out an extreme position in the hope of stimulating the most change (as Newt Gingrich often does) or to preach moderation in order to avoid being rejected outright (as Bill Clinton tends to do)? There are two answers to this question. First, it's vital to ensure that one's arguments are based on premises that are at least acceptable to an audience (Holtgraves & Bailey, 1991). Second, communicators should argue for positions that are only moderately discrepant from that of the audience. Generally, the more discrepant the message, the greater the change. But there's a breaking point, beyond which too much discrepancy produces less change (Siero & Doosje, 1993).

A second common question concerns the arousal of emotion. Is it better to recite only facts and rational arguments or to stir up primitive emotions? This issue is often raised in discussions of the persuasive effects of fear, a common device. Magazine ads for condoms often use fear appeals—the most extreme being "I enjoy sex but I don't want to die for it" (Struckman-Johnson et al., 1990). Similarly blunt ads tell us that smoking "is a matter of life and breath" and that "this [a fried egg] is your brain on drugs." So does fear persuade? If so, is it better to arouse just a little nervousness or a full-blown anxiety attack? Over the years, researchers have measured the amount of attitude change produced by messages varying in fearfulness. Their results suggest that high-fear messages produce more change than low-fear messages—but only when they provide reassurance and instructions on how to avoid the threatened danger (Gleicher & Petty, 1992; Leventhal, 1970). Without guidance on how to cope, people panic and tune out. But when clear instructions are given, fear arousal is effective. Antismoking films thus work better when they show gory scenes of lung-cancer patients rather than charts filled with dry statistics. Similarly, driving-safety films have more impact when they show bloody human victims instead of controlled collisions involving crash dummies (Rogers, 1983).

It's interesting that just as fear sparks change, so does positive emotion. Food, drinks, a soft reclining chair, tender memories, pleasant music, and a breathtaking view can all lull us into a positive emotional state—ripe for persuasion. Why? One reason is that when people are in a good mood, they want to savor the moment, so they get mentally lazy and uncritically accepting of persuasive arguments (Isen, 1987). A second reason is that a good mood can be distracting, causing the mind to wander and making it more difficult to scrutinize a persuasive message (Mackie & Worth, 1989). Weakened in the motivation and the ability for critical thinking, people are easier to persuade when they're in a positive emotional state (Schwarz et al., 1991).

The Audience Source and message factors are important, but no persuasion strategy is complete without a consideration of the audience. Presentations that work on some people may fail with others. Are some individuals easier to persuade than others? No, not as a general rule. But people are responsive to different types of messages. For example, some people are more likely than others to take the central route to persuasion—and, therefore, to be focused on content. According to Cacioppo and Petty (1982), individuals differ in terms of how much they enjoy and engage in effortful cognitive activities or, as they call it, the *need for cognition*. Research shows that people with a high need for cognition are influenced by strong informational messages, while those who are low in the need for cognition are swayed more by a speaker's reputation, the applause of an audience, and other peripheral cues (Cacioppo et al., 1996).

According to Mark Snyder (1987), people who are highly concerned about their public image exhibit *self-monitoring*: a tendency to modify their behavior from one social situation to the next. As measured by the Self-Monitoring Scale, high self-monitors tend to say that "in different situations and with different people, I often act like different persons." As targets of influence, high self-monitors are thus drawn to messages that promise a desirable social image. In one study, subjects read information-oriented or image-oriented magazine advertisements. As predicted, high self-monitors were willing to pay more for products that were presented in image-oriented than in informational ads. To be persuasive, a message should meet the psychological needs of its audience (Snyder & DeBono, 1985).

Self-Persuasion   Anyone who has ever acted on stage knows how easy it is to become so absorbed in a role that the experience seems real. Forced laughter can make an actor feel happy, and fake tears can turn to sadness. Even in real life, the effect can be dramatic. In 1974, Patty Hearst—a sheltered young college student from a wealthy family—was kidnapped by a revolutionary group. By the time she was arrested months later, she was carrying a gun and calling herself Tania. How could someone be so totally converted? In Hearst's own words, "I had thought I was humoring [my captors] by parroting their clichés and buzzwords without believing in them. . . . In trying to convince them I convinced myself."

The Patty Hearst case reveals the powerful effects of role playing. You don't have to be terrorized to be coaxed into doing something that contradicts your inner convictions. People often engage in attitude-discrepant behavior—as part of a job, for example, or to please others. This raises a profound question: What happens when people behave in ways that do not follow from their attitudes? We know that attitudes influence behavior. But can the causal arrow be reversed? That is, can a forced change in behavior spark a change in attitude?

cognitive dissonance An unpleasant psychological state often aroused when people behave in ways that are discrepant with their attitudes.

Cognitive Dissonance Theory   The answer to this question was provided by Leon Festinger's (1957) **cognitive dissonance** theory. According to Festinger, we hold many cognitions about ourselves and the world around us—and sometimes these cognitions clash. For example, you say you're on a diet, and yet you just dove head-first into a chocolate mousse. Or you waited in line for hours to get into a concert, but then the band was disappointing. Or you baked under the hot summer sun, even though you knew of the health risks. In each case, there is inconsistency and conflict. You committed yourself to a course of action, but you realize that your behavior contradicts your attitude.

According to Festinger, these kinds of discrepancies often produce an unpleasant state of tension that he called cognitive dissonance. Attitude-discrepant behavior doesn't always arouse dissonance. If you broke a diet for a holiday dinner or if you thought that the mousse you ate was low in calories, you would be relatively free of tension. Attitude-discrepant behavior that is performed *freely* and with *knowledge* of the consequences, however, does arouse dissonance—and the motivation to reduce it. There are different ways to cope with this unpleasant state. Often the easiest is to change your attitude so that it becomes consistent with your behavior.

To understand dissonance theory, imagine for a moment that you are a subject in the classic study by Leon Festinger and J. Merrill Carlsmith (1959). The experimenter tells you that he is interested in various measures of performance. He hands you a wooden board containing forty-eight pegs in square holes and asks you to turn each peg to the left, then to the right, then back to the left, and again to the right. The routine seems endless. After thirty minutes, the experimenter comes to your rescue. Or does he? Just when you think things are looking up, he hands you another board, another assignment. For the next half-hour, you are to take twelve spools of thread off the board, put them back on, take them off, and so on. By now, you're just about ready to tear your hair out. As you think back over better times, even the first task begins to look good.

Finally, you've finished. After one of the longest hours of your life, the experimenter lets you in on a secret: There's more to this study than meets the eye. You were in the control group. To test the effects of motivation on performance, the experimenter will tell other subjects that the experiment is fun. You don't realize it, but you're being set up for a critical part of the study. Would you tell the next subject that the experiment is enjoyable? As you hem and haw, the experimenter offers to pay for your lie. Some subjects, like you, are offered a dollar; others, twenty dollars. Before you know it, you're in the waiting room trying to dupe an unsuspecting fellow student.

By means of this staged presentation, subjects were goaded into an attitude-discrepant behavior, an act that contradicted their private attitudes. They knew the experiment was dull, but they raved. Was cognitive dissonance aroused? It depended on how much subjects were paid. Suppose you were one of the lucky ones offered twenty dollars. Even by today's standards, that amount provides sufficient justification for telling a little white lie. Being well compensated, these subjects did not feel dissonance. But wait. Suppose you were offered only one dollar. Surely your integrity is worth more than that, don't you think? In this case, you do not have sufficient justification for going along. So you cope by changing your view of the task. If you can convince yourself that the experiment was interesting, then there is no conflict.

When the experiment was presumably over, subjects were asked to rate the pegboard tasks. Control-group subjects, who did not mislead a confederate, admitted the tasks were boring. So did those in the twenty-dollar condition, who had ample justification for what they did. Those paid only one dollar, however, rated the tasks as more enjoyable. After engaging in an attitude-discrepant behavior without sufficient justification, these subjects felt internally pressured to change their attitudes in order to reduce cognitive dissonance (see Figure 27.2).

Cognitive dissonance theory makes another interesting prediction: that people will change their attitudes to justify effort, money spent, time, or suffering. In the first test of this hypothesis, Eliot Aronson and Judson Mills (1959) invited female students to join a discussion group about sex. To get into the group, subjects were told they would have to pass an "embarrassment test." One set of subjects underwent a severe test (they had to recite obscene words and lurid passages), a second set took a mild test (they read a list of mildly sexual words), and a third set was admitted without an initiation. Subjects then listened in on a dreadfully boring discussion. How much fun was this discussion group? As predicted, those who had to endure a severe initiation liked the group more than the others did. There are some interesting implications. Research shows, for example, that the harder psychotherapy patients work at their treatment, the better they say they feel later (Axsom, 1989). Cognitive

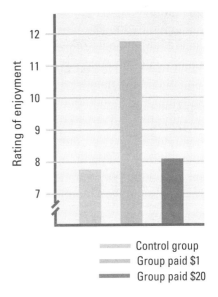

Control group
Group paid $1
Group paid $20

FIGURE 27.2 Festinger and Carlsmith's classic dissonance study How interesting is a boring task? Compared to subjects who did not have to lie and those paid $20 to do so, those paid only $1 later rated the task as more enjoyable. Having engaged in an attitude-discrepant behavior, these latter subjects reduced dissonance by changing their attitude.

Naval Academy photo courtesy of United States Naval Academy Photographic Laboratory.

dissonance theory may also explain why college fraternities and sororities foster such lifelong loyalties or why 58 percent of Vietnam veterans, compared to 29 percent of others, say that "the U.S. was right to get involved in the Vietnam war" (Witteman, 1990). Perhaps even today, those who had risked their lives need to justify the nightmare they experienced.

Alternative Routes to Self-Persuasion   Following Festinger, a generation of social psychologists has studied and refined the basic theory. Nobody disputes the fact that when people are coaxed into performing an attitude-discrepant behavior, they often go on to change their attitudes. In fact, people who have a high need for consistency are most likely to show the effect (Cialdini et al., 1995). But under what conditions, and why? According to Joel Cooper and Russell Fazio (1984), four conditions are necessary for change to occur: (1) The behavior has *negative consequences*; (2) the person feels *responsible* for these consequences; (3) the person becomes *physiologically aroused*, experiencing tension that needs to be reduced; and (4) the person *attributes* that arousal to his or her behavior.

The "why" question is still a matter of controversy. Some theorists argue that the attitude change is not fueled by a need to justify our actions but instead occurs as a rational process through which people draw conclusions about how they feel by observing their own behavior. In other words, subjects who lied about the boring task for a dollar reflected upon their actions and concluded that the task must have been interesting—or else why would they have said so (Bem, 1967)? Other theorists claim that the predominant motive is not to be consistent but to *appear* consistent, or favorable, to others. In this view, the subjects who lied simply did not want the experimenter to think they had sold out for a paltry sum of money (Tedeschi et al., 1971). Still others claim that the change in attitude is necessary for one's self-concept—that the subjects who lied had to view the task as fun in order to repair the damage done to their self-esteem (Steele, 1988; Thibodeau & Aronson, 1992).

28 *The Successful Military Leader*

Objectives

1. Describe the Rational Emotive Theory of emotional disturbance.

2. List the major irrational beliefs and cognitive errors.

3. Give examples of cognitive-behavioral strategies for managing your thoughts and emotions.

4. Define five qualities that, according to General Bradley, a leader adds to a situation.

The Nature of Psychological Disturbance and Health

Psychological disturbance

Irrational beliefs and their derivatives. Rational-emotive theory posits that at the heart of psychological disturbance, lies the tendency of humans to make devout, absolutist evaluations (i.e., irrational beliefs) of the inferred in their lives. As has been shown, these evaluations are couched in the form of dogmatic 'musts', 'shoulds', 'have to's', 'got to's', and 'oughts'. These absolutist cognitions represent a philosophy of religiosity which, according to rational-emotive theory, is the central feature of human emotional and behavioural disturbance (c.f. Ellis, 1983 a). As has been shown, these beliefs are deemed to be irrational in that they usually (but not invariably) impede and obstruct people in the pursuit of their basic goals and purposes. Absolute musts do not invariably lead to psychological disturbance because it is possible for a person to devoutly believe 'I must succeed at all important projects', have confidence that he or she will be successful in these respects, and actually succeed in them and thereby not experience psychological disturbance. However, the person remains vulnerable because there is always the possibility that he or she may fail in the future. So while on probabilistic grounds RET theory argues that an absolutist philosophy will frequently lead to psychological disturbance it does not claim that this is absolutely so. Thus, even with respect to its view of the nature of human disturbance rational-emotive theory adopts an anti-absolutist position.

Rational-emotive theory goes on to posit that if humans adhere to an absolutist and devout philosophy they will strongly tend to make a number of core irrational conclusions which are deemed to be derivatives of their 'musts'. These major derivatives are viewed as irrational because they too tend to sabotage a person's basic goals and purposes.

The first major derivative is known as *awfulizing*. This occurs when an inferred event is rated as being more than 100 per cent bad—a truly exaggerated and magical conclusion which stems from the belief: 'This must not be as bad as it is'.

The second major derivative is known as *I-can't-stand-it-itis*. This means believing that one cannot experience virtually any happiness at all, under any conditions, if an event which 'must' not happen actually occurs, or threatens to occur.

The third major derivative, known as *damnation* represents a tendency for people to rate themselves and other people as 'sub-human' or 'undeserving' if they or other people do something that they 'must' not do, or fail to do something which they 'must' do. 'Damnation' can also be applied to the world or life conditions which are rated as being 'rotten' for failing to give the person what he or she 'must' have.

While RET holds that 'awfulizing', 'I-can't-stand-it-itis' and 'damnation' are secondary irrational processes, in that they stem from the philosophy of 'musts', these processes can sometimes be primary (Ellis, 1984 a). Indeed, Wessler (1984) has argued

After two hours of trying to remember which to salute first -- the OOD or the flag, Ensign Sampson began contemplating a hotel room.

that they are more likely to be primary and that 'musts' are derived from them. However, the philosophy of 'musts', on the one hand, and those of 'awfulizing', 'I-can't-stand-it-itis' on the other, are, in all probability, interdependent processes and often seem to be different sides of the same 'cognitive coin'.

Other forms of distorted thinking stemming from irrational beliefs. Rational-emotive theory notes that humans also make numerous kinds of illogicalities when they are disturbed (Ellis, 1985 b). In this respect it agrees with cognitive therapists (Beck, *et al.*, 1979; Burns, 1980) that such cognitive distortions are a feature of psychological disturbance. However, rational-emotive theory holds that such distortions almost always stem from the 'musts', although this hypothesis has yet to be empirically tested. Some of the most frequent distortions are:

All-or-nothing thinking: 'If I fail at any important task, as I *must* not, I'm a *total* failure and *completely* unlovable!'.
Jumping to conclusions and negative non-sequiturs: 'Since they have seen me dismally fail, as I *should* not have done, they will view me as an incompetent worm'.
Fortune telling: 'Because they are laughing at me for failing, they know that I *should* have succeeded, and they will despise me forever'.
Focusing on the negative: 'Because I *can't stand* things going wrong, as they *must* not, I can't see any good that is happening in my life'.
Disqualifying the positive: 'When they compliment me on the good things I have done, they are only being kind to me and forgetting the foolish things that I *should* not have done'.
Allness and neverness: 'Because conditions of living *ought* to be good and actually are so bad and so intolerable, they'll *always* be this way and I'll never have any happiness'.
Minimization: 'My good shots in this game were lucky and unimportant. But my bad shots, which I *should* never have made, were as bad as could be and were totally unforgivable'.
Emotional reasoning: 'Because I have performed so poorly, as I *should* not have done, I feel like a total idiot, and my strong feeling proves that I *am* no damned good!'.
Labelling and overgeneralization: 'Because I *must* not fail at important work and have done so, I am a complete loser and failure!'.
Personalizing: 'Since I am acting far worse than I *should* act and they are laughing, I am sure they are only laughing at me: and that is *awful!*'.
Phoneyism: 'When I don't do as well as I *ought* to do and they still praise and accept me, I am a real phoney and will soon fall on my face and show them how despicable I am!'.
Perfectionism: 'I realize that I did fairly well, but I *should* have done perfectly well on a task like this, and am therefore really an incompetent'.

Although RET counsellors at times discover all the illogicalities just listed—and a number of others that are less frequently found with clients—they particularly focus on the unconditional shoulds, oughts, and musts that seem to constitute the philosophic core of irrational beliefs that lead to emotional disturbance. For they hold that if they do not get to and help clients surrender these core beliefs, the clients will most probably keep holding them and create new irrational derivatives from them.

RET counsellors also particularly look for 'awfulizing', for 'I-can't-stand-it-itis', and for 'damnation': and they show clients how these almost invariably stem from their 'musts' and can be surrendered if they give up their absolutist demands on themselves, on other people, and on the universe. At the same time, rational-emotive counsellors usually encourage their clients to have strong and persistent desires, wishes, and preferences, and to avoid feelings of detachment, withdrawal and lack of involvement.

More importantly, RET holds that unrealistic and illogical beliefs do not in themselves create emotional disturbance. Why? Because it is quite possible for people to unrealistically believe, 'Because I frequently fail, I always do' and it is possible for them also to believe illogically, 'Because I have frequently failed, I always will'. But they can, in both these instances, rationally conclude, 'Too bad. Even though I always fail, there is no reason why I must succeed. I would prefer to but I never have to do well. So I'll manage to be as happy as I can be even with my constant failure'. They would then rarely be emotionally disturbed.

To reiterate, the essence of human emotional disturbance, according to rational-emotive theory, consists of the absolutist *musts* and *must nots* that people think *about* their failure, *about* their rejections, *about* their poor treatment by others, and *about* life's frustrations and losses. Rational-emotive counselling therefore differs from other forms of cognitive-behavioural counselling—such as those inspired by Beck (1976), Bandura (1969, 1977), Goldfried and Davison (1976), Janis (1983), Lazarus (1981), Mahoney (1977), Maultsby (1984), and Meichenbaum (1977)—in that it particularly stresses therapists looking for clients' dogmatic, unconditional *musts*, differentiating them from their preferences, and teaching them how to surrender the former and retain the latter (Ellis, 1984 a).

Psychological health

If the philosophy of religiosity is at the core of much psychological disturbance then what philosophy is characteristic of psychological health? Rational-emotive theory argues that a philosophy of relativism or 'desiring' is a central feature of psychologically healthy humans. This philosophy acknowledges that humans have a large variety of desires, wishes, wants, preferences, etc., but if they refuse to escalate these non-absolute values into grandiose dogmas and demands they will not become psychologically disturbed. They will, however, experience appropriate negative emotions (e.g. sadness, regret, disappointment, annoyance) whenever their desires are not fulfilled. These emotions are considered to have constructive motivational properties in that they both help people to remove obstacles to goal attainment and aid them to make constructive adjustments when their desires cannot be met.

Three major derivatives of the philosophy of desiring are postulated by rational-emotive theory. They are deemed to be rational in that they tend to help people reach their goals, or formulate new goals if their old ones cannot be realized.

The first major derivative is known as *rating or evaluating badness*. Here, if a person does not get what she wants she acknowledges that this is bad. However, because she does not believe 'I have to get what I want' she contains her evaluation

Naval Academy photo courtesy of United States Naval Academy Photographic Laboratory.

along a 0–100 percent continuum of 'badness' and does not therefore rate this situation as 'awful'—a magical rating which is placed on a nonsensical 101 percent—∞ (infinity) continuum. In general, when the person adheres to the desiring philosophy, the stronger her desire the greater her rating of badness will be when she does not get what she wants.

The second major derivative is known as *tolerance* and is the rational alternative to 'I-can't-stand-it-itis'. Here the person acknowledges that an undesirable event has happened (or may happen); believes that the event should occur empirically if it does (i.e. does not demand that what exists must not exist); rates the event along the badness continuum; attempts to change the undesired event, or accepts the 'grim' reality if it cannot be modified; and actively pursues other goals even though the situation cannot be altered.

The third major derivative known as *acceptance* is the rational alternative to 'damnation'. Here the person accepts herself and others as fallible human beings who do not have to act other than they do and as too complex and fluid to be given any legitimate or global rating. In addition, life conditions are accepted as they exist. People who have the philosophy of acceptance fully acknowledge that the world is highly complex and exists according to laws which are often outside their personal control. It is important to emphasize here that acceptance does not imply resignation. A rational philosophy of acceptance means that the person acknowledges that whatever exists empirically should exist, but does not have to exist in any absolute sense forever. This prompts the person to make active attempts to change reality. The person who is resigned to a situation usually does not attempt to modify it.

Perpetuation of psychological disturbance

While rational-emotive theory does not posit an elaborate view to explain the acquisition of psychological disturbance, it does deal more extensively with how such disturbance is perpetuated.

The three RET insights. First, people tend to maintain their psychological problems by their own 'naive' theories concerning the nature of these problems and to what they can be attributed. They lack what RET calls *RET Insight No. One:* that psychological disturbance is primarily determined by the absolutist irrational beliefs that people hold about negative life events. Rather they consider that their disturbances are 'caused' by these situations. Since people make incorrect hypotheses about the major determinants of their problems, they consequently attempt to change the events rather than their irrational beliefs. Second, people may have Insight No. One but lack *RET Insight No. Two:* that people remain disturbed by re-indoctrinating themselves *in the present* with their irrational beliefs. While they may see that their problems are determined by their beliefs they may distract themselves and thus perpetuate their problems by searching for the historical antecedents of these beliefs, instead of directing themselves to change them as currently held. Third, people may have Insights Nos. One or Two but still sustain their disturbance because they lack *RET Insight No. Three:* only if people diligently work and practise in the present as well as in the future to think, feel and act against their irrational beliefs are they likely to change them, and make themselves significantly less disturbed. People who have all three insights clearly see that they had better persistently and strongly challenge their beliefs cognitively, emotively and behaviourally to break the perpetuation of disturbance cycle. Merely acknowledging that a belief is irrational is usually insufficient to effect change (Ellis, 1979 c).

The philosophy of low frustration tolerance (LFT).   Rational-emotive theory contends that the major reason why people perpetuate their psychological problems is because they adhere to a philosophy of low frustration tolerance (LFT) (Ellis, 1979 b, 1980 a). Such people believe that they must be comfortable, and thus do not work to effect change because such work inevitably involves experiencing discomfort. They are short-range hedonists in that they are motivated to avoid short-term discomfort even though accepting and working against their temporary uncomfortable feelings would probably help them to reach their long-range goals. Such people evaluate cognitive and behavioral therapeutic tasks as 'too painful', and even more painful than the psychological disturbance to which they have achieved some measure of habituation. They prefer to remain with their 'comfortable' discomfort rather than face the 'change-related' discomfort which they believe they must not experience. Maultsby (1975) has argued that people often back away from change because they are afraid that they will not feel right about it. He calls this the 'neurotic fear of feeling a phoney' and actively shows clients that these feelings of 'unnaturalness' are in fact the natural concomitants of relearning. Another prevalent form of LFT is 'anxiety about anxiety'. Here, individuals believe that they must not be anxious, and thus do not expose themselves to anxiety-provoking situations because they might become anxious if they did so—an experience they would evaluate as 'awful'. As such, they perpetuate their problems and restrict their lives to avoid experiencing anxiety.

Disturbances about disturbances.   'Anxiety about anxiety' constitutes an example of the clinical fact that people often make themselves disturbed about their disturbances. Having created secondary (and sometimes tertiary) disturbances about their original disturbance, they become pre-occupied with these 'problems about problems' and thus find it difficult to get back to solving the original problem. Humans are often very inventive in this respect. They can make themselves depressed about their depression, guilty about being angry, as well as anxious about their anxiety, and so on. Consequently, people often need to tackle their disturbances about their disturbances before they can successfully solve their original problems (Ellis, 1979 b, 1980 a).

Naval Academy photo courtesy of United States Naval Academy Photographic Laboratory.

Defences.   Rational-emotive theory endorses the Freudian view of human defensiveness in explaining how people perpetuate their psychological problems (Freud, 1937). Thus, people maintain their problems by employing various defence mechanisms (e.g., rationalization, avoidance) which are designed to help deny the existence of these problems, or to minimize their severity. The rational-emotive view is that these defences are used to ward off self-damnation tendencies and that under such circumstances, if these people were to honestly take responsibility for their problems, they would severely denigrate themselves for having them. In addition, these defence mechanisms are also employed to ward off discomfort anxiety: again, if such people admitted their problems they would rate them as 'too hard to bear' or 'too difficult to overcome'.

Payoffs.   Rational-emotive theory notes that people sometimes experience a form of perceived payoff for their psychological problems other than avoidance of discomfort (Ellis, 1979 a). The existence of these payoffs serves to perpetuate these problems. Thus, a woman who claims to want to overcome her procrastination may avoid tackling the problem because she is afraid that should she become successful she might then be criticized by others as being 'too masculine', a situation she would evaluate as 'awful'. Her procrastination serves to protect her, she believes, from this 'terrible' state of affairs. It is important to note that rational-emotive theory considers that people are affected by payoffs because they make inferences and evaluations about the consequences, or likely consequences, of their behaviour. They are not influenced directly by these consequences.

Self-fulfilling prophecies.   Finally, the well-documented 'self-fulfilling prophecy' phenomenon helps to explain why people perpetuate their psychological problems (Jones, 1977; Wachtel, 1977). Here, people act according to their evaluations and consequent predictions, and thus often elicit from themselves or from others responses which they then interpret in a manner which confirms their initial hypotheses. Thus, a socially anxious man may believe that other people would not want to get to know 'a worthless individual such as I truly am'. He then attends a social function and acts as if he were worthless, avoiding eye contact and keeping away from others. Unsurprisingly, such social behavior does not invite approaches from others—a lack of response which he interprets and evaluates thus: 'You see, I was right. Other people don't want to know me. I really am no good'.

In conclusion, rational-emotive theory holds that people 'naturally tend to perpetuate their problems and have a strong innate tendency to cling to self-defeating, habitual patterns and thereby resist basic change. Helping clients change then poses quite a challenge for RET practitioners' (Dryden, 1984 a, p. 244).

Leadership

General of the Army Omar N. Bradley

(Editor's Note: General of the Army Omar N. Bradley visited Carlisle Barracks on 7–8 October 1971 to meet with members of the 12th Army Group Association. While he was at Carlisle, he addressed the Army War College faculty and students on the subject of Leadership. His address contained observations that were gleaned during a long and significant career. A careful reading of his remarks gives us some insight into the qualities that made General Bradley the great soldier and human being that he is.

General Bradley's thesis is that leadership is an intangible that involves a constant interplay between the leader and the led. When this interplay is successful we have the ingredients for great accomplishments.)

All of you here this evening are leaders. I am pleased to meet you. What you do may well dignify the past, explain today, and secure for all of us—tomorrow.

Perhaps I can touch upon a few factors that will underscore the value of good leadership. Leadership is an intangible. No weapon, no impersonal piece of machinery ever designed can take its place.

This is the age of the computer, and if you know how to program the machine you can get quick and accurate answers. But, how can you include leadership—and morale which is affected by leadership—into your programming? Let us never forget the great importance of this element—leadership, and while we use computers for certain answers, let us not try to fight a whole war or even a single battle without giving proper consideration to the element of leadership.

Another element to be considered is the Man to be led, and with whose morale we are concerned. I am constantly reminded of this point by a cartoon which hangs over my desk at home which depicts an infantryman with his rifle across his knees as he sits behind a parapet. Above him is the list of the newest weapons science has devised and the soldier behind the parapet is saying: "But still they haven't found the substitute for ME."

Of course, with this particular group of service personnel, I am considering leadership as it applies to a military unit. However, having been associated with industry for some time now, I find it difficult to completely separate the principles of military and industrial leadership. They have much in common.

In selecting a company in which to invest our savings, we often give primary consideration to the company with good leadership. In similar manner, a military unit is often judged by its leadership. Good leadership is essential to organized action where any group is involved. The one who commands—be he a military officer or captain of industry—must project power, an energizing power which coordinates and marshals the best efforts of his followers by supplying that certain something for which they look to him, be it guidance, support, encouragement, example, or even new ideas and imagination.

The test of a leader lies in the reaction and response of his followers. He should not have to impose authority. Bossiness in itself never made a leader. He must make his influence felt by example and the instilling of confidence in his followers. The greatness of a leader is measured by the achievements of the led. This is the ultimate test of his effectiveness.

Too frequently, we use the words leader and commander synonymously. We should not forget that there are far more staff officer assignments than there are command billets, and a good staff officer can and should display the same leadership as a commander. While it takes a good staff officer to initiate an effective plan, it requires a leader to ensure that the plan is properly executed. That is why you and I have been taught that the work of collecting information, studying it, drawing a plan, and making a decision, is 10 percent of the job: seeing that plan through is the other 90 percent. A well-trained officer is one who can serve effectively either as a staff officer or as a commander.

I can recall a former vice-president of one of the companies with which I am associated. He would formulate some good plans but never followed up to see that his plans got the expected results. I knew he had served in World War II so, out of curiosity, I looked into the nature of his service and found that his entire period of service was as a staff officer. He had never had the advantage of a command job, so his training was incomplete. Maybe if he had remained in the service longer, we could have developed his leadership qualities as well—and this man would still be with the company.

You may have heard this story about General Pershing in World War I. While inspecting a certain area, he found a project that was not going too well, even though the second lieutenant in charge seemed to have a pretty good plan. General Pershing asked the lieutenant how much pay he received, and when the lieutenant replied: "$141.67 per month, Sir," General Pershing said: "Just remember that you get $1.67 for making your plan and issuing the order, and $140.00 for seeing that it is carried out."

I am not sure that I would go to that extreme. Certainly in these days, problems are complex and good staff work plays a large part in resolving them. I have known commanders who were not too smart, but they were very knowledgeable about personnel and knew enough to select the very best for their staffs. Remember, a good leader is one who causes or inspires others, staff or subordinate commanders, to do the job.

Furthermore, no leader knows it all (although you sometimes find one who seems to think he does!). A leader should encourage the members of his staff to speak up if they think the commander is wrong. He should invite constructive criticism. It is a grave error for the leader to surround himself with a "Yes" staff.

General George C. Marshall was an excellent exponent of the principle of having his subordinates speak up. When he first became Chief of Staff of the Army, the secretariat of that office consisted of three officers who presented orally to General Marshal the staff papers, or "studies" coming from the divisions of the General Staff. I was a member of that secretariat. We presented, in abbreviated form the contents of the staff studies, citing the highlights of the problem involved, the various possible courses of action considered, and the action recommended.

At the end of his first week as Chief of Staff, General Marshall called us into his office and opened the discussion by saying: "I am disappointed in all of you." When we inquired if we might ask why, he said: "You haven't disagreed with a single thing I have done all week." We told him it so happened that we were in full agreement with every paper that had been presented, that we knew what he wanted, and that we would add our comments to anything that we considered should be questioned.

The very next day, we presented a paper as written and then expressed some thoughts which, in our opinion, made the recommended action questionable. General Marshall said: "Now that is what I want. Unless I hear all the arguments against an action, I am not sure whether I am right or not."

If you happen to be detailed to a staff, try to be a good staff officer and, if possible, avoid being a "Yes" man. I would suggest to all commanders that they inform the members of their staffs that anyone who does not disagree once in a while with what is about to be done, is of limited value and perhaps should be shifted to some other place where he might occasionally have an idea.

Of course, I am thinking about the decision-making process. After a decision is made, everyone must be behind it 100 percent. I thought the British were admirable in this respect during World War II. No matter how much discussion there had been on a subject, as soon as a decision was made you never heard any doubts expressed. You had to believe that everyone involved in making the decision had never entertained any ideas except those expressed in the decision.

I don't want to overemphasize leadership of senior officers. My interest extends to leaders of all ranks. I would caution you always to remember that an essential qualification of a good leader is the ability to recognize, select, and train junior leaders. I would like to quote from a book entitled *Born at Reveille* and written by Colonel Red Reeder. Colonel Reeder was on a trip for General Marshall and one of his assignments was to inquire into junior leadership. This is an account of his conversation with Colonel Bryant Moore on Guadalcanal. And I quote:

> "Colonel Moore," I said, "tell me something about leadership." I had hit a sensitive spot. He forged ahead. "Leadership! The greatest problem here *is* the leaders, and you have to find some way to weed out the weak ones. It's tough to do this when you're in combat. The platoon leaders

who cannot command, who cannot foresee things, and who cannot act on the spur of the moment in an emergency are a distinct detriment.

"It is hot here, as you can see. Men struggle; they get heat exhaustion. They come out vomiting, and throwing away equipment. The leaders must be leaders and they must be alert to establish straggler lines and stop this thing.

"The men have been taught to take salt tablets, but the leaders don't see to this. Result, heat exhaustion.

"The good leaders seem to get killed; the poor leaders get the men killed. The big problem is leadership and getting the shoulder straps on the right people."

Sixty-millimeter Japanese mortar shells fell about thirty yards away and attacked a number of coconut trees. I lost interest in taking dictation and the colonel stopped talking. When the salvo was over and things were quiet again, Bryant Moore said, "Where was I? You saw that patrol. I tell you this, not one man in fifty can lead a patrol in this jungle. If you can find out who the good patrol leaders are before you hit the combat zone, you have found out something."

"I have had to get rid of about twenty-five officers because they just weren't leaders. I had to *make* the battalion commander weed out the poor junior leaders! This process is continuous. Our junior leaders are finding out that they must know more about their men. The good leaders know their men."—Unquote.

What then, are the distinguishing qualities of a leader? There are many essential characteristics that he must possess, but I will mention a few that come to mind as perhaps the most important. First, he must know his job, without necessarily being a specialist in every phase of it. A few years ago it was suggested that all engineering subjects be eliminated from the required studies at West Point. I objected. For example, bridge building is a specialty for engineers; yet, I think every senior officer should have some idea of what is involved. When we reached the Rhine in World War II, it was not necessary that I know how to build a bridge, but it was very helpful that I knew what was involved so that I could see that the bridge engineers received proper support in tonnage allowed and an idea of the time involved.

Specialties dominate almost every problem faced today by the military leader or the business manager. This individual must get deeply enough into his problem that he can understand it and intelligently manage it, without going so far as to become a specialist himself in every phase of the problem. You don't have to be a tank expert in order to effectively use a tank unit of your command.

Thomas J. Watson of IBM once said that genius in an executive is the ability to deal successfully with matters he does not understand. This leads to another principle of leadership which I have often found neglected, both in the military and in business. While you need not be a specialist in all phases of your job, you should have a proportionate degree of interest in every aspect of it—and those concerned, your subordinates, should be aware of your interest.

You must get around and show interest in what your subordinates are doing, even if you don't know much about the technique of their work. And, when you are making these visits, try to pass out praise when due, as well as corrections or criticism.

We tend to speak up only when things go wrong. This is such a well recognized fact that a "Complaint Department" is an essential part of many business firms. To my knowledge, no comparable facility exists anywhere to expedite the handling of praise for the job well done—it need not be extravagant.

We all get enough criticism and we learn to take it. Even Sir Winston Churchill, despite his matchless accomplishments, found occasion to say: "I have benefited enormously from criticism and at no point did I suffer from any perceptible lack thereof." But let us remember that praise also has a role to play. Napoleon was probably the finest exponent of this principle of recognition through his use of a quarter inch of ribbon to improve morale and get results.

Both mental and physical energy are essential to successful leadership. How many really good leaders have you known who were lazy, or weak, or who couldn't stand the strain? Sherman was a good example of a leader with outstanding mental and physical energy. I cite him with some trepidation because some of you may be from Georgia! However, during the advance from Chattanooga to Atlanta, he often went for days with only two or three hours of sleep per night and was constantly in the saddle reconnoitering, and he often knew the dispositions and terrain so well that he could maneuver the enemy out of position without a serious fight and with minimum losses.

Conversely, a sick commander is of limited value. It is not fair to the troops under him to have a leader who is not functioning 100 percent. I had to relieve several senior commanders during World War II because of illness. It is often pointed out that Napoleon didn't lose a major battle until Waterloo where he was a sick man.

A leader should possess human understanding and consideration for others. Men are not robots and should not be treated as though they were machines. I do not by any means suggest coddling. But men are highly intelligent, complicated beings who will respond favorably to human understanding and consideration. By this means their leader will get maximum effort from each of them. He will also get loyalty—and in this connection, it is well to remember that loyalty goes down as well as up. The sincere leader will go to bat for his subordinates when such action is needed.

A good leader must sometimes be stubborn. Here, I am reminded of the West Point cadet prayer. A leader must be able to choose the harder right instead of the easier wrong. Armed with the courage of his convictions, he must often fight to defend them. Then he has come to a decision after thorough analysis—and when he is sure he is right—he must stick to it even to the point of stubbornness. Grant furnishes a good illustration of this trait. He never knew when he was supposed to be licked. A less stubborn man might have lost at Shiloh.

Maybe you have heard the story of Grant in the Richmond Campaign when after being up all night making his reconnaissance and formulating and issuing orders, he lay down under a tree and fell asleep. Sometime later, a courier rode up and informed the General that disaster had hit his right flank and that his troops at that end of the line were in full retreat. General Grant sat up, shook his head to clear the cobwebs and said: "It can't be so," and went back to sleep—and it wasn't so. He had confidence in himself and in his subordinate leaders.

I do not mean to infer that there is always just one solution to a problem. Usually there is one best solution, but any good plan, boldly executed, is better than indecision. There is usually more than one way to obtain results.

Another quality of leadership that comes to mind is self-confidence. You must have confidence in yourself, your unit and your subordinate commanders—and in your plan.

This recalls a couple of incidents. Just before the invasion of Normandy in 1944, a story went around in some of the units that were making the assault on the beaches that they would suffer 100 percent casualties—that none of them would come back. I found it necessary to visit these units and talk to all ranks. I told them that, of course, we would suffer casualties, but certainly our losses would not be 100 percent and that with our air and naval support we would succeed. After our landing, a correspondent told me that on his way across the Channel in one of the leading LST's he had noticed a sergeant reading a novel. Struck by the seeming lack of concern of the sergeant, he asked: "Aren't you worried, how can you be reading at a time like this?" The sergeant replied: "No, I am not worried. General Bradley said everything would go all right, so why should I worry."

I can't recall just what I had said, but it had accomplished its purpose, at least where one man was concerned.

I might relate another incident where there was a lack of confidence. I had to relieve a senior commander because I learned that his men had lost confidence in him. This meant, of course, that we could not expect maximum performance by that division. After being relieved, the officer came back through my headquarters and showed me a file of statements given him—by request, I am sure—by the burgomaster of all towns his division had passed through. If he had had confidence in himself, he would not have felt the need for those letters.

After seeing the letters, I told the officer that if I had ever had any doubts as to whether I had to relieve him, those doubts were now removed. His letters proved beyond question that he had lost confidence in himself, so it was no wonder the men had lost confidence in him.

A leader must possess imagination. Whether it be an administrative decision, or one made in combat, the possible results of that decision must be plain to the one making it. What will be the next step—and the one after that?

While there are many other qualities which, contribute to effective leadership, I will mention just one more—but it is a very important one—Character. This word has many meanings. I am applying it in a broad sense to describe a person who has high ideals, who stands by them, and, who can be trusted absolutely. Such a person will be respected by all those with whom he is associated. And, such a person will readily be recognized by his associates for what he is.

Circumstances mold our character. These circumstances affect different people in different ways. From exactly the same set of circumstances one man may theoretically build a palace, while another may have difficulty building a lean-to.

It has been said that a man's character is the reality of himself. I don't think a man's strength of character ever changes. I remember a long time ago when someone told me that a mountain might be reported to have moved, I could believe or disbelieve it, as I wished, but if anyone told me that a man had changed his character, I should not believe it.

All leaders must possess these qualities which I have been discussing, and the great leaders are those who possess one or more of them to an outstanding degree. Some leaders just miss being great because they are weak in one or more of these areas. There is still another ingredient in this formula for a great leader that I have left out, and that is LUCK. He must have opportunity. Then, of course, when opportunity knocks, he must be able to rise and open the door.

Some may ask: "Why do you talk about the qualities of leadership?" They maintain that you either have leadership or you don't—that leaders are born, not made. I suppose some are born with a certain amount of leadership. Frequently, we see children who seem inclined to take charge and direct their playmates. The other youngsters follow these directions without protest. But I am convinced, nevertheless, that leadership can be developed and improved by study and training.

There is no better way to develop leadership than to give the youngster or other individual a job involving responsibility and let him work it out. Try to avoid telling him how to do it. That, for example, is the basis of our whole system of combat orders. We tell the subordinate unit commander what we want him to do and leave the details to him.

I think this system is largely responsible for the many fine leaders in our services today. We are constantly training and developing younger officers and teaching them to accept responsibility.

However, don't discount experience. Someone may remind you that Napoleon led armies before he was 30; and that Alexander the Great died at the age of 33. Napoleon, as he grew older, commanded even larger armies. Alexander might have been even greater had he lived longer and had more experience. In this respect, I especially like General Bolivar Buckner's theory that "Judgment comes from experience and experience comes from bad judgment."

I have been asked to speak on leadership in the past. I have fairly well covered these same thoughts with other groups.

Somehow, however, at the moment, these thoughts take on added significance for me. You see, my first great-grandson was born a year ago. We call him "Fat Henry." What happens to his life, and to the lives of his contemporaries, may well be in your hands.

Thank you.

General of the Army Omar N. Bradley was born in Clark, Missouri 12 February 1893. Following graduation from the U.S. Military Academy in 1915 he served with the Infantry in a variety of assignments, and at the Military Academy as an instructor and a tactical officer. Early in World War II he commanded the 82d and later the 28th Infantry Divisions. In 1943 he was Corps Commander, II Corps, during the Tunisian and Sicilian Campaigns; and in 1943 was Commanding General of the First U.S. Army, during its famed Normandy invasion. In 1944 and 1945 he served as Commanding General, 12th Army Group during campaigns in France and Germany.

In 1946, General Bradley was named Administrator, Veterans Affairs, until he was recalled to active duty in 1948 to serve as Chief of Staff, U.S. Army. In 1950, he was appointed General of the Army while serving as Chairman of the Joint Chiefs of Staff.